Advantage™
Database Server:
The Official Guide

About the Authors

Cary Jensen   Cary Jensen is President of Jensen Data Systems, Inc. In addition to his consulting and development duties, he is an award-winning, best-selling author of 19 books, including *Building Kylix Applications* (McGraw-Hill/Osborne), *Oracle JDeveloper* (Oracle Press), *JBuilder Essentials* (McGraw-Hill/Osborne), *Delphi In Depth* (McGraw-Hill/Osborne), and *Programming Paradox 5 for Windows* (Sybex). Cary is a featured Web columnist for the Borland Developers Network (bdn.borland.com), where his column "The Professional Developer" appears, and is Contributing Editor of *Delphi Informant* Magazine. He is an internationally respected speaker and trainer, and was the author and principal speaker for the 2001–2003 Developer Days Seminars and Workshops, the 2000–2001 Delphi Development Seminars, the 1999–2000 Borland Developer Days, and the 1995–1999 Borland/Softbite Delphi World Tours. Cary has a Ph.D. from Rice University in Human Factors Psychology, specializing in human-computer interaction.

Loy Anderson   Loy Anderson is Vice President of Jensen Data Systems, Inc., a Houston-based consulting and training company. She is an award-winning, best-selling co-author of 19 books with Cary Jensen and has served as coordinating editor on several books. Loy manages the Delphi Developers Days Seminars and Workshops, which won the 2002 and 2003 Delphi Informant's Readers Choice Awards for Best Training. Her company's latest workshops include .NET development, Delphi development, and Advantage Database Server training. She was also an event coordinator for the 1999–2000 Borland Developer Days and the 2000–2001 Delphi Development Seminars. Loy has a Ph.D. from Rice University in Human Factors Psychology, specializing in human-computer interaction.

About the Lead Technical Editor

Brad Schmidt   Brad Schmidt is an R&D Project Manager at Extended Systems, Inc. Prior to becoming project manager for the Advantage Database Server product line, as well as other software products at Extended Systems, he was a lead developer on the Advantage Database Server. He has worked on the Advantage product line since its inception in 1992, and has been the lead architect and developer on many of its significant features, including the Transaction Processing System, the port of the server to Windows NT, the Advantage Local Server, the Advantage proprietary file format (ADT/ADI/ADM files), and the Advantage OLE DB Provider. Brad holds a patent on functionality available in the Advantage Transaction Processing System. In addition to his current project management responsibilities, he has significant influence on new product features, contributes to all facets of Advantage documentation, and delivers several developer training sessions a year on Advantage Database Server. Brad lives in Eagle, Idaho, with his wife, Judy, two sons, Kellen and Nicholas, and a daughter, Lindsey. He has a bachelor's degree in Computer Science from Montana State University.

Advantage™ Database Server: The Official Guide

Cary Jensen
Loy Anderson

McGraw-Hill/Osborne

New York   Chicago   San Francisco
Lisbon   London   Madrid   Mexico City   Milan
New Delhi   San Juan   Seoul   Singapore   Sydney   Toronto

The *McGraw-Hill* Companies

McGraw-Hill/Osborne
2100 Powell Street, 10 Floor
Emeryville, California 94608
U.S.A.

To arrange bulk purchase discounts for sales promotions, premiums, or fund-raisers, please contact
McGraw-Hill/Osborne at the above address. For information on translations or book distributors
outside the U.S.A., please see the International Contact Information page immediately following the
index of this book.

Advantage™ Database Server: The Official Guide

1234567890 FGR FGR 019876543

Book p/n 0-07-223085-1 and CD p/n 0-07-223086-X
parts of
ISBN 0-07-223084-3

Publisher	Brandon A. Nordin
Vice President & Associate Publisher	Scott Rogers
Editorial Director	Wendy Rinaldi
Project Editor	Jennifer Malnick
Acquisitions Coordinator	Athena Honore
Coordinating Editor	Loy Anderson
Technical Editor	Brad Schmidt
Contributing Technical Editors	Chris Franz, Patrick Harper, Jeremy "J.D." Mullin, Lance Schmidt, Chuck Vertrees, Mark Wilkins, and Alex Wong
Copy Editors	Jan Jue, Dennis Weaver
Proofreader	Linda Medoff
Indexer	Loy Anderson, Cary Jensen
Composition	Carie Abrew, Tara Davis
Illustrators	Kathleen Edwards, Michael Mueller, Melinda Lytle
Series Designer	Roberta Steele
Cover Illustration	Pattie Lee

This book was composed with Corel VENTURA™ Publisher.

We dedicate this book to our dance instructors,
Al Lena and Ronny Roch, for sharing with us
this beautiful expression of life.

Contents at a Glance

Contents

Part II	**Using Advantage SQL**

Acknowledgments

We want to take this opportunity to express our heartfelt thanks to everyone who made this book possible. From Osborne Media Group, we want to thank Scott Rogers, who got this project rolling; Wendy Rinaldi, who made sure it happened; Jennifer Malnick, for her professionalism and dedication in moving this book quickly through production; as well as Dennis Weaver, our favorite copyeditor; and Jan Jue, for her meticulous work. We also want to thank Athena Honore.

We are also deeply indebted to the wonderful people at Extended Systems, Inc. In particular, we want to thank Katie Moser, Advantage Marketing Manager, and Chuck Vertrees, Advantage Product Manager, for inspiring this project and promoting it at Extended Systems. We are also deeply indebted to, and grateful for, the technical editing team, who gave us, hands-down, the best technical edit and support that we have ever had on a book. This team was lead by this book's Technical Editor, Brad Schmidt. During the course of this book, not only did Brad, the Advantage R&D Project Manager, review these chapters, but he also had each chapter reviewed by several, and sometimes all, of the following people (listed in alphabetical order): Chris Franz, Patrick Harper, Jeremy "J.D." Mullin, Lance Schmidt, Chuck Vertrees, Mark Wilkins, and Alex Wong. In addition, we appreciate the unflinching help of Lance, J.D., Chris, and Alex for their advice and assistance in writing the applications that appear in Part III of this book. Other people at Extended Systems we want to thank include Charles Jepson, Justin Borg, Joachim Dürr, Dirk Erickson, Peter Funk, Phil Ruebel, Lee Stigile, Bryce Twitchell, Jay Wendt, and last, but not least, master salesman Bill Schuler.

We also want to thank the many wonderful people who use and champion the Advantage Database Server. This is a really great community, and your enthusiasm for this product is nothing less than contagious. Thanks also to our colleague Bill Todd. Finally, we want to thank our friend Corey Wood, who provided us with technical assistance when we wrote our first training course on the Advantage Database Server.

Introduction

I have considered myself a database developer since Loy Anderson and I launched our business in 1988. During that time, I have had the pleasure of working on a large number of different and exciting database projects in almost every field imaginable, from medical to legal, from financial to aerospace, from manufacturing to distribution.

I also started training corporate software developers in 1988, and in the intervening years have trained thousands of database developers. In the early days, most of these developers used a local, file server–based database engine, such as Paradox, dBase, FoxPro, Clipper, or MS Access, though over time an increasingly greater proportion used a client/server architecture. But even to this day there are a surprisingly large number of developers still using a local database engine.

Over the years, as the limitations of the file server–based architecture became more widely understood, a specific interaction repeated itself over and over, and does so to this day. A developer in one of my seminars will approach me during a break and relate that they are still using a local database engine. Realizing that they need greater stability and performance, they will tell me that they are switching to a particular database server, almost always one of the big-name database servers. When I ask them how many users are on their system, they often reply that they have three or five or ten. Rarely more than twenty.

This exchange always leaves me feeling a little shocked. Do they know what they are getting themselves into? Sure, the client/server architecture offers greater stability and increased performance, but are they going to be able to allocate the resources that most of the high-end database servers require? Do they have a DBA (database administrator) already? If not, can they afford to hire a DBA? Can they afford the continuing training and certification? Is the expense worth it when they have only five users?

I'm sharing this background with you so that you will understand why I am such a huge fan of Advantage Database Server (ADS). For almost every developer with whom I have had the preceding interaction, ADS is a better solution for implementing their application using a client/server architecture, one that can easily handle hundreds of users. Not only does ADS offer the reliability and performance of a remote database server, it does so with a very minimum of administration. In a world where we often confuse sophistication with complexity, ADS is the perfect exception to the rule. But isn't this the way it should be? Simple sophistication. Wouldn't it be great if all software were like this?

But there is something else about the Advantage Database Server that originally attracted my attention—the company that makes it. From my very first contacts with the Advantage group at Extended Systems, all the way through the writing of this book, I have been continuously impressed with the level of professionalism and commitment by the people behind the product. From the individuals in marketing and sales, through the management and development team, there is a culture of pride that permeates this group. Ask anyone who uses ADS and you'll likely hear the same thing. This product is great, and so is the company behind it. What a combination.

Don't get me wrong: My admiration for the people behind ADS is not intended as a slight to other software companies. Indeed, I have had in the past, and continue to have, great respect for a number of the software companies that I deal with, the people who work at them, and an appreciation for the culture of excellence that they engender. Borland Software Corporation is an outstanding example of what I am talking about. But the fact remains that ADS is backed by a first-rate company that respects and supports its customers. You can't say that about every software company.

—*Cary Jensen*

About This Book

This book is designed to get you started using the Advantage Database Server, organized into three parts. In Part I, you learn how ADS gives you the performance of a world-class, relational, remote database server without the complexity normally associated with the client/server architecture. Topics discussed here include what ADS is, what your data access options are, how to build tables and indexes, and how to set up a data dictionary in order to create a secure and feature-rich database.

In Part II, you learn the ins and outs of Advantage SQL, the particular dialect of ANSI/92 SQL used by the Advantage Database Server. And in Part III, you learn how to access your ADS data from the most popular development environments, including Delphi, Java, Visual Basic, C#, and more.

The CD-ROM that accompanies this book includes code samples as well as a set of database files. As you progress through the chapters of Part I, you will make modifications to this database, adding tables, indexes, a data dictionary, constraints, stored procedures, triggers, and more. Each chapter contains step-by-step instructions that walk you through the process of creating these various objects. Consequently, in most cases, you will want to start this book from the beginning and work your way through the chapters in sequence.

There is one thing to note about this database that you will be working with in this book: The examples described do not add all of the objects that you would probably want to add to this database if you were creating a production application. For example, the step-by-step instructions only have you add the indexes that are necessary for the other objects you will create later in the book, such as referential integrity definitions.

In other words, if you were actually going to deploy this database, you would likely add many more indexes than we have you add here. But that point, and other similar points related to the creation of objects, is made repeatedly throughout. For a real database, you create those objects that support the features that you want to implement in your client applications. Importantly, the chapters in Part I explain what these features are and show you how to define them.

Who This Book Is For

This book is for anyone who wants to create better database applications without the complexity normally associated with the client/server architecture. If you are not currently using a remote database server, you are cheating yourself if you do not give ADS a look. If you are currently using another database server, and are unhappy with the level of maintenance that it requires, you too will benefit from considering the advantages of ADS.

The CD-ROM that accompanies this book includes everything you need to give ADS a try; it includes a single-user license for the Windows NT/2000/2003, Linux, Novell NetWare, and Windows 98/ME platforms. It also includes all utilities and associated client drivers, permitting you to access this server from almost every development environment imaginable. You will also find a link on the CD-ROM that permits you to download a 5-user trial version of the ADS server, in case you want to test ADS in a multiuser environment.

If you do not need a remote database server just yet, this CD-ROM also includes ALS, the Advantage Local Server. (ALS is installed when you install any of the client drivers, with the exception of the Java client. Read the license.txt file located in the directory in which you install a client driver for further information.) ALS is a file server–based database engine that supports up to five simultaneous users, and can be deployed royalty-free. (Note, however, that the free ALS cannot be used in Internet applications or with the Advantage JDBC Java Driver.) Importantly, ALS and ADS have identical APIs (application programming interfaces), permitting you to effortlessly convert an ALS client to an ADS client. The CD-ROM also includes the sample code listings and applications described in this book.

In short, the CD-ROM has everything you need to get started with ADS today.

So buckle your seatbelt and return your seat to its full, upright position. The fun is about to begin

ADS and the Advantage Data Architect

Part I of this book shows you how to build and configure the tables, indexes, and data dictionaries that you access from ADS (Advantage Database Server). Chapter 1 begins with a broad overview of ADS, providing you with a detailed understanding of the power, performances, and flexibility of ADS.

Chapters 2 and 3 show you how to create the basic building blocks of a high-performance database. In Chapter 2, you discover how to define tables, the data structures in which your data is stored. And in Chapter 3, you explore indexes, the means to fast and efficient data access.

In Chapter 4, you learn the power of ADS data dictionaries, including the many advanced features that data dictionaries provide. This chapter also shows you how to implement security using a data dictionary, including how to add users and groups to control access to your data.

Chapter 5 provides you with an in-depth look at constraints, record and field-level definitions that improve the accuracy of the data managed by ADS. And in Chapter 6, you discover how to create custom views of your tables. Included in this discussion is how you can modularize your access to data using views, simplifying what would otherwise require sophisticated data manipulations.

The final two chapters in this section provide you with everything you need to know in order to use two of ADSs most advanced features: stored procedures and triggers. Not only do these chapters provide you with a detailed examination of the role that these features play in your applications, but they also show you how to implement these objects using some of today's hottest development languages, including Delphi, Visual C# .NET, and Visual Basic .NET.

Introduction to Advantage Database Server

IN THIS CHAPTER:

Overview of Advantage Database Server

Advantage Database Server Versus Advantage Local Server

Advantage Tools

Building Database Applications Using ADS

Features Added in ADS Version 7

T his chapter is designed to provide you with an overall picture of the Advantage Database Server (ADS), including what makes it special, a quick tour of the tools that you will likely use with it, as well as how to build database applications using ADS. If you are new to ADS, you will want to read this chapter carefully. Doing so will show you how you can use ADS in your database applications.

If you are already familiar with ADS, you probably already know much of what is discussed in this chapter. In that case, you might want to quickly skim this chapter before continuing on to Chapter 2. In particular, you might want to read the section "Features Added in ADS Version 7," the latest release of ADS at the time of this writing.

Overview of Advantage Database Server

Advantage Database Server (ADS) is a relational database management system (RDBMS) marketed by Extended Systems, Inc., a company based in Boise, Idaho. ADS has been around since 1993, when it was introduced to provide a stable solution for Clipper developers who were tired of slow performance and corrupt indexes inherent to file server–based databases. Over the years, ADS has grown in both popularity and features. With the release of Advantage Database Server version 7.0, ADS finds itself a mature product with an impressive collection of features that rivals many of the more expensive and complicated database servers.

But what exactly is ADS? In a nutshell, the Advantage Database Server is a high-performance, low-maintenance, remote database server that permits you to easily build and deploy client/server applications. A lot of information is in that description, but what does it all mean? The following sections consider each of the points in this description.

ADS Is High Performance

First of all, ADS is a high-performance server. It permits you to manage very large quantities of data, and to access that data in a multiuser environment with unbelievable speed. For example, so long as you have designed your tables and indexes correctly, you can usually locate a particular record or subset of records in your database in a fraction of a second.

ADS's performance derives from its underlying architecture. Unlike many of the more complicated and expensive database servers, such as Microsoft's SQL Server and Oracle, ADS is not a traditional set-based relational database server based on SQL (structured query language). Instead, ADS is an ISAM (indexed sequential access method) relational database server. ISAM databases use indexes extensively, permitting them to perform high-speed table searches, filtering, and table joins.

Even though it is an ISAM server, ADS provides extensive support for the SQL language. Indeed, with ADS you can use the industry standard SQL language to perform almost any task related to the management of your data. When it comes to data access, these SQL statements are translated by ADS into optimized, index-based operations, providing you with an unbeatable combination of speed and accessibility.

The ISAM architecture has a long history. It is the same architecture that is used by venerable databases such as dBase, FoxPro, and Clipper. However, those databases were file server databases, while ADS is a client/server database server. In other words, ADS provides the unbeatable combination of proven performance and client/server reliability.

Unlike traditional ISAM databases, however, ADS supports many of the features that you find in high-end, set-based SQL database servers. For example, ADS supports views, stored procedures, triggers, referential integrity, and domain integrity constraints.

NOTE

Extended Systems also has an Advantage Replication server, a separate product from ADS, for companies who need to keep multiple databases synchronized. Information about this replication server can be found at www.AdvantageDatabase.com.

Another performance-related ISAM feature distinguishes ADS from set-based SQL databases. ISAM databases support a navigational model of data access, whereas set-based SQL databases do not. In the set-based database model, in theory at least, there is no record order. As a result, the SQL language does not support the concept of navigating a database. While some set-based SQL databases know that record B follows record A, the only way to move to a record that is 100 records after record A is to retrieve the record that follows A, then retrieve the record that follows that one, and again, and again, until this task is performed 100 times. Consider the Delphi language, which supports a navigational model of data access, a legacy of the BDE (Borland Database Engine). Imagine that a Delphi DBGrid (a grid-like component used for displaying a result set) displays data from a SELECT * FROM CUSTOMER query against a set-based SQL server where the CUSTOMER table contains a million records. If the end user presses CTRL-END while the DBGrid displaying this result set is active, the DBGrid will navigate to the last record—but in order to do so, it must fetch every single record. Anyone who has seen this knows that it will take a very, very long time before the user arrives at the last record. Furthermore, both the server and the network will be kept busy by this operation.

By comparison, records in an ISAM database have a record order, based on a selected index. If you point a Delphi DBGrid to an ADS table with a million records, and press CTRL-END, you will move immediately to the last record. This is because ADS can use the current index or the table's natural order to go to the last record, and then return only those last records needed to fill the display of the DBGrid.

This is an important point, especially if you are coming to ADS from a file server database, such as Paradox, dBase, or Access. File server databases permit a navigational approach. If you want to migrate one of these databases to a set-based SQL database server, unless your database is very small, you will likely have to reprogram your user interface to remove any navigational features. Otherwise, users' attempts to navigate can have serious consequences for your application's performance.

The problem is that end users love the navigational interface. Having a grid that displays some records from a table, and having the impression that they can easily jump to somewhere in the middle of that table (or anywhere in the table they want to) is very appealing to end users. With ADS, you can provide that feature, but with set-based SQL servers, you should not.

Here is another way to look at it. With ADS you have a choice. You can write your applications using the portable and more or less standardized SQL language, or you can use a navigational model, or you can use both. With SQL-based remote database servers, you are limited to the set-oriented SQL language.

A number of the Advantage data access mechanisms permit you to build client applications that use the navigation model. These include the Advantage TDataSet Descendant, which can be used by Borland's Delphi, Kylix, and C++Builder, as well as languages that can make direct calls to the Advantage Client Engine, which include Borland's products as well as Microsoft's Visual Basic and Visual C++.

NOTE

Development environments that can use ADO (Active X data objects) can leverage most of the navigational model through the Advantage OLE DB Provider. What is missing with ADO is that you cannot set ranges.

ADS Is Low Maintenance

Most database servers require a database administrator to keep them running smoothly and efficiently. And database administrators often require advanced training and certification. But with ADS, most applications require little or no maintenance. In most cases, once the ADS server is installed, you can pretty much forget about it, other than ensuring that your data gets backed up regularly.

"How can this be?" you ask. Once again, this is largely due to the underlying architecture of ADS. For example, so long as you use the Advantage proprietary format for your data tables, space previously occupied by deleted records is automatically recovered when new records are added. Similarly, ADS's legendary stability makes it unnecessary to rebuild indexes, in most cases.

That ADS-based databases require little or no maintenance makes this server particularly attractive for applications that are distributed to many different locations. For example, if you license your application to many different clients, the less you or they have to worry about managing the database server, the better. This is why ADS is a good choice for vertical market applications and for applications that are deployed to many different systems.

ADS Is a Remote Database Server

A remote database server like ADS is an application specifically designed to provide other applications with access to one or more databases. Those other applications are referred to as *clients,* and most client applications are end user applications. This configuration, where clients request data from a remote server, is referred to as *client/server architecture*.

The client/server architecture offers many advantages, but the most important is reliability. With ADS, you have confidence that your data is secure and accessible.

Advantage Database Server Versus Advantage Local Server

In addition to ADS, Extended Systems also provides a database engine called the Advantage Local Server (ALS). ALS is very similar to Microsoft's Jet Engine, which is used by MS Access, and Borland's BDE (Borland Database Engine) when the BDE is using local tables. All of these database engines are file server database engines.

Unlike a database server, which is a stand-alone application, a database engine is essentially a library of data access routines that runs in the same process as the client application. Each client application will load its own copy of these database engine files, and each client application is responsible for all data manipulation.

Extended Systems makes ALS available to developers free of charge. Developers can use ALS with their stand-alone and small, multiuser applications, and can even distribute these applications to their clients without paying any royalty fees. The only applications that you are prohibited from using ALS with are those applications that run on the Internet, such as CGI (common gateway interface) Web server extensions. For those types of applications, you must use ADS.

Why, you are probably wondering, should you use ADS if you can use ALS for free? The answer is straightforward. ADS is better.

Actually, the benefits of a database server like ADS over database engines like ALS are associated with four factors. These are reduced network traffic, improved performance, enabled transactions, and unparalleled stability. Each of these factors is examined in the following sections.

Reducing Network Traffic

In short, the Advantage Local Server is not a database server, in the true client/server sense. With file server–based systems, all data processing is performed on the individual workstations. For example, to select all records from a customer table for customers in a particular city, the entire customer table index must be transferred across the network to the workstation, which then finds the record based on the index locally. The located records are then retrieved from the file server.

The problem is worse if an appropriate index does not exist for the table. In that case, the entire table must be transmitted across the network.

While this overhead is negligible if the customer table includes several dozen records, the strain that it places on the network increases with the size of the table. For example, selecting the hundred or so records for customers from Des Moines, Iowa, from a million record table requires that the entire index for all one million records be transmitted across the network.

The problem is particularly bad when you consider that the network load increases in direct proportion to the number of people who are using the application simultaneously. Every single client needs to read indexes and tables across the network in order to get its work done.

By comparison, Advantage Database Server performs its processing on the database server, which is typically the machine on which the shared data files are located. There is no need to copy entire indexes or tables across the network when the client application is interested in only a few records. Specifically, in a client/server environment, the client requests the records that it needs, and the server uses the indexes and tables to locate the needed data. Once the data is identified, that data, and only that data, is transmitted across the network to the client.

Improved Performance

Performance is another area where file server–based systems suffer. Specifically, the individual workstations are responsible for all processing. In other words, all user interface interaction as well as database manipulation is performed on each client workstation in a file server–based system. The file server itself performs no processing, other than transferring files from the server to the workstation.

By comparison, client/server systems perform nearly all data manipulation on the database server, efficiently distributing the processing across multiple machines. When using ADS, your workstations are primarily responsible for the user interface, while the remote server takes care of data manipulation.

Most database applications are multiuser, and it is in these situations where the performance advantages of the client/server architecture are most profound. However, note that in stand-alone applications, where the data is used by only one workstation, ALS-based applications might actually outperform client/server applications. In short, if the data is used by only one workstation, and the data is stored on that workstation, ALS often provides the greatest level of performance. For these applications, ADS provides you with a seamless, high-performance migration path when these applications are converted to multiuser use.

Available Transactions

A transaction is an operation that treats two or more changes to a database as a discrete unit, saving those changes in an all-or-none fashion. If all of the operations involved in the transaction can be completed, the transaction itself is committed. However, if even one operation cannot be successfully completed, all operations within the transaction are canceled, ensuring that your data remains consistent.

Transactions require centralized control of data access, and file server–based systems cannot provide that. Every change in a file server–based system is independent of every other change. As a result, it is entirely possible for a file server–based system to complete some, but not all, operations.

One very important feature of a transaction comes into play if the database server, the client workstation, or the network across which they communicate, fails before the transaction is committed. In those cases, the edits of the transaction are rolled back automatically by the Advantage Database Server once the problem is detected, or the server is restarted (if the server crashed).

Though ALS does not support transactions, you can write your applications that use ALS as if it did. Specifically, when using ALS, your code can include calls to begin, commit, and roll back transactions. These statements will be ignored. However, if you then migrate that application to use ADS, no changes are necessary in your code, and the transactions will be observed.

Improved Stability

The final drawback to file server–based systems is stability. Because there is no centralized control over locking and transactions, the failure of a single workstation can corrupt parts of the database. Developers familiar with BDE-based local table applications occasionally encounter errors such as corrupt or out-of-date indexes.

The issue of stability disappears almost completely when the Advantage Database Server is involved. In these applications, ADS itself is managing the data, and failure of an individual workstation or the network simply cannot harm the data.

When to Use the Advantage Local Server

If ADS is so much better than a database engine solution like ALS, why does Extended Systems bother making ALS available? Well, There are several, but they are all related to a simple fact. Not all applications require the benefits of ADS.

Imagine that you have written a database application that you plan on licensing to many different clients. Your software is probably pretty expensive, and pricing may be an issue for some of your customers. For example, consider a customer who will have only one or two users on the system. The additional cost of an ADS license may make the difference between selling the software or not. For those customers, you can deploy the application using ALS.

Imagine this same customer at some later time. Maybe they now have four simultaneous users, and they cannot tolerate the occasional corruption of an index due to a workstation crash. For a relatively small amount of money, you can upgrade their application to use the Advantage Database Server, and your customer can say "goodbye" to corrupt indexes.

For other customers, especially those who have a large number of users, there is no question about it—you will deploy their applications using ADS.

What is so great about this scenario is that there is no difference, from a development standpoint, between your application using ALS or ADS. The API (application programming interface) for ALS and ADS is exactly the same. And most of the time, upgrading an ALS application to use ADS is simply a matter of installing the server (a process that can be automated).

To put this another way, whether an application uses ALS or ADS is a deployment issue, not a development issue. You will write your application the same way regardless of which deployment option you choose.

Actually, there are a couple of differences, but they really serve more to underscore how similar the two interfaces are. As you have already learned, you can write your application to employ transactions, but only when you deploy with ADS will those statements actually do something.

There is another difference. If you are using the Java language and want to use the Advantage JDBC (Java database connectivity) Driver, you can only use ADS. This is because the Advantage JDBC Driver is a class 4 driver, which is to say that it communicates directly with the server, without going through a client API. If you want to use Java with ALS, you must use the JDBC-ODBC bridge (a class 1 driver), in conjunction with the Advantage ODBC (open database connectivity) Driver.

The second difference is related to triggers and extended stored procedures. With ADS, both triggers and stored procedures execute on the server. Since ALS is not a remote database server, any triggers or stored procedures will actually execute on the client workstation, so you lose the major benefits of distributed computing and reduced network traffic.

The bottom line is that ALS is a wonderful option for database developers. It provides you with a low-cost deployment option that effortlessly scales to client/server when client/server features are required.

Throughout this book we will assume that you are going to deploy your applications using ADS. But we will try to point out when a feature we are describing works differently between ADS and ALS.

Advantage Tools

There is more to Advantage than just ADS and ALS. You will also use several support tools to configure your database server, as well as to create your actual databases. Among these are the Advantage Configuration Utility, the Advantage Data Architect, and the Advantage ANSI Collation Utility. Each of these tools is described in the following sections.

The Advantage Configuration Utility

When ADS is installed on your server on Windows NT/2000/2003, the Advantage Configuration Utility is also installed. This utility provides you with several important capabilities. It permits you to view statistics about your server's operation, and it also permits you to manually set many of the server's configurable properties. Because the Windows NT/2000/2003 server is the most popular server version, the Advantage Configuration Utility is described in this section.

Windows 98/ME, Linux, and Novell NetWare installations of ADS do not include the Advantage Configuration Utility. Windows 98/ME installations are configured from the server application itself, and Linux and NetWare installations are configured from command-line parameters and/or configuration files. For these installations, refer to the documentation for information on configuring ADS.

ON THE CD

The ADS documentation is located on this book's CD-ROM. The ADS documentation can also be downloaded in PDF format from http://devzone.AdvantageDatabase.com.

All OS (operating system) versions of ADS have an Advantage Database Server Management Utility available from within the Advantage Data Architect. (A stand-alone version of this utility is also available with ADS 7.0 and later.) The Management Utility contains information similar to the Advantage Configuration Utility described in this section. See the ADS documentation for additional information on the Advantage Database Server Management Utility.

NOTE

The purpose of the following descriptions is to show you where you can get information about the server. This section is not designed to provide a detailed description of how these settings are used. For that information, please refer to the ADS documentation.

To use the Advantage Configuration Utility in Windows NT/2000/2003, select the Start button, and then select Programs | Advantage Database Server | ADS Configuration Utility. The Advantage Configuration Utility shown in Figure 1-1 is displayed. There are three main tabs: Database Info, Installation Info, and Configuration Utility. These pages are described in the following sections.

Database Info Page

The Database Info page, shown in Figure 1-1, contains basic statistics about attached users, connections, work areas, as well as open tables and indexes. The Current column

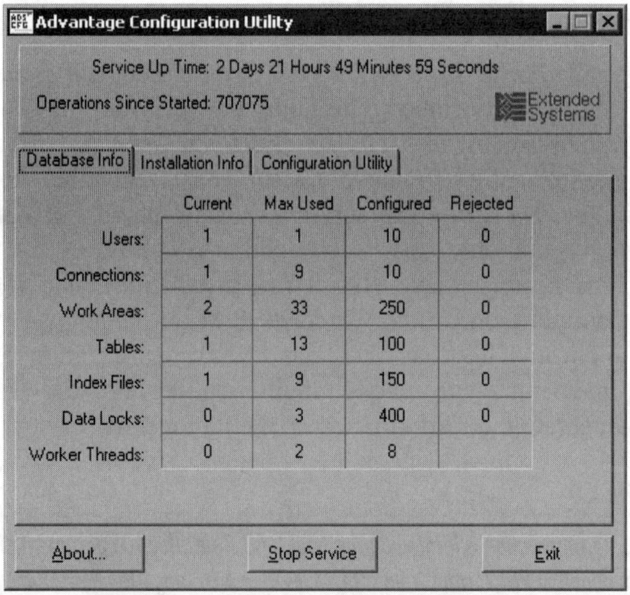

Figure 1-1 *Use the Advantage Configuration Utility to view statistics for and to configure your ADS server.*

on the Database Info page displays current usage statistics, while the Max Used column shows the highest value for each statistic since the server was started.

This information can help you determine whether you need to make adjustments to any of the configurable parameters of the server. For example, if you find that the maximum number of configured connections were used, and that some connections were rejected, you can use the Configuration Utility pages to increase the number of available connections. The Configuration Utility pages are described later in this section.

The Installation Info Page

The Installation Info page, shown in Figure 1-2, contains information about the installed server, including the licensed number of users, your serial number, and the server version you are running.

The values on the Installation Info page are not configurable. If you need to change these values, you can either reinstall your server, or use a special utility that ships with ADS. This utility, called adsstamp.exe, permits you to install a new license key and to change your character sets and a few other settings. For information on using adsstamp.exe, refer to the ADS help.

ON THE CD

Many of the settings that you can control from the Advantage Configuration Utility can also be adjusted using command-line parameters and/or configuration files. For information about these options, see the Advantage Database Server documentation on this book's CD-ROM.

Advantage Configuration Utility		
Service Up Time: 2 Days 21 Hours 50 Minutes 28 Seconds		
Operations Since Started: 707075		Extended Systems

Database Info | Installation Info | Configuration Utility |

Registered to:	Cary Jensen
Serial Number:	774422
User Option:	10
ADS Revision:	7.0
OEM Character Set:	USA
ANSI Character Set:	ENGL(AMER)
Install Date:	
Eval Expiration Date:	
Log Entries:	77

About...   Stop Service   Exit

Figure 1-2   *The Installation Info page of the Advantage Configuration Utility*

The remaining pages of the Advantage Configuration Utility are used to set the parameters used by the server. You display these additional pages by clicking on the Configuration Utility tab of the Advantage Configuration Utility.

In most cases, once you have adjusted the settings of the Advantage Database Server, you will not need to make further changes. However, after the server has been running for a while, you should inspect the Database Info page of the Advantage Configuration Utility to ensure that your initial settings are sufficient. If you find that you have to make adjustments to one or more of the settings found on the Configuration pages of the Advantage Configuration Utility, you will need to stop and then restart your server before your changes take effect.

The Database Settings Page

Use the Database Settings page, shown in Figure 1-3, to adjust the maximum permitted connections, work areas, and simultaneously opened tables and indexes. Note that the maximum number of connections is not the same as the maximum number of users. Each machine that is currently accessing the server counts as a user. Each user can have multiple connections. You should set Number of Connections to the maximum user count times the average number of connections each user requires.

The File Locations Page

Use the File Locations page, shown in Figure 1-4, to change the location of the error and transaction log files, as well as the semaphore connection file path.

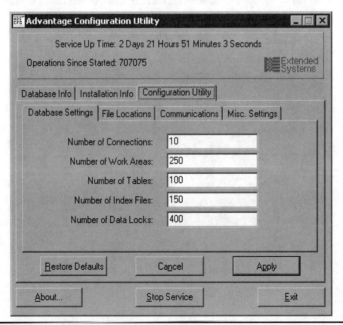

Figure 1-3   *The Database Settings page of the Advantage Configuration Utility*

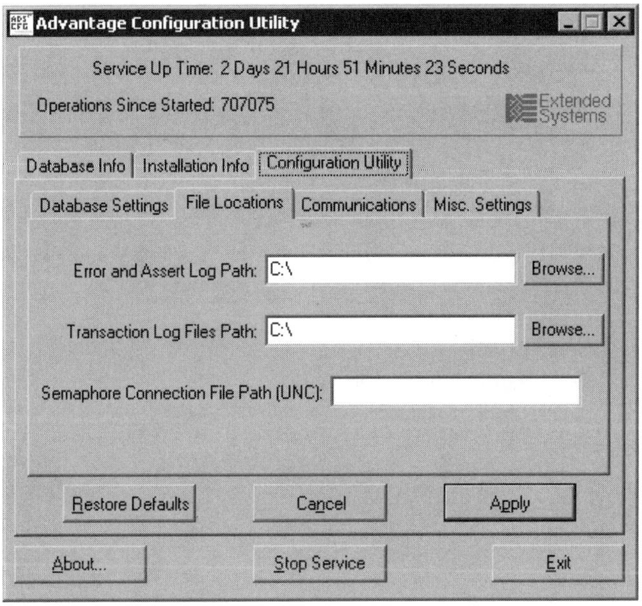

Figure 1-4   *The File Locations page of the Advantage Configuration Utility*

The error file, ads_err.dbf, is updated when ADS encounters a problem at runtime. This log file is a simple DBF file that you can open as a free table using the Advantage Data Architect, or using any other utility capable of viewing DBF files.

Transaction log files are files that the ADS TPS (transaction processing system) creates while updates to a database are being performed within the context of a transaction. These important files permit ADS to either commit or roll back changes if there is a failure somewhere in the system before the transaction is complete. These files, which have the .tps extension, are deleted by ADS when the associated transaction is complete.

Unlike the ads_err.dbf files, TPS files are intended for the internal use of ADS. You should not manually delete or attempt to view these files.

The Communications Page

If you want to permit applications to connect to your server over the Internet, use the Communications page to define how this communication will be permitted. The Communications page of the Advantage Configuration Utility is shown in Figure 1-5.

IP Port permits you to set the UDP and TCP ports on which the server will listen for client connections. ("IP," "UDP," and "TCP" stand for Internet protocol, universal datagram protocol, and transmission control protocol, respectively.) If IP Port is set to the default 0, it will try to use UDP and TCP port 6262. If you want to specify the UDP/TCP IP Port, set IP Port to a port that is available for both UDP and TCP.

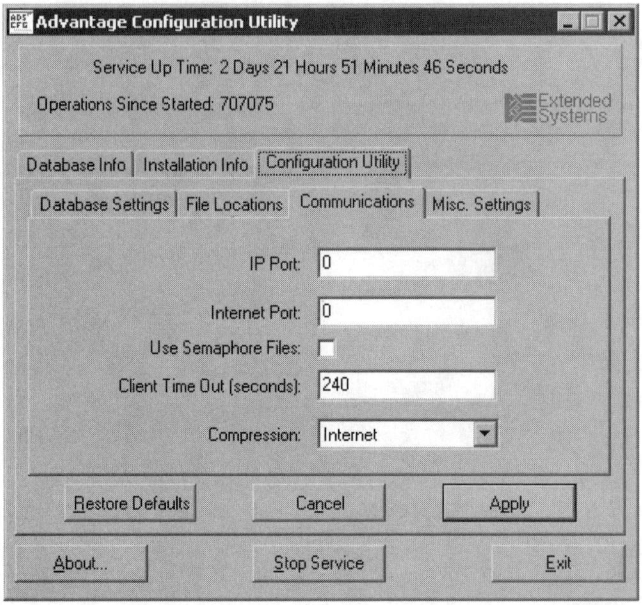

Figure 1-5   *The Communications page of the Advantage Configuration Utility*

If you want to connect to ADS over the Internet, you set Internet Port to the UDP port that applications (Windows and Linux clients) will use to connect to your server, or to the TCP/IP (transmission control protocol/Internet protocol) port that Java applications will use to connect to your server. This port (TCP/IP for Java clients or UDP/IP for Windows and Linux clients) must also be opened in any firewalls separating the server and the applications that need to access it. Leaving Internet Port set to the default of 0 disables Internet access.

NOTE

There are plans to include full TCP/IP support with Windows and Linux clients in an ADS release sometime after 7.0.

You also use this page to configure whether to use a semaphore file, the client connection timeout, and level of data compression.

NOTE

To enable Internet access to the Advantage Database Server, you must also configure the data dictionary used to access the data to accept Internet connections. Depending on the data access mechanism or the specifics of your connection, each client machine may also require an ADS configuration file that contains additional information about the connection. For information on setting up client applications to connect over the Internet, see the topic "Advantage Internet Server" in the ADS documentation.

The Misc. Settings Page

Use the final page of the Advantage Configuration Utility, Misc. Settings, shown in Figure 1-6, to set the maximum number of worker threads, as well as the maximum size of the error log.

Advantage Data Architect

The Advantage Data Architect, whose main screen is shown in Figure 1-7, is a graphical tool that simplifies the creation and configuration of your tables and databases. The Advantage Data Architect is also referred to as *ARC*. The Advantage Data Architect also includes a wide variety of support features, including the ability to import and export data, execute ad hoc queries, perform checks on your development environment, and much, much more. As a developer, you are likely to use the Advantage Data Architect more than any other tool that ships with ADS.

While the Advantage Data Architect makes it easy to design your tables and data dictionaries, there are alternatives. Specifically, all of the database-related configuration capabilities provided by Advantage Data Architect can also be performed using Advantage SQL, as well as by programming directly to the ADS API using ACE (the Advantage Client Engine).

The Advantage Data Architect provides another benefit, albeit one that is not immediately obvious. It can provide you with insight on how to create and manage

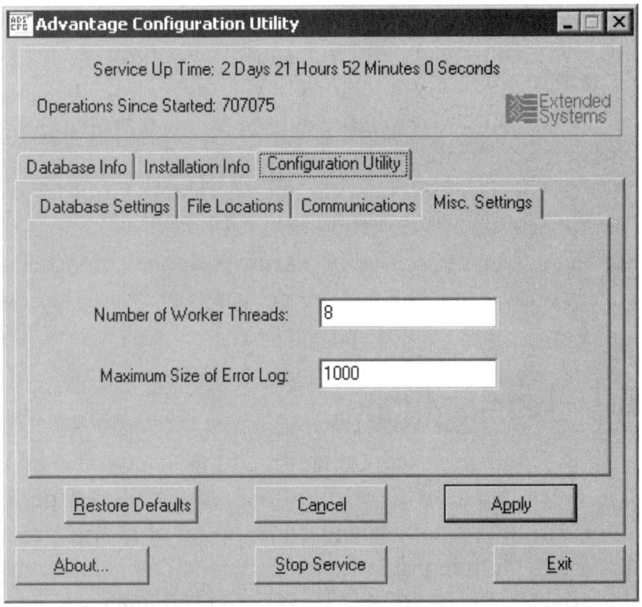

Figure 1-6   *The Misc. Settings page of the Advantage Configuration Utility*

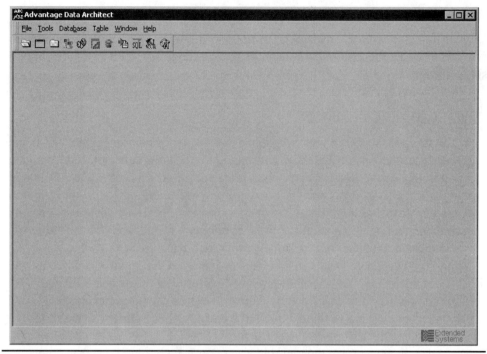

Figure 1-7   *The main screen of the Advantage Data Architect*

your tables and data dictionaries programmatically. The Advantage Data Architect was written in the Delphi language, and the source code for this Delphi project is available on the CD-ROM that accompanies this book. The Delphi language is easy to read, so even if you are not a Delphi developer, you can probably figure out how specific operations were performed.

Because the Advantage Data Architect is such a valuable tool for working with tables and data dictionaries, a large portion of this book discusses its use. In other words, there is no chapter that specifically discusses the Advantage Data Architect. Instead, almost all examples in this book where tables and data dictionaries are manipulated use the Advantage Data Architect.

Advantage ANSI Collation Utility

ADS ships with the Advantage ANSI Collation Utility, shown in Figure 1-8, a tool that permits you to create custom ANSI collations. The ANSI (American National Standards Institute) character set is a standard mapping of characters to numeric values. These characters include printable characters and special control characters, such as tabs and carriage returns. An ANSI collation sequence defines the order, or precedence, of characters for the purpose of making string comparisons.

Character Sets and Collations

File   Help

File Name:

C:\Program Files\Extended Syste   [Browse]

Display: [✓] Hex

Select a current Collation Language: Danish

Create a new Language Collation: [Create]

[Open File]

Collation Table | Org Table | Upper Table | Lower Table

0()	1()	2()	3()	4()	5()	6()	7()	8()	28(()	29())	2A(*)	2B(+)	2C(,)	9()	A()
B()	C()	D()	E()	F()	10()	11()	12()	13()	14()	15()	16()	17()	18()	19()	1A()
26(&)	2D(-)	2E(.)	2F(/)	30(0)	31(1)	32(2)	21(!)	33(3)	34(4)	35(5)	58(X)	36(6)	22(")	37(7)	38(8)
73(s)	77(w)	79(y)	7B({)	7D(})	7E(~)	7F()	80(€)	81()	82()	39(9)	3A(:)	59(Y)	5A(Z)	5B([)	3B(;)
3C(<)	84()	8F()	91(')	95()	99()	A3(£)	A6()	A8(¨)	AA(ª)	B4(´)	B6(¶)	B8(¸)	BA(º)	BC(¼)	C0(À)
CD(Í)	CF(Ï)	D1(Ñ)	D3(Ó)	D8(Ø)	DD(Ý)	E5(å)	E7(ç)	E9(é)	EB(ë)	F3(ó)	3D(=)	3E(>)	3F(?)	40(@)	42(B)
43(C)	83()	8E()	90()	94()	98()	A2(¢)	A5(¥)	A7(§)	A9(©)	B3(³)	B5(µ)	B7(·)	B9(¹)	BB(»)	BF(¿)
CC(Ì)	CE(Î)	D0(Ð)	D2(Ò)	D7(×)	DC(Ü)	E4(ä)	E6(æ)	E8(è)	EA(ê)	F2(ò)	44(D)	45(E)	46(F)	47(G)	1B()
72(r)	1C()	52(R)	A4(¤)	55(U)	70(p)	6D(m)	6E(n)	41(A)	71(q)	D5(Õ)	56(V)	CB(Ë)	1D()	F5(õ)	1E()
1F()	50(P)	51(Q)	53(S)	54(T)	6F(o)	24($)	25(%)	4F(O)	DB(Û)	D4(Ô)	57(W)	CA(Ê)	20()	F4(ô)	EF(ï)
27(')	48(H)	61(a)	62(b)	63(c)	64(d)	49(I)	65(e)	4A(J)	66(f)	85()	5D(])	67(g)	23(#)	68(h)	4B(K)
69(i)	5C(\)	7A(z)	7C(|)	4C(L)	6A(j)	6B(k)	6C(l)	4D(M)	78(x)	C1(Á)	5E(^)	74(t)	75(u)	76(v)	4E(N)
89()	87()	8B()	8D()	F9(ù)	FF(ÿ)	F7(÷)	93()	9D()	9B()	9F()	A1(¡)	AE(®)	AC(¬)	B0(°)	B2(²)
97()	BE(¾)	C5(Å)	C3(Ã)	C7(Ç)	C9(É)	FD(ý)	5F(_)	FB(û)	E1(á)	DF(ß)	E3(ã)	F1(ñ)	ED(í)	DA(Ú)	D6(Ö)
88()	86()	8A()	8C()	F8(ø)	FE(þ)	F6(ö)	92(')	9C()	9A()	9E()	A0()	AD()	AB(«)	AF(¯)	B1(±)
96()	BD(½)	C4(Ä)	C2(Â)	C6(Æ)	C8(È)	FC(ü)	60(`)	FA(ú)	E0(à)	DE(Þ)	E2(â)	F0(ð)	EC(ì)	D9(Ù)	EE(î)

Figure 1-8   *The ANSI Collation Utility*

Few developers will ever need to use the Advantage ANSI Collation Utility. For most applications that use the English language, you will install one of the provided English collation sequences. Similarly, for most non-English applications, Extended Systems provides localized character sets that ensure proper string comparisons.

For those non–English speaking developers for whom there is no localized character set, the Advantage ANSI Collation Utility is an essential tool for defining character precedence.

When installing ADS or ALS, you will choose either a localized character set or an ANSI collation sequence. Which options you have depends on the version of the Advantage Database Server that you are installing. For example, if you are installing the domestic version of ADS, you will be able to select only between an American English collation, a Canadian English collation, and a French Canadian collation.

Regardless of which character set or collation sequence you install, keep one very important issue in mind. The server, and all client applications that use it, must use the same character set or collation sequence. Doing so ensures that both clients and server agree on how strings are compared.

Because both client and server must use the same character set or ANSI collation sequence, it is particularly important for non-English applications to use the ANSI character set provided by Extended Systems, instead of choosing "default on machine." This is especially important for Advantage Local Server users. Each version of Windows (95, 98, NT, 2000, and so on) has different "default on machine" ANSI collation sequences, even when the same language is configured. Consequently, if one ALS client is using Windows 98 and another is using Windows 2000, collation mismatch errors will result.

CAUTION

If you change the character set or collation sequence being used by your clients and server, you must rebuild all indexes before you access any of your tables.

Building Database Applications Using ADS

The Advantage Database Server is a RDBMS (relational database management system), but it is not a full-scale database development environment. While ADS includes a varied set of tools for creating and configuring the files that will be used by a database application, you do not use it directly to build the actual client applications. For that purpose you use one of a wide range of development environments.

This section is designed to provide you with a broad understanding of the role that ADS, and the tools that come with it, play in application development. To meet this end, this discussion is broken down into two parts: creating the database and creating the client applications.

In reality, this discussion could have been organized in a number of different, yet equally correct, ways. For example, database development is often described as a four-part process of design, development, testing, and deployment. While true, that description focuses on the process, and not the tools. Since this book is specifically about the Advantage Database Server, we felt that a tool-based view is more appropriate.

Creating the Database

A *database,* as the term is used here, is a collection of files used by the Advantage Database Server. With ADS, these files include tables, memo files, indexes, and in most cases, data dictionaries.

NOTE

If you are unfamiliar with what the parts of a database are, you might want to take a quick look at Chapter 2 (creating tables), Chapter 3 (defining indexes), and Chapter 4 (using data dictionaries). The introductions to each of these chapters define what these various files are, and what roles they play in a database.

In most cases, you use the Advantage Data Architect to create your database. Specifically, you either import existing data into one or more tables, or you design the tables from scratch. You then consider how your data will be accessed by the client applications, and design the indexes that will make that access fast.

In many cases, you also design a data dictionary. A data dictionary, as far as ADS is concerned, is a special file that is used to access all of the tables within a given application. Data dictionaries provide your client applications with a number of powerful features, such as security, constraints, and referential integrity, to name just a few. Here again, you will probably use the Advantage Data Architect to create your data dictionary.

Instead of using the Advantage Data Architect to create your database, you can also create your database at runtime from one or more of your client applications. To do this, your client applications would need to include code that defines new tables, indexes, and data dictionaries, as needed, on-the-fly. Your client applications would not explicitly create memo files. Memo files are created automatically when data is inserted into memo or BLOB (binary large objects) fields.

Creating databases on-the-fly from within a client application requires a lot of programming, compared with creating databases with the Advantage Data Architect. Fortunately, creating a database at runtime is normally only necessary in special situations. For example, some applications need to store separate data in separate databases. If these applications need to be able to create a new database at any time, then you will probably need to take the extra effort to create the new database at runtime.

Before a client application can access the tables, indexes, and data dictionaries of an application, the client workstation must be able to send IP packets to the server upon which Advantage Database Server is running. Client applications don't even need the rights to access the individual files. The server does this. The exception is when the client is using ALS, in which case the client application must have rights to the shared table, index, and memo files.

The server on which you install your database and the Advantage Database Server can be running one of the following operating systems: Windows 98, Windows ME, Windows NT 4.0 (Service Pack 6 or later), Windows 2000, Windows 2003, Novell NetWare 4 or later, or Linux.

Actually, there are four versions of the ADS server. The most popular version is designed for Windows NT 4.0 or later, which includes 2000 and 2003. For Novell networks, there is a NLM (NetWare loadable module), which requires NetWare version 4 or later. The Linux version of ADS requires glibc 2.1.2-11 or newer and kernel version 2.2 or newer. Finally, there is a Windows 98/ME version. However, Windows 98 and ME are poor hosts for a server, so you should consider one of the other versions of ADS.

NOTE

Windows XP is not listed as a supported OS since XP is marketed by Microsoft as a client operating system only, not as a server operating system. ADS for Windows NT/2000/2003 runs on XP, although XP is not a supported OS.

Some final comments about creating a database are in order before continuing on to the discussion about building client applications. First, while creating tables, indexes, and data dictionaries is not hard, the design of the tables, indexes, and data dictionaries is often the result of research and thoughtful consideration.

For example, you need to take into account what kind of data your need to store and how it will be used. This will lead you to consider how many tables you will need to create, and what indexes you will add to them. Likewise, how you set up a data dictionary, including what groups and users to add, what views to define, and whether to use referential integrity, can have a big impact on the success of your database application.

A second consideration is that the design of your database is something that will likely change over time. In short, database design is often an iterative process.

As your design begins to take shape, you often will discover that a particular table is missing one or more fields, or that additional indexes need to be created, or that entirely new tables must be added.

These changes, when they happen, will often affect both the server and the client parts of the application. For instance, if you find that you have to add a new field to a table, you might use the Advantage Data Architect to update the table file. In most cases you will then also need to change your client applications so that they can use the newly added field.

Creating the Client Applications

The Advantage Data Architect is a pretty powerful piece of software. You will learn as you work through the later chapters in this book, that not only does the Advantage Data Architect provide you with the tools to design a database, but also that it permits you to work with the database. Specifically, using the Advantage Data Architect, you can add new records to your tables, change existing records, and delete records. It also provides you with a number of tools to sort the data in your tables, as well as to filter your data to display only a subset of the records in a given table. Indeed, it even permits you to export your data to HTML (hypertext markup language), which you can then print, using this feature as a simple reporting mechanism.

Here is another way to look at it. The Advantage Data Architect is an ADS client application. However, it is a very general ADS client whose primary purpose is to give you the ability to easily design and test your database. In most cases, you will create one or more custom client applications to work with your ADS databases.

Custom client applications are all about making your data accessible to your end users. Sure, an end user could use the Advantage Data Architect to view just a subset of records, but that would require that your end user know SQL. Similarly, while an end user could export the results of a SQL query to HTML, and then print this from a Web browser, the output would lack the quality and sophistication that most people want to see in a report.

With a custom client application, your end users are presented with data options that make sense in the context of the data. For example, your application can display a form from which the end user enters a customer account number. Once the number is entered, your application can perform a query to select the data for that customer, and display the customer data in an easy to view format. Similarly, your application can include a menu item that, when selected, creates and prints an attractive report that makes the data easily digestible.

You can create custom client applications that use ADS from a wide variety of application development platforms. Examples of languages from which you can access ADS include Borland products Delphi, C++Builder, C#Builder, Kylix, and JBuilder; Microsoft products Visual Basic, Visual C++, Visual C#, FoxPro, Visual J#, and Visual Studio.NET; IBM's VisualAge for Java; Sun Microsystems' Sun ONE Studio; Computer Associates' Clipper; Grafx Software's Visual Objects; and Corel's Paradox. For Web-based development, many of the preceding products can be used to create CGI or ISAPI (Internet server application programming interface) Web server extensions. In addition, you can access ADS from PHP and Perl.

In short, you can use any application development environment for which Extended Systems supplies a data access mechanism. Fortunately, Extended Systems provides a large number of data access mechanisms. These are listed in Table 1-1, which includes a description of the development environments best suited for each mechanism.

Several of the data access mechanisms listed in Table 1-1 refer to groups of drivers. For example, there are two Advantage ODBC drivers, one for 32-bit Windows and another for Linux. Similarly, there are Windows and Linux versions of both the Perl and PHP drivers.

As you can see from this list, you have an impressive selection of data access options with the Advantage Database Server. As a result, you can access your data from Advantage Database Server with nearly every modern software development environment.

There is another point that deserves mention here. Each of these data access options can access any version of the Advantage Database Server. Specifically, even though the Advantage OLE DB Provider is only available for Windows clients, it can access ADS running under Linux as well as Novell NetWare. Similarly, a Java client using the Advantage JDBC Driver running on a Macintosh can access any ADS server, regardless of the operating system the server is running on.

Data Access Mechanism	Supported Development Environments
Advantage TDataSet Descendant	Any language that supports Borland's VCL (visual component library) or CLX (component library cross-platform). These include Delphi, C++Builder, and Kylix.
Advantage ODBC Driver	Any language that supports ODBC drivers. These include almost all Windows-based development environments such as Visual Basic, Visual C++, Visual FoxPro, Delphi, and C++Builder, to name a few. There is also a Linux ODBC version for ODBC-enabled Linux applications.
Advantage OLE DB Provider	Any language that supports ADO (ActiveX data objects). These include Visual Basic, Visual C++, Delphi, C++Builder, and any .NET development tool such as Visual Studio .NET and C#Builder.
Advantage Client Engine (ACE) API	Any language that can make an API call into a Windows DLL (dynamic link library) or Linux SO (shared object) file, such as Visual Basic, Delphi, Kylix, and C/C++.
Advantage Clipper RDDs (replaceable database drivers)	Clipper.
Advantage Visual Objects RDDs	Visual Objects.
Advantage JDBC Driver	Any Java development environment that supports JDBC drivers such as JBuilder, Sun ONE Studio, and VisualAge for Java.
Advantage .NET Data Provider	Any .NET-enabled development environment including, but not limited to, Visual Studio.NET and C#Builder.
Advantage DBI Driver	Perl under Windows or Linux.
Advantage PHP Extension	For PHP version 3 or later under Windows or Linux.
Advantage Crystal Reports Driver	Seagate Crystal Reports versions 6 and later.

Table 1-1   *Data Access Mechanisms for the Advantage Database Server*

ON THE CD

The drivers listed in Table 1-1 can be found on the CD-ROM accompanying this book.

Features Added in ADS Version 7

The Advantage Database Server is a mature product, and version 7.0 is the latest release at the time of this writing. With this release, Extended Systems has continued the tradition of adding powerful new features to the server, while maintaining the ease of use that is its hallmark. These features are discussed in the following sections.

Triggers

A trigger is a compiled routine that executes on the server in response to a data-related event. ADS supports record-level triggers on insert, update, and delete events. For each of these events there are three trigger event types: a *before,* an *instead of,* and an *after* event type. As a result, there are a total of nine trigger events.

Like AEPs (Advantage Extended Procedures), ADS's stored procedure mechanism, triggers can be implemented in a wide variety of languages. Specifically, Advantage triggers can be written as standard Windows DLLs (dynamic link libraries), COM (component object model) servers, Linux SO (shared object) libraries, or .NET managed assemblies. Unlike AEPs, Advantage triggers can also be implemented using SQL scripts.

Creating and installing triggers is discussed in Chapter 8.

Full Text Search

Full text search (FTS) permits you to conduct high-speed, index-based searches of text, memo, and BLOB fields. Using full text search, you can add sophisticated search-engine functionality to your client applications. Full text search is discussed in detail in Chapter 3.

Data Dictionary Upgrade Functionality

Two versions of a data dictionary can be compared. The result of this comparison is a script of SQL statements that you can use to transform one data dictionary to another.

The purpose of these generated SQL scripts is to permit you to easily upgrade a data dictionary from within a client application. Once an upgraded SQL script has been generated, you can customize it, if necessary, and then include that script in your application. For example, within your application you can determine the current version of a data dictionary, and execute the appropriate upgrade if you find it to be an older version. This capability is particularly beneficial to developers who deploy their applications to many different sites and who need to provide a mechanism to upgrade older data dictionaries.

Comparing data dictionaries is discussed in Chapter 4.

The Advantage .NET Data Provider

While .NET developers can use the Advantage OLE DB Provider with the classes of the System.Data.OleDb third-level namespace to connect to ADS, Extended Systems has created a custom .NET Data Provider for optimized access to ADS using ADO.NET. These classes can be found in the AdsProvider namespace and include AdsConnection, AdsCommand, AdsDataReader, AdsParameter, AdsParameterCollection, AdsCommandBuilder, and AdsDataAdapter.

The Advantage .NET Data Provider is discussed in Chapter 15.

The Advantage JDBC Driver

Prior to the release of ADS 7.0, Java developers had to rely on the JDBC class 1 JDBC-ODBC bridge in order to use ADS from their Java applications. Although this solution works, it is limited to clients running on ODBC-enabled operating systems. It also creates a more complicated client install, since not only does the Advantage ODBC driver need to be installed, but so does the ACE (Advantage Client Engine). In ADS 7.0 and later, Java developers have a class 4 JDBC driver for ADS, the Advantage JDBC Driver. A class 4 JDBC driver is one that is written entirely in Java, and that does not require a client API. As a result, Java client applications using a class 4 driver are very convenient to install.

The Advantage JDBC Driver is discussed in Chapter 13.

Extended SQL Support

With each release of ADS, more of ADS's functionality has been exposed through Advantage SQL. With ADS 7.0, support has been extended to almost every aspect of the product. Now you can obtain metadata about databases and data dictionaries, create and remove users, set user access rights, and more, all using the SQL language. Now there is almost nothing you can do with ADS that cannot be done using SQL.

To learn more about the syntax and semantics of SQL with Advantage, please refer to Chapters 9, 10, and 11.

Other Enhancements

While not as spectacular as triggers or full text search, a number of additional enhancements to ADS are sure to be welcomed by pre-7.0 ADS users. The first of these is a new compression algorithm that will improve the speed of data transfer over networks. While this feature will improve the already fast performance of ADS over local area networks (LANs), it will be most welcome by developers needing to access ADS from client applications across the Internet and in other WAN (wide area network) environments.

Another welcome addition is a MONEY field type in ADS tables. The money field is similar to the CURDOUBLE field. However, unlike CURDOUBLE fields, which are internally stored as IEEE (Institute of Electrical and Electronics Engineers, a standards body) double values, all calculations with those fields are done using doubles. IEEE doubles can easily lose precision. With the MONEY data type, all storage and calculations are performed using 64-bit integer fields, which lose no precision.

Another notable upgrade applies only to the NetWare version of ADS. With ADS 7.0 and later, NetWare ADS servers will no longer be limited to files smaller than 4GB. The maximum file size is now 16 exabytes for tables, 35 terabytes for index files, and 4 terabytes for memo files. You will also need to be using NetWare 5 or later for this feature.

NOTE

An exabyte is a billion gigabytes.

In the next chapter, you will learn how to use ADS to create tables.

CHAPTER

2

Creating Tables

IN THIS CHAPTER:

A table is a structured file that holds raw data about a particular subject. For example, you might have one table that contains information about customers and another table that contains information about sales.

Tables are organized by rows and columns. Each row contains information about one object. The customer table, for example, will contain one row for each customer. These rows are commonly referred to as *records,* but the terms are interchangeable.

A table may have zero or more records. A table with zero records is referred to as an *empty table*.

Each row in a table consists of one or more columns, with every row in a given table having the same number of columns. Each column is used to hold a particular piece of information about the subject associated with the table. For example, the customer table may have one column that holds the customer account number, and another column that holds the customer's name, and so on. Columns are also referred to as *fields*.

Memo files are special files that hold a table's variable-length binary data (binary, image, and memo fields in ADS). These types of fields are collectively referred to as BLOB (binary large object) fields. For example, your customer table may have a memo field used to hold a description of each customer. While some, or even all customer records may not have a description, whenever a description is present, it is stored in the memo file. With ADS tables, all binary, image, and memo fields for a particular table are stored in a single memo file. In addition, a table and its associated memo file (if present) have the same name. Only their file extensions differ.

In most cases, your application will reference the tables directly, but does not have to explicitly refer to any index or memo files. In most cases, ADS (Advantage Database Server) takes complete responsibility for accessing the indexes and memo files. For example, so long as you have only one structural index file for a table, any time you access that table through ADS, ADS opens the table, and opens its structural index and memo files, if present.

NOTE

The term "structural index" is originally a FoxPro term used to refer to the index file that has the same filename as its associated table. We have adopted that term to refer to any index file for an ADS table that has the same name as its associated table. While some people prefer to refer to these index files as "auto-open" index files, we feel that the term auto-open is less appropriate now that all of a table's indexes are auto-opened when you access the ADS table through a data dictionary.

ADS Supported Table Types

The Advantage Database Server supports three different table formats: Clipper and FoxPro DBF formats (compatible with dBASE III + format), and a proprietary ADT format. The two DBF formats are useful for developers who want to maintain backward compatibility with legacy applications, particularly those still running in DOS. In this book, the ADS-supported formats are referred to collectively as *ADS tables*.

The ADT format, on the other hand, is the preferred ADS format for ADS-based applications that no longer need to maintain backward compatibility. This is because the ADT format provides superior features, flexibility, and performance.

While there are still some legacy Clipper and FoxPro applications out there that can benefit from the stability and performance offered by ADS, most developers using ADS should use the ADT format.

DBF Formats

DBF format databases employ tables in DBF format. These tables use indexes in either FoxPro IDX or CDX formats, or the Clipper NTX format. Similarly, memo fields employ the FPT (FoxPro) and DBT (Clipper) memo field files. Because the index and memo files are associated with either FoxPro or Clipper, which format you use depends on the Advantage driver you are employing. For example, you use the Advantage NTX driver to create and work with NTX indexes. By comparison, you use the Advantage CDX driver to use IDX and CDX indexes.

Both the FoxPro and Clipper formats have well-known characteristics and limitations. For example, the maximum field name length is 10 characters, deleted records are merely marked for deletion and can still be accessed up until a table is packed, unique indexes do not enforce record uniqueness, and memo files can include large amounts of wasted space.

In short, except for legacy application support, the use of the DBF file formats is discouraged. In fact, if you are building a new application with no need for backward compatibility with existing Clipper or FoxPro applications, you are much better off using the ADS proprietary format. For more information on Clipper and FoxPro DBF formats, including their characteristics, refer to the ADS help or a third-party book on Clipper or FoxPro.

The Advantage Proprietary (ADT) Format

As noted in the preceding section, the traditional DBF format has well-documented limitations, making its use less attractive than many of the alternatives available today. In response to these limitations, Extended Systems introduced a new, proprietary format in 1998. This format is referred to as the *ADT format*.

Tables of the ADT format employ the .adt file extension, with the associated memo file and structural index having the same filename, but with the .adm and .adi file extensions, respectively. Among the enhancements introduced with the ADT format are long field names, superior memo file space utilization, improved index options, and more flexible table structures. Also, whereas FoxPro and Clipper field names are limited to alpha characters, 0–9, and underscore (_), ADS table field names can include all but null values, semicolons, and commas.

Table 2-1 lists some of the basic ADT table specifications. For more information, refer to the Advantage documentation, which is available on the CD-ROM that accompanies this book.

Free Tables Versus Database Tables

There is a second major distinction between the various ADS table types, but this is not related to table format. Instead, it is associated with how ADS interacts with the tables. There are two data access mechanisms. Tables can either be accessed directly,

Table Characteristic	Specification
Maximum field name length	128 characters.
Maximum table size	4 gigabytes (16 exabytes using Windows NT/2000/XP/2003 NTFS or NetWare NSS file systems; 8 exabytes using Linux).
Maximum number of records per table	2.2 billion.
Maximum record length	64 kilobytes.
Maximum record filter expression length	64 kilobytes.
Maximum index file size	4 gigabytes (35 terabytes in Windows NT/2000/XP/2003 NTFS, NetWare NSS file systems, or Linux).
Maximum memo file size	4 gigabytes (4 terabytes in Windows NT/2000/XP/2003 NTFS, NetWare NSS file systems, or Linux).
Maximum number of fields per record	Dependent on the average field name length. For example, if the average field name length is 10 characters, you can have 3256 fields. If the average field name is 40 characters, you can have 1302 fields per table.

Table 2-1   *Characteristics of the ADT Table Format*

or they can be accessed through a data dictionary. When tables are accessed directly, they are referred to as *free tables*. Tables accessed using a data dictionary are referred to as *database tables*.

Free tables provide far fewer features than database tables. Because ADS accesses free tables directly, the only features available with free tables are those associated with the tables, indexes, and memo files. Security is provided by the free table's encryption (if encrypted), and validation is provided for by the table's structure, that is, the data types of the columns of the table. If any other security or validation features are desired, you must program those manually into your client application.

Database tables are those ADS tables that are bound to a data dictionary. By binding a table to a data dictionary, the properties defined in the data dictionary are used by ADS when you access the table, which is how some of ADS's more advanced features are implemented. For example, a data dictionary permits you to define constraints, which further define what data can be posted to a record. For example, you can use a constraint to prevent a negative number from being posted to an integer field. With a free table, by comparison, if you want to prevent a negative number from being posted to an integer field, you must add code to your client application.

When an ADT table is bound to a data dictionary, additional information is written into its header, and that information prevents the ADT from being accessed directly. This restriction ensures that the properties you set for the data dictionary to which the table is bound are respected.

Unlike an ADT database table, which can only be accessed through the data dictionary to which it is bound, there is no way to attach custom information to a DBF format table that would prevent ADS from accessing the database table directly. As a result, even though a DBF table may be bound to a data dictionary, ADS as well as legacy applications can continue to access that table directly. This can compromise the integrity of your data since data dictionary definitions will not necessarily be enforced. Here again is yet another argument in favor of using ADT tables over DBF format tables.

The remainder of this chapter discusses how to create ADT tables. These operations apply to both free tables and database tables, unless noted. Creating a data dictionary, and binding ADT tables to it, is discussed in detail in Chapter 4.

Creating ADS Tables

There are a number of ways that you can create tables for use by ADS. At runtime you can execute a CREATE TABLE SQL statement. Alternatively, if you are using either the Advantage TDataSet Descendant or the ACE (Advantage Client Engine) API, you can invoke AdsCreateTable.

The most convenient way to create an ADS table at design time is to use the Creating Table dialog box of the Advantage Data Architect. Actually, since you can execute SQL statements in the Advantage Data Architect, you can also create a table by executing a CREATE TABLE statement. However, the Creating Table dialog box provides a graphical user interface making it far easier to use than using SQL, which requires you to code a long SQL statement.

NOTE

If your table already exists in another database format, the Advantage Data Architect provides you with an import facility that permits you to convert a wide range of table types into the ADT format. Using the import feature of Advantage Data Architect is described later in this chapter.

The following steps demonstrate how to create a new ADT table using the Creating Table dialog box:

1. Launch the Advantage Data Architect if it is not already running by selecting Programs | Advantage Database Server | Advantage Data Architect from the Windows Start menu.

2. Select File | New Table from the Advantage Data Architect main menu, or alternatively, press CTRL-N. The Advantage Data Architect displays the Table Type dialog box shown here:

3. Leave the Table Type field set to Advantage Database Table (ADT) and click OK. The Advantage Data Architect opens the Creating Table dialog box shown in Figure 2-1.

4. You use the Creating Table dialog box to define the fields of your new table's structure. You define each field by setting the Field Name, Data Type, Field Size, Decimals, and Starting Value fields, and then clicking Add Field. Not all field types require you to define values in Field Size, Decimals, or Starting Value fields. Table 2-2 describes the valid data types for ADT tables.

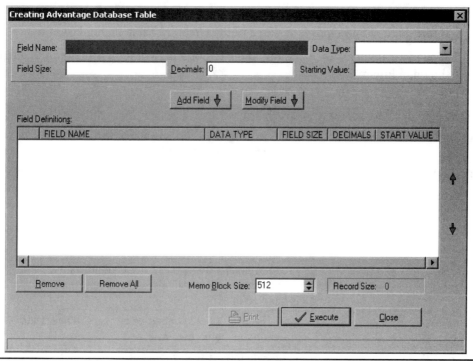

Figure 2-1   *The Creating Table dialog box of the Advantage Data Architect*

CAUTION

Auto-increment fields, such as the ADT AUTOINC field, automatically generate a unique value for the associated field. You specify a starting value in the Starting Value field of the Creating Table dialog box. Some developers use auto-increment fields to assign a unique value to a record, such as a customer ID number or a part number. However, auto-increment fields are notorious for creating headaches, since as a developer you have little control over the generation of the unique value. The problem is particularly noticeable when you add data from one table with an auto-increment field into another that also contains an auto-increment field. Most developers prefer to generate their own unique values, rather than relying on auto-increment fields, thereby influencing the unique values and eliminating potential conflicts.

5. Use the data in Table 2-3 to create six fields for your new table. Add these fields, one at a time, by entering the provided Field Name and Field Type, and optionally, Field Size and Decimals. Once you have defined a field's parameters, click the

Add Field button on the Creating Table dialog box. Each added field will appear in the Field Definitions area of the Creating Table dialog box.

When you are done, the Creating Table dialog box will look something like that shown in Figure 2-2.

Data Type	Size	Description
AUTOINC	4	A unique, four-byte, unsigned, internally generated integer from 0 to 4,294,967,296.
BINARY	10	Variable-length field containing binary data. Data is stored in the memo file.
CHARACTER	1 to 65530	Fixed-length text field.
CURDOUBLE	8	Same as DOUBLE, but designed to hold monetary values.
DATE	4	Integer representing a date.
DOUBLE	8	Floating-point value with 15 digits of precision. Field Size is ignored, and Decimals affects how the field value is handled in expressions.
IMAGE	10	Variable-length field containing a binary image. Data is stored in the memo file.
INTEGER	4	Four-byte integer with a range from –2,147,483,647 to 2,147,483,647.
LOGICAL	1	Boolean value. Valid case-insensitive values are T, True, F, and False.
MEMO	10	Variable-length text field stored in the memo file. Can hold up to 4 gigabytes of text.
MONEY	8	Use to store monetary data to an accuracy of four decimal places with a range from –922,337,203,685,477.5807 through 922,337,203,685,477.5807.
RAW	1 to 65530	Fixed-length raw data field.
SHORTINTEGER	2	Two-byte short integer with a range from –32,767 to 32,767.
TIME	4	Four-byte integer representing number of milliseconds since midnight.
TIMESTAMP	8	Eight-byte value where the high-order four bytes contain an integer representing a date, and the low-order four bytes contain the number of milliseconds since midnight.

Table 2-2   *The Allowable Field Types for ADT Table Fields*

Field Name	Field Type	Field Size	Decimals
Customer ID	SHORTINT		
First Name	CHARACTER	12	
Last Name	CHARACTER	18	
Date Account Opened	DATE		
Active	LOGICAL		
Comments	MEMO		

Table 2-3   *Use This Data to Add Six Fields to the Table*

6. Click the Execute button. The Advantage Data Architect responds by displaying the Save As dialog box. Using this dialog box, either specify a directory or create a new directory into which you will store your database-related files. You can use any directory you like, but we recommend that you use the same

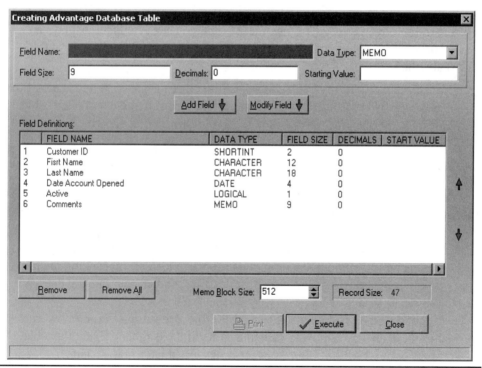

Figure 2-2   *The Creating Table dialog box with the structure of a new table defined*

directory in which the sample database described in Appendix B is stored: c:\Program Files\Extended Systems\Advantage\ADSBook. Save this new table using the name **CUST.ADT** in this directory, as shown here:

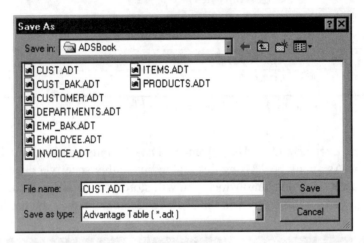

7. Once you have saved your table, the Advantage Data Architect displays an information message indicating that the table has been created. Accept this dialog box.

8. Now close the Creating Table dialog box by clicking Close. A new dialog box is now displayed, asking if you would like to open the newly created table. Select Yes to open the new table in the Table Browser, as shown in Figure 2-3.

Working with Tables

The Table Browser is a tool for working with tables. You can use the Table Browser to enter and edit data in the table. In addition, you can use the toolbar on the left side of the Table Browser to perform a variety of table-related maintenance tasks including modifying the table's structure, adding one or more index orders, packing the table (removing deleted records), rebuilding its index files, and encrypting and decrypting the table.

This section describes the basic use of the Table Browser including how to open tables in it, as well as how to navigate and edit those tables. Using the table maintenance features of the Table Browser is discussed later in this chapter.

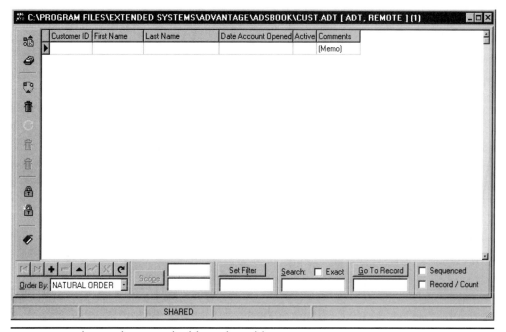

Figure 2-3   *The newly created table in the Table Browser*

Opening a Previously Created Table

After you have finished creating a table structure, you are given the opportunity to open the newly created table in the Table Browser. This feature is useful if you immediately want to enter some data into the newly created table, or to perform some maintenance function such as defining indexes for the table. Once you are through working with your new table, you simply close the Table Browser.

The Table Browser can also be used on tables that already exist. To open a table in the Table Browser, select File | Open Table from the Advantage Data Architect main menu.

The following steps demonstrate how to open a previously created table:

1. If your CUST.ADT table is already open in the Table Browser, close the Table Browser by clicking the Close button in the upper-right corner of the Table Browser window.

2. Select File | Open Table from the Advantage Data Architect main menu. The Advantage Data Architect responds by displaying the Open Table(s) dialog box, shown in Figure 2-4.

Figure 2-4 *Use the Open Table(s) dialog box to display an existing ADS table in the Table Browser.*

3. Select the Path radio button in the top portion of the Open Tables(s) dialog box, and then click the Browse button. Use the displayed Browse for Folder dialog box to select the directory into which you saved the CUST.ADT table you created in the preceding section of this chapter. Click OK once you have selected the path to return to the Open Table(s) dialog box.

4. Click the Browse button associated with the File(s) field, and then select CUST.ADT from the displayed dialog box. Click OK to return to the Open Table(s) dialog box.

5. You probably do not have to change any of the settings in the Open Options section of the Open Table(s) dialog box, but make sure that Table Type is set to Auto Sense, and that all three checkboxes are enabled in the Server Type section. If they are not, make the necessary changes.

6. If you are opening a free table for editing, as you are in this instance, and there is more than one index for the table you are opening (which there is not in this case), you would need to click the Additional Indexes button, and choose all of the indexes that are associated with this table. Failure to do so would make it likely that those indexes would become corrupt if you were to post any changes to the table. This is only a problem with free tables, as additional indexes are

automatically opened when you work with database tables. Click OK to open this table in the Table Browser, as shown in Figure 2-3.

> **TIP**
>
> *You can open two or more tables at the same time from the Open Table(s) dialog box, as long as these tables are in the same directory or the same data dictionary. To open more than one table, select the two or more tables that you want to open from the Open dialog box (which you display by clicking the Browse button associated with the Files field). Or, you can enter a semicolon-separated list of table names in the File(s) field.*

Once you have opened a table in the Table Browser, the caption in the Table Browser title bar provides you with information about the table. In addition to the fully qualified filename of the table you opened, the type of table (ADT in this case) and the type of connection used to open the table (REMOTE in Figure 2-3) are displayed in brackets following the filename. After the brackets are parentheses, indicating the total number of connections that were currently viewing this table at the time the Table Browser was opened.

Navigating and Editing Data in a Table

Using the Table Browser, you can add, remove, and modify records in a table. For all basic data types, such as CHARACTER, INTEGER, LOGICAL, and DATE, you can simply navigate to the field whose data you want to change and enter or edit the data using your keyboard. The standard keyboard shortcuts allow you to cut (CTRL-X), copy (CTRL-C), and paste (CTRL-V) data. For MEMO fields, simply double-click on the MEMO field, and a small editor window will be displayed. Close this window when you are done changing the contents of the MEMO field. You can also double-click IMAGE fields to view their contents in a small editor window, although it displays a limited subset of the data. You can add, remove, and modify IMAGE data using the keyboard shortcuts.

Basic navigation is supplied by the navigator control (shown next) that appears in the lower-left corner of the Table Browser. The available navigator buttons, from left to right, perform the following tasks: First record (go to the first record), Last record (go to the last record), Insert record, Delete record, Post edit (post additions or changes), Cancel edit (cancel additions or changes), and Refresh data. Pause your mouse pointer over one of the buttons of the navigator briefly to see a fly-by help window describing the purpose of that button.

NOTE

In addition to posting changes to a record using the Post edit button of the navigator, any changes that you made to a record are posted if you then navigate to another record in the Table Browser.

You can also navigate your table using the cursor keys on your keyboard. For example, LEFT ARROW and RIGHT ARROW and TAB and SHIFT-TAB permit you to navigate between columns on the current record. Similarly, UP ARROW and DOWN ARROW and PAGE UP and PAGE DOWN permit you to scroll between records.

You can also navigate with your mouse. To select a particular record/column cell that is currently visible in the Table Browser, click on the cell. To navigate to a record that is not currently visible in the grid, click on the grid's scrollbar until the record you want is visible.

So long as you have not opened a table in exclusive mode, the Table Browser permits you to modify the contents of a table in a multiuser environment, meaning that other users could possibly be viewing and even editing this same table at the same time you are. In order to coordinate the edits by multiple users, just as you begin editing a record, a record lock is placed on that record, meaning that while other users will be able to view that record, no other user can edit that same record until you have released the lock. The lock is released when you click the Post edit button of the navigator, or move to another record, in which case your changes will be automatically posted.

Use the following steps to demonstrate the editing of a table's contents:

1. With the new CUST table still open in the Table Browser, move to the Customer ID field and enter **12688**. For First Name enter **Frank**, and for Last Name enter **Jones**. Similarly, set Date Account Opened to **5/9/1983** and Active to **T**.

2. Now double-click the Comments field for this first record. The blank memo opens in a window, like this:

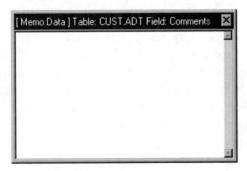

Customer ID	First Name	Last Name	Date Account Opened	Active
18744	Peter	van Clive	4/2/1999	F
15198	Juanita	Zapata	9/12/1987	T
22799	Jamie	Lutz	12/1/2003	T

Table 2-4   *Sample Data for the CUST.ADT Table*

3. Enter the following text into the memo window: **Our first customer**. Close the memo window when you are done.

4. Click the Post edit button on the navigator (the button with the checkmark). Notice that after the record is posted, the contents of the memo field now display "(MEMO)." The capital letters indicate that there is data in the Comments field.

5. Select the first record in the table and press DOWN ARROW. Doing this opens a new record. Enter data for three more records using these same techniques. The data that you should enter can be found in Table 2-4. Once you have entered data for the last record, click the Post edit button or move to a different record to post the last record's data.

Other Table Support Features

In addition to viewing and editing data, the Table Browser is your primary tool for controlling a number of features of a table. These include data security and table maintenance. Using these features is discussed in the following sections.

Data Security

ADS provides security for your data in a number of important ways. Some of these are associated with how ADS transmits data across the network, and others are associated with access rights conferred by a data dictionary. But the most fundamental of data security features is provided at the table level. Specifically, individual tables can be encrypted with a password.

When a table is encrypted with a password, both the table and its memo file are encoded using the password. The effect of this encoding is that the raw table and memo files appear scrambled to anyone who attempts to view their contents. Without encryption, it would be possible for someone with a file viewer, or even Windows Notepad (for small tables), to open the table and read its contents.

Once the table is encrypted, you must provide the password for the table before you attempt to use it for the first time. For database tables, which can only be accessed through a data dictionary, the data dictionary supplies the password automatically. Note, however, that a data dictionary itself provides security, and when the data dictionary is configured correctly, you will not be able to access the data dictionary without supplying a user name and password. The data dictionary user name and password are separate from a table's password.

If you want to view an encrypted free table using the Advantage Data Architect, you will be prompted for the password when you open the table. Similarly, before an encrypted table can be accessed from a client application, your code will be responsible for submitting the password.

How you submit a table's password from a client application depends on the data access mechanism you are using. For example, if you are using the ACE API, you must make a call to AdsEnableEncryption (for ADS tables) or AdsStmtSetTablePassword (for executing SQL statements against the table), passing the table name and the password as the arguments to the function call. You need to make one of these calls once per ADS table, prior to accessing it for the first time.

The following section describes how to encrypt and decrypt a free ADS table. For information about encrypting database tables, see Chapter 4.

NOTE

You must be able to obtain exclusive access to a table in order to encrypt or decrypt it. Specifically, if a table is already in use by at least one other user, you will not be permitted to either encrypt or decrypt that table.

Encrypting ADS Tables

To encrypt an ADS table, open that table in the Table Browser, and then click the Encrypt button in the Table Browser toolbar. Use the following steps to encrypt the CUST.ADT table created earlier in this chapter:

1. If the CUST.ADT table is not currently open in the Table Browser, open it.

2. Click the Encrypt Table button in the Table Browser toolbar, located on the left side of the Table Browser. This toolbar button displays a picture of a padlock. The Table Browser responds by displaying the Encryption Password dialog box:

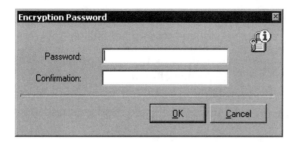

3. You use this dialog box to enter the table encryption password twice, the second time for verification purposes. In the Password field, enter the value **password**. Confirm this password by entering **password** in the Confirmation field. Click OK when you are done.

NOTE

The simple password "password" is used throughout this book since it is one that is easy to remember. This password would be a very poor choice for use in a real application since it is also easy to guess. Proper passwords should be difficult to guess.

CAUTION

You should take steps to protect and remember any passwords you use to encrypt your tables. If you forget the password for a free table, the data encrypted in it will be inaccessible. You might want to write your passwords down, and place them in a secure location, such as a safety deposit box or safe that only trusted individuals have access to.

Once a table is encrypted, a picture of a padlock will appear in the status bar of the Table Browser when you are viewing the table.

Use the following steps to see the effects of encryption:

1. If the CUST.ADT table is currently open in the Table Browser, close it.

2. Select File | ReOpen Tables | CUST.ADT from the Advantage Data Architect main menu. The Advantage Data Architect displays the Encryption Password dialog box:

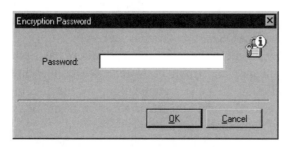

3. Click Cancel without entering a password. While the CUST.ADT table is opened in the Table Browser, it contains scrambled data, as shown in Figure 2-5.

4. Close the Table Browser. Select File | ReOpen Tables | CUST.ADT once again from the Advantage Data Architect main menu. This time enter **password** into the Encryption Password dialog box. Now when the Table Browser opens the table, the unencrypted data is visible and can be edited, as shown in Figure 2-6.

Decrypting ADS Tables

If you want to remove the password from a previously encrypted table, open that table in the Table Browser and click the Decrypt Table button in the Table Browser toolbar. When you do, the Encryption Password dialog box is displayed. Enter the table's current password into this dialog box to decrypt the table. Note that you need exclusive access to a table to decrypt it.

Since the CUST.ADT table is one that we are using for demonstration purposes only, the following steps demonstrate how to remove the encryption. This will permit you to work with this table without having to continually provide a password.

1. If the CUST.ADT is not currently open in the Table Browser, open it.

2. Click the Decrypt Table button in the Table Browser toolbar. The Encryption Password dialog box is displayed.

3. Enter **password** in the password field of the Encryption Password dialog box, and click OK to decrypt the CUST.ADT table.

Table Maintenance

Depending on the type of ADS table you are working with, and whether or not you are using ADS versus ALS, there are a couple of maintenance tasks that you will have to perform periodically on tables.

For example, if you are using DBF tables, you will probably need to pack them from time to time, in order to recover space occupied by deleted records. With ADT tables, packing is rarely necessary.

Similarly, if you are using ALS, there exists a real possibility that a hardware or software problem may cause one or more of a table's indexes to become corrupt. If this happens, you will have to rebuild the table's indexes. Index corruption is very rare when you are using ADS.

The following sections describe how to perform these basic table maintenance tasks from the Advantage Data Architect. Note, however, that these same tasks can be performed at runtime from a client application. See the documentation for the particular data access mechanism you are using for information on how to add these maintenance tasks to your client applications.

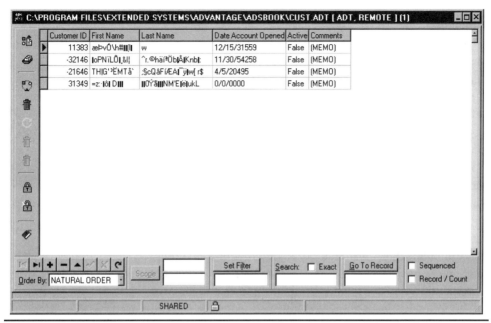

Figure 2-5   *If you do not supply a valid password for an encrypted free table, its data is scrambled.*

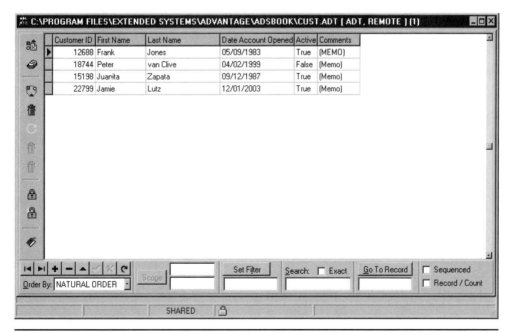

Figure 2-6   *The Table Browser displaying data after a valid password has been entered.*

Changing a Table's Structure

A table's structure consists of its field definitions, and you design this structure based on your application's storage needs. Unfortunately, these needs tend to change over time. In a simple case, while testing your client application, you might find that you did not allocate enough space for one or more of your character fields. For example, you might find that 20 characters is insufficient for your Last Name field, making it necessary for you to increase this field's size to 28 characters.

A more complicated situation may require you to add one or more fields to a table. As an application enters its prototype stage, it is not unheard of to discover that data essential to the application was not considered in the original design. Such a realization may require you to add one or more fields to one or more of your application's tables.

Fortunately, the Advantage Data Architect makes it relatively easy to modify the structure of an existing table, whether you need to simply change the size or precision of an existing field, or to add fields to or remove fields from the table.

The following steps show you how to change the structure of the CUST.ADT table you created earlier in this example:

1.   If you do not currently have the CUST.ADT table open in the Table Browser, open it now.

2.   Click the Table Management button in the Table Browser toolbar to open the View\Modify Table Structure dialog box, shown in Figure 2-7. This dialog box is essentially the same as the Creating Table dialog box shown in Figure 2-1.

3.   Select the Last Name field in the Field Definitions section of the View\Modify Table Structure dialog box. When the field is selected, its currently defined parameters appear in the Field Name, Data Type, Field Size, Decimals, and Starting Value fields. Change the Field Size value from 18 to **28**, and click the Modify Field button. In response, a dialog box is displayed, asking you to confirm the modifications to the field. Select Yes to save the new definition for the Last Name field in the table's structure.

4.   Now enter **Last Access** in the Field Name field, and set Data Type to **TIMESTAMP**. Click Add Field. The newly added field will be placed

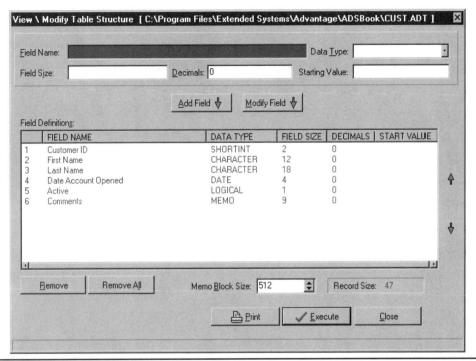

Figure 2-7   *You change an existing table's structure using the View\Modify Table Structure dialog box.*

at the end of the table structure. Your View\Modify Table Structure dialog box should look something like that shown in Figure 2-8.

In addition to changing field definitions and adding fields, you can remove fields, as well as change the order of fields in the table's structure. To remove a field, select the field you want to remove and click the Remove button. To change a field's position in a table's structure, select the field whose position you want to change, and click the Up or Down buttons to the right of the Field Definitions area (Move Field Definition Up and Move Field Definition Down, respectively) to move the selected field.

5. When you are done, click Execute to apply the changes to your table's structure. When asked to confirm that you want to continue with the restructure, select Yes from the displayed dialog box.

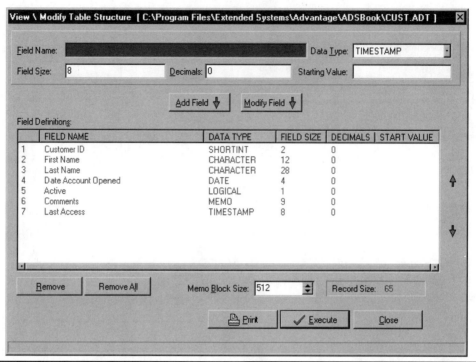

Figure 2-8   *The View\Modify Table Structure dialog box after the size of the Last Name field was changed and the Last Access field was added.*

NOTE

ADS also creates backup files of table, index, and memo files. They are given names identical to your original files but with the extensions .~adt, .~adi, and .~adm, respectively.

A couple of comments about restructuring a table are in order. First, you must be able to obtain exclusive access to a table before you can restructure it.

The second point is related to your client applications. Changing the structure of a table will often have an impact on the client applications that use the table. It is very important that you test all client applications following the restructuring of a table to ensure that the applications are running correctly, and to correct any problems that the restructuring may have introduced.

Adding Indexes

Indexes play a very important role in the design of ADS tables. Not only do they permit you to view a table sorted by one or more fields, but they also are the source of much of ADS's performance. Consequently, once you create a table, you will nearly always add one or more indexes to it.

You add one or more indexes to a table by clicking the Index Management button in the Table Browser toolbar. Creating indexes is discussed in detail in Chapter 3.

Restoring Deleted Records

With DBF tables, records that have been deleted may be recoverable. With DBF tables, deleted records are simply marked as deleted, and can be restored, or *recalled,* so long as you have not packed a table since the records were deleted.

The Table Browser actually provides you with two options for recalling deleted records for DBF tables. The first is to recall a deleted record that is currently active in the Table Browser. To recall the currently active deleted record, click the Recall Deleted Record button in the Table Browser toolbar. If you want to recall all recoverable records in a DBF table, select the Recall All Records button in the Table Browser toolbar. These toolbar buttons are disabled if no recallable records exist in the DBF table.

With ADT tables, you cannot recall deleted records in the Table Browser, and the recall toolbar buttons are disabled. This is consistent with deleted record management in other mainstream DBMSs (Database Management Systems). However, with ADS 7.0 and later, you can use the ACE API AdsRecallAllRecords to programmatically recover the desired deleted data to your table (such as situations of accidentally executing the SQL statement DELETE * FROM TABLE). See the ADS help for more information on AdsRecallAllRecords.

Packing Tables

As you have learned, records deleted from a DBF file are marked for deletion, but continue to occupy space in the underlying table. Unlike ADT tables, which reuse the space occupied by deleted records when new records are added, you must take explicit steps to recover the space occupied by deleted records with DBF files. This process is referred to as *packing.*

To pack a table, open it in the Table Browser, and click the Pack Table button in the Table Browser toolbar. You must be able to obtain exclusive access to a table in order to pack it. Also, if the table has a large number of records, packing can be a time-consuming operation.

While packing is a process often associated with DBF files, you can also pack an ADT table. As with DBF tables, packing an ADT table removes all records that have been deleted. Since an ADT table can reuse deleted records automatically, packing an ADT table is usually only necessary if you have deleted a large number of records, do not plan to add many new records, and want to recover available space in the underlying ADT file.

One very specific scenario in which you may want to pack ADS tables occasionally occurs if you are using memo files. A memo file will have orphaned memo pages if a memo field's contents for a record (any binary, image, or memo data) are added and are then deleted, and that record's memo field now has no data in it. Packing an ADS table with frequent changes of this type to a memo file will recover disk space.

NOTE

If you delete an entire record with data in binary, image, or memo fields, the space in the memo file will be available for reuse when future data is written to the memo file.

CAUTION

Packing a table permanently destroys any records deleted prior to the packing, making them unrecallable.

Re-Indexing Tables

Re-indexing a table rebuilds the table's indexes from scratch. In most cases, there are three conditions under which you will need to re-index a table. First, you need to re-index a table if you have changed the ANSI collation or the localized OEM character set that your server and all of its client applications are using. The rebuilt indexes will then use the new collation sequence or OEM character set.

The second condition under which you will want to re-index is when your current indexes become highly fragmented. An index can become fragmented over time if the fields involved in one or more of an index's tags, or index orders, have had unusual patterns of data. For example, if an indexed field of a large table has a great variety of different values, and then over time that same field becomes somewhat homogenous, and then later becomes varied again, the index can get fragmented.

The effect of a fragmented index is that operations using that index are slow compared to when the index was originally built. If you suspect that your database performance is being hurt by fragmented indexes, you should rebuild the indexes to restore your database's performance.

The third condition under which re-indexing is indicated is when one or more of your index files become corrupt. This can happen when you fail to open all index files for a free table prior to editing the table. (With database tables, all index files are auto-open indexes, thereby preventing index corruption from this source.) Index files can also become corrupt if there is a failure in a workstation or the network when a client application is accessing data using the Advantage Local Server. Re-indexing rebuilds the indexes, removing any corruption in the process.

To re-index a table, open the table in the Table Browser, and then click the Re-Index button in the Table Browser toolbar. Note that you must obtain exclusive access to a table to re-index it. Also, if your table has many records and/or many indexes, re-indexing may be a time-consuming process.

Emptying Tables

When you empty, or *zap,* a table, you permanently remove all records from that table, losing the data forever. In order to empty a table, open it in the Table Browser and click the Empty Table of ALL Data button in the Table Browser toolbar. When you do, the Table Browser will display the following warning dialog box asking you to confirm that you want to remove all data from the table:

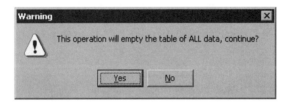

Select Yes on the Warning dialog box. A second dialog box is displayed, asking you to repeat your confirmation. Select Yes to permanently remove all data from the table. Note that you must be able to obtain exclusive access to a table to zap it.

Importing and Exporting Data

Earlier in this chapter you learned how to create a table from scratch. But that is not always necessary if your data already exists. For example, if you are converting an old Paradox application to ADS, you can import your existing data, creating an ADT table with a structure based on the existing table. Better still, the newly imported table will be populated with the data from the existing table.

Data can go the other way, as well. The Advantage Data Architect permits you to export data to a wide variety of formats. This permits you to share your data with other applications. For example, you can export data from an ADS table to an Excel spreadsheet, permitting you to use the business graphing capabilities of Excel to create a pie chart, a bar chart, or whatever kind of chart is suitable for your data.

Alternatively, you can export your data in HTML format, permitting you to quickly publish it on your company's Web site.

The following sections describe how to import and export data using ADS. This discussion begins with importing.

Importing Data into ADS Tables

When you import data, you are making a copy of an existing data source, placing that copy into one or more ADT tables. Whether you get one or more tables depends on what you import. If you are importing a Microsoft Access database (an MDB file), you will end up with one ADT table for each table in the Access database. By comparison, if you are importing from Paradox tables using the Borland Database Engine, you will get one ADT table for each Paradox table you select to import.

The Advantage Data Architect permits you to import data using a wide variety of data access mechanisms. One of the most flexible involves ADO (ActiveX data objects), which you can use if you have the necessary OLE DB provider. This is the most flexible approach since most Windows databases have an OLE DB provider. There are also mechanisms to import Paradox tables, xBASE tables, Pervasive SQL (Btrieve) tables, and to import both fixed-length and CSV (comma-separated value) text files.

NOTE

If you have an ODBC driver for a data format that you want to import, you can import that data using Microsoft's OLE DB Provider for ODBC.

You begin the import process by selecting Tools | Import from the Advantage Data Architect main menu. The Advantage Data Architect responds by displaying the Advantage Data Import dialog box shown in Figure 2-9.

There are four tabs on the Advantage Data Import dialog box. You use the Select Import Type tab to identify which data import mechanism you want to use. Once you select the mechanism you want to use to import the data, either click Next or click the Select Import Data tab. The contents of the Select Import Data page depend on the data access mechanism you chose on the Select Import Type page. For example, if you selected ADO Data Source, you are asked to enter or build an ADO connection string, as shown in Figure 2-10.

If, on the other hand, you choose to use the Borland Database Engine and select BDE Alias on the Select Import Type page, you are asked to identify the BDE alias from which to import the data, as shown in Figure 2-11.

After you provide the Advantage Data Import dialog box with the information it needs to connect to your original data source, click Next or select the Select

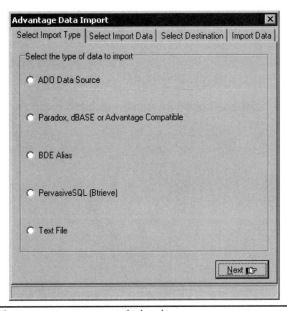

Figure 2-9   *The Advantage Data Import dialog box*

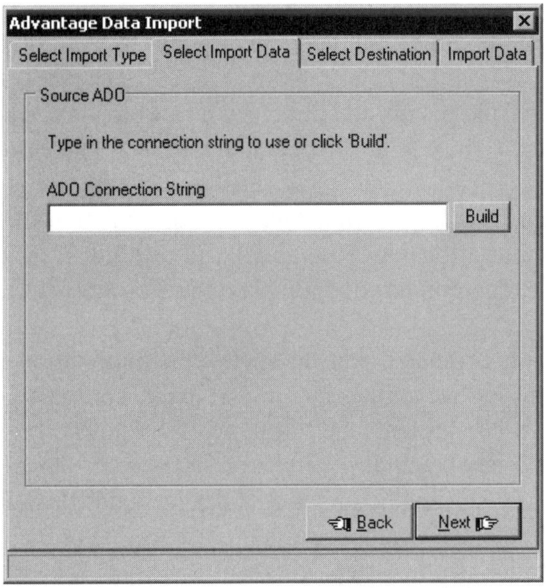

Figure 2-10   *ADO requires an ADO connection string to connect to data.*

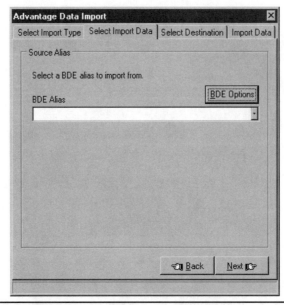

Figure 2-11 *The BDE requires a BDE alias to connect to data.*

Destination tab to display the Destination page shown in Figure 2-12. Select the directory where ADS should create the table or tables to hold the data you are importing.

You can either type the path of the directory into which you want these tables stored, or you can click Browse to select a directory using the Browse for Folder dialog box.

Click Next or select the Import Data tab. The Import button shown in Figure 2-13 initiates the data importation. Once you click Import, the Advantage Data Import Utility will begin the data importation, displaying its progress as the importation proceeds.

Once importation is complete, you can review the importation progress log and even print it out. This log sometimes includes valuable comments about the data it imports. For example, it notes that tables imported from indexed Paradox tables, which necessarily have a primary key index, will be given an index named PRIMARY. It goes on to warn you that if you want the imported index named PRIMARY to be designated as the primary index in a data dictionary, you must set that property manually.

Note that importation is a two-step process if you want to bind the imported tables to a data dictionary. In the first step, you import your data into ADT free tables.

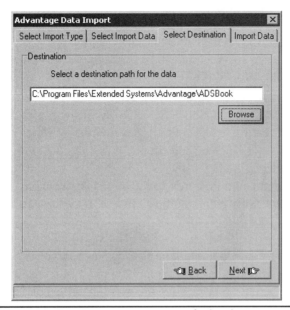

Figure 2-12   *Use the Select Destination page to specify the directory path where imported table(s) are stored.*

Figure 2-13   *Click Import to begin the data importation.*

Once you have your free ADT tables, you can add them to a data dictionary. Adding existing free ADS tables to a data dictionary is discussed in Chapter 4.

Exporting Data from ADS Tables

The Advantage Data Architect permits you to export data from ADS tables using either the Table Browser or the Native SQL Utility. Using the Table Browser, you can either export the entire table's contents, or you can set either a scope (an index-based range) or a filter (a Boolean selection expression) to export only a subset of records from the table. Using the Native SQL Utility, you can execute a SQL SELECT statement to select some or all records and columns from a table, and then export only the selected data. Only by using the Native SQL Utility can you export fewer than all columns of your data.

Whether you use the Table Browser or the Native SQL Utility, there are three general categories of export options. The first is to export your data to another, new ADT table, and the second is to export your data to an existing ADT table. If you want to export to an existing ADT table, the existing table must have a structure that is compatible with the table from which you are exporting. These first two export options make it easy to copy and append data, but are not useful if you want to make your data available to other programs.

The third export option is to export to a non-ADS format. This export option permits you to export your data into a variety of useful formats, including Excel, comma-delimited text, tab-delimited text, and HTML, among others. Most applications that you might want to use your data with will likely support at least one, if not more, of the export format options provided for by this feature.

Use the following steps to demonstrate the export feature of the Advantage Data Architect:

1. Open the Native SQL Utility by selecting Tools | Native SQL Utility from the Advantage Data Architect main menu.

2. Set Connection Type to Path, and then enter or select the path to the directory into which you stored your CUST.ADT table you created earlier in this chapter.

3. Click Connect. When you successfully connect, the Connect button label will change to Disconnect.

4. Enter the following SQL statement into the SQL editor:

```
SELECT "First Name", "Last Name", "Date Account Opened"
FROM CUST WHERE "Customer ID" = 12688
```

5. Click the Execute SQL button to execute the entered query. The query results will be displayed in the Results pane.

6. Right-click in the Results pane to display a popup menu with the following three options for exporting the result set: Export Results To New Table, Export Results To Existing Table, Export Results To HTML, Excel, …. Select Export Results To HTML, Excel,…. The Native SQL Utility responds by displaying the Export Items dialog box:

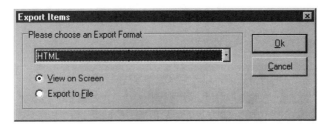

7. Select Comma-Delimited Text (CSV) from the Export Format dropdown list, and set the radio button group to Export to File. Click OK.

8. You will now see a browser window that you can use to provide the filename and directory to which to export the data. Use this browser to navigate to the directory where your CUST.ADT table is stored, and set File Name to **CUST.CSV**. Click Save.

9. Now use Windows Notepad, or any other text file viewer, to open the CUST.CSV file you just exported. This file should look like that shown in Figure 2-14. Close this window or viewer.

10. Click Disconnect on the Native SQL Utility to drop your connection, and then close the Native SQL Utility window.

The preceding example demonstrated how to export specific rows and columns from an existing ADS table using the Native SQL Utility. To export using the Table Browser, set a scope or a filter if you want to export fewer than all rows of data, and then right-click the grid. Select the export option that you want from the displayed popup menu, and then proceed as you did with the Native SQL Utility.

Exporting Table Structures as Code

At the beginning of this chapter, you learned that you can either create tables at design time using the Advantage Data Architect, or you can create tables in code

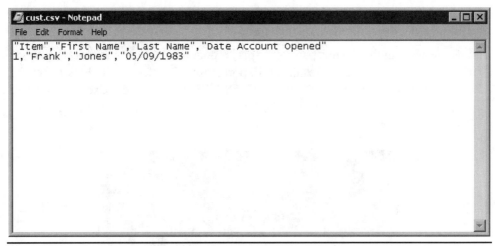

Figure 2-14   *The exported data from the CUST.ADT in CSV format.*

at runtime. As mentioned during that discussion, creating tables in code at runtime requires that you create, debug, and maintain the code that defines the table structures.

Fortunately, the Advantage Data Architect can help. Specifically, so long as you have an existing ADS table structure, the Tables to Code dialog box of the Advantage Data Architect can generate code that will create that table at runtime, including indexes. You can then use that code in your client application to create the table and its indexes at runtime.

Use the following steps to generate a SQL script that can re-create your CUST.ADT table at runtime from a client application:

1. From the Advantage Data Architect main menu, select Tools | Export Table Structures as Code. The Advantage Data Architect responds by displaying the Tables to Code dialog box shown in Figure 2-15.

2. Click the Add Table(s) button to display a browser window. Navigate to the directory into which you saved your CUST.ADT, and select that table. (You can actually select two or more tables at a time if you want, but there is currently only one table in this directory.) Click Open to continue.

3. The name of your selected table appears in the Tables to Code dialog box. If your free table has more than one index file, you can right-click and select additional indexes to generate code for. Currently there are no index files for the CUST.ADT table, so skip this step.

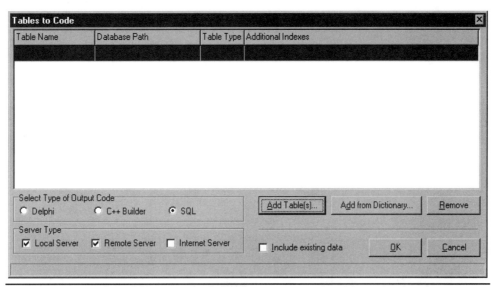

Figure 2-15   *Use the Tables to Code dialog box to generate table and index creation code that you can use in your client applications.*

4. You can generate code in one of three formats: Delphi, C++Builder, or SQL script. At Select Type of Output Code, select SQL.

5. The generated code can either create the table, or it can create the table and populate it with data. If you have selected to output the generated code using SQL scripts, you can check the Include Existing Data checkbox to populate the generated table with its current data. Leave this checkbox unchecked for this demonstration. Click OK to continue with your code generation.

6. After clicking OK, the Output Code window appears as shown in Figure 2-16. From this window you can copy the code to the Windows clipboard, or click Save As to save the code to a file. When you output your code as SQL, there is an additional button that will open the code in the Native SQL Utility, which permits you to test the code.

CAUTION

Testing the code output by the Table to Code generator may produce errors if you attempt to create a new table using the same name as your existing table. This code is normally intended to be executed from a client application to create a table where no table currently exists.

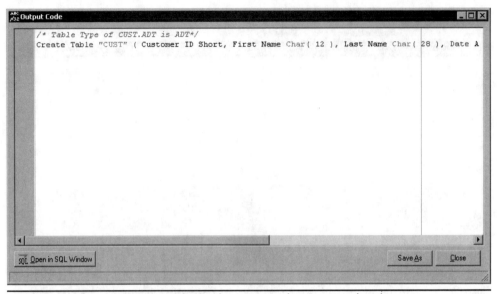

Figure 2-16   *Use the Output Code window to save the generated code.*

In the next chapter, you will learn about the importance of ADS indexes and how to create them for your tables.

Defining Indexes

While a table's structure defines what kind of data it can hold, it's a table's indexes that influence how that data is accessed. Except in the most trivial of databases, a major design issue in most applications involves the definition of indexes. Done properly, indexes can give your applications unparalleled speed and advanced features.

This chapter provides you with an overview of indexes. It begins with an introduction to the terms used to describe indexes. It continues with a look at the various types of indexes supported by ADS, as well as how to create and test indexes for your tables.

Toward the end of this chapter, you will find a detailed discussion of a new, special type of index called an *FTS index*. "FTS" stands for full text search, and these indexes permit you to quickly locate records based on the contents of text fields, including memo and binary fields.

Overview of Index Files

An index file is one that contains one or more index orders, also referred to as *tags*. An index file that contains only one index order is called a *single-order* index, but these are rare. Because you often need to access a table in a number of different ways, most developers include many index orders in a given index file. An index file that has two or more index orders is referred to as a *multiple-order* index file, or *compound* index file. A given index file can contain up to 50 index orders.

Not all index files are alike. Index files that have the same name as their associated table are known as *structural indexes*. The primary advantage of structural index files is that they are auto-open index files. Specifically, if you open a table, the Advantage Database Server (ADS) automatically opens that table's structural index. Likewise, when you close the table, the structural index is closed for you.

A given table can have up to 15 index files. However, only the structural index file is an auto-open index file. Any additional index files associated with a given table must be explicitly opened and closed through code (or the appropriate utility in the Advantage Data Architect). If you make any changes to a table without opening all of its indexes, those indexes that were left closed would likely be logically corrupt, in which case they would need to be rebuilt.

NOTE

When a table is associated with a data dictionary, and the table is being opened using the data dictionary, all of the table's indexes are opened automatically.

Index orders consist of zero or more *keys*. A key has two parts, an index key expression and a reference to a record in a table. The *index key expression* is used to sort and search the keys in the index. Most index key expressions consist of data from one or more fields in a table. For example, an index key expression may consist of the data from the customer ID field of the customer table. The associated index could then be used to order customers by their customer ID, as well as to search for records based on customer ID. But index key expressions can also be more involved, and may include two or more field values, constants, functions, and a variety of operators, including concatenation, arithmetic, and Boolean.

Every record in an ADS table has a unique *record number,* and each key points to a single record using this record number. Some types of index orders, such as expression indexes, have one key in the index order for each record in the associated table. Other index orders, such as conditional index orders and custom index orders, may have far fewer keys than records in the associated table. As a result, these index orders refer only to some of a table's records. Finally, an FTS index may have many keys for each record, with one key for each indexed word in each record.

Why Create Indexes?

There are two reasons for creating an index order. The first is to provide a meaningful view of the records in a table. The views may be related to the order of a table's records, or they may be related to the specific contents of individual records. The second reason is related to database performance.

The physical order of records in a table, sometimes called the *natural order,* is rarely very useful. The natural order is a consequence of the order in which the records were added in conjunction with records that were deleted. For example, when using ADT tables, a newly added record may be placed in a position where a previously deleted record appeared.

Using index orders, you can provide many different and meaningful orderings for your records. For example, there may be times when you want to access your customer table in order of the customer ID number. At other times, you may want to work with your customer records sorted by the customer's last name. Both of these orders are possible by creating one index order that organizes records by customer ID, and another that orders records by customer last name. Which sort order the customer table appears in depends on which of these two indexes is currently active.

Index orders that are based on the contents of individual records can be used to work with a subset of records from a table. For example, you may have a table that contains records for employees, both past and present. One of the fields in this table may indicate the status of the employee, whether the employee is a current employee or a former employee. If you regularly want to work only with current employees, you can create an index order that ignores former employees. When that index order is active, the table will appear to contain only records for current employees.

As noted earlier in this section, the second reason to create an index order is to enable high-performance operations on your data. Imagine, for instance, that you need to work with a record where the customer ID number is 10304. If you have an index order whose index key expression is based on the customer ID field, ADS will locate the record using this index order. Specifically, it will locate the record by first searching for the customer ID in the keys of this index order, and then use the key's pointer to the record to retrieve the data. In other words, the underlying table is not even touched until the server knows which record it needs to read. This approach is much faster than if the server had to read every record in the table looking for the particular customer ID.

While the preceding example considered the location of a single record, these indexes also allow groups of records to be quickly identified. For example, if you have an index key expression based on the customer table's Last Name field, you can quickly locate all customers whose last name begins with a given letter, such as *W*. Likewise, if you have an index on the City Name field, you can very quickly obtain a list of customers who reside in a particular city—New York City, for example. In both of these cases, ADS can quickly find the appropriate customer records by reading the keys of the associated index orders, which is always faster than reading the individual customer records.

It is this second characteristic of index order, the identification of record locations using the indexes directly, that is the source of ADS's blinding performance.

Here's another way to look at it. If you design your indexes correctly, ADS will provide you with the best performance possible. On the other hand, if you fail to define indexes based on how your application needs to work with its data, your application's performance will suffer. For example, if you do not have an index order whose index key expression is based on the City Name field, searching for customers who live in New York City will be significantly slower.

Types of Index Orders

ADT tables support four types of index orders. These are expression indexes, conditional indexes, custom indexes, and FTS indexes. Each of these types is described in the following sections.

Expression Indexes

An expression index is a simple index order that consists of one key for each record. As is the case with all ADS index orders, with the exception of FTS indexes, the value of each key is defined by an index key expression.

A common type of index key expression is one that is based on one or more fields of a table. For example, assuming that there is a table that includes a field named Country, the following index key expression builds an index order based on this field:

```
Country
```

When building an index key expression on two or more fields of an ADT table, you separate the field names with a semicolon. For example, the following index key expression defines an index based on the Invoice Number and Part Number fields:

```
Invoice Number;Part Number
```

For DBF index files, this same expression index would be represented by something like the following:

```
INVNUM + PARTNO
```

> ### NOTE
> *For the preceding DBF index order to be meaningful, both INVNUM and PARTNO would need to be string fields. If they were numeric fields, it would be necessary to the expression engine STR function to convert them to a string before concatenating the two values. The resulting expression would look like* $STR(INVNUM) + STR(PARTNO)$. *If the fields were not converted to a string, the resulting expression would be the sum of the INVNUM and PARTNO fields, which would be worthless. This conversion is not necessary for ADT tables when a semicolon is used to concatenate fields. With ADT index order expressions, a semicolon can concatenate expressions of differing types. For example, a string field can be concatenated with an integer field.*

While expression indexes based on one or more fields are the most common, these indexes can also include more complicated expressions. For example, they can include two or more expressions, as well as basic arithmetic, string, and Boolean operators. These operators include the following:

+	–	*	/
AND	OR	NOT	

In addition, expressions can use a variety of functions supported by the ADS expression engine. The following is the list of these functions as of this writing:

ABS	ALLTRIM	AT	CHR	CTOD	CTOT
CTOTS	DATE	DAY	DELETED	DESCEND	DTOC
DTOS	EMPTY	I2BIN	IIF	L2BIN	LEFT
LEN	LOWER	LOWERW	LTRIM	MAX	MIN
MONTH	NOW	PAD	PADC	PADL	PADR
RAT	RECNO	REVERSE	RIGHT	ROUND	RTRIM
SPACE	STOD	STOTS	STR	STRZERO	SUBSTR
TIME	TRIM	TODAY	TRANSFORM	TRIM	UPPER
UPPERW	VAL	YEAR			

Consider this: expression indexes are case sensitive. To create an expression index that can be used to sort and search a text field without regard to case, you can use the UPPER function (or LOWER function). The following expression defines an index that can be used to create a case-insensitive filter on a field named Last Name:

```
UPPER(Last Name)
```

It is important to note, however, that with an index like this, your filter expression or SQL SELECT WHERE clause must also use the UPPER function. Otherwise, the selection operation will not be optimized. More is said about this later in this chapter.

In addition to their other features, expression indexes can be descending indexes and they can be unique. When you make a descending expression index active, the records in your table are sorted in descending order.

What a unique expression index does depends on whether the associated table is an ADT table or a DBF table. With DBF tables, a unique index contains one key for each distinct value on the index expression, but the index does not enforce uniqueness among records. For example, if you define a unique index on a DBF table field named Customer ID, it is still possible for this table to contain two different records that had the same value in the Customer ID field. However, when this index is active, only one of those records would be accessible. (This behavior is similar to a SQL SELECT statement that uses the DISTINCT keyword.)

By comparison, a unique index on an ADT table enforces uniqueness. For example, if you have a unique index on the Customer ID field of an ADT table, an attempt to write another record to this table using the same customer ID value as one that already exists in the table will fail.

Expression indexes are the workhorse indexes of your database applications. In fact, conditional, subindex, and custom index orders are really just special cases of expression indexes. In short, they provide you with ordered, high-speed access to your table's records based on index key expressions.

Conditional Indexes

A conditional index is similar to an expression index. The major difference is that while an expression index has a key for every record in the underlying table, a conditional index may not.

There are two parts to a conditional index: the index key expression and the condition expression. The index key expression serves the same purpose as in an expression index. Specifically, it defines the contents of the index key, which is used both for sorting and for high-speed access to the underlying records.

The second part is the condition expression. The condition expression is a Boolean expression, and it typically compares values in one or more fields to one or more expressions. A conditional index has one key for each record where the condition evaluates to a Boolean True.

When a conditional index is made the current index of a table, only those records for which there are keys appear visible in the table. Those records appear in the order defined by the index key expression. For example, if you want to create an index that includes only customers from the USA, and you want those records to be sorted by the customer ID, you define the index key expression as

```
Customer ID
```

and the condition expression as

```
Country='USA'
```

At first glance, conditional indexes sound appealing. But in practice, there are more flexible mechanisms for achieving the same result. For example, you can use a SQL SELECT statement to select a subset of records as well as to sort the records that are displayed. Since SQL SELECT queries can contain parameters in their WHERE clauses, the Boolean expression that selects the subset of records can be controlled at runtime. By comparison, the Boolean expression employed by a conditional index is fixed when the index is created.

An even more flexible solution is to use an expression index in conjunction with a *scope* (sometimes called a *range*) or a *filter*. Like a conditional index, a scope on an expression index can limit which records appear in the table, as well as provide a sorted view of the records that do appear. Filters provide a similar feature, and while slightly slower than scopes, enable more flexible expressions than scopes. Specifically, a filter expression can include more fields than are contained in the index key expression. Importantly, both scopes and filters can be modified at runtime. Furthermore, unlike SQL SELECT statements, expression indexes provide for index-based, high-speed access to a table's records.

This discussion is not meant to suggest that you should avoid conditional indexes. Indeed, they are high-performance indexes with many valuable characteristics. However, there are alternatives. Which indexes and filtering mechanism are best for your application depends on the nature of your data and how you need to access it.

Custom Indexes

A custom index is an initially empty index whose keys are added at runtime. For example, you can have a custom index named ShowCustomers. You can then add keys for each customer that you want displayed in the table when the index is applied. As is the case with the other indexes discussed in this section, the keys of a custom index are defined using an index key expression.

You add a custom key using the ACE (Advantage Client Engine) API by calling AdsAddCustomKey. This method adds a key to the custom index that references the current record of a table. Similarly, AdsDeleteCustomKey removes a key for the current record from the custom index. Some of the other Advantage data access mechanisms provide additional functions for adding and removing keys from a custom index.

While a custom index might sound like a useful tool, you need to be careful when using a custom index in a multiuser environment. Specifically, all client applications that are using the same custom index can add or remove keys from that index, so long as the index is opened in a shared mode. Also, keys that are added to a custom index are based on the data in the associated record at the time that the key was added.

FTS Indexes

FTS indexes enable high-speed searches of text-based fields in ADT and FoxPro DBF tables. (Clipper NTX indexes do not support FTS indexes.) Unlike the other indexes introduced in this section, the keys of an FTS are not based on an index key expression. Instead, they are based on the words of the text-based field on which they are built.

Each FTS index applies to only a single text-based field. You can create an FTS index on any of the following field types: BINARY, CHARACTER, MEMO, RAW (ADT tables only), and IMAGE.

FTS indexes are used by filter expressions and the WHERE clause of SQL SELECT statements to select records based on their text content. These filter expressions must use the CONTAINS scalar function, and WHERE clauses must contain one or more of the following scalar functions: CONTAINS, SCORE, and SCOREDISTINCT.

NOTE

See the section "Full Text Search Indexes" later in this chapter for in-depth coverage of these indexes.

Creating Indexes

You have a number of ways to create indexes. At runtime, you can create indexes using SQL, and many of the Advantage data access mechanisms provide additional functions for this same purpose. At design time, it is easiest to use the Advantage Data Architect to add indexes to a table.

The following steps walk you through the process of creating indexes for the CUST.ADT table you created in Chapter 2.

Several expression indexes and a conditional index are created in the following steps. Custom and subindexes are not recommended for most applications, so those types of indexes will not be created in this section. (Subindexes are found in some legacy DBF database applications, and are supported by ADS, but are virtually unknown in modern applications, which is why they are not discussed in this chapter.) Creating FTS indexes is described later in this chapter.

Use the following steps to add four index orders to the table created in the section "Creating ADS Tables" in Chapter 2:

1. Launch the Advantage Data Architect if it is not already running.

2. Open the CUST.ADT table that you created in Chapter 2 in the Table Browser. If you have opened that table recently, you can select File | ReOpen Table | CUST.ADT from the Advantage Data Architect main menu. If not, select File | Open Table, and use the displayed dialog box to choose the CUST.ADT table. When you are done, the CUST table will appear in the Table Browser.

3. Click the Index Management button on the Table Browser toolbar. The Advantage Data Architect opens the Index Management dialog box shown in Figure 3-1.

   The Index Management dialog box has three tabs: View Index Structures, Create New Index, and Create New FTS Index. If you had already created one or more

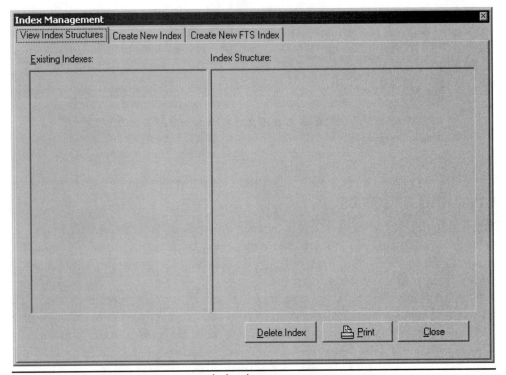

Figure 3-1   *The Index Management dialog box*

index orders for this table, you can select the View Index Structures tab to see their names and properties. You add a new index using the Create New Index or Create New FTS Index pages.

4. You create an expression index by using the Create New Index page of the Index Management dialog box, shown in Figure 3-2. If this page is not currently selected, click the Create New Index tab.

5. Leave Index File Name set to CUST. This will result in the creation of an index file named CUST.ADI, which is the structural index for the CUST.ADT table. As you learned earlier in this section, the structural index is automatically opened when you open its associated table.

6. We will begin by creating a unique expression index that will guarantee that every customer will have a different ID. Double-click Customer ID in the Available Fields list. This sets the Index Name field to Customer ID, and sets the Index Key Expression field to Customer ID. In other words, the index order

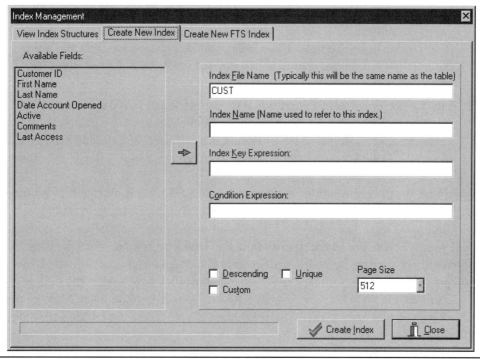

Figure 3-2   *Use the Create New Index page to define indexes.*

will be named Customer ID, and it will be based on the Customer ID field. If you wanted to give the index a different name, you can do this using the Index Name field.

To make this index unique, click the Unique checkbox at the bottom of the Index Management dialog box. Finally, click the Create Index button to create this index.

7. You are now ready to create another index. Note that the Create New Index page still contains the values you used to create the Customer ID index, including the Unique checkbox, which is still checked. The first thing you should do is uncheck the Unique checkbox.

8. The next expression index you are going to create is based on the customer's full name. At Index Name, enter **Full Name**. Next, set Index Key Expression to **First Name** + ' ' + **Last Name**. When you are done, click Create Index.

9. You will now create another expression index that can be used to perform a case-insensitive sort of the table by Last Name and then by First Name. Set Index Name to **By Customer** and Index Key Expression to **UPPER(Last Name);UPPER(First Name)**. When you are ready, click Create Index to create this index.

10. Finally, you will create a conditional index. Set Index Name to **Active Customers** and Index Key Expression to **Date Account Opened**. Next, set Condition Expression to **Active=True**. Finally, select the Descending checkbox to sort the Date Account Opened keys in descending order. Click Create Index.

An index file (with the .adi file extension) for an ADT table is created the first time you add an index order to an index file. You can set the Page Size field on Figure 3-2 at the time you create this index file. Unless your index order expressions are unusually large, you will typically not need to change the default page size. Also, the Page Size option will not appear after the index file has been created and you close the Index Management dialog box. If you need to change the index page size in the future, you can do this programmatically with ACE API functions. Or, in the Index Management dialog box, you will need to delete the ADI index file, re-create it, and add your index orders back to it.

If you want to view or remove an index, you do this from the View Index Structures tab. While this tab is selected, you can select a particular index to view information about it in the Index Structure pane. Figure 3-3 shows how this page of the Index Management dialog box looks with the Active Customers index selected.

Deleting or Changing Index Orders

To delete an index order, use the View Index Structures page of the Index Management dialog box, shown in Figure 3-3. Select the index that you want to delete in the list of Existing Indexes, and then click Delete Index.

You cannot change an existing index; you can only remove it. If you are unhappy with a particular index definition, you need to delete it as just described. You then add the new index with the modifications you want using the Create New Index page of the Index Management dialog box.

Testing Indexes

You can test the indexes that you create using the Table Browser. As you learned earlier in this chapter, the primary features provided by indexes are customized

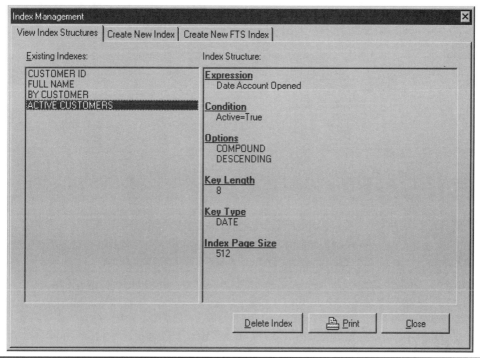

Figure 3-3 *You can view and remove indexes using the View Index Structures page of the Index Management dialog box.*

views and high-speed searches (FTS indexes only provide high-speed searches). The Table Browser permits you to test both of these aspects of your indexes.

Use the following steps to test the indexes that you created in the preceding section:

1. With the CUST.ADT table displayed in the Table Browser, note the natural order of the records.

2. Using the Order By dropdown list that appears in the lower-left corner of the Table Browser, select the CUSTOMER ID index. Note that the records are displayed sorted by Customer ID, as shown in Figure 3-4, confirming that this index is providing the proper order view.

3. To test the speed aspect of the index, enter **Customer ID = 15198** in the field below the Set Filter button (shown in Figure 3-4). Now click Set Filter. Two things should happen. First, only the record for the customer whose Customer ID field contains the value 15198 will be displayed, as shown in Figure 3-5. Second, a green circle should appear to the right of the Set Filter button.

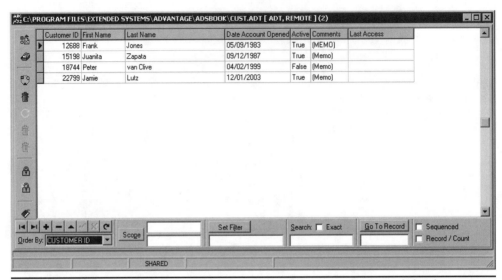

Figure 3-4   *Setting the index to CUSTOMER ID sorts the customer records by the Customer ID field.*

(The button's caption changes to "Clear Filter.") This green circle indicates that the filter used an AOF (Advantage Optimized Filter). AOFs are one of the important performance-related objects that ADS can create from indexes. Click Clear Filter to remove the filter.

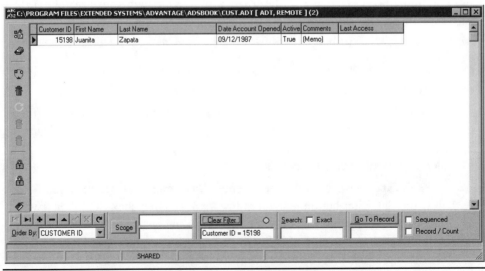

Figure 3-5   *An optimized filter displays a subset of records in the table.*

4. Now enter **Active = False** in the field below the Set Filter button, and then click Set Filter. Although a filter is applied, displaying only customers whose accounts are no longer active, the circle to the right of the Set Filter button is red. This red circle indicates that no indexes were used to build this filter. In other words, none of the table's indexes contributed to the location of the matching record. As a result, this operation was much slower than the filter applied in the preceding step. If there were many more records in this table, the difference would have been noticeable. Click Clear Filter to remove the filter.

5. Now set the Order By dropdown list to By Customer. Notice that a case-insensitive ordering of the customer records appears, first by last name and then by first name.

6. Next set Order By to Full Name. Notice that this also provides a sorting by customer, but this one is sorted by first name and then by last name. What is not obvious about this view is that this is a case-sensitive sort. You can verify this by changing the first name of customer 4 from "Jamie" to "jamie." If you click the Post edit button in the navigator after making this change, you will see this record reordered to the last position in the table. This is because case-sensitive sorts place uppercase letters before lowercase letters. Change customer 4's first name back to "Jamie" and click Post edit again.

7. Finally, let's test the Active Customers index. Set Order By to Active Customers. As shown in Figure 3-6, the table now appears only to contain customers where

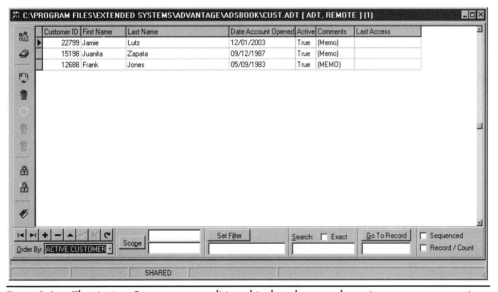

Figure 3-6   *The Active Customers conditional index shows only active customers, sorting these records by Date Account Opened and in descending order.*

the Active field contains the value True. Also note that the records in the displayed view are sorted by Date Account Opened, in descending order.

> ### TIP
> ---
> *If you double-click on the field below the Set Filter button, the Filter dialog box is displayed. This dialog box provides a larger field for entering filter expressions, making the testing of filter expressions more convenient.*

Indexes and Performance

Indexes and database performance are intimately tied, which is why it is so important that you provide your tables with the appropriate indexes, given your application's needs. Since speed is such an important issue in many applications today, this section takes an extended look at indexes and database performance.

How Many Indexes Should You Define?

As is the case with so many issues in software development, there are trade-offs between the number of indexes and performance. The more indexes you have on a table, the more work ADS has to perform in the background as you modify the contents of your table. For every record that is inserted, deleted, or modified, the table's associated indexes must be updated.

In the end, it is a balancing act. You don't want to have too few or too many indexes. In general, you want to ensure that you have indexes to support those operations that are performed frequently, and that must be performed quickly. For those operations that are performed only occasionally, or for which performance is not an issue, additional indexes should be defined only if they do not reduce performance in other areas.

For instance, if your table has only a few indexes, and their update at runtime is not noticeable, it won't hurt to add an additional index for non-critical tasks. On the other hand, if your table already has many indexes, and their runtime update is a performance concern, you cannot afford to add additional, non-essential indexes.

Scopes, Seeks, and AOFs

Another performance-related issue concerns how indexes are used. Some operations, such as scopes (ranges) and seeks (single-record locates), are performed directly on indexes. Other operations, such as filtering, involve special bitmap files that are referred to as *AOFs (Advantage Optimized Filters)*.

Let's start by considering scopes and seeks, which in the terminology of the Advantage TDataSet Descendant are called *ranges* and *findkeys*. A *scope* is a subset of records, based on an index order. A *seek* is the selection of a given record in a table, based on an index order.

Both scopes and seeks use indexes directly, and provide the highest attainable level of performance. Before you can set a scope or perform a seek, you must make the index that will be used for the operation the active index. This permits the keys of the active index to be used for the operation.

For example, if you have an index whose index expression consists of two fields, Last Name and First Name, you can select this index and then set a scope to include all records where the last name is Smith. This operation uses the index directly to set the scope. This same index could be used to select all customers whose last name is Jones and whose first name begins with the letters *A* through *G*. Again, this scope uses the active index directly.

Not all ADS developers can use scopes and seeks directly. For example, if your only interface to ADS is through SQL, such as when you are using an ODBC or Java JDBC driver, you have no way to execute scopes and seeks directly. Scopes and seeks are available to developers who can use the Advantage Client Engine API, the Advantage Clipper RDD, the Advantage OLE DB Provider, the Advantage Visual Objects RDD, and the Advantage TDataSet Descendant.

Even if you cannot create scopes and seeks directly, ADS may be creating them for you. For example, a SQL SELECT statement including a WHERE clause may set a scope in order to satisfy the WHERE clause, but only if the appropriate index is available. If a scope cannot be used, ADS will try to create an AOF instead.

AOFs are special, bitmap filters that are created from available indexes in order to create filtered views of a table. Unlike the use of scopes and seeks, where you as the developer must specifically choose the index, AOFs are constructed at runtime based on the available indexes. Once constructed, they can be used by multiple client applications to select one or more records based on a filter. AOFs are never faster than a scope, but they are often much faster than if an optimized AOF cannot be created.

Each bit in an AOF corresponds to a record in a table. If an AOF is fully optimized, a bit that is set means that the corresponding table record passes the filter, and a clear bit means that the record does not. These values are then used to retrieve the filtered records from the table.

If an AOF is partially optimized or not optimized, a set bit in the AOF means that the record might be in the filter, and a clear bit means that it is not. In these cases,

ADS must read each record associated with a set bit in order to determine whether to include the record in the filtered set.

You may recall that earlier in this chapter, in the section "Testing Indexes," you entered a filter expression and a green circle appeared. When the circle is green, ADS is using a fully optimized AOF. If the circle is red, the AOF is not optimized. If a partially optimized AOF can be created, a yellow circle appears. As a result, the Set Filter feature of the Table Browser is an invaluable tool for verifying that your indexes are providing ADS with the information it needs.

While a given index order can be based on one or more expressions in the index key expression, optimized AOFs are based only on the first expression in the index key expression.

Consider the following index key expression: Last Name;First Name. This index order can participate in creating an optimized AOF based on the Last Name field only. The existence of the First Name field in this index key expression cannot be used to create an optimized AOF on the First Name field. Only an index order where the First Name field is the first expression in the index key expression can be used for that purpose. Consequently, if your application requires an AOF that will search both First Name and Last Name fields, there must be at least one expression index order where the First Name field is the first expression in the index key expression.

For more details concerning AOFs, and what you can do to ensure that your application will use optimized AOFs, see the ADS documentation.

Full Text Search Indexes

Full text search (FTS) is one of the more powerful and exciting features introduced in ADS 7.0. With FTS you can find records based on the words in your text fields, including the presence or absence of specific words, the number of instances of specific words, and the proximity of specific words to each other. For example, you can select all records in which the word "punctual" appears in a comment field. Alternatively, you can select all records in which the word "performance" appears near the word "database."

Like an AOF, an FTS may be fully or partially optimized, or not optimized at all. When an FTS is not optimized, it means that ADS must read data from every record in the table, searching for the selection criteria. As you can imagine, unless your table is relatively small, an FTS that is not optimized can be very slow.

To have a fully or partially optimized FTS, you must create one or more FTS index orders. An FTS index order contains one key for each search word in each record. A fully optimized FTS can determine which records contain the search words from the

FTS index alone. A partially optimized FTS refers to the records that might satisfy the search criteria, but ADS must read the individual records identified by the index to complete the operation.

For example, imagine that you want to search for all records that contain the word "database" in the Comments field. If you have created an FTS index order on the Comments field, the selection of which records contain this word can be performed exclusively through the index.

However, to find those records in which the word "performance" appears in proximity to the word "database," an FTS is used initially to identify those records that contain both words in the Comments field, but a record by record examination of those identified records is necessary to make a final determination. Such a search is partially optimized.

You can create FTS index orders for both ADT tables and for FoxPro DBF tables that use CDX indexes. You cannot create FTS index orders for Clipper DBF tables that use NTX indexes. You can still perform FTS selections on Clipper tables, but they will not be optimized by definition.

Creating FTS Index Orders

You create FTS index orders using the Create New FTS Index page of the Index Management dialog box. This section demonstrates how to create FTS index orders by walking you through the process of creating an FTS index on a table. For this process to be meaningful, it is best if the table on which you are creating the FTS has either a large text field or a memo field. And although the simple CUST.ADT table that you have been working with up to this point does have a Comments field of type MEMO, that field contains very little data.

The following steps makes use of one of the free tables located on the CD-ROM associated with this book.

ON THE CD

Before you continue, you should copy the tables in the sample database from the CD-ROM to a directory on your computer's hard drive. See Appendix B for a description of these files, including how you can download these files from the Internet if you have lost your CD-ROM.

Use the following steps to demonstrate the creation of an FTS index:

1. Select File | Open Tables to display the Open Table(s) dialog box. Set Path to the directory into which you copied the sample ADT tables for this book, and set File(s) to CUSTOMER.ADT. Click OK. The CUSTOMER.ADT table is opened in the Table Browser, as shown in Figure 3-7.

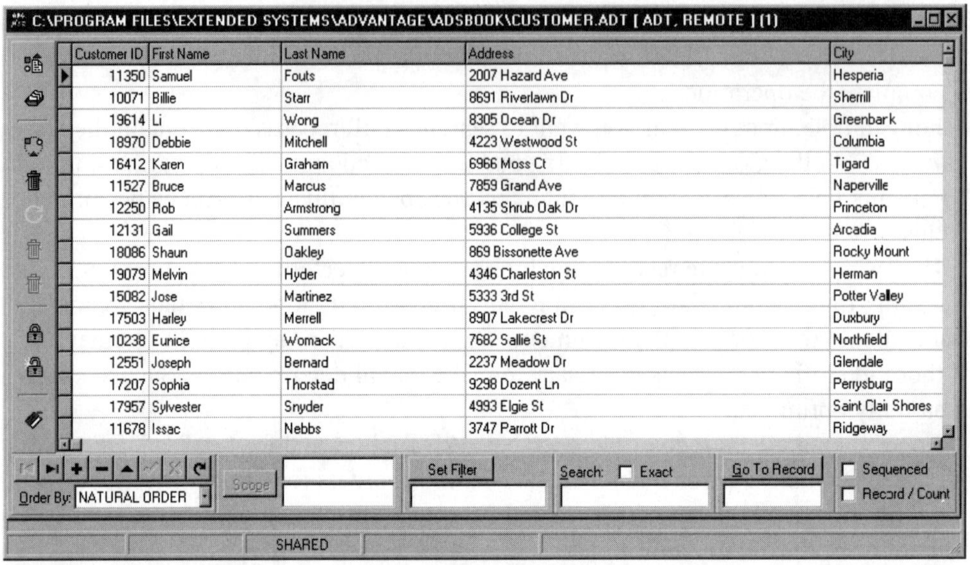

Figure 3-7   *The CUSTOMER.ADT table opened in the Table Browser*

2. Click the Index Management button from the Table Browser's toolbar.

3. From the Index Management dialog box, select the Create New FTS Index tab. The Create New FTS Index page is displayed, as shown in Figure 3-8.

4. You use the options on the Create New FTS Index page of the Index Management dialog box to set the options for your FTS index. Leave Index File Name set to CUSTOMER in order to create this FTS index in the structural index.

5. Use the Index Key Field dropdown list to choose the Notes field for the FTS Index. This dropdown list only includes the names of the text fields for which you can build an FTS index. Select Notes.

6. When you set Index Key Field to Notes, the Index Name field is automatically set to Notes as well. You can keep this index name, or set this index name to any other valid name. In this case, keep Index Name set to Notes.

7. Leave all other options set to their defaults, and click Create Index to create the FTS index. How these FTS index options affect your FTS index order is discussed later in this section.

8. Click Close.

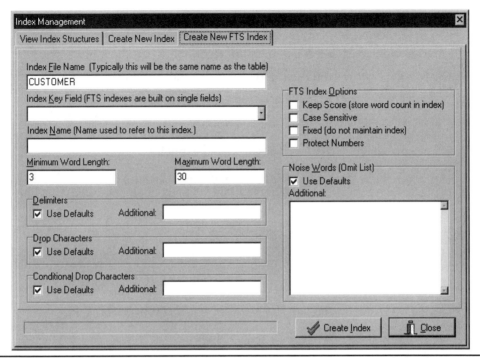

Figure 3-8   *The Create New FTS Index page of the Index Management dialog box*

Now that you have created your FTS index, you are ready to test it.

Testing FTS Index Orders

FTS index orders, unlike the expression-based indexes you created earlier in this chapter, are used for filtering records, and not for sorting data. Therefore, you test an FTS index by setting filters and executing queries. The following steps demonstrate how to test an FTS-based filter:

1. With the CUSTOMER.ADT table open in the Table Browser, enter **contains(Notes, 'birthday or anniversary')** in the field below the Set Filter button and click Set Filter. (Note that the word "Notes" in the CONTAINS function is the name of the field on which to perform a full text search. It is not the index name.)

2. The Table Browser responds by displaying only those records whose Notes field contains the words "birthday" or "anniversary" or both. You can

double-click the Notes field to examine the memo and verify that at least one of the search words is present. You will also notice that the green circle appears, indicating that this is an optimized filter. Click Clear Filter.

3. Change the filter to **contains(*, 'train*')** and click Set Filter.

4. Once again a green circle indicates that an optimized FTS index was used. In this case, the asterisk (*) instructed ADS to use all FTS indexes available for this table in its search. Since there was only one FTS index, this had the same effect as when you specified the Notes field explicitly. Click Clear Filter.

5. Finally, try searching on a field for which there is no FTS index order. Enter **contains(Last Name, 'zap*')** in the filter field and click Set Filter. This time the red circle indicates that a non-optimized filter was used. In this case, ADS searched the Last Name field record-by-record to locate the matching values.

The preceding example demonstrated how to test FTS filters. Use the following steps to demonstrate the use of FTS indexes in SQL SELECT statements:

1. Begin by closing the Table Browser for the CUSTOMER.ADT table.

2. Next, Select Tools | Native SQL Utility from the Advantage Data Architect main menu.

3. Set Connection Type to Path, and use the browse button (…) to choose the directory into which you exported the CUSTOMER.ADT table.

4. Click Connect to make a connection to this directory. You should see a message indicating that the connection succeeded. If not, fix your directory path and click Connect again.

5. Enter the following SQL statement in the SQL editor pane located at the top-left corner of the Native SQL Utility:

```
SELECT * FROM CUSTOMER WHERE CONTAINS(Notes, 'birthday NEAR card')
```

6. Click the Execute SQL button. Two records are returned, as shown in Figure 3-9.

7. Now, edit the SQL statement to look like the following:

```
SELECT * FROM CUSTOMER WHERE CONTAINS(Notes, 'birthday')
  and SCORE(Notes, 'birthday') > 1
```

8. Click the Execute SQL button again. This time only records where the word "birthday" appears more than once are displayed.

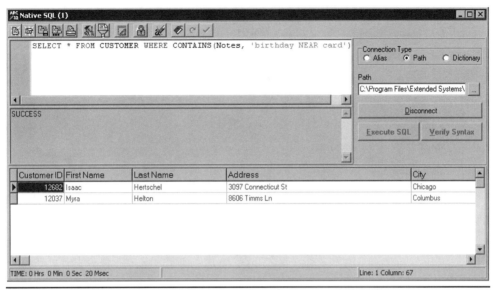

Figure 3-9   *A SQL query using full text search in the Native SQL Utility*

Options for FTS Index Orders

The Notes FTS index order created in the earlier section "Creating FTS Index Orders" used the default settings for FTS indexes. As you can see on the Create New FTS Index page of the Index Management dialog box (shown previously in Figure 3-8), there are many different options, and they can dramatically influence what keys the FTS index order contains.

Each of the options associated with FTS index orders is discussed briefly here. Note, however, that some of these options have somewhat complicated implications. For a complete discussion of FTS index order options, please refer to the Advantage documentation.

After an FTS index is created, you can view its options by selecting the index from the View Index Structures page of the Index Management dialog box. The options for the Notes index are shown in Figure 3-10. You should refer to this information if you have any questions about the default values for FTS indexes.

Minimum Word Length

Keys in an FTS index are not created for any words shorter than the minimum word length. The default minimum word length is 3.

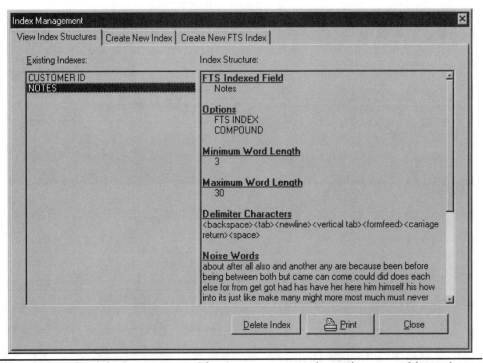

Figure 3-10   *The default settings used for the Notes FTS index order are visible on the View Index Structures page of the Index Management dialog box.*

Maximum Word Length

The maximum word length value identifies the longest key that will be stored in an FTS index order. If your text field contains a word longer than the maximum word length, that value is truncated to the maximum word length. Consequently, words longer than the maximum word length affect an FTS index, but only up to the maximum word length. The default maximum word length is 30.

Delimiters

Delimiters are the ANSI characters that separate words in a text-based field. For example, if you stored Java language code segments in a memo field, and wanted to search for specific Java class members, you would want to include the period (.) as a delimiter, since a period separates member references in Java's dot notation.

The default delimiters are the following:

backspace   tab   newline   vertical tab   form feed   carriage return   space

If you want to use the default delimiters, leave the Use Defaults checkbox of the Delimiters section checked. If you want to define your own delimiters, uncheck Use Defaults and enter your own delimiters in the Additional field. To use the default delimiters in addition to some of your own, leave Use Defaults checked, and enter your additional delimiters in the Additional field.

Drop Characters

Drop characters are those that are unconditionally ignored when the index is being created. The default drop characters are the double quote, single quote, and apostrophe characters.

You can use the default drop characters, replace the drop characters with your own, or add your own to the defaults, as described in the preceding section, "Delimiters."

Conditional Drop Characters

Conditional drop characters are those that are dropped only if they appear at the beginning or end of a word. A good example of a conditional drop character is a comma, which can appear in numbers, for example, 3,000. By making this character a conditional drop character, it will be dropped if it appears at the end of a word, as it did in the preceding phrase, but will be retained if it appears in a number.

The default conditional drop characters are the following:

comma	period	question mark	exclamation point
semicolon	colon	at sign (@)	pound or hash sign (#)
dollar sign	percent sign	caret or hat (^)	ampersand
open paren	close paren	n-dash or minus sign (–)	underscore

You can use the default conditional drop characters, replace the conditional drop characters with your own, or add your own to the defaults, as described in the earlier section "Delimiters."

Keep Score

Score refers to the number of times a key appears in a text-based field. If you use the SCORE function on a field regularly, you can improve the speed of your FTS index order by checking the Keep Score checkbox. Doing so causes ADS to include the score in the index.

Including the score in the index means that ADS must constantly calculate the score as records are updated. If you do not keep score, and use the SCORE function,

ADS uses the index to locate the records in which the word or words appear, but then must read the individual records to calculate the score at runtime.

Scores are not included in FTS index orders by default.

Case Sensitive

By default, the keys of an FTS index order are not case sensitive. If you want case-sensitive index orders, check the Case Sensitive checkbox.

Fixed

A fixed FTS index order is not maintained, meaning that the index is not updated during write operations to the associated table. The index is only rebuilt by explicit request.

If you make frequent changes to text fields in a table, and only occasionally need to perform full text searches, you may be able to improve the speed of table updates by using a fixed FTS index, requesting that the index be rebuilt in code prior to performing a full text search.

FTS index orders are maintained by default.

Protect Numbers

Protect numbers is used when you need to include periods and/or commas as delimiter characters. Consider the previous example of Java code. If you added a period as a delimiter, the floating-point constant 1.000 would be divided into two values, 1 and 000. If periods or commas are used as delimiters, check the Protect Numbers checkbox to treat numbers that include these delimiters as the original numbers.

Protect numbers is not enabled by default.

Noise Words

Noise words are common words that you do not want to appear as keys in an FTS index order. For example, it is extremely unlikely that you would search a text field for the word "the." To prevent this word from being treated as a content word, it is included as a default noise word.

The default noise words are as follows:

about	after	all	also	and	another	any	are	because	been	before
being	between	both	but	came	can	come	could	did	does	
each	else	for	from	get	got	had	has	have	her	
here	him	himself	his	how	into	its	just	like	make	many
might	more	most	much	must	never	now	only	other	our	

out	over	said	same	see	should	since	some	still	such
take	than	that	the	their	them	then	there	these	they
this	those	through	too	under	use	very	want	was	way
well	were	what	when	where	which	while	who	will	with
would	you	your							

You can add additional noise words by entering them into the Additional area of the Noise Words section, separated by spaces. If you want to specify your own set of noise words, uncheck the Use Defaults checkbox.

In the next chapter you will learn how to create and use data dictionaries.

Understanding and Using Data Dictionaries

IN THIS CHAPTER:

Data Dictionary Overview

Creating a Data Dictionary

Adding Tables to a Data Dictionary

Data Dictionaries and Table Encryption

Implementing Security with Data Dictionaries

Comparing Data Dictionaries

A data dictionary is a special file that serves as the sole access point for database tables. Although the use of a data dictionary is optional, it is hard to imagine anyone creating a serious database without one. This is because a data dictionary provides access to many of the Advantage Database Server's most powerful and advanced features.

This chapter has two goals. First, it provides you with an overview of data dictionaries, including a tour of the features that they make available. The second purpose of this chapter is to show you how to set up a data dictionary with tables and security. This dictionary will be used in many of the later chapters of this book to demonstrate some of ADS's most advanced features, including AEPs (Advantage Extended Procedures) and Advantage Triggers.

Data Dictionary Overview

A *data dictionary* is a special file that contains a wide range of definitions that are used by ADS to access your data. Some of these definitions apply to individual tables of your database. For example, a data dictionary can be used to associate one or more non-structural indexes with a table. This permits ADS to auto-open these indexes any time the associated table is opened. With free tables, you are responsible for opening these non-structural indexes yourself, and risk index corruption if your fail to do so.

Other definitions in a data dictionary apply to two or more tables. For example, a data dictionary permits you to create referential integrity definitions. *Referential integrity definitions* specify how data in related tables is maintained.

When your client applications connect to ADS in order to use free tables, you connect to a directory in which your free tables are stored. By comparison, when your data is stored in database tables—those bound to a data dictionary—you make your connection to the data dictionary itself. Using this connection, ADS enforces the definitions found in the data dictionary, assuring that the tables associated with that data dictionary are maintained correctly.

When you are using ADT tables, the recommended table type for ADS, the use of a data dictionary is an all or none proposition. Specifically, an ADT table is either a free table or a database table. Once an ADT table is associated with a data dictionary, it cannot be accessed as a free table anymore (unless you specifically free it from the data dictionary).

Data dictionaries provide a great wealth of features, making them an indispensable part of almost all ADS applications. The following is a list of many of the capabilities that data dictionaries provide you and your applications:

▶ You can configure database tables and/or index files to be auto-created. The table structures of auto-created tables are stored in the data dictionary. At runtime, if an auto-created table is not found, the data dictionary will create it and its indexes the first time a client attempts to open that table. This feature simplifies database deployment for those developers who normally distribute their databases empty.

▶ Data dictionaries permit you to define default values for fields for newly inserted records. If a value is not assigned to the field when the record is being inserted into the table, that field will be assigned the specified default value.

▶ When using a data dictionary with encrypted tables, your client applications do not have to supply each table with a password. The data dictionary does this automatically.

▶ Data dictionaries provide your client applications with access to stored procedures. Stored procedures are precompiled subroutines that run on the server and are ideal for data intensive operations. Stored procedures (Advantage Extended Procedures) are described in Chapter 7.

▶ Data dictionaries permit you to define views. A *view* is a SQL SELECT statement that resides on the server, and that can be treated like a table from your client applications. Views are described in Chapter 6.

▶ Data dictionaries permit you to implement sophisticated security. Every user can have a different user name and password that they use to access the data dictionary. Furthermore, you can customize the access rights of each user to the tables, fields in the tables, stored procedures, links, and views in the data dictionary.

▶ Data dictionaries enable you to create triggers. *Triggers* are server-side subroutines similar to stored procedures. Unlike stored procedures, which are invoked by the client application, triggers are executed when changes are posted to a database table. Triggers permit you to implement sophisticated actions in response to changes in your data. Triggers are described in Chapter 8.

▶ Up to 14 non-structural index files can be associated with each database table in a data dictionary. The data dictionary will automatically open these index files any time you open the table, closing them when the associated table is closed.

▶ Data dictionaries permit you to associate record-level and field-level constraints with tables. *Constraints* are rules that prohibit invalid data from being posted. Defining constraints is described in Chapter 5.

▶ Data dictionaries permit you to enforce referential integrity. Referential integrity is described in Chapter 5.

▶ Data dictionary definitions can only be updated through a special data dictionary administrator account, which can be password protected. This allows you to prevent unauthorized changes to your data dictionary definitions.

▶ Using a data dictionary, you can permit your client applications to connect to your tables over the Internet directly without having to resort to a Web browser interface.

▶ You can assign to your data dictionary a major and minor version number. If you update your data dictionary in the future, for example, adding or removing tables, or changing existing table structures, a special Advantage Data Architect utility can generate SQL scripts that you can use to upgrade older data dictionaries. This feature is particularly valuable when you need to upgrade data dictionaries remotely. However, the major and minor versions are for your benefit and are not used by this utility.

▶ When using data dictionaries, ADS can ensure that all of your indexes use the same ANSI collation sequence or OEM character set. If ADS discovers a mismatch among ANSI collation sequences or OEM character sets, it automatically rebuilds your indexes.

▶ You can work with data dictionaries through the Advantage Database Manager in the Advantage Data Architect. This graphical tool allows you to easily manage all of your data dictionary's definitions.

NOTE

Actually, you can also work with data dictionaries using SQL and the ACE (Advantage Client Engine) API. However, the Advantage Data Architect provides a much more convenient and graphical way to work with data dictionaries.

Data dictionaries can be used with both ADS and ALS (Advantage Local Server). The only data dictionary feature that is not also available for ALS is data access over the Internet. This feature requires ADS.

Creating a Data Dictionary

Like tables and indexes, data dictionaries can be created at runtime from your client applications. However, most developers will create their data dictionaries at design time as part of their overall database design process. You use the Advantage Data Architect to create data dictionaries at design time.

NOTE

The following steps will instruct you to save your data dictionary in the same directory where you copied the sample tables for this book. (See Appendix B for information on accessing these tables if you have not yet installed them.) This is being done for convenience. In short, as long as you can refer to the location where a table is stored using a UNC (universal naming convention) path from the location of the data dictionary, the data dictionary will have no problem accessing your table.

The following steps demonstrate how to create a data dictionary. This data dictionary will be used in this and future chapters to demonstrate data dictionary features.

1. Select Database | New Database from the Advantage Data Architect main menu. In response, the Advantage Data Architect opens the Advantage Database Manager shown in Figure 4-1. You are only required to provide information for the fields identified by an asterisk (*). However, most developers provide additional information.

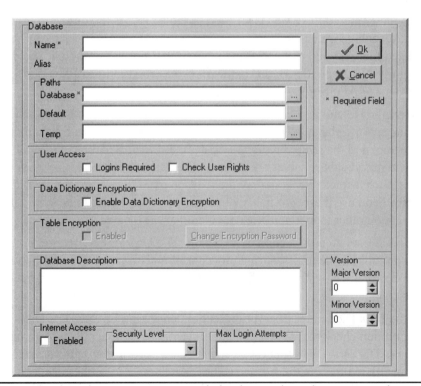

Figure 4-1   *The data dictionary properties dialog box in the Advantage Database Manager*

2. At the Name field, enter **DemoDictionary**. This is the name of the data dictionary. The Advantage Database Manager creates several files using this filename, including DemoDictionary.ADD, DemoDictionary.AI, and DemoDictionary.AM. The ADD file contains the fixed-length data dictionary metadata, and the AM file contains the variable-length metadata.

   Only the ADD and AM files should be deployed. ADS will re-create the AI file the first time it accesses the data dictionary. If you were to deploy the AI file, and there are collation sequence differences between the ADS server to which you are deploying and the server against which the ADD file was created, you will have problems.

3. Next, set the Alias field to **DemoDD**. This alias provides a shorthand reference to the data dictionary. Many of the Advantage Data Architect's utilities permit you to connect to a data dictionary using an alias, so this definition will come in handy later. Aliases are stored in a file named ADS.INI.

4. In the Paths section, set the Database field to the directory in which you previously stored the CUSTOMER.ADT table. This is the directory in which the Advantage Database Manager will store the DemoDictionary.ADD and related files. If you are using Windows and you stored this table in the directory suggested in Appendix B, this path will be c:\Program Files\Extended Systems\ Advantage\ADSBook.

5. Leave the Default and the Temp fields blank in the Paths section. When these fields are left blank, ADS uses the Database directory as both the default directory and the temp directory. The default directory defines the location where new database tables are created. The temp directory is where temporary files, such as those generated by the Advantage SQL engine, are created and stored. You use these two fields when you want these files to be stored in a location other than where the data dictionary is located.

6. Skip the User Access section at this point. The User Access section is used to control how the tables, stored procedures, and views of the data dictionary can be accessed by client applications. These features are discussed later in this chapter.

7. In the Data Dictionary Encryption section, check the Enable Data Dictionary Encryption checkbox. When you encrypt a data dictionary, the data dictionary files (ADD and AM) are encrypted, and cannot be viewed without using the proper password from the Advantage Data Architect. This is the only opportunity that you will have to encrypt the data dictionary. After creating the data dictionary, you cannot go back and enable encryption.

8. Skip the Table Encryption section. Table encryption can be enabled only after you create the data dictionary so its checkbox is disabled at this point. We will come back to this option later in this chapter.

9. You use the Database Description field to provide a description of the data dictionary. In this case, enter **Sample ADS Data Dictionary**.

10. You use the Internet Access section to configure whether or not your database can be accessed over the Internet. We are not going to enable Internet access in this example, but to do so, you check the Enabled checkbox in the Internet Access section.

    If you enable the Internet Access option, you will also want to set the Security Level option to Level 0, Level 1, or Level 2. Security Level 0 provides no authentication or encryption and is recommended only for intranet access. Security Level 1 requires authentication, but the data is not encrypted before it is transferred across the network. Security Level 2 provides both authentication and 160-bit encryption, which is most appropriate when transmitting sensitive data across the Internet. If you set the Security Level option to Level 1 or Level 2, then you can use the Max Login Attempts field to disable a user's Internet access privileges if they fail to log on after the specified number of attempts.

    In addition to enabling Internet access for a data dictionary and the database itself, you must enable Internet access for individual data dictionary users, as well as for the ADS server. Enabling Internet access for individual users is described later in this chapter. You enable Internet access for ADS by defining an Internet IP Port via the Advantage Configuration Utility. This utility is described briefly in Chapter 1. See the ADS documentation for additional information on the Advantage Configuration Utility.

11. Finally, set the Major Version and Minor Version fields. Set Major Version to **1** and Minor Version to **0**.

12. Click OK.

13. At first you will see a message indicating that the data dictionary was created. Accept this dialog box. Next, the following message is displayed:

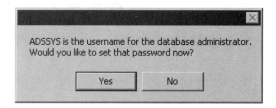

14. Click Yes to assign a password to the data dictionary administrator's account. Assigning a password to the ADSSYS user name of the data dictionary prevents unauthorized people from changing the data dictionary definitions. Set the password for the ADSSYS user name to **password**. (If this were a real database that you were adding a password to, you would use a more secure password than this one.)

> ### NOTE
> *Passwords for data dictionaries are case sensitive. If you attempt to access this data dictionary using the administrative user name, and the Advantage Data Architect reports that your user name or password is not correct, check to see if your CAPS LOCK key is on.*

15. Once you have entered the password twice and click Save to accept the Change Password dialog box, you will see the following dialog box, informing you of the name of the data dictionary:

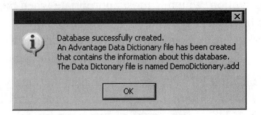

16. After you accept this final dialog box, the Advantage Data Architect displays the new data dictionary in the Advantage Database Manager, as shown in Figure 4-2.

As you can see in Figure 4-2, the Advantage Database Manager is roughly divided into two sections. On the left side is a tree view that displays the various elements of a data dictionary. The pane on the right side is used for displaying the various dialog boxes for configuring the object selected on the left. There is also a toolbar along the top that provides you with easy access to a number of the Advantage Database Manager features.

The Advantage Database Manager is also where you can enable the display of additional confirmation dialog boxes that are shown while you are working with the Advantage Data Architect. These additional dialog boxes are not displayed, by default. If you would like the additional confirmation dialog boxes displayed, which

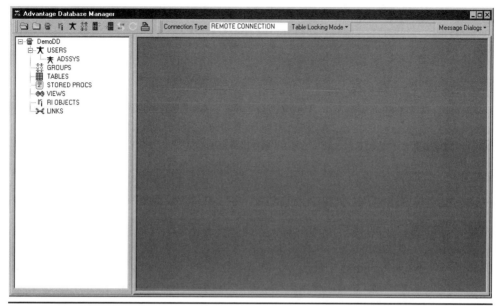

Figure 4-2   *The DemoDictionary data dictionary in the Advantage Database Manager*

will give you more feedback while you are working with the Advantage Data Architect, select Yes for the Message Dialogs option, which is located at the top right of the Advantage Database Manager shown in Figure 4-2. At a later time, you can set the Message Dialogs option to No to once again suppress the display of these additional confirmation dialog boxes.

When you first create a data dictionary, it contains only a single definition, a user named ADSSYS, which is the data dictionary administrator's user name. This user name cannot be changed.

> **TIP**
>
> *When you created this data dictionary, you had the option of assigning an alias to this data dictionary. An alias simplifies the process of connecting to ADS data. Not only can aliases be associated with data dictionaries, but they can also be associated with file directories containing ADS tables. Aliases also simplify your configuration of Advantage TDataSet Descendants. To create an alias for a directory, select Tools | Alias Configuration from the Advantage Data Architect main menu. The Alias Configuration Utility permits you to create, update, and remove aliases. All alias information is stored in the ADS.INI file.*

Adding Tables to a Data Dictionary

While a data dictionary provides you with access to a number of different types of objects, these aren't very useful unless you have tables for them to work with. As a result, adding tables to a newly created data dictionary is often one of your first tasks.

You can add any of the ADS-supported table types to a data dictionary, but it is nearly always preferable to use ADT tables. Not only do ADT tables have superior characteristics, compared to DBF tables, but when used with data dictionaries, the definitions for that table that you save to your data dictionary will always be respected. This is because when an ADT table is added to a data dictionary, information stored in the table's header prevents it from being accessed as a free table (unless you later free that table from the data dictionary).

The same cannot be said about DBF tables. Specifically, while you can add one or more DBFs to a data dictionary, there is nothing to prevent applications from accessing those tables directly, without using the data dictionary. Obviously, when accessed without the data dictionary, it is possible to perform tasks that a data dictionary would have otherwise prevented.

For example, imagine that you have configured a data dictionary to prevent a particular user from accessing a specific DBF table. So long as the user is working with a client application that uses the data dictionary, access will be prevented. However, if another application uses the DBF table directly, it is entirely possible that the user would then be given access to the table.

There are a number of different ways that tables can be added to a data dictionary. You can right-click the TABLES node in the Advantage Database Manager tree view and select Create New Table. Doing so displays the Creating Table dialog box described in Chapter 2. You use this dialog box to define the structure of the new table you want created. When you click Execute from this dialog box, the new table is created as a database table.

Alternatively, you can add existing free tables to the data dictionary. This second approach is the one that you are going to use in the following section.

Opening a Data Dictionary

Before we add tables to a data dictionary, it makes sense to learn how to open a data dictionary in the Advantage Database.

1. If the DemoDictionary is still open in the Advantage Database Manager, click the Close icon in the upper-right corner of the Advantage Database Manager to close this window.

2. Now, select Database | Open Database from the Advantage Data Architect main menu. The Advantage Data Architect displays the Select a Database dialog box:

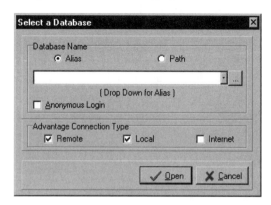

NOTE

ADS uses a remote connection as shown in the Advantage Connection Type option of the Select a Database dialog box. If you are using ALS, you would select Local for the Advantage Connection Type option. If you have both options checked, the Advantage Data Architect will first attempt to connect to ADS, and then attempt to connect to ALS if ADS is not available.

3. Select the Alias radio button. Next, select DemoDD from the Database Name dropdown list and then click Open. The Advantage Data Architect displays the Database Login dialog box:

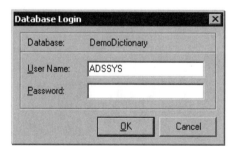

4. Set User Name to **ADSSYS** and Password to **password**. Click OK. Assuming that you entered the user name and password correctly, DemoDictionary.ADD (with alias DemoDD) will be opened in the Advantage Database Manager.

Adding Existing Tables to a Data Dictionary

Adding existing tables to a data dictionary is easy. The following steps show you how:

1. With the DemoDictionary data dictionary open in the Advantage Database
   Manager, right-click the TABLES node in the Advantage Database Manager
   tree view, and select Add Existing Table(s). The Open dialog box is displayed.

2. Use the Open dialog box to navigate to the directory into which you copied
   the sample ADT tables, as described in Appendix B (this is the same directory
   in which DemoDictionary.ADD is stored).

3. Select the CUSTOMER.ADT and the EMPLOYEE.ADT tables. To do
   this, hold down the CTRL key and click on CUSTOMER.ADT and on
   EMPLOYEE.ADT. With both tables selected, click the Open button.
   The two newly added tables should now appear as nodes beneath the
   TABLES node, as shown in Figure 4-3.

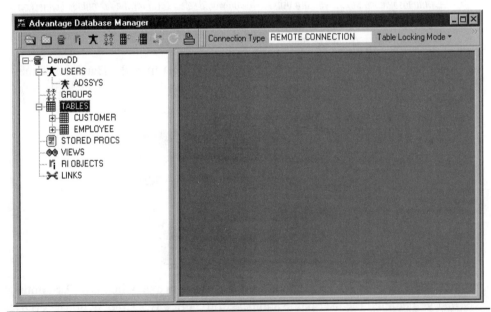

Figure 4-3   *The CUSTOMER and EMPLOYEE tables have been bound to the
DemoDictionary data dictionary.*

Removing a Table from a Data Dictionary

You remove a table from a data dictionary using the Advantage Database Manager. To remove a table, right-click the desired table node in the tree view of the Advantage Database Manager and select Remove.

CAUTION

There is also a utility called FREEADT.EXE that can be used to free tables from a data dictionary. However, there are few occasions when it should be used since tables you free using this utility still remain in the data dictionary definition even though they are freed. To remove tables from the data dictionary definition, you will most likely use the Advantage Database Manager, although you can also remove tables programmatically using the ACE API, or using the SQL DROP TABLE command (which both deletes the table and removes the table from the data dictionary definition).

Data Dictionaries and Table Encryption

Data dictionaries significantly simplify the process of working with encrypted tables. With free tables, each table can have a different password, and this password must be submitted to ADS prior to accessing the associated table.

With data dictionaries, a single password is applied to all encrypted tables. Better still, there is no longer any need to pass the table password to ADS prior to accessing an encrypted database table. Instead, ADS reads the password from the data dictionary.

Enabling Table Encryption

Before you can encrypt the tables of your data dictionary, you must enable table encryption for your database tables and define the encryption password. Use the following steps to enable table encryption for the DemoDictionary data dictionary:

1. Right-click the data dictionary node (labeled "DemoDD," our alias for DemoDictionary) in the Advantage Database Manager tree view, and select Properties from the displayed popup menu. The data dictionary node is the root node of the tree view, and its label is the alias DemoDD. The Advantage Database Manager responds by displaying the data dictionary properties dialog box, shown in Figure 4-4.

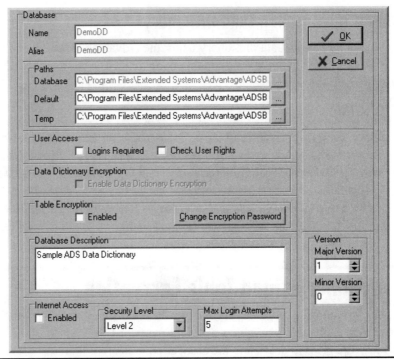

Figure 4-4 *You display the data dictionary properties dialog box by right-clicking the data dictionary node in the tree view, and selecting Properties.*

2. Check the Enabled checkbox in the Table Encryption section of the data dictionary properties dialog box.

3. Next, click the Change Encryption Password button to display the Change Password dialog box.

4. At New Password, enter **password**. Click Save when you are done.

5. Now click OK on the data dictionary properties dialog box to save the data dictionary's properties.

NOTE

The table encryption password and your data dictionary administrator's password are separate and serve different purposes. The table encryption password provides the key for encrypting your data. The data dictionary administrator's password provides you with administrative access to the data dictionary. We are using the same word, "password," for these two passwords merely as a convenience, one that is intended to simplify the number of passwords that you have to remember while working with the examples in this book. Typically, you would want to use two different passwords in your applications, as well as passwords that are more difficult to guess.

Encrypting Database Tables

Once you have enabled encryption for the data dictionary, you can selectively encrypt tables in the data dictionary. Once encrypted, a table's contents are scrambled on disk, which prevents someone from examining your data with a low-level file viewer.

Table encryption also is beneficial because all table and memo data transmitted over the network (including the Internet) are in encrypted form, so that someone using network sniffer utilities cannot see your raw table and memo data.

Use the following steps to encrypt the two tables of this data dictionary:

1. If the TABLES node in the Advantage Database Manager tree view is not expanded, click the + next to this node to display the nodes for the CUSTOMER and EMPLOYEE tables.

2. Right-click the CUSTOMER node and select Encrypt. After a brief moment, the glyph that appears to the left of the CUSTOMER table node will change. The new glyph depicts an encrypted table.

3. Now right-click the EMPLOYEE node and select Encrypt. The glyph for this node will soon reflect that this table is also encrypted.

Binding Tables with Table Encryption Enabled

If you enable encryption for a data dictionary after binding tables to it, you must manually encrypt each table using the technique demonstrated in the preceding section. However, if you enable encryption prior to adding existing tables, those tables will be encrypted as they are added to the data dictionary. As a result, if you are creating a data dictionary from existing tables, you can save yourself some time by enabling encryption prior to adding the tables.

Use the following steps to add four more tables to the data dictionary:

1. Right-click the TABLES node and select Add Existing Table(s).

2. Using the Open dialog box, navigate to the directory in which you copied the sample tables, if necessary. Then, while keeping the CTRL key depressed, click the DEPARTMENTS.ADT, INVOICE.ADT, ITEMS.ADT, and PRODUCTS.ADT tables to select them. With these four tables selected, click Open.

3. The Advantage Database Manager binds these four tables to the data dictionary, encrypting them in the process.

4. Your data dictionary should now contain six tables, as shown in Figure 4-5.

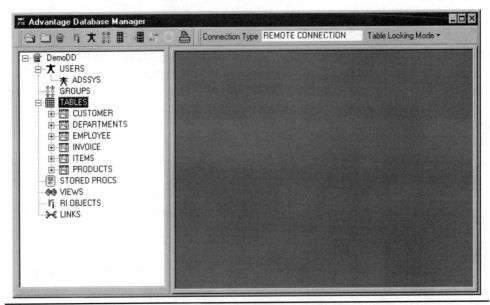

Figure 4-5   *A total of six tables have been bound to this data dictionary.*

Implementing Security with Data Dictionaries

While encrypting your database tables prevents someone from viewing the data in your table files directly, it does nothing to prevent those tables from being accessed by client applications designed to work with a data dictionary. If you want to control who can access your tables, you have to implement security for your data dictionary.

You can take a number of specific steps to ensure that your data is accessed only by authorized users. These include requiring users to log in prior to providing them with access to your database tables, as well as setting up the user names and passwords that users use to log in. These topics are covered in the following sections.

Controlling User Access

Unless you take specific steps, any user who can connect to your data dictionary can access the data dictionary's database tables. Encrypting the tables does not help, since the data dictionary provides ADS with the password for the bound tables.

You can easily demonstrate this using the following steps:

1. Close the Advantage Database Manager.

2. Select Database | Open Database from the Advantage Data Architect main menu.

3. With the Alias radio button selected, and Alias set to DemoDD, check the Anonymous Login checkbox, and then click Open. The Advantage Data Architect responds by opening the data dictionary in the Advantage Database Manager. You can now view and edit the tables in this data dictionary if you like.

4. Close the Advantage Database Manager.

NOTE

So long as anonymous login is permitted by the data dictionary, a user can log in anonymously and view and edit data. However, a user logged in anonymously cannot change data dictionary definitions, such as table structures, index orders, and data dictionary properties.

If you want to control access to a data dictionary, you must configure the data dictionary to require a valid user name and password before access is granted. Use the following steps to restrict access to the data dictionary:

1. Open the Advantage Database Manager again, this time with the Anonymous Login checkbox unchecked. When prompted, log in using the data dictionary administrative user name **ADSSYS** and the password **password**.

2. Right-click the data dictionary node in the Advantage Database Manager tree view and select Properties. As you may recall from earlier in this chapter, the data dictionary node is the root node in the Advantage Database Manager tree view. In our example, DemoDD, the alias for DemoDictionary, is displayed as the root node. The Advantage Database Manager displays the data dictionary properties dialog box.

3. In the User Access section, check the Logins Required checkbox. When Logins Required is checked, ADS will not accept a connection to the data dictionary unless the user has provided a valid user name and password.

4. The User Access section also includes a Check User Rights checkbox. If this checkbox is not checked, a valid user name and password will provide the user with unlimited access to all objects in the data dictionary. If this checkbox is checked, the user will be limited by whatever user rights are expressly granted for their user name. For the time being, do not check the Check User Rights checkbox. Assigning user rights is discussed in the following section.

5. Click OK to save the new data dictionary properties.

It is now impossible to log in anonymously. You can test this by closing the Advantage Database Manager, and then attempting an anonymous login, as demonstrated earlier in this section. This time you will get an ADS 7078 error. Because ADS could not authenticate you, it denied you access to the data dictionary.

Defining Users and Groups

An administrative user is created when you first create a data dictionary. The user name for the user is ADSSYS, and this user is specifically designed to manage the configuration of the data dictionary.

In most cases, you should not use this user name for regular data access. The ADSSYS connection consumes additional resources on your ADS server and increases the amount of network traffic between server and clients.

In addition, transaction processing is not allowed by ADS using the ADSSYS connection.

The only time that your client application should connect to a data dictionary using this administrative user account is when it needs to make runtime changes to your data dictionary. For example, you can build functionality into your client applications that permits users to be added to a data dictionary, passwords to be changed, access rights to be added or revoked, and so on. These capabilities are only available, however, when the connection to the data dictionary is made using the ADSSYS user name and associated password. As a result, your client application would likely offer these capabilities to select users, and establish an administrative connection only while administrative activities are being performed.

For all other, non-administrative access to a data dictionary, you should establish one or more "regular" users. (*Regular user,* as the term is used here, is any user other than ADSSYS.) In the simplest case, you create a single regular user and provide that user name and password (the password could even be blank) for all of your users. If there is going to be only one user, and that user is you, this approach is usually more than adequate.

NOTE

Some applications, such as Web server extensions, are inherently more secure as long as you've installed them correctly — for example, placing them in a virtual directory of your Web server, and configuring that directory with execute, but not read, rights. For applications like these, a single regular user account is sufficient to permit your application to connect to the data dictionary through ADS while preventing access by unauthorized local users.

If your client application is used by more than one user, you should consider having more than one non-administrative user. Having more than one user permits you to exert greater control over access to your database.

For example, imagine that you are writing a database application that will be used by several employees in your company. If one of those employees is subsequently terminated, you probably want to revoke their access to the database, particularly if the database contains sensitive information. If each employee has their own user name and password, you can revoke the former employee's access by removing their associated user from the data dictionary.

Granted, if security is not an issue, you may conclude that the benefits of multiple passwords are not worth the additional administration. Nonetheless, if you do opt for multiple user names, you should also consider making use of groups. Groups are discussed later in this section.

Adding Users

Adding users from the Advantage Database Manager is quite simple, as shown in the following steps:

1. Open the DemoDictionary data dictionary in the Advantage Database Manager if it is not already open.

2. Right-click the USERS node in the Advantage Database Manager tree view and select Add User. The Advantage Database Manager displays the Create New User dialog box:

3. Set User Name to **adsuser**.

4. Set both Password and Verify Password to **password**, and then click Continue. The User Description dialog box is displayed:

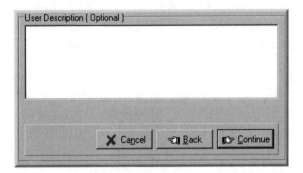

5. Set User Description to **Basic user name for data access**. Click Continue to display the Set User Rights dialog box:

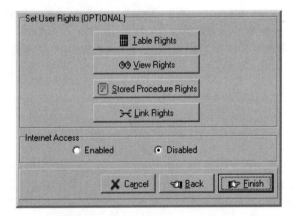

6. You use the Set User Rights dialog box to grant specific access privileges to the user. These privileges are only meaningful, however, if you have checked the Check User Rights checkbox of the data dictionary's properties dialog box. Enabling user rights checking is discussed later in this section.

    The Set User Rights dialog box is also where you enable Internet access for the user. If you want to grant this user access to the data dictionary and the database over the Internet, check the Enabled checkbox in the Internet Access area. This right is only meaningful if you have enabled the data dictionary and database for Internet Access from the data dictionary's properties dialog box, and have also configured ADS to provide Internet access by specifying an Internet IP port through the Advantage Configuration Utility. Do not enable Internet access for this user at this time.

7. Click Finish to finalize the adsuser's properties and to add this user to the USERS node in the Advantage Database Manager tree view.

Any number of end users can use the same user name and password at the same time, which is why you can get by with a single non-administrative user if you want. But if you want more than one user, you can repeat the preceding steps for each of the additional users that you want to add.

In addition to providing you with greater control over your application's security, having more than one user permits you to leverage another feature of data dictionaries. This feature is user rights, and it is discussed in the following section.

Checking User Rights

User rights refer to access permissions associated with the tables, fields, views, stored procedures, and database links associated with a data dictionary. For some objects, such as stored procedures, rights refer to whether or not a connection for that particular user has the right to execute the stored procedure. For other objects, such as tables, these rights are more involved. For example, you can permit one user to view a particular table, but that is all. You might provide another user with complete access to that table, permitting them to view and edit the data.

The rights for tables can be extended down to the field level. For example, for the user who can only read a particular table, you can further define that there are one or more fields that this user is not even allowed to see. For example, you might let a user view the records of the employee table, but deny them the ability to view the Salary field.

There are two parts to controlling user rights. The first is to configure the data dictionary to check a user's rights prior to providing access to a data dictionary's objects, such as a table or a stored procedure. The second part involves explicitly granting rights to those resources. Use the following steps to configure the DemoDictionary data dictionary to check user rights. Granting rights is discussed later in this chapter.

1. Right-click the DemoDictionary (alias DemoDD) node in the Advantage Database Manager tree view and select Properties. The data dictionary's properties dialog box, similar to that shown in Figure 4-4, is displayed. (The Logins Required and the Enabled checkboxes were enabled in previous steps.)

2. Check the Check User Rights checkbox and then click OK.

If you are considering limiting a user's access to one or more resources, you should consider whether you want to employ groups.

Understanding Groups

A group is like a user template for access rights. You begin by creating a group and defining what access rights members of that group require. You can then assign group membership to individual users. By default, a user inherits the rights associated with the groups they belong to.

Groups are especially valuable when you have multiple users and want to easily administer their rights. For example, you can create one group and explicitly grant that group the rights that all group members will need to the data dictionary's resources. You can then make each of your users a member of that group.

If at some later date you need to change the rights of all users in the particular group, you simply update the group's rights. The members of that group automatically inherit those changes (unless you have overridden this behavior for a particular user; overriding inherited rights is discussed later in this chapter). By comparison, if you do not use groups, and explicitly set rights for each individual user, any changes that you make to user privileges will need to be applied to each user's rights separately.

The benefits of using groups increase when you have two or more types of users of your database. For example, some applications have three levels of users: those who can only view data, those who can view and add data, and those who have full access (including delete privileges).

To accommodate this scenario, you begin by creating three groups, with each group being granted the rights associated with the type of user who will be a member. Then, for each user you add to the data dictionary, you assign them to whichever group they belong.

Actually, you can get pretty fancy about how you use groups. For example, a given user can belong to two or more groups. That user's rights are the sum of the rights conveyed to the groups to which they belong.

Using Access Rights and Groups

As you probably concluded from the preceding discussions concerning users, groups, and access rights, how you set up the security for your data dictionary depends largely on your application's needs. In the case of the data dictionary created in this chapter, a simple security model will be employed. You will create two groups, one with readonly access to the data dictionary's tables, and one with complete access. You will then assign adsuser to the group that grants complete access.

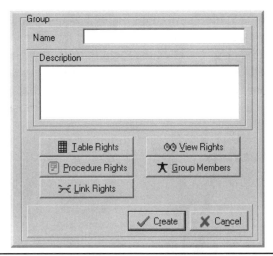

Figure 4-6   *The Group dialog box allows you to define access rights for a group as well as to display existing properties for the group.*

Use the following steps to configure security for this data dictionary:

1. Right-click the GROUPS node in the Advantage Database Manager tree view and select Add Group. The Group dialog box, shown in Figure 4-6, is displayed.

2. Set Name to **ReadOnly** and Description to **Sample group with readonly permissions**. Click Table Rights to view the Table Permissions dialog box.

3. Click the Set All Read button to check the Read checkbox associated with every table in the data dictionary. Leave the Insert, Update, and Delete checkboxes unchecked:

Permissions	Effective Permissions				
		Read	Insert	Update	Delete
EMPLOYEE		☑	☐	☐	☐
CUSTOMER		☑	☐	☐	☐
PRODUCTS		☑	☐	☐	☐
DEPARTMENTS		☑	☐	☐	☐
INVOICE		☑	☐	☐	☐
ITEMS		☑	☐	☐	☐

Clear All Read   Set All Insert   Set All Update   Set All Delete

Field Permissions   ✓ OK   ✗ Cancel

The settings on the Table Permissions dialog box apply to entire tables. If you want to configure field-level permissions, select a table name from the Table Permissions dialog box, and click the Field Permissions button. For example, if you select the ITEMS table in the Table Permissions dialog box and click Field Permissions, you will see the Field Permissions dialog box. This dialog box permits you to set the Read, Insert, and Update permissions for the fields in the ITEMS table:

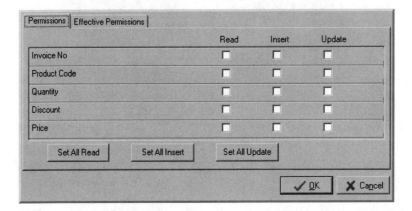

As long as no checkboxes are checked on the Field Permissions dialog box, the group members can have any access to the table's fields granted by the table's rights. If at least one checkbox is checked, that group's members will have only those permissions explicitly granted by the field-level permissions. Click OK to close the Field Permissions dialog box and return to the Table Permissions dialog box.

NOTE

This field-level permissions behavior differs from that of the SQL GRANT statement, which is described in Chapter 11.

4. Click OK to close the Table Permissions dialog box and return to the Group dialog box. From here you can add other permissions, but in our example, there are currently no other objects for which permissions can be granted. You can also click the Group Members button in order to add a user to this group, but we are not going to add a user to the ReadOnly group at this time. Click Create to create the group.

5. Right-click the GROUPS node in the Advantage Database Manager tree view and select Add Group once more.

6. Set Name to **ALL** and Description to **Sample group with rights to everything**.

7. Click the Table Rights button to display the Table Permissions dialog box. Click the Set All Read, Set All Insert, Set All Update, and Set All Delete buttons to enable all rights to the tables of the data dictionary. Click OK when done to return to the Group dialog box.

8. Click Create to create this group.

Once you create a group, you add users to the group. The following steps add the adsuser to the ALL group:

1. If the USERS node is not already expanded, click the + sign next to it to expand it.

2. Click the adsuser user node to display this user's properties, as shown in Figure 4-7.

3. Click the Group Membership button from the User dialog box. The User Group List displays all defined groups. Check the ALL group to add adsuser to the

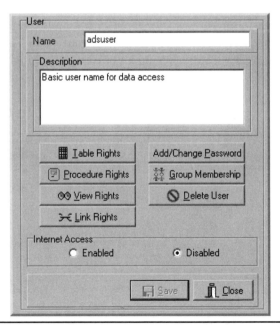

Figure 4-7   *The User dialog box displays the properties for the user selected in the Advantage Database Manager tree view.*

ALL group. Click Save, and then click Close to close the User Group List dialog box.

4. Click the Table Rights button on the User dialog box to view the user's Table Rights dialog box, as shown in Figure 4-8. Notice that the last column of checkboxes is labeled "Inherit," and each of the checkboxes in this column is checked by default. When Inherit is checked, the rights of this user for the associated table are inherited from the sum of the groups the user is a member of.

   If you want to override this behavior, assigning table rights explicitly rather than using the inherited rights, uncheck the Inherit checkbox for each table whose rights you want to define explicitly. Note that you can view the effective rights by clicking the Effective Permissions tab of this dialog box. The Effective Permissions page is a readonly view of the current permissions, taking into account group membership and inherited rights.

5. Do not make any changes to this user's Table Rights dialog box. Click Cancel once to close the Table Rights dialog box. Click Close to close the User dialog box.

Changing Objects and Permissions

Creating users, groups, and enabling user rights checking is often one of the final steps that you will take in the testing and deployment of a database application. The creation of users and groups, and the enabling of rights checking were performed in this chapter since these issues are closely related to the creation and control of

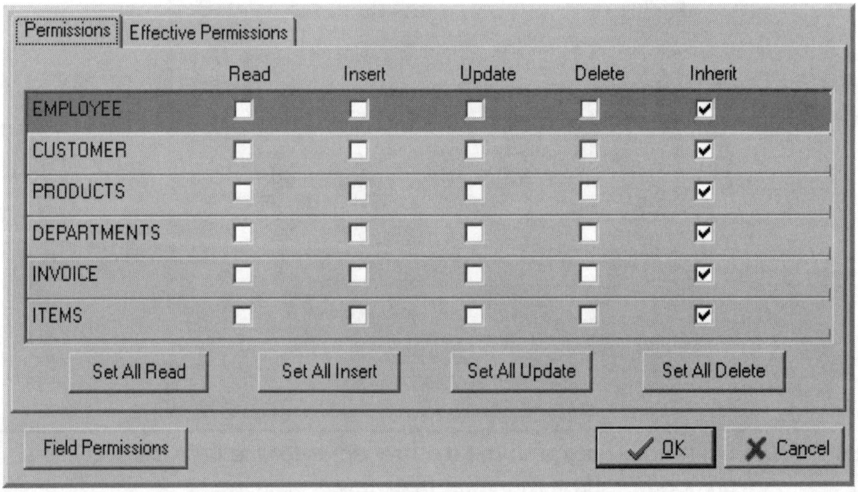

Figure 4-8   *Use the Table Rights dialog box to customize a user's rights as well as to view effective permissions.*

a data dictionary. The problem is that you have not completed the construction of this data dictionary. In later chapters of this book, you will add new objects, such as stored procedures and views, to this data dictionary.

Each time you add a new object (stored procedure, view, or link), you will also need to update group and/or user access rights in order to permit access to the added object. By comparison, if you had waited to enable access rights until after all of the data dictionary's objects were created, you would have had to configure access rights only once.

To update group or user access rights for a newly added object, you display the Advantage Database Manager and select the desired group or user in the tree view. If you select a group, you will see a Group dialog box similar to the one shown in Figure 4-6. If you select a user, you will see a User dialog box similar to the one shown in Figure 4-7. The Procedure Rights, View Rights, and Link Rights options on these dialog boxes allow you to define group or user access rights for stored procedures, views, and links, respectively.

Setting rights for stored procedures, views, and links is discussed later in this book when these objects are discussed.

How Field-Level Permissions Are Enforced

We did not assign field-level permissions to any of the tables in this data dictionary. In fact, some developers avoid using field-level permissions altogether, and use alternative mechanisms to restrict access to certain fields. Consider the example given earlier in this chapter in which a user can view the EMPLOYEE table, but is not permitted to view the Salary field of the EMPLOYEE table. Instead of using field-level permissions, the user could be denied read access to the EMPLOYEE table, but be granted read access to a view that includes all fields other than the Salary field from the EMPLOYEE table. In the end, the results are similar. That user cannot access the Salary field.

But what happens when you do employ field permissions to limit a user's access to a field? Specifically, what would happen if you try to show a user a record that contains a field whose field-level permissions prohibit the field from being read?

The answer depends on the permissions level associated with the table to which the field belongs. You can view and change a table's permission level by right-clicking the node associated with the table under the TABLES node, and selecting Properties from the displayed menu. Figure 4-9 shows the table properties dialog box for the EMPLOYEE table.

There are three possible values for the Permission Level table property. These are Level 1, Level 2, and Level 3, where Level 1 is the least restrictive and Level 3 is the most.

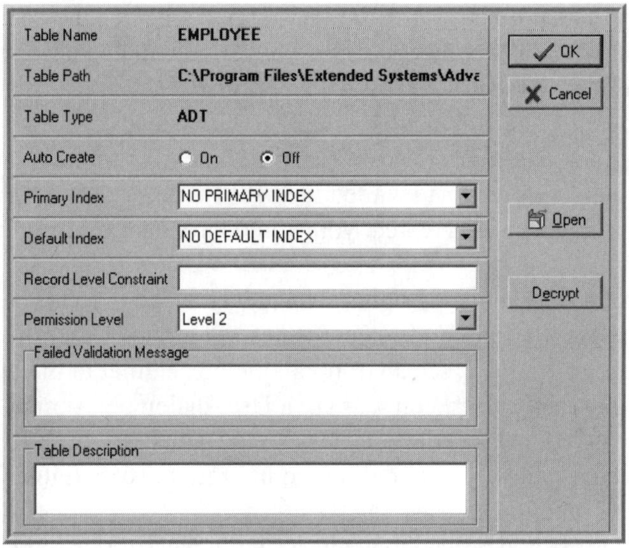

Figure 4-9   *The table properties dialog box for the EMPLOYEE table*

If you set a table's Permission Level property to Level 1, reading a field that does not have read permissions does not cause an error, it simply returns a null value. If you try to display that data to a user who does not have read permissions, the field appears empty. However, you can use the field in a SQL WHERE clause, a filter, or a scope, which means that a user could possibly infer the value of the field based on the results of one of these operations.

The Level 2 Permission Level also returns a null value if you attempt to read a field that does not have read permissions. However, attempting to use that field in a SQL WHERE clause, a scope, or a filter will generate an error. This is the default permission level.

The Level 3 Permission Level is very restrictive. Tables with this permission level can only be accessed using SQL. Furthermore, any field without read rights cannot appear in a WHERE, HAVING, or ORDER BY clause. Otherwise, the SQL statement will produce an error.

Comparing Data Dictionaries

Because data dictionaries contain many of the essential definitions that are used by your client applications, changes to your database nearly always involve changes to its associated data dictionary. If your database is deployed to a single location, making changes to your data dictionary is not a major issue. However, when a database is deployed to a large number of sites, such as is often the case with vertical market applications, updating the data dictionary can be a complicated task.

The simplest way to update a data dictionary would be to change an existing data dictionary, and then deploy the update. In many applications, however, this is not a reasonable solution. Specifically, some client applications permit an administrative user to add users, make them members of groups, grant additional access rights to users or groups, and so forth. If you were to replace the data dictionary that the client applications were using, these customizations would be lost.

Fortunately, since ADS 7.0, the process of updating data dictionaries is much more straightforward. The Advantage Data Architect in ADS 7.0 and later includes the Dictionary Differentiator, a utility that can examine two data dictionaries. Moreover, as a result of this examination, the Dictionary Differentiator can generate a SQL script that contains instructions that can be executed to update a data dictionary.

You use the SQL scripts generated by the Dictionary Differentiator to write a utility that you distribute to your Customers. Within this utility, which each customer only needs to run once, your code examines the version number of the current data dictionary. If it determines that an older version of the data dictionary is present, it executes the SQL script, which applies the updates.

The following steps describe how you can use the Dictionary Differentiator:

1. From the Advantage Data Architect's main menu, select Database | Compare Data Dictionaries. The Dictionary Differentiator, shown in Figure 4-10, is displayed.

2. Use the First Dictionary section to select one version of your data dictionary.

3. Use the Second Dictionary section to select the second data dictionary.

4. If there are objects that you do not want to include in the comparison and SQL script generation, click the Exclude Objects button. If you click Exclude Objects, you may be asked to log into one or both data dictionaries. Provide an administrative user name and password for each data dictionary you are asked to log into. Once you have provided any requested passwords, the Select Objects for Exclusion dialog box is displayed:

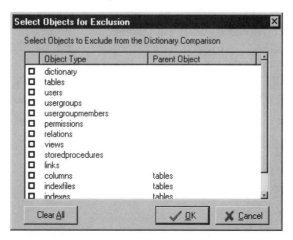

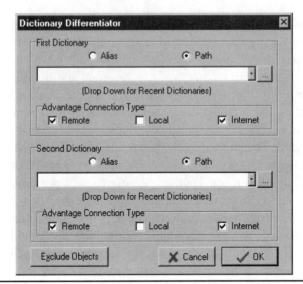

Figure 4-10   *Use the Dictionary Differentiator to compare two data dictionaries.*

5. Using the Select Objects for Exclusion dialog box, place a checkmark next to any category of object that you do not want to be included in the comparison. For example, if user names and groups are something that can be administered through client applications, you probably do not want to include these in the comparison. Click OK to close the Select Objects for Exclusion dialog box when you are done to return to the Dictionary Differentiator.

6. When you are ready to continue, click OK to display the Object Differences dialog box shown in Figure 4-11.

    The objects that the Dictionary Differentiator can generate code for appear as nodes in the Object Differences dialog box. Examine a node to see the objects that both data dictionaries share, as well as those objects that are included in only one data dictionary. For example, consider Figure 4-11, in which the tables node has been expanded. The dictionary on the left includes the tables CUST_BAK and EMP_BAK, while the data dictionary on the right does not. The table glyphs associated with the data dictionary on the left show + signs, indicating that this dictionary has objects that the other does not. The glyphs for these same tables in the data dictionary on the right show – signs, which indicates that this data dictionary does not have these objects.

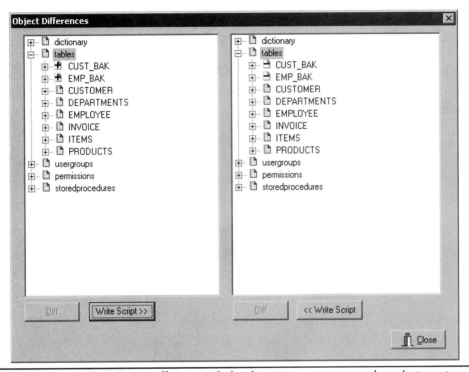

Figure 4-11   *Use the Object Differences dialog box to compare your data dictionaries.*

7. To generate a SQL script that will convert the selected node for the data dictionary on the left side, tables in the example shown in Figure 4-11, to match the structure of the corresponding node on the right side, click the button labeled Write Script >>. This script would contain SQL DROP TABLE statements, which would remove these two tables from the data dictionary on the left.

To generate a SQL script that will convert the node on the right to the node on the left, click the << Write Script button. This script would contain a series of SQL CREATE TABLE statements, and any other statements that would apply, such a CREATE INDEX, CREATE TRIGGER, as well as the execution of one or more system stored procedures, such as sp_ModifyTableProperty, to name a few of the items you might expect in this script.

8. Save each script that you generate, until you have created scripts to update the one data dictionary from the other. Click Close when you are done.

In the next chapter, you will learn how to define field-level and record-level constraints for your database tables and implement referential integrity, a special type of constraint.

Defining Constraints and Referential Integrity

C onstraints are server-side rules that the Advantage Database Server (ADS) can use to validate your data as it is being posted to a table. Referential integrity is a special type of constraint that ensures that the data residing in two or more related tables remains consistent.

This chapter provides you with a broad overview of constraints and referential integrity. It begins with a discussion of data validation in your applications. It then shows you how to improve the integrity of your data using constraints and referential integrity.

Understanding Constraints

Constraints are declarations that you attach to a table to ensure that your data is consistent and accurate. For example, imagine that you have a database that is used to manage the inventory of a warehouse. Using a constraint, you can prevent negative quantities from being entered into a field used to store the number of items on hand. From an inventory perspective, a negative quantity doesn't make sense. You either have some quantity of a particular object (a positive integer) or you have none. (This example assumes that back orders are handled separately from the field used to maintain the number of items on hand.)

This type of constraint applies to a single field in a table. As a result, a constraint like this one is called a *field-level constraint*.

Another type of constraint supported by ADS is one that can consider the data in one or more fields of a record when determining whether data is valid or not. For example, in an invoice table you can make sure that a value has been entered into the credit card number field when payment type is credit, and that the credit card field is blank when payment type is cash. This type of constraint is called a *record-level constraint*.

Referential integrity constraints apply to two related tables. For example, imagine that you have a table that holds invoices for sales made to customers, and another table where each customer's information, such as their ID, name, address, and credit limit, is stored. Using a referential integrity constraint, you can ensure a new invoice added to the invoice table includes the customer ID for one of your valid customers. If a user attempts to post a new invoice record, but the customer ID that they entered is not one found in the customer table, the invoice record will be rejected.

In all three of these cases, the purpose of the constraint is to improve the accuracy and consistency of the data in your database. But constraints are not the only source of data integrity in database applications. In order to put this into perspective, it is worthwhile spending a few minutes considering the alternatives to constraints in ADS applications.

Alternatives to Constraints

In addition to constraints, the consistency and accuracy of your data derives from a number of other sources. These include the structures of your data files, unique indexes, client-side code, and triggers. Each of these is discussed in this section.

Table Structures

Even without constraints, there are inherent limits to the data that can be added to a table. These are derived from the table's structure. For example, you cannot post a text string to an integer field. Similarly, you cannot add a string of 100 characters to a 20-character field. Attempting to post data like this will cause an error, and the data will be rejected.

These limits, however, are very general. A 12-character field that is used to hold a product code doesn't discriminate between text strings that are 12 characters or less. Unless some other mechanism is used, such as referential integrity, an invalid product code cannot be detected based solely on the field's type.

Unique Indexes

Another source of data integrity is the use of unique indexes on ADT tables. For ADT tables, at least, a unique index prevents two records with the same unique key from being posted to the table. (DBF unique indexes do not enforce record uniqueness.) For example, if you have a unique index on the customer ID field in the customer table, an attempt to post a second customer with the same ID will fail. This type of integrity, sometimes referred to as *entity integrity*, guarantees that no two customers can share the same customer ID.

Client-Side Validation

Another significant source of a data validation is code that you program into your client application. This type of validation, referred to as *client-side validation*, involves the programmatic inspection of data prior to posting it to the database. The data that is evaluated may be information entered into a graphic user interface (GUI) by an end user, or it may be data that is read from a data-collection device or a file.

Client-side validation is one of the most flexible of all the validation mechanisms. In short, your code can perform any test and apply any criteria available in your programming language to verify that the data is acceptable before continuing with a post operation.

Although it is very flexible, client-side validation has two serious drawbacks. These are related to development and consistency.

Let's consider the development side of things first. Client-side code must be written and debugged. In some cases this is a minor matter, and in other cases it represents a significant investment of time.

A whole new set of problems arises if you later need to change how the validation is performed. Not only do you have to modify and test your client applications, but you must also deploy your updated applications to every client machine. If only a few users use your application, the deployment may not be a big problem. However, if many people in many different locations use your application, the redeployment itself may represent an enormous investment of resources.

The second drawback to client-side validation is related to consistency. In short, the rules applied through client-side validation are applied consistently only to the extent that you ensure that they are. For example, imagine that you have several different client applications that work with a particular database. It is your responsibility to ensure that all client applications apply the validation rules the same way. If you make a change in the rules of validation in one client application, you need to do so in all others that work with the same database; otherwise, the data posted by one application may be inconsistent with that posted by another.

Triggers

Like client-side validation, triggers are programs that you write. Unlike client-side validation, however, you install triggers on your server, and configure the data dictionary to call them in response to a data action. For example, a trigger can be executed prior to a record being updated in your database.

From within a trigger, your code has access to all of the data associated with the data event. For example, if the trigger is being executed because a record is being updated in your database, your trigger code has access to both the original record and the updates that the client is attempting to post.

You can use the information passed to your trigger to perform almost any action you can imagine. In most cases, though, the purpose of the trigger is to validate the data. If the data is determined to be good, the record is accepted. On the other hand, if your code finds that the record is invalid, an error can be returned, and the record can be rejected.

Triggers have many advantages over client-side code. While providing the same level of flexibility in how you validate the data, triggers reside on the server. There are several advantages to this. First, triggers can be modified without requiring any changes to individual client applications. There is no need to redeploy your client applications in response to updates to triggers.

Second, since triggers are executed by ADS, and not at the discretion of the client applications, triggers are always applied consistently.

Third, triggers are also run if someone updates the database via the Advantage Data Architect or some other application that the developer has no control over.

Triggers were added to ADS in version 7.0, and represent one of the most valuable features in the product. Triggers are discussed in detail in Chapter 8.

Advantages of Constraints

Constraints have two primary advantages. First, they are declarative in nature. With the exception of the Boolean expressions that you use to specify record-level constraints, they require no programming. Compared to client-side validation and triggers, constraints are simple to create and document.

The second major advantage of constraints is that they reside in the data dictionary. As a result, ADS enforces the constraints regardless of how the data is accessed. No matter how many client applications you have that use the database, the constraints within the data dictionary are enforced.

That constraints reside on the server has another benefit. Specifically, if you need to change one or more constraints after deployment, you only need to update the data dictionary. No changes to client applications are necessary.

Creating Constraints

Data dictionaries support three types of constraint definitions: field-level, record-level, and referential integrity. While there are some similarities between these various types of constraints, the steps you take to implement them are quite different. As a result, the creation of each constraint type is described in its own section.

Defining Field-Level Constraints

You define field-level constraints using a table's Fields dialog box. Figure 5-1 shows the Fields dialog box for the CUSTOMER table in the DemoDictionary project.

NOTE

The steps for creating the DemoDictionary data dictionary are explained in Chapter 4. If you did not create this data dictionary, and want to follow along with the examples in this chapter, you should return to Chapter 4 and create this data dictionary before continuing.

The Fields dialog box serves several purposes. First, it displays a list of the fields of the associated table, ordered by the table's structure. When you select one of the fields from this list, you can view its metadata, including its name, its type, its width (in bytes), and its precision (where applicable).

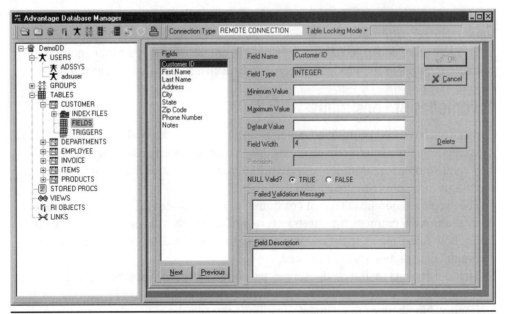

Figure 5-1 *The Fields dialog box for the CUSTOMER table in the DemoDictionary data dictionary*

The second purpose that this dialog box serves is that it permits you to set a default value for fields. When a new record is being inserted, fields that have not been assigned a value will be assigned the default value. If no default value is specified, fields that are not assigned a value when the record is being inserted will contain the value of NULL.

Imagine, for instance, that you have a sales rep table, and that one of the fields of the sales rep table is the code for the office to which the employee is assigned. You may define that the default value for the office field is a value, say 100, that indicates that no office has yet been assigned. In a situation like this one, this default value would be a valid key field in the related table that contains information about offices.

A third feature of this dialog box is that it permits you to assign a description to each field in the table. This feature is especially useful when the purpose of a field cannot be easily determined by its field name. It can also be useful for validation. The following SQL statement can be used to retrieve this description:

```
SELECT * FROM system.columns
```

The final feature offered by this dialog box is the assignment of field-level constraints. The three field-level constraints are minimum value, maximum value, and required (NULL valid).

These field-level constraints are pretty self-explanatory. The minimum and maximum values define the acceptable range for data. Fields containing data that exceed either of these limits are rejected. If no minimum or maximum value is set, the data type of the field will define the field's limits.

The NULL valid radio buttons permit you to define whether or not it is acceptable to post a record where the associated field does not contain data. The default value is True, meaning NULLs are acceptable values for the field. If you set Null Valid to False, posting a record where the associated field has not been assigned a value will produce an error, and the record will be rejected.

When a record cannot be posted because at least one field's field-level constraints is violated, ADS generates an error that includes the ADS error code as well as a description of the error. For example, if you set a minimum value of 0 for a field named Retail Price, and then a client application attempts to post a record where the Retail Price value is a negative number, ADS will generate an error message similar to the one shown here:

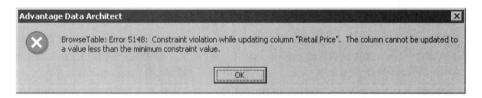

When you configure at least one of the field-level constraints for a particular field, you have the option of providing a custom error message that will be displayed in place of the descriptive text that ADS would have added to the error message. For example, if you assign the text **Retail Price must be a positive integer** to the Failed Validation Message field, attempting to post a record with a negative retail price will produce this error message:

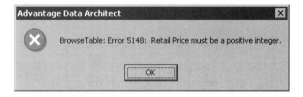

How Field-Level Constraints Are Applied

From the Fields dialog box, the Advantage Database Manager keeps track of each field to which you define one or more field-level constraints. After you are through setting field-level constraints for one or more fields in your table, and you click the

OK button on the Fields dialog box, the Advantage Database Manager will apply the constraints to the table.

These constraints are applied one field at a time, using the order in which you first defined the constraints. For example, if you are applying at least one field-level constraint to three different fields, there will be three independent operations on the table, with the first operation applying all of the constraints you defined for the first field you set constraints for, the second operation applying constraints to the second field you set at least one constraint for, followed by the third operation on the last field to which you defined constraints.

The Advantage Database Manager permits you to define how the constraints are applied to each field individually. For example, if you applied at least one field-level constraint for three different fields, you must decide how each of those fields will be validated. For some fields you might want to remove invalid records from the table, for others you might want to ignore invalid data, and for another you might want to abort the application of the constraints if even one record contains data in that field that does not pass the constraints.

You make the decision on how to validate a particular field once you are done setting one or more constraints for it. Specifically, the Advantage Database Manager displays the Validation Method dialog box for a particular field if you have changed one or more constraints when you select another field to set constraints for, or you click OK to begin applying your constraints. You must select from this Validation Method dialog box before you can set constraints to another field, or save your work and begin applying the constraints.

Using the Validation Method dialog box to apply your constraints is discussed later in this section.

Field-Level Constraint Example

The following steps demonstrate how to add field-level constraints to a table. Begin by opening the DemoDictionary data dictionary in the Advantage Data Architect:

1. Select the PRODUCTS node under the TABLES node in the Database Tree View, and expand it.

2. Select the FIELDS node to display the Fields dialog box.

3. Select the Product Code field in the Fields list, and then set NULL Valid to FALSE.

4. Select the Retail Price field in the Fields list. At this point, the Validation Method dialog box is displayed so that you can define what the Advantage Database Manager should do if one or more records contain data in the Product Code field that does not pass the newly selected constraints. Select VALIDATION WITH ERROR from the dropdown list and click OK. You are now shown the current constraints for the Retail Price field.

5. Set NULL Valid to FALSE, and set the Minimum Value field to **0**.

6. Finally, set Failed Validation Message to **Retail Price must be a positive integer**. Your screen should look similar to that shown in Figure 5-2.

7. Click OK. The Advantage Data Architect now displays the Validation Method dialog box once more, permitting you to define how to apply these constraints to the Retail Price field. Set Validation Option to VALIDATION WITH ERROR, and then click OK, as shown here:

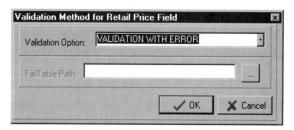

The Validation Method Dialog Box

Constraints are formal declarations of what constitutes bad data. If you apply one or more constraints to an existing table, there is a real possibility that some of the existing data is inconsistent with the constraints. You use the Validation Method

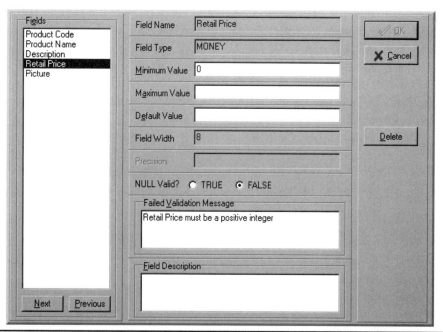

Figure 5-2   *The Fields dialog box for the PRODUCTS table*

dialog box to instruct the Advantage Database Manager how to handle invalid data if it is encountered when you first define the constraint.

You select from five options on the Validation Method dialog box: NO VALIDATION, VALIDATION WITH APPEND TO FAIL TABLE, VALIDATION WITH FAIL TABLE CREATE, VALIDATION WITHOUT RECORD SAVE, and VALIDATION WITH ERROR.

Set Validation Option to NO VALIDATION if you want the Advantage Data Architect to ignore invalid data that currently exists in the table. Any records whose data violates any of the constraints you are applying will remain in the table.

That constraint-violating records may remain in the table when you choose NO VALIDATION makes this option very unattractive in most cases. Imagine what would happen if one of these invalid records needed to be modified. Unless the modification fixed the validation problem, it would be impossible to post those changes. This may place the end user in the unfortunate position of having to fix a problem that they did not cause. In fact, if the user doesn't have field-level access rights to the field where the constraint violation exists, they would not be able to correct this problem.

Three of the Validation Method dialog box options provide for the removal of any records that would otherwise violate the constraints you are adding to the table. Two of these, VALIDATION WITH APPEND TO FAIL TABLE and VALIDATION WITH FAIL TABLE CREATE, save the offending records to an ADT table called the *fail* table.

The VALIDATION WITH APPEND TO FAIL TABLE option adds the offending records to an existing fail table, although a fail table will be created if an existing fail table does not exist when the first offending record is encountered. The second option, VALIDATION WITH FAIL TABLE CREATE, should only be used when you want to create a new fail table, overwriting any previous fail table with the same name. Do not select VALIDATION WITH FAIL TABLE CREATE if you are setting constraints on more than one field, since a second fail table creation will cause the loss of records saved in a previous creation.

If you select either of these fail table–creating options, examine the fail table to see if records were placed there once the constraints have been applied. If one or more constraint-violating records were removed to the fail table, you can edit these records, correcting whatever problem they have, and then add them back to the original table.

The next option that removes constraint-violating records from your table is VALIDATION WITHOUT RECORD SAVE. When you select this option, records that violate one or more of the constraints that you are applying are deleted from the table, and are permanently lost. Use this option only if you are certain that you don't want any records that violate your constraints.

The final option is VALIDATION WITH ERROR. If you select this option, and your table contains at least one record that contains invalid data in a field to which constraints are being applied, the process halts. Specifically, constraints are not applied to this field, nor are they applied to any remaining field to which constraints have not yet been applied. Furthermore, an error message is displayed, indicating which field caused the error. Under these circumstances, it is possible that some, but not all, of your constraints may have been applied.

What some developers do when applying constraints is to always choose VALIDATION WITH ERROR. If the Fields dialog box reports that the constraints could not be applied, they then examine the data to locate and fix the errors, after which they attempt to apply the constraints again. Occasionally during this examination, the developer concludes that an adjustment needs to be made to one or more of the constraints, and not the table's data.

If you really want to have control, use VALIDATION WITH ERROR, but apply constraints to only one field at a time, clicking OK to initiate the application of the constraints on only that field before attempting to apply constraints to the next field. Using this technique, you will get your constraints applied in an all or none fashion.

Defining Record-Level Constraints

Record-level constraints are defined using a Boolean expression. This expression can include field references, constants, and comparison operators, as well as any of the functions associated with the Advantage expression engine. This expression is evaluated each time a record is being posted to a table. If the filter expression evaluates to a Boolean False, an error is generated and the record is rejected.

You define a table's record-level constraint from the table's properties dialog box. Right-click the table's node and select Properties to display this dialog box. The CUSTOMER table's properties dialog box is shown in Figure 5-3.

Like the Fields dialog box, a table's properties dialog box permits you to configure a number of characteristics of a table. For example, the Auto Create radio buttons permit you to define this table as an auto-create table.

When Auto Create is set to On, the data dictionary uses information it stores about the table's metadata and indexes to re-create the table and all of its indexes at runtime if the table is not found when a client application attempts to open the table. This is a particularly useful feature for developers who distribute empty databases. For these developers, they can deploy only the data dictionary, permitting the tables and indexes to be created on-the-fly when needed.

In addition, if a table exists, but its index files do not, setting Auto Create to On causes index files to be auto-created when that table is opened by the client application as long as the indexes were previously included in the data dictionary definition.

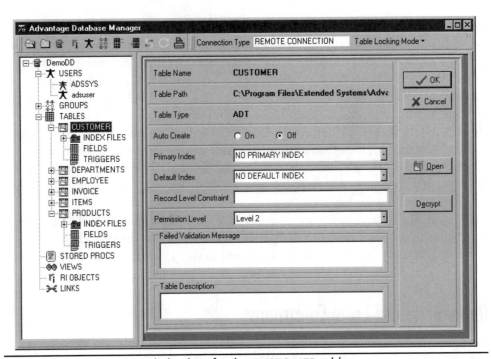

Figure 5-3 *The properties dialog box for the CUSTOMER table*

NOTE

ADS writes an error 5168 to the error log file whenever a table or index is auto-created. The client application never sees an error message, however, since this is not a true error and is only written to the log file to let the developer know that auto-creation has occurred.

The table properties dialog box also permits you to designate primary and default indexes. The primary index definition is used by the Advantage Database Manager to create referential integrity constraints. A primary index must be a unique index. More will be said about primary indexes later in this chapter.

A default index, when accessed using the Advantage TDataSet Descendant or the Advantage OLE DB provider (when using ADO and opening a table directly using adCmdTableDirect), is the index order that a table will make active by default. In other words, if you have not specifically set an active index, the default index order, if designated, will be used. If you do not select a default index, a table that has no active index is displayed in its natural order.

Two additional features that you can set from the table properties dialog box are the table's permissions level and description. Permissions Level is associated with field-level access privileges. Field-level access privileges and permissions levels are discussed in Chapter 4. You use the Table Description to document the purpose of the table.

The final feature that you can configure on the table properties dialog box is the record-level constraint. You enter your record-level constraint in the Record Level Constraint field. You can also supply a custom error message in the Failed Validation Message field.

Once the record-level constraint has been applied, if you attempt to post a record that violates a record-level constraint to the table, ADS will generate a 5150 error that will look something like the following:

This particular error is the one that is generated if you do not specify a failed validation message. If you do specify a failed validation message, your custom message appears in the error along with the error code. For example, if your failed validation message is "You must supply a value for either the Product Name or Description field (or both)," the error will look like the following:

Record-Level Constraint Example

Use the following steps to add a record-level constraint to the PRODUCTS table:

1. Right-click the PRODUCTS table node in the Advantage Database Manager tree view and select Properties.

2. Set Record Level Constraint to the following value:

   ```
   NOT ((Product Name=NULL) AND (Description=NULL))
   ```

3. Set Failed Validation Message to **You must supply a value for either the Product Name or Description field (or both)**.

4. Click OK. Similar to field-level constraints, the Advantage Data Architect now displays a Validation Option dialog box.

5. Set Validation Option to VALIDATION WITH ERROR and click OK.

The Validation Option dialog box options are identical to those that apply to field-level constraints. Refer to the preceding section for a discussion of these options.

Defining Referential Integrity Constraints

Where field-level and record-level constraints define rules concerning the data stored in a single table, referential integrity refers to rules that define relationships between tables. Before continuing with the discussion of referential integrity, it is worthwhile to pause for a moment and consider how tables in an application are related.

In almost all but the simplest application, many tables that make up your database contain related data. For example, you may have one table that contains customer records and another table that contains records of the individual invoices for your customers. These tables are related, in that a given invoice is associated with a specific customer.

This relationship is embodied in the invoice table through the invoice table's customer ID field. Assuming that the invoice table's customer ID field is limited to those customer ID values appearing in the customer ID field of the customer table, and that the customer ID field in the customer table is unique for each customer, if you know that value of the invoice table's customer ID field, you know which customer the invoice is for.

In most applications there are many of these types of relationships. The invoice table records are also likely associated with an employee who made the sale, and that employee will have a record in an employee table. The order may also include a part number or service code, and those will be associated with records in a parts table or a services table, and on and on.

When a primary key index order of one table uses the same key expression as a nonprimary index order of a second table, the fields of the second table's index order are referred to as a *foreign key*. Tables that include one or more foreign keys represent *associations*. The invoice table, for example, represents an association between an invoice and a customer. It also represents an association between an invoice and an employee responsible for the invoice, so long as the invoice table has at least two foreign keys—one for the customer table and one for the employee table.

The relationship between the customer and invoice tables in this example is often called a *master-detail relationship*, a *one-to-many relationship*, or a *parent-child relationship*. These terms are interchangeable, but the term "parent-child relationship" is used by ADS.

NOTE

The discussion here assumes that you are familiar with the issues related to relational database design. If you are going to be responsible for designing the new tables for an application, and are not familiar with relational database design issues, you should read a book on the topic or engage the services of a qualified consultant before you begin. The success of a database application is greatly influenced by the soundness of the original design.

Referential integrity (RI) refers to index-based rules that define how the related data in your collective tables is managed. RI is useful because the associations between data in the tables of an application are valuable in that, together, they represent important information. For example, if a customer record is deleted from the customer table, and that record was associated with one or more records in the sales table, the deletion of the customer record makes the previously associated sales records less informative. Specifically, you would have a record of a sale, but no information about who made the purchase.

With referential integrity definitions, you can explicitly define what happens when data in related tables is changed. For example, you can use referential integrity to prohibit the deletion of a customer record if that customer is associated with one or more sales in the sales table. To put it another way, referential integrity definitions can prevent loss of data.

The Advantage Data Architect provides you with two mechanisms for defining referential integrity: one is declarative and the other is more visual in nature. Both of these approaches are demonstrated in the following sections.

Defining Referential Integrity Using RI Objects

In order to define a referential integrity relationship, you must specify which two tables participate in the relationship. In addition, you must specify which indexes embody the relationship. Specifically, you must identify which index order of the child table defines the foreign key, and which index order of the parent table defines the primary key.

Obviously, the two index orders—the child table's foreign key index order and the parent table's primary index order—must exist prior to your defining the referential integrity relationship. But there is a related issue that is not obvious. You must specifically designate which parent table index order is the primary index. A given table can have only one primary index, and you must explicitly identify which one it is.

You designate a table's index to be its primary index using the table's properties dialog box. Using this dialog box is discussed in the preceding section. Setting a table's primary index is demonstrated here.

Use the following steps to define a referential integrity relationship between the customer (parent) and the invoice (child) tables:

1. Begin by identifying the primary index of the CUSTOMER table. Right-click the CUSTOMER table's node and select Properties. Set the Primary Index drop-down list to CUSTOMER ID. (Alternatively, you can expand the CUSTOMER table's INDEX FILES node in the Advantage Database Manager tree view, right-click the node for the CUSTOMER ID index order, and select Make Primary Index, which displays the Index Structure dialog box. Click OK.) Your table properties dialog box now looks something like that shown in Figure 5-4.

2. Click OK to close the table properties dialog box.

3. Next, we need to add some foreign key indexes to the INVOICE table. To do this, expand the INVOICE node under the TABLES node. Expand the INDEX FILES node, then right-click INVOICE.adi and select Add Index. The Index Management dialog box is displayed.

4. Double-click Customer ID to create a single order expression index on the Customer ID field. Click Create Index.

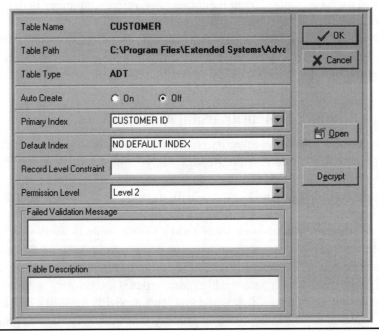

Figure 5-4   *The CUSTOMER ID index has been selected as the primary index using the table properties dialog box.*

5. Now double-click Employee ID to create an index order on this field. Click Create Index again.

6. Click Close to close the Index Management dialog box. You are now ready to define your referential integrity object.

7. Right-click RI OBJECTS and select Create.

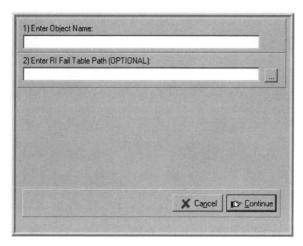

8. Set Enter Object Name to **Customer Invoices**. Set RI Fail Table Path to **c:\Program Files\Extended Systems\Advantage\ADSBook\RIFAIL.ADT**. The RI fail table is described later in this section. Click Continue to display the Parent Table/Primary Key dialog box.

9. Set Database Tables to CUSTOMER. The Primary Index field is automatically set to the designated primary index, Customer ID. Click Continue to display the Child Table/Foreign Index dialog box.

10. Set Database Tables to INVOICE. Set Foreign Index to Customer ID.

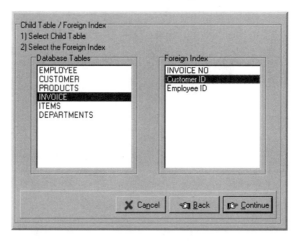

11. Click Continue to advance to the Update/Delete Rules dialog box. Set Update Rule to Cascade. Set Delete Rule to Restrict. (The update and delete rules are described in the next section.)

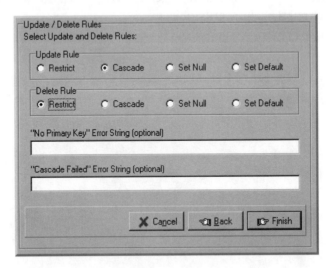

12. Click Finish to complete the RI definition. The Advantage Data Architect responds by displaying the RI definition using an ER (entity-relationship) diagram, as shown in Figure 5-5.

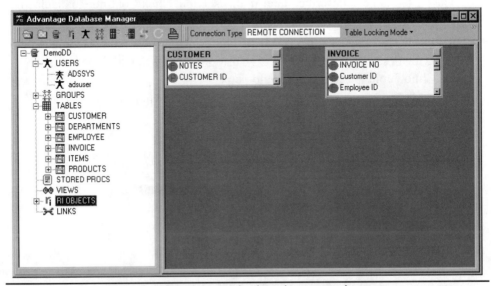

Figure 5-5   *The newly defined RI object is displayed in an ER diagram.*

When you complete this definition, the RI rules will be applied to the table. If the child table contains data when these rules are applied, depending on the specific rules that you applied, there is a possibility that one or more records in the child table violate the RI rules.

If one or more records of the child table violate your RI rules, what happens depends on whether or not you defined an RI fail table path. If you did not specify an RI fail table path, and records exist in the child table that don't have a corresponding primary key, a dialog box reports that the RI object cannot be created and the Advantage Database Architect (ARC) will ask you if you want to see the first offending record.

If you defined an RI fail table, and one or more records of the child table violate the RI rule you defined, those records are deleted from the child table and placed into the RI fail table. In the preceding steps, you set the RI fail table to RIFAIL.ADT. This table, if created, will be saved to the default directory. Because of the way that the DemoDictionary data dictionary was configured, this directory is the same directory in which the DemoDictionary.ADD file is stored.

TIP

After you have applied your RI rules, check to see if any records have been placed in the RI fail table. If records were added to the RI fail table, you should inspect them to see if they can be corrected and returned to the child table. In addition, since an RI fail table will be overwritten with each RI rule creation, it is a good idea to specify a different RI fail table for each RI rule you create.

Update and Delete Rules

You use the update and delete rules of an RI definition to control what kind of changes are permitted to the parent table when associated child records exist, as well as what to do if changes would otherwise disassociate the relationship.

Understanding Update Rules

The update rule defines what happens when you want to post a change to a parent table record that has one or more associated child records. Selecting an update rule of Restrict prevents a parent table's key fields from being changed for any record for which there are related child records. Using our current tables for example, if you use a restrict rule and there are invoices for a particular customer in the invoice table, you cannot change that customer's Customer ID field.

If you set Update Rule to Cascade, changes made to a parent table's key fields are propagated to the corresponding fields of existing child records. For example, using a cascade rule, you can change the Customer ID field for customer records, even when there are associated child records. The changed Customer ID field will be applied both to the customer table as well as the associated invoice table records.

Both the Restrict and the Cascade update rules ensure that the parent/child relationship in your tables is maintained. The remaining two options, Set Null and Set Default, permit you to sever the relationship. These rules control what happens to the fields of the child table foreign key when the relationship ends.

If you set Update Rule to Set Null, changing a parent key will cause the associated child table record's foreign key fields to be set to a null value. For example, if you were to change the Customer ID field in the customer table, any related invoice table records would have their Customer ID fields set to null values. This has the effect of orphaning the child table records.

If you set Update Rule to Set Default, changing a parent key causes the associated child table record's foreign key to be set to the default value defined using the Fields dialog box. This default value must be a legitimate primary key in the parent table, so although an Update Rule of Set Default will sever the relationship, it will create a new relationship to some other parent.

Understanding Delete Rules

Delete rules are similar to update rules, but apply when you attempt to delete a parent table record for which there are associated child records. Set Delete Rule to Restrict to prevent a parent record from being deleted if at least one associated child record exists. When this rule is in place, you must first delete any associated child table records before you can successfully delete the parent table record.

Set Delete Rule to Cascade if you want ADS to automatically delete associated child records when a parent record is deleted. Considering the example tables of the DemoDictionary data dictionary, if a cascade delete rule is enforced, deleting a customer would cause the automatic deletion of the invoices for that customer.

Set Delete Rule to Set Null if you want the foreign key of the associated child table records to be set to a null value upon deletion of the parent record. Finally, set Delete Rule to Set Default to set the foreign key of the associated child table records to the default value defined using the Fields dialog box.

> #### NOTE
>
> *When you use update and delete rules other than Restrict, changes or deletions made to the parent table can potentially introduce unique key violations in the child table if the child table's foreign key field is part of another unique index.*

Defining RI Rules Using the ER Diagram Tool

An ER (entity relationship) diagram is a visual tool for representing tables and their relationships. Specifically, it represents the RI links between tables based on primary/foreign key associations.

As you saw in Figure 5-5, an ER diagram is created from your RI object definition. Instead of creating an RI object, you can define your referential integrity relationships using the ER diagram directly. This is demonstrated in the following steps:

1. Before you can define the RI relationship, you must set the primary index for the EMPLOYEE table. (You already added a foreign key index to the INVOICE table for the Employee ID field in the preceding section.) Begin by expanding the TABLES node of the Advantage Database Manager tree view.

2. Right-click the EMPLOYEE node and select Properties. Use the table properties dialog box to set Primary Index to Employee Number. Click OK.

3. You are now ready to define the RI constraint. Start by making sure that the ER diagram is displayed. If you do not see it, expand the RI OBJECTS node and select Customer Invoices.

4. Now, drag the EMPLOYEE table node (under TABLES) and drop it into the ER diagram. (Drag by left-clicking the employee node, and while keeping the mouse button depressed, move the mouse into the ER diagram area. Drop the EMPLOYEE table by releasing the mouse button once you are over the ER diagram.) Your screen should now look something like that shown in Figure 5-6.

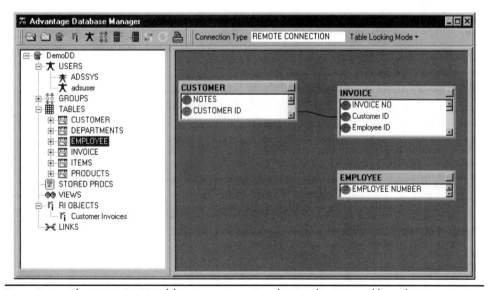

Figure 5-6   *The EMPLOYEE table now appears in the ER diagram, although it is not yet part of an RI definition.*

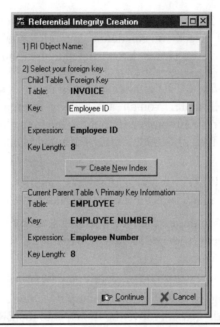

Figure 5-7 *The RI Object Name page of the Referential Integrity Creation dialog box*

5. Click on the Employee ID Foreign Key index order in the INVOICE table. When you do so, your cursor will appear as though you are performing a drag operation. Now click on the EMPLOYEE NUMBER index order of the EMPLOYEE table. The Advantage Data Architect responds by displaying the Referential Integrity Creation dialog box shown in Figure 5-7.

6. Set RI Object Name to **Employee Sales**. Click Continue to display the Update/Delete rules page of the Referential Integrity Creation dialog box, shown in Figure 5-8.

7. Set Update Rule to Cascade and Delete Rule to Restrict. Set the fail table path to **c:\Program Files\Extended Systems\Advantage\ADSBook\RIFAIL.ADT**. Set Primary Key Violation to **You must provide an Employee ID**, and leave the Cascade Error field blank. Click Finish.

The ER diagram now displays this new RI definition, with the link between the EMPLOYEE (parent) table's primary index Employee ID and the INVOICE (child) table's foreign key index Employee ID.

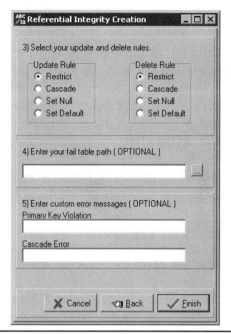

Figure 5-8   *The Update/Delete rules page of the Referential Integrity Creation dialog box*

Comments About Constraints and Referential Integrity

As pointed out at the beginning of this chapter, there are a number of benefits to constraints and referential integrity. They are easy to configure, all client applications must abide by them, and they can improve the overall integrity of your data.

But the ease with which constraints can be added to a data dictionary can lead to their overuse. When overused, they can prevent valid data from being entered into your database. And in the case of referential integrity constraints, they can produce an unexpected increase in resource use on the server.

The following sections take a final look at each of the type of constraints provided by a data dictionary. In each case, the limits of each approach are discussed.

Using Field-Level Constraints

Field-level constraints permit you to improve the integrity of data in individual columns by defining meaningful limits to the range of values that a field can store. They are especially useful for fields designed to hold data that have a fixed range. For example, a field designed to hold the relative humidity of a meteorological measurement has a fixed range of between 0 and 100. Relative humidity cannot be lower than 0, nor can it be greater than 100 percent. Placing a minimum and maximum value on a relative humidity field of 0 and 100, respectively, makes some sense.

But some domains do not have clear limits. For example, imagine that you have a date of birth (DOB) field in your employee table. Should you put a minimum date on the field? Probably not. In this case, the use of a minimum value on a date of birth field doesn't help your data much. On the one hand, if you set the minimum value on a date of birth field to 1/1/1920, you might actually prevent an employee's valid birthday from being entered. On the other, permitting DOB values as early as 1/1/1880 does little to prevent inaccurate data.

The issue here is fixed limits versus artificial ones. Percentages, such as relative humidity, have well-defined limits. When a field represents a domain that does not have physical limits, it is probably best to avoid using minimum and maximum limits. Instead, you may want to employ client-side code to ask the user to confirm data values that lie in extreme, yet potentially valid, ranges.

You should also be careful when setting the Null Valid field to False, meaning that NULL values are not allowed for a particular field. In reality, most tables have only a few fields whose values absolutely must be entered before you can accept the record. Most of these are fields that uniquely identify a record, such as the fields associated with a table's primary key.

What you want to avoid doing is setting Null Valid to False for fields that are not actually essential. For example, you may need the invoice date in your invoice table. But if the end user does not have the order date when they are entering the record, requiring them to supply a non-null value for this field either provokes them to enter fake data or prevents them from entering the record altogether.

Using Record-Level Constraints

Record-level constraints are more flexible than field-level constraints in that they can include some basic conditional logic. For example, a record-level constraint can be used to verify that a credit card field has been assigned a value, but only when the payment type is credit card.

The problem with record-level constraints is that it can be challenging to embody a complicated condition using a Boolean expression. When you must use a complicated Boolean expression with several conditional parts, it is very important to test the expression thoroughly to ensure that it does not reject records that are valid, and at the same time does not accept invalid records.

An alternative to using a complex record-level constraint is a trigger. Triggers can be written in a variety of high-level languages that can express complex conditional logic more easily than a Boolean expression. In addition, you can embed comments in your trigger code that identify what exactly your conditions are testing for. This is not something that you can do with a record-level constraint. Using triggers is described in Chapter 8.

Using Referential Integrity

Referential integrity definitions are valuable, but they tend to get overused. Most database applications contain many related tables. But just because two tables contain related data does not mean that there is a parent/child relationship that needs to be managed through referential integrity.

There are two primary problems caused by the overuse of referential integrity definitions. The first is that few related tables require the tight controls imposed by referential integrity. Referential integrity restricts your ability to delete and change parent table records, as well as prohibiting the insertion of child records for which there is no parent. When applied to the wrong tables, a user's attempt to add, edit, or delete data may be rejected, even when that operation is legitimate.

The second problem is related to resources. Whenever a table involved in a referential integrity definition is written to, the associated tables and their auto-open indexes are opened. This happens even if you are making a change only to the one table you opened.

Extensive use of referential integrity may require you to configure ADS to use additional work areas to handle the increases in table usage, and can also make it more difficult to obtain an exclusive lock on a table. (A table opened as a result of a referential integrity definition cannot be opened exclusively by another user.)

The solution is to use referential integrity sparingly. Most applications have only one or two pairs of tables whose related data is so critical to the application that referential integrity definitions are required. For many other related but nonessential tables, the data integrity provided by referential integrity is not worth the restrictions and increased resource usage they produce.

In the next chapter you will learn how to create and use views.

CHAPTER

6

Working with Views

IN THIS CHAPTER:

A view is an object that contains a SQL SELECT statement that produces a result set containing zero or more records and at least one field. From the perspective of your applications, a view is like a table in your database. This chapter shows you how to create and configure views. It begins by showing you how to define views. Later topics in this chapter include testing views, controlling view rights, querying views, and using views to link to tables outside of your data dictionary.

NOTE

If you are unfamiliar with SQL, you may also want to refer to Chapters 9, 10, and 11 while reading this chapter.

Overview of Views

A view is a customized row/column selection from one or more ADS tables. Depending on how the view is defined, this result set may or may not be editable.

Views serve several valuable purposes. First of all, they provide a convenient way to define prepackaged queries that are available to all of your client applications. These queries reside on the server, and are executed from a client application by opening the view, just like you would open a table.

Because views are stored on the server, you can update them by updating the data dictionary in which they are defined. By comparison, when your data selections are defined in your client applications through SQL queries, any changes to those queries require that you update and redeploy all of your client applications.

Views also permit you to modularize data access in your application. This is possible because one view can select data from one or more other views. For example, you can create one view that includes all records but only selected fields from a table. Another view can query the first view, calculating statistics about the selected fields. A third view can select a subset of the calculations for the purpose of building a report. A fourth view can select a different subset of the calculations for use in another report.

Another feature of views is that they permit you to work with ADT tables from two or more data dictionaries with a single connection. As you learned in Chapter 2, when an ADT table is bound to a data dictionary, you must connect to that data dictionary in order to access the table. Views, in conjunction with a feature called *data dictionary links*, permit you to access data in two or more data dictionaries through a single connection. (Tables from two or more data dictionaries can also be accessed using a SQL query, but with views you can navigate the result as if it were a table.)

Creating views that access data from multiple data dictionaries or data dictionary tables is described later in this chapter in the section "Views That Use Other Database Tables."

Creating Editable Views

An editable view is one that can be used to edit data in the underlying data dictionary tables. In short, an editable view is one where the SQL SELECT statement used to create the view produces an editable result set.

SQL SELECT statements that produce editable result sets select data from only one table or view. If selecting from a table, that table must be in the same data dictionary as the view, and there must be a one-to-one correspondence between the individual records and columns in the query result set and the table being queried. In other words, you cannot use SQL keywords like DISTINCT, UNION, or GROUP BY, and only a list of one of more fields, or all fields (using the * operator), may appear in the SELECT clause. Similarly, you cannot use aggregate functions or subqueries in a view if you want to edit the results.

If selecting from a view, the view being queried must produce an editable result set.

The following steps show you how to create a simple, editable view using the sample files you have been working with in preceding chapters:

1. Open the DemoDictionary data dictionary (with the DemoDD alias) in the Advantage Database Manager.

2. Right-click the VIEWS node in the Advantage Database Manager tree view, and select Create. The View dialog box is displayed, as shown in Figure 6-1.

3. Set Name to **Employee Tab**.

4. Enter the following SQL statement in the SQL section:

   ```
   SELECT "Employee Number", "First Name", "Last Name", "Department Code"
   FROM EMPLOYEE
   ```

5. Set Description to **View of EMPLOYEE table without the Salary field**.

6. Click Create. After a moment, a dialog box is displayed indicating that the view was created successfully. Accept this dialog box.

> **NOTE**
>
> *You will not see the final confirmation dialog box if you have set the Message Dialog dropdown list to No in the Advantage Database Manager.*

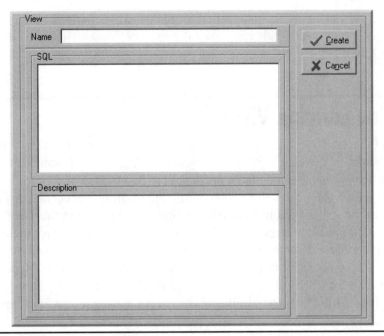

Figure 6-1   *Creating a new view*

Testing a View

You test a view by opening it, or by querying it. Either way, the result set created by the view is returned. Both of these techniques are shown in this section.

Opening a View

Use the following steps to demonstrate opening a view:

1. If the VIEWS node in the Advantage Database Manager tree view is not already expanded, expand it.

2. Click the Employee Tab node. The View dialog box is displayed. Unlike when you initially created the view, this dialog box now has one additional button, as shown in Figure 6-2. This button is labeled Open.

3. Click the Open button. After a moment the result set created by the view is opened in the Table Browser, as shown in Figure 6-3.

Notice that the Salary field, which was not included in the SELECT clause of the query, is not in this view.

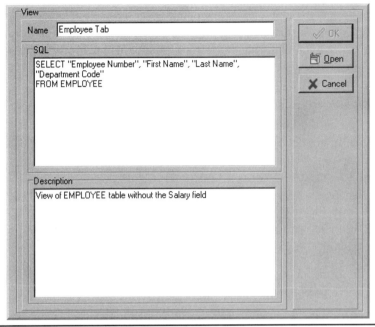

Figure 6-2 *After a view has been created, you can select and open it.*

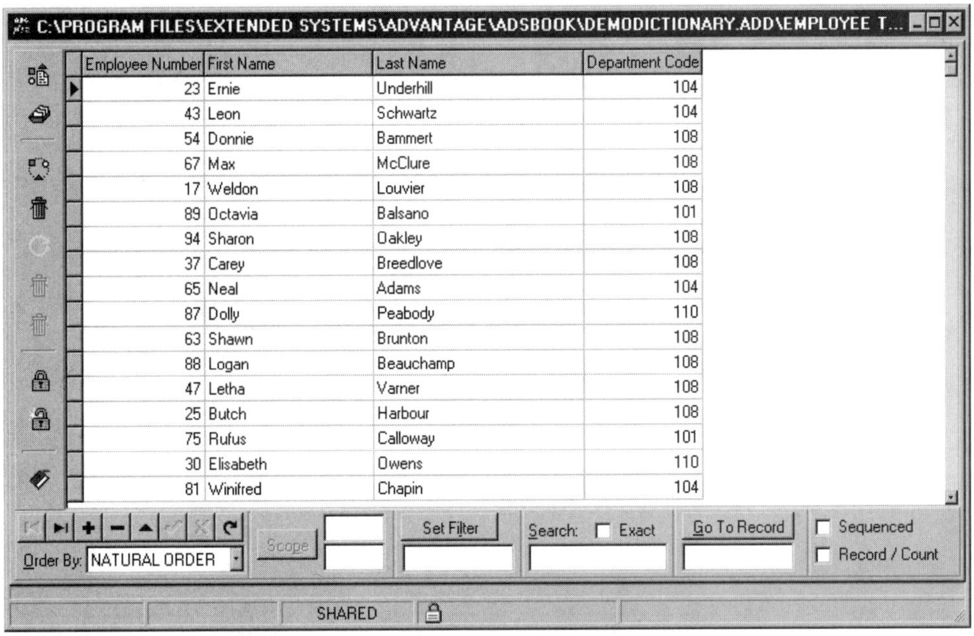

Figure 6-3 *A result set returned by a view in the Table Browser*

This view is an editable view. For example, if you wanted to change the department code for one of the employees, you could do so from this view using the Table Browser. Any changes that you write to the view will be applied directly to the underlying table from which the records were obtained.

Querying a View

Views are often used in the FROM clause of SQL queries in client applications, and in other views. In both of these situations, the view itself is being treated as though it were a table in your database.

Use the following steps to demonstrate querying a view:

1. Select Tools | Native SQL Utility from the Advantage Data Architect main menu. The Native SQL Utility is shown in Figure 6-4.

2. Set Connection type to Alias and set Alias to DemoDD.

3. Click the Connect button. When prompted, set User Name to **ADSSYS** and password to **password**.

4. In the SQL pane in the upper-left corner of the Native SQL Utility, enter the following SELECT statement:

```
SELECT * FROM "Employee Tab"
```

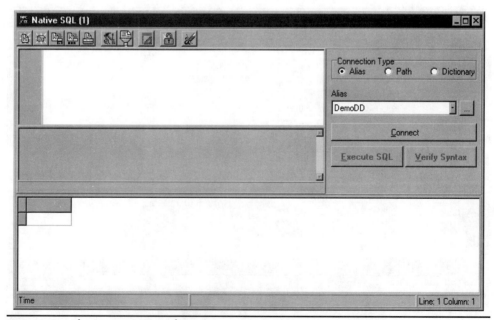

Figure 6-4   *The Native SQL Utility*

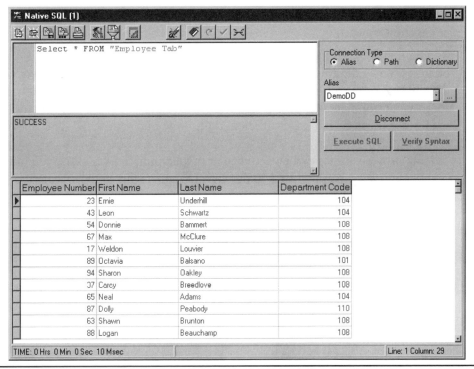

Figure 6-5   *A SQL SELECT statement that selects all fields from a view.*

5. Click the Execute SQL button to execute this query. After a moment, the query result is returned, as shown in Figure 6-5.

Making Views Accessible

As described in Chapter 4, it is possible to restrict groups and specific users access to data dictionary objects. Doing so provides you with additional security in your database.

If you followed the steps in Chapter 4 to enable security for your data dictionary, the view that you just created is accessible to the data dictionary administrator, but not to any of your defined users. Specifically, since you entered the data dictionary administrator's user name and password when you opened the Native SQL Utility, you were permitted to execute a query against the view. However, if you log in using the adsuser user name, access would be denied.

Use the following steps to demonstrate this:

1. If the Native SQL Utility is still open, click the Disconnect button to drop your connection using the data dictionary administrator account (ADSSYS). If you closed the Native SQL Utility, select Tools | Native SQL Utility to open it again.

2. Click the Connect button. This time enter the user name **adsuser**, and the password **password**.

3. The SQL statement that you entered in the preceding section should still be in the SQL Editor. If it is not, reenter the SQL SELECT statement provided in step 4 of the preceding section. Now click Execute SQL. This time you will receive an error message. This error message indicates a 7079 error, which results when you do not have sufficient rights to the table or view.

In order to provide access to views to regular (nonadministrative) users, you must either explicitly grant the users rights to the view or grant rights to the view to the one or more of the groups to which the users are members.

The following steps show you how to add access rights to the Employee Tab view:

1. Open the DemoDictionary in the Advantage Database Manager if it is not already open.

2. Expand the GROUPS node of the Advantage Database Manager tree view and select the ALL group. The Group dialog box is displayed:

3. Click View Rights to display the Permissions dialog box:

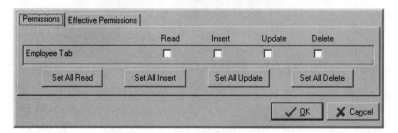

4. Click the Set All Read, Set All Insert, Set All Update, and Set All Delete buttons to enable all rights for this view to this group. Click OK to close the Permissions dialog box.

5. On the Group dialog box, click Save to save these rights.

6. Click the READONLY group to display the Group dialog box again.

7. Click the View Rights button to display this group's Permissions dialog box.

8. Click the Set All Read button, and then click OK to close the Permissions dialog box.

9. Click the Table Rights button from the Group dialog box to display the table Permissions dialog box. Uncheck the Read checkbox associated with the Employee table. Click OK to close the Permissions dialog box.

10. Click Save from the Group dialog box to save these rights.

Since the adsuser user inherits rights from the ALL group, anyone connecting to this data dictionary using the adsuser user name and password will be able to work with the EMPLOYEE table data using either the table itself or the Employee Tab view. However, any user belonging only to the READONLY group will be able to view the EMPLOYEE data using the Employee Tab view, but will not be able to change the data in any way and will be denied any kind of direct access to the EMPLOYEE table.

Changing a View

You can change the SQL that defines a view, so long as the new SQL that you provide is valid for a view. To change a view, select the node for the view you want to change under the VIEWS node in the Advantage Database Manager tree view. Using the View dialog box, modify the SQL that appears in the SQL section. When you are done, click OK to save the view.

One change that you cannot make to a view is changing its name. If you want to change the name of a view, copy the SQL text from your original view, and then create a new view and paste the copied text into the SQL area.

Once you have created a new copy of the view using a new name, you can delete the old view. To delete a view, right-click the node for the view you want to delete under the VIEWS node and select Delete.

CAUTION

You should exercise caution when changing a view that is used by deployed client applications. If your client applications refer to specific fields by name or position in the result set, changes you make to column names, or changes to the order and/or number of columns in the result set, can cause errors in your client applications. Make sure to test all client applications before deploying data dictionaries with updated views where these types of changes have been applied.

Views That Use Views

Earlier in this chapter, you learned how to execute a SQL SELECT statement against the Employee Tab view using the Native SQL Utility. Since a view itself is defined using a SQL statement, there is no reason why the SQL SELECT statement used in a view cannot query a view.

Views that use views can be employed in a number of interesting ways. Two of these are covered in this section. In the first technique, you will learn how views can be used to modularize operations on your data. In the second, you will see how a view can be used as a temporary table.

Modularizing Operations with Views

One reason for creating a view that selects from a view is that it permits you to break up data operations into manageable modules. For example, you may have a view that performs a calculation for each record in a table. You can then create another view that performs an aggregation, such as a SUM operation, on the calculation performed by the first view. This view, in turn, can be used in a third query to perform additional manipulation.

One of the advantages to this approach is that some views may get used over and over by other views.

The following steps demonstrate how to create views that are used by other views:

1. If the DemoDictionary data dictionary is not open in the Advantage Database Manager, open it.

2. Right-click the VIEWS node in the Advantage Database Manager's tree view and select Create.

3. Set Name to **Sum by Invoice**.

4. Enter the following SQL statement in the SQL section:

   ```
   SELECT SUM(Quantity * Price) as "Inv Total", "Invoice No"
     FROM ITEMS GROUP BY "Invoice No"
   ```

5. Click Create to save this new view. You should see a node for this Sum by Invoice view under the VIEWS node in the Advantage Database Manager tree view.

6. Right-click VIEWS again and select Create.

7. Set Name to **Sales by Employee**.

8. Enter the following SQL statement in the SQL section:

   ```
   SELECT SUM(SInv."Inv Total") as "Total Sales", Inv."Employee ID",
     Emp."First Name", Emp."Last Name" FROM "Sum by Invoice" SInv,
     INVOICE Inv, EMPLOYEE Emp
   ```

```
WHERE SInv."Invoice No" = Inv."Invoice No" and
   Inv."Employee ID" = Emp."Employee Number"
GROUP BY Inv."Employee ID", Emp."Last Name", Emp."First Name"
```

9. Click Create to save this view. You should see a node for this Sales by
    Employee view under the VIEWS node in the Advantage Database Manager
    tree view.

10. Right-click Views once more and select Create.

11. Set Name to **Purchases by Customer**.

12. Enter the following statement in the SQL section:

```
SELECT SUM(SInv."Inv Total") as "Total Purchases", Inv."Customer ID",
   Cust."First Name", Cust."Last Name" FROM "Sum by Invoice" SInv,
   INVOICE Inv, CUSTOMER Cust
   WHERE SInv."Invoice No" = Inv."Invoice No" and
      Inv."Customer ID" = Cust."Customer ID"
   GROUP BY Inv."Customer ID", Cust."Last Name", Cust."First Name"
```

13. Click Create to save the view. You should see a node for this Purchases by
    Customer view under the VIEWS node in the Advantage Database Manager
    tree view.

14. Select the Sales by Employee view node under the VIEWS node. Click
    the Open button to execute the view. The results, shown in Figure 6-6, are
    displayed in the Table Browser. Close the Table Browser when you are done
    inspecting the data.

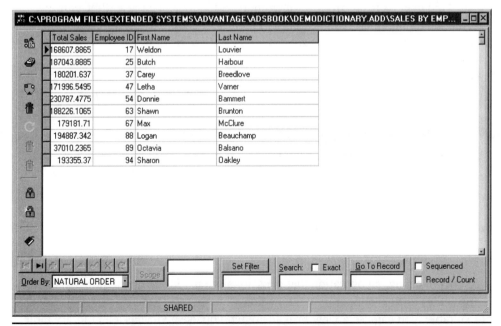

Figure 6-6   *The Sales by Employee view in the Table Browser*

15. Now select the Purchases by Customer view node. Click Open to display this data in the Table Browser. Close the Table Browser when you are done.

16. Take a moment now to grant read access rights to the three views that you just created to both the ALL and the READONLY groups. (The steps you use to enable view rights were discussed earlier in this chapter in the section "Making Views Accessible.") It is not necessary to enable any further rights, since the use of aggregate operations and joins in these views renders them readonly.

This example demonstrates the modular aspect of views. Both the Sales by Employee and the Purchases by Customer views select data from the Sum by Invoice view. If one or more future views also need to work with the summary data in the Sum by Invoice view, they can easily select from it.

> **NOTE**
> _____
>
> *Views that query views may execute more slowly than a single complicated view. If performance is important for your application, you may want to compare the performance of your views with alternative data access mechanisms, such as SQL queries and scopes (ranges).*

Views as Temporary Tables

Some operations cannot be performed using a single query. For example, you may need to execute one query to create a result set with intermediate results. You then use the first query's result from another query. Situations like these often call for the creation of a temporary table that will be used to store the intermediate results, so that the second query can be executed against these records.

Creating temporary tables in a client application requires careful planning, considering the multiuser environment in which most applications are running. At a minimum, the use of a temporary table involves the following steps:

▶   The creation of a temporary table into which records can be inserted.

▶   Devising a mechanism to guarantee that this temporary table name is unique on a connection-by-connection basis. This is necessary in order to isolate the operations initiated by one client application from any others that happen to be running.

▶   Deleting the temporary table when it is no longer needed.

Failure to correctly implement these steps can result in one of the most difficult problems to debug: an operation that occasionally fails for no apparent reason.

Instead of using a temporary table, which requires you to manage the lifecycle of that table, you can use a view instead. When you use a view as a temporary table,

ADS is responsible for creating, naming, and destroying the temporary table. Fortunately, ADS does this reliably, with no danger of conflict between client connections.

Consider the Sum by Invoice view created in the preceding section. This view returns the type of data that you could have placed into a temporary table. Then, a query similar to the one you entered into the Sales by Employee view could have been used to process the records in this temporary table. Thankfully, the use of views made all of that complexity unnecessary.

Selecting Record Subsets from Views

You learned at the beginning of this chapter that views look like tables to client applications. This similarity extends to SQL queries that you can execute against views. In particular, the use of WHERE clauses to select a subset of records from a view can be very powerful.

Consider the Sales by Employee view that you created in the preceding section. That view produces a total of sales for each employee. However, what if you were interested in the sales by employees who are in the Sales and Marketing department? Or, what if you were interested in the sales of a specific employee? Using a SQL SELECT statement, you can query the Sales by Employee view, using a WHERE clause to return only those records of interest.

For example, consider the following query:

```
SELECT SEmp."Employee ID", SEmp."Last Name", SEmp."First Name",
   SEmp."Total Sales" FROM "Sales by Employee" SEmp, "Departments" Dep,
   EMPLOYEE Emp
   WHERE SEmp."Employee ID" = Emp."Employee Number" and
        Emp."Department Code" = Dep."Department Code" and
        Dep."Department Code" = 108
```

This query uses the totals calculated by the Sales by Employee view, and then uses a WHERE clause to select only those employees whose department code is 108, the Sales and Marketing department.

The preceding query was a bit involved, since it was necessary to link from the view to the EMPLOYEE table and then to the DEPARTMENT table to select those employees from the specific department. If the selection can be made based on data in the view itself, the SQL SELECT statement would be considerably shorter.

For example, imagine that you want to get the total sales for a specific employee. If you can perform your selection based on the employee's ID, first name, last name, or any combination of those field values, the query can reference the view alone.

For example, the following query returns the sales totals for the employee associated with employee ID 89:

```
SELECT "Employee ID", "First Name", "Last Name", "Total Sales"
  FROM "Sales by Employee"
  WHERE "Employee ID" = 89
```

Views That Use Other Database Tables

Most client applications need to work with data in a single data dictionary. But what do you do if you want to work with data in two different data dictionaries? Actually, this is not hard if you are willing to use more than one connection. For example, you can establish one connection to one data dictionary, and another connection to the other data dictionary. Because the licensing of the Advantage Database Server permits a single workstation to make any number of connections, there is no monetary cost associated with this approach.

As you learned in Chapter 2, ADS tables that are bound to a data dictionary cannot be accessed directly. They must be accessed through the data dictionary to which they are bound. As a result, references to database tables in a view must include a reference to the data dictionaries to which they are bound.

There are two ways to qualify a table name with the data dictionary to which it is bound, and both of these use dot notation. The first way is to qualify the table from the other data dictionary by including the name of the data dictionary in which the table resides, separating this path from the table name using a dot, or period.

The second way to qualify a data dictionary–bound table name is to precede the table name with a data dictionary link. As is the case when you use a data dictionary path, this data dictionary link is separated from the table name by a period.

Before continuing, it is worth noting that the issue of referring to tables in other data dictionaries is not actually a view issue, but a SQL issue. Specifically, the linking that is discussed in this section can be used in views and in SQL statements that you send directly to ADS.

Qualifying a Table Using a Dictionary Path

You might recall that in Chapter 2 you created a free table called CUST.ADT. Imagine that instead of being a free table, CUST.ADT was in a data dictionary other than DemoDictionary. For example, suppose that CUST.ADT was stored in a data dictionary named Shared.ADD.

NOTE

You are free to create a data dictionary with this name and add the CUST.ADT table to it. This would permit you to try linking to another data dictionary using a view. However, when you are done, remove CUST from that data dictionary. You remove a table from a data dictionary by right-clicking the table's node in the Advantage Database Manager's tree view and selecting Remove.

If the Shared.ADD data dictionary is located in the same directory as DemoDictionary, you can use CUST.ADT by preceding the CUST table name with the name of the Shared.ADD data dictionary, enclosed in double quotation marks and separated from the table name using a period. This is demonstrated in the following SQL statement:

```
SELECT "Customer ID", "First Name", "Last Name"
FROM "Shared.ADD".CUST
```

Of course, this view could include links between tables in the Shared and DemoDictionary data dictionaries, as shown in this example:

```
SELECT CDB."Customer ID", CDB."First Name", CDB."Last Name",
  Cust.Address, Cust.City, Cust.State
FROM "Shared.ADD".CUST CDB, CUSTOMER Cust
WHERE CDB."Customer ID" = Cust."Customer ID"
```

If the data dictionaries are not in the same directory, the reference to the data dictionary table must include the path to the data dictionary. For example, if Shared.ADD is not in the same directory as DemoDictionary, instead residing in the directory C:\MyData, the preceding view would have to be represented as follows:

```
SELECT CDB."Customer ID", CDB."First Name", CDB."Last Name",
  Cust.Address, Cust.City, Cust.State
FROM "C:\MyData\Shared.ADD".CUST CDB, CUSTOMER Cust
WHERE CDB."Customer ID" = Cust."Customer ID"
```

When you include a data dictionary name as the qualifier for an external database table, ADS uses the user name and password of the connection from which the view is being accessed to connect to the external data dictionary. If you cannot ensure that the external data dictionary includes user names and passwords for all users who will access the view, you must use a data dictionary link. Using data dictionary links is discussed in the following section.

Qualifying a Table Using Data Dictionary Links

Data dictionary links, sometimes referred to as *link aliases*, are objects that you define in a data dictionary that refer to another data dictionary. These links can then be used in SQL statements to refer to tables in the linked data dictionary, including SQL statements used in views. You use the link in dot notation in place of the data dictionary name described in the preceding section.

One of the more interesting characteristics of a link is that you can associate a user name and password with it. If you do this, that user name and password is used to connect to the external data dictionary to which the link refers.

Following are the steps involved in creating a data dictionary link:

1. To create a data dictionary link, right-click the LINKS node in the Advantage Database Manager tree view, and select Add. The Advantage Database Manager responds by displaying the Link dialog box shown in Figure 6-7.

2. Set the Alias field to a string that you will use in your views to qualify the other data dictionary. Set Linked Data Dictionary to the path of the data dictionary to which this link will refer. This path can be either a Windows path or a UNC path.

3. Check the Static Path checkbox if you want the link to save the fully qualified path, or leave it unchecked to save only the relative path.

4. Check Authenticate Active User if you want to pass the user name and password of the connection that is accessing the link to the other data dictionary. If you do not check Authenticate Active User, and the data dictionary you are linking to requires user login, you need to set the User Name and the Password fields.

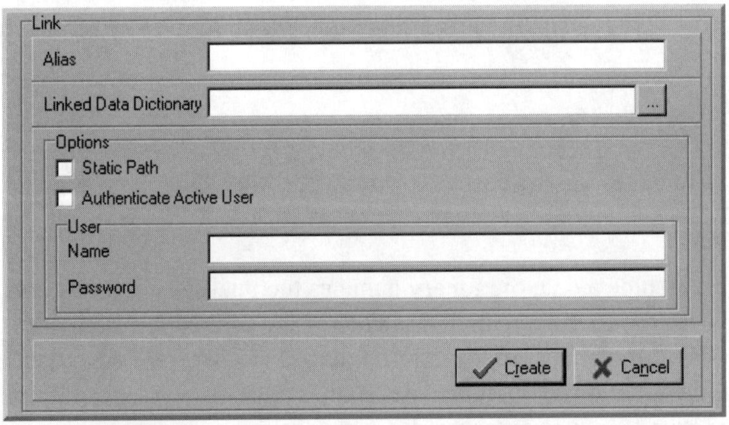

Figure 6-7 *The Link dialog box*

The values you provide in the User Name and Password fields must be associated with a user who has at least read rights to the tables that you will use in your views.

5. Click Create when you are done.

Once you have defined a link, you must grant rights to that link to all users who also have rights to the views that use the link. The following image shows the View permissions for the ALL group, one that grants link access rights to a link named ToShared:

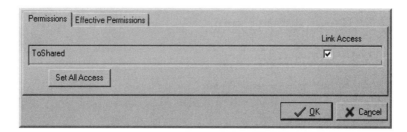

As mentioned earlier, links are used in place of data dictionary references in the dot notation in your view queries. For example, assuming that the link named ToShared has been created to point to the Shared.ADD data dictionary, and access rights have been assigned to this link, the following SQL statement produces a result identical to the SQL statement shown in the preceding section:

```
SELECT Link."Customer ID", Link."First Name", Link."Last Name",
  Cust."Address", Cust."City", Cust.State
FROM
  ToShared.CUST Link, CUSTOMER Cust
WHERE Link."Customer ID" = Cust."Customer ID"
```

NOTE

If your data dictionary link name includes spaces or other special characters, you would need to enclose that link name in double quotation marks in your view's SQL statement.

Once you define a link, you cannot change its name or the name of the data dictionary to which it points. If you want to change this information, you must delete the link and add a new link with the updated information. To delete a link, right-click the node for the link and select Delete.

In the next chapter, you will learn how to create stored procedures, called Advantage Extended Procedures (AEPs) in ADS.

Creating Advantage Extended Procedures (AEPs)

IN THIS CHAPTER:

Overview of Stored Procedures

The Structure of AEPs

Writing AEPs

Using AEPs

A stored procedure is a compiled subroutine that is installed on the server. While a stored procedure is called from your client applications at runtime, it is actually executed on the server.

Unlike most other relational database servers, which provide you with limited means for developing stored procedures, the stored procedures that ADS (Advantage Database Server) uses can be written in almost any development environment that can compile Windows DLLs (dynamic link libraries), Linux SO (shared object) libraries, in-process COM (component object model) servers, or .NET class libraries. These stored procedures are referred to collectively as Advantage Extended Procedures, or AEPs for short. In addition, since each of these libraries can contain more than one stored procedure function, they are referred to as *AEP containers* for convenience.

This chapter provides you with an in-depth look at stored procedures and AEPs. It begins with a detailed overview of the benefits that stored procedures can bring to your applications. This is followed by a thorough discussion of the structure of AEPs.

Later in this chapter, you will find step-by-step instructions on how to create AEPs using Delphi, C#, and VB.NET. This chapter concludes by describing how to install, test, debug, and deploy your newly created stored procedures.

Overview of Stored Procedures

A stored procedure is a compiled module that can be loaded by the Advantage Database Server and executed at the request of a client application. A given stored procedure is loaded only once—the first time it is called from one of the database's clients. From that point forward, the stored procedure remains in memory and can be invoked by any client application. Stored procedures created as DLLs, shared object libraries, and COM objects are unloaded when the clients using them disconnect from ADS. When implemented as a .NET class library, loaded stored procedures remain in memory until ADS is stopped.

To say that stored procedures are useful is a gross understatement. Simply put, stored procedures provide your applications with speed, efficiency, and power, all in a reusable package that can be updated independently of your client applications.

The following is a list of the benefits that stored procedures provide your applications:

▶   Any client that has permission to use a stored procedure can execute it. This ensures that the operations embodied in the stored procedure are performed consistently regardless of which client application invokes the procedure.

By comparison, if those same operations were performed by client applications, it would be up to you to ensure that each client performs the task the same way.

▶ You can design your stored procedure to accept parameters, and then use those parameters to customize the operation that the procedure performs. For example, you can design a stored procedure to perform some operation on records associated with a particular customer. This stored procedure would likely require at least one parameter, which would identify the customer whose records the procedure should process.

A given stored procedure has a fixed number of parameters, but how many it has is something that you define when you register it in a data dictionary. These parameters can be of any data type supported by ADT tables.

▶ You can design your stored procedure to return data. This data is in the form of a result set consisting of rows and columns. In fact, when a stored procedure returns a result set, that result set can be treated like a readonly table.

▶ Your stored procedure can perform any operation supported by the development environment it was written in, even if that same operation is not supported by your client application's development environment. For example, if you write your stored procedure using a language that can spawn new threads, the stored procedure can spawn a new thread even if a language that does not support multithreaded development, such as Visual Basic 6, invokes the procedure.

▶ Stored procedures can be updated and deployed without requiring changes to your client applications. So long as you do not change the number of parameters that your stored procedure accepts, or the number of columns your stored procedure returns in its result set, your existing client applications can invoke the updated stored procedure and immediately benefit from your updates.

▶ For many types of data-intensive operations, stored procedures can dramatically reduce network traffic compared to performing those same operations from your client applications. For example, imagine that you need to generate a report that prints 100,000 records. If you print that report from your client application, it will need to retrieve all 100,000 records from the server. By comparison, printing that report from the stored procedure invoked from ADS means that no records need to be transferred across the network.

▶ The use of stored procedures permits you to benefit from distributed computing. Your client applications run on the individual workstations, but the stored procedures execute on the server.

▶ With ADS 7.0 and later, stored procedures have unlimited access to the objects
   in a data dictionary. This permits you to define tables and views, for example,
   that a user cannot access directly, but can access through the controlled
   environment of a stored procedure.

NOTE

*Using stored procedures with ALS (Advantage Local Server) does not provide all of the benefits
realized when used with ADS. When used with ALS, stored procedures execute on the workstation
with your client application. As a result, you do not benefit from reduced network traffic and
distributed computing. However, the use of stored procedures with ALS ensures that these benefits
will be gained when you scale your application to use ADS. Stored procedures also execute on the
client when used with ADS for NetWare, due to the limitations of this operating system.*

The Structure of AEPs

Most database servers that support stored procedures limit how you can create them.
For example, most database servers support only one, or maybe two, languages to
write stored procedures. In most cases, these languages are a mixture of SQL and
rudimentary control structures. These stored procedures are often written using
tools provided by the database vendor, which in some cases have to be purchased
separately. In addition, typically only the database administrator can create and
install stored procedures.

   ADS provides you with great flexibility when it comes to creating and installing
stored procedures. As mentioned earlier in this chapter, AEPs can be written as
Windows DLLs, in-process COM objects, .NET class libraries, or Linux shared
object libraries. It does not matter which language you use to create these AEPs.

   Because you can use your language of choice to create your stored procedures,
AEPs can be far more sophisticated than those used by most other database servers.
Instead of being restricted to conditional SQL, your stored procedures can use the
full breadth of capabilities of the development tool you choose. You can even perform
tasks that have little or nothing to do with your database, such as sending an automated
email message, if your development environment supports that.

   For example, a Delphi developer can use practically any VCL (visual component
library) class or RTL (runtime library) routine. Similarly, developers using a .NET
language, such as C#, VB.NET, C#Builder, or Delphi for .NET can use any of the
classes in the FCL (framework class library), as well as any invokable managed or
unmanaged code.

Being able to use your development language of choice provides you with additional benefits. First, you do not have to learn another language before you can write stored procedures. Second, you get to use the tools with which you are already comfortable.

While ADS supports four distinct types of libraries for creating AEP containers, as described earlier in this chapter, all have similar characteristics. Each library type must export at least four functions: Startup, Shutdown, GetInterfaceVersion, and one or more stored procedure functions. The names used by the stored procedure functions are arbitrary.

NOTE

ADS 7.0 introduced version 2 AEPs, which greatly improved the performance of stored procedures. AEPs prior to ADS 7.0 are now called version 1 AEPs, and both their functions and the function parameters are significantly different from version 2 AEPs. Since version 1 AEPs have been deprecated, they are not discussed further in this book. For information on version 1 AEPs, refer to the Advantage documentation.

In addition to these functions, all AEP containers have an object that is used to manage one or more client connections. This object is created when the AEP container is first loaded, and destroyed when the AEP container is released. The name of this object depends on which AEP template you use to create your AEP container. For example, with .NET languages, this object is a HashTable named colClientInfo. For the convenience of the following discussion, we will refer to this object as the *connection manager*.

The following sections describe the four types of functions in greater detail.

The Startup Function

The startup function is called the first time a given client application calls one of the stored procedure functions in a particular AEP container using a specific connection. If a client application has two connections to ADS, and calls a particular AEP from each connection, the startup function will be called twice, once for each connection. The purpose of the startup function is to initialize an object that is used to maintain client state information about the connection, and to save this object to the connection manager.

The startup function is passed two parameters. The first parameter is a unique integer that is generated by the server prior to the invocation of the startup function. This value uniquely identifies the client's connection that is invoking the AEP. This same value is passed as the first parameter in the shutdown function and as the first parameter in the stored procedure functions for all subsequent calls from the same client over the same connection. Consequently, this value is used to store the state maintenance object to, and retrieve the state maintenance object from, the connection manager.

The second parameter is a handle to an active ADS connection. This ADS connection has a one-to-one mapping to the connection on which the client is communicating with the AEP. As a result, if the client's connection has an active transaction, any data manipulation performed with the connection whose handle is passed in the second parameter will be performed in that same transaction.

In most AEP containers, the startup function will create an instance of a state maintenance object, initialize a connection using the connection handle passed in the second parameter, and then save the state maintenance object so that it can be retrieved within the stored procedure functions and the shutdown function.

The startup function returns a 32-bit integer. With ADS 7.0, this value is not actually used, but should be set to the value 0 (zero) in order to maintain compatibility with potential changes in later releases of ADS.

The Shutdown Function

The shutdown function is called when a client that had invoked at least one of the stored procedure functions in the AEP container is closing its connection. The shutdown function is used to perform any cleanup operations on connection-specific objects that were created during the client's use of the AEP.

Like the startup function, the shutdown function is passed two parameters. The first parameter is the unique connection ID for this client connection. The second parameter is a handle of an active connection. The shutdown function uses the connection ID to remove the state maintenance object for this connection from the connection manager, and to destroy it, if necessary. With automatic garbage collecting languages, such as .NET languages, the state maintenance object is destroyed automatically once there are no remaining references to it. With languages like these, you do not have to explicitly destroy the state maintenance object.

The shutdown function returns a 32-bit integer value. As with the startup function, this value should be 0 (zero).

The GetInterfaceVersion Function

This simple function returns a 32-bit integer, and is used to inform ADS of the AEP version of the library. With AEPs created for ADS 7.0, this function should return a value of 2. If this function is absent from the AEP, ADS will assume that the AEP version is 1.

The GetInterfaceVersion function takes no parameters.

NOTE

If you are using a version of ADS later than version 7.0, and Extended Systems has updated its AEP support, it is possible for GetInterfaceVersion to return a value other than 1 or 2.

Stored Procedure Functions

Each AEP container can have one or more stored procedure functions. These functions contain the code that performs the operations that you want to execute on the server when the stored procedure is called by the client application.

Stored procedure functions are passed three parameters. The first and second parameters contain the connection ID and the associated connection handle, respectively. The connection ID is typically used to retrieve the state maintenance object for the connection that is calling this procedure. In most cases, this state maintenance object holds an active connection, so usually you do not need to use the second parameter of your stored procedure object.

The third parameter is a 32-bit integer that serves as an optional output parameter. If your stored procedure can modify one or more records, you can use this parameter to return the number of records affected by the stored procedure's execution.

As you learned earlier, stored procedures can be passed parameters and can return one or more rows of data. Both input parameters and results sets returned by stored procedures are passed between the AEP and ADS using ADT tables. The table containing the input parameters is named _ _input, and the table you use to return a result set is named _ _output. (Both of these table names are preceded by two underscore characters.)

These tables can be accessed from within your stored procedure function through the connection handle. Recall that this same connection handle is passed to the startup and shutdown functions, as well as to the stored procedure functions. For efficiency, most developers initialize this connection in the state maintenance object that is saved in the startup function. From within a given stored procedure, the state maintenance object for this connection ID is retrieved, and the connection is then used to read the input parameters from the _ _input table, if necessary. Not all stored procedures use input parameters.

As the stored procedure executes, any data that it needs to return to the invoking client is inserted into the _ _output table. As must be obvious, the _ _output table is always an empty table when the stored procedure function begins executing.

The structures of the _ _input and _ _output tables are defined when you register your stored procedure in a data dictionary. When registering a stored procedure in a data dictionary, you provide names and data types for all of your input and output parameters. The __input table will have one field for each input parameter, and the __output table will have one field for each output parameter.

There is a third temporary table accessible through the connection handle. This table, named __*error*, is an in-memory table. Unlike the __input and __output tables, the __error table is available to the startup and shutdown functions as well.

The __error table has two fields. The first field is an integer field named ERRORNO, and the second is a memo field named MESSAGE. If you want to return a custom error message, you add a single record to this table, setting ERRORNO to your custom error number and setting MESSAGE to your error message. If you want to return a custom message, but want to use ADS's standard AEP error code, leave ERRORNO empty.

Writing AEPs

You can write AEPs using any language that supports the creation of the types of executable files supported by ADS. To simplify the task of creating AEPs, Advantage provides templates for the most popular development environments. One of these templates is used for Delphi, Kylix, and C++Builder. There is another template for Visual Basic. Additional templates are used for VB.NET and Microsoft C#. There is also a template for Borland's C#Builder.

You do not need to begin with one of these templates, but doing so is highly recommended. These templates are well designed and can significantly reduce the amount of time it takes for you to create AEPs. If you decide instead to write your own AEPs from scratch, you should examine the AEP templates both for the signatures of the included functions, as well as for the helpful comments that appear throughout the code.

The following sections in this chapter show you how to create AEPs using Delphi, C#, and VB.NET. The descriptions in these sections assume that you are already familiar with using the development environment being described. Consequently, only high-level steps are provided, such as "create a new project from the AEP template."

The primary focus of these sections is the code that produces the AEP. If you are new to one or more of these development environments, and want to follow along with the examples, you may want to refer to the development environment's documentation, or get a good introductory book on the tool.

The AEP container that is created in the following sections contains only a single stored procedure function. This function is named Get10Percent, and it will return every tenth invoice number for a given customer. If a customer has fewer than ten invoices overall, Get10Percent returns an error.

A function like Get10Percent might be used to select records for auditing purposes. If this were a real function, you would probably want to select ten percent of the records by randomly selecting the records to return. Implementing Get10Percent using random selection would require much more code, which is why this example simply returns every tenth record.

Nevertheless, this stored procedure demonstrates the value of server-side processing provided when you use AEPs with ADS. Specifically, if you were to write a function like Get10Percent in a client application, all of a customer's records need to be transferred across the network before the ten percent of records can be selected. Implementing Get10Percent as an AEP permits the selection to be performed on the server, and only the ten percent of records is transferred to the client.

Get10Percent takes a single integer input parameter that will identify the customer whose records need to be processed. This stored procedure has a single output parameter, which holds the invoice numbers that are returned. In this case, zero or more records are returned by the function.

From within the function, the input parameter is read from the _ _input table and is used to select all of that customer's records. Next, the invoice number for every tenth record is written to the _ _output table. Once this processing is complete, if the output table contains no records because there were less than ten records for that customer, an error code and a message is written to the _ _error table.

The final step is optional in your stored procedures. If your stored procedure affected one or more records, the number of affected records can be assigned to the third parameter of the stored procedure, a parameter provided for just this purpose.

But before we get to the examples, there are a couple of warnings about AEPs to consider. These are related to the multithreaded nature of AEP execution, as well as exception handling in your AEPs.

ADS is a multithreaded server. When a client invokes an individual stored procedure in an AEP container, that invocation is performed by one of the server's threads.

Most AEPs can be invoked simultaneously from different threads on the ADS server. (Only COM servers created in Visual Basic 6 cannot be invoked concurrently. More about that is said in the section "Creating AEPs Using Visual Basic 6.") As a result, it is extremely important that you use good multithreading programming techniques.

In short, you should not refer to global variables or other resources that are not thread-safe from within your stored procedures without using a synchronization object such as a critical section. The state maintenance object, however, is thread-safe (at least as it is employed in the code generated by AEP templates).

> **NOTE**
>
> *Two or more stored procedure calls from a given client's connection will not necessarily be made using the same thread. In other words, do not use the thread ID of the thread from which a stored procedure is invoked to identify a client. Only use the connection ID parameter passed to the stored procedure to identify which client connection the stored procedure is being invoked from. Also, for the same reason, thread local storage cannot be used for state maintenance. If you need to maintain state, add that feature to your state maintenance object that is created in the startup function.*

Another concern for AEP developers is exceptions. It is considered bad form to permit an unhandled exception to escape your AEP container. Consequently, your AEP code should always be placed inside an exception trapping block. If an exception occurs, your code should insert an error into the _ _error table.

Creating AEPs Using Delphi

You create a Windows DLL when you create an AEP in Delphi using the template provided. This template is installed when you install the Advantage TDataSet Descendant. This template is also available when you install the TDataSet Descendant for C++Builder or the TDataSet Descendant for Kylix. With Kylix, however, the template will create a shared object library.

> **NOTE**
>
> *The extension of this DLL or shared object library will be .aep.*

Creating the AEP Project

You can use the following steps to create an AEP using Delphi:

1. Select File | New | Other to display the Object Repository.
2. Click Projects to view the Project templates page of the Object Repository.

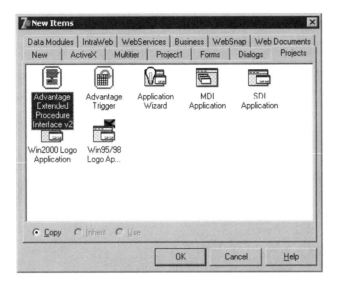

3. Select the Advantage Extended Procedure, and click OK. When prompted, use the displayed browser to select a directory in which this project will be stored.

The copied template is now your current project in Delphi.

NOTE

The steps given here for creating AEPs using Delphi are also applicable to Kylix. For C++Builder, the steps are similar, and the object properties and methods are the same, but you need to write the code in C++ instead of the Delphi language.

Saving the Project Using a New Name

When you use a project template, you are using an exact copy of a project that was installed in your Object Repository. If you were to create another AEP, it would have exactly the same project name, and this could lead to confusion. Consequently, one of your first tasks should be to rename the project. To do this:

1. Select File | Save Project As from the main menu.
2. Save the project using the name **AEPDemoD.dpr**.

Changing Your Stored Procedure Function Name

Initially the AEP template includes one stored procedure named MyProcedure. You should change the name of this procedure to something meaningful. In this case, the new procedure name will be **Get10Percent**. This must be done in two places in the .DPR file as described here:

1. Search the AEPDemoD.dpr file for the line that begins function MyProcedure.
2. Change the name of the function from MyProcedure to **Get10Percent**.
3. Locate the exports clause at the end of this unit. Change the entry for MyProcedure to **Get10Percent**.

Writing Your Stored Procedure

You are now ready to update the Get10Percent function and compile your project. Use the following steps:

1. Locate the beginning of the Get10Percent function in AEPDemoD.dpr.
2. Modify this procedure to look like that shown in Listing 7-1.
3. When you are done updating the procedure, select Project | Compile AEPDemoD.dpr from the main menu.

   You are now done. Your compiled DLL, named AEPDemoD.aep, will be located in the directory where you saved your AEP project. While it is not required that you do so, we recommend that you set your output directory to the same directory where your DemoDictionary data dictionary is stored. That way, a new copy of the DLL will be written to this directory each time you compile, and it will also make debugging easier, if necessary.

ON THE CD

This listing is also located in listing7-1.txt located on this book's CD-ROM (see Appendix B).

Listing 7-1

```
function Get10Percent( ulConnectionID: UNSIGNED32;
                       hConnection: ADSHANDLE;
                       pulNumRowsAffected: PUNSIGNED32 ): UNSIGNED32;
                       {$IFDEF WIN32}stdcall;{$ENDIF}
                       {$IFDEF LINUX}cdecl;{$ENDIF}
var
   DM1 : TDM1;
   InvoiceTable: TAdsTable;
   Counter: Integer;
```

```
    CustID: Integer;
begin

    Result := AE_SUCCESS;

    {* Get this connection's data module from the session manager. *}
    DM1 := TDM1( AEPSessionMgr.GetDM( ulConnectionID ) );
    try
      with DM1 do
      begin
        InvoiceTable := TAdsTable.Create(nil);
        try
          //Get customer's invoices
          InvoiceTable.DatabaseName := DataConn.Name;
          InvoiceTable.TableName := 'invoice';
          InvoiceTable.Open;
          InvoiceTable.IndexName := 'customer ID';
          tblInput.open;
          CustID := tblInput.Fields[0].AsInteger;
          InvoiceTable.SetRange([CustID], [CustID]);
          tblInput.Close;

          //Write 10 percent of customer IDs to output
          tblOutput.Open;
          InvoiceTable.First;
          Counter := 0;
          repeat
            inc(Counter);
            if Counter = 10 then
            begin
              Counter := 0;
              tblOutput.Append;
              tblOutput.Fields[0].Value :=
                InvoiceTable.Fields[0].Value;
              tblOutput.Post;
            end;
            InvoiceTable.Next;
          until InvoiceTable.Eof;

          //Generate error if no records
          if tblOutput.IsEmpty then
            begin
              DataConn.Execute( 'INSERT INTO __error VALUES ' +
```

```
                    '( 2500, ' +
                    QuotedStr( 'There are less than 10 records for ' +
                    IntToStr(CustID) ) + ' )' );
                  Exit;
                end;
             pulNumRowsAffected^ := tblOutput.RecordCount;
          finally
            InvoiceTable.Free;
            tblOutput.Close;
          end;
        end;    {* with DM1 *}

   except
     on E : EADSDatabaseError do
        {* ADS-specific error, use ACE error code *}
        DM1.DataConn.Execute( 'INSERT INTO __error VALUES ( ' +
          IntToStr( E.ACEErrorCode ) +
            ', ' + QuotedStr( E.Message ) + ' )' );
     on E : Exception do
        {* other error *}
        DM1.DataConn.Execute( 'INSERT INTO __error VALUES ( 1, ' +
          QuotedStr( E.Message ) + ' )' );
   end;
end;
```

If you wanted to create additional stored procedure functions in this AEP container, you would make one or more copies of the original MyProcedure function. You would then change the names of these functions so that they are unique in the project, and then add these names to your exports clause.

Creating AEPs Using C# with Visual Studio .NET

When you create an AEP using C# with Visual Studio .NET, you begin with a template that is installed when you install the Advantage .NET Data Provider. You'll see how to do this next.

NOTE

Extended Systems also provides a template for C#Builder developers. Using that template and the code provided in Listing 7-2, you can create this same project using C#Builder.

Creating the AEP Project

Use the following steps to create a new AEP project in Visual Studio using the AEP
template:

1. Begin by selecting File | New | Project. Visual Studio responds by displaying
    the New Project dialog box. In the Project Types tree view, select Visual C#
    Projects. The available templates are displayed in the Templates pane, which
    appears to the right of the Project Types tree view, as shown here:

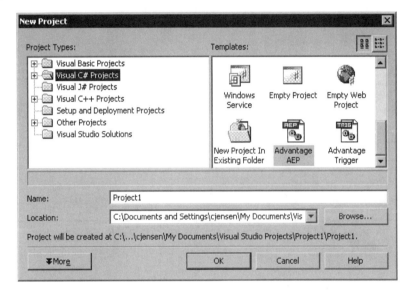

2. Scroll the Templates pane until you see the Advantage AEP template. Select
    this template.

3. Set Project Name to **AEPDemoCS**.

4. Next, use the Browse button to choose the directory in which you want to save
    this project.

5. Click OK to continue.

Your new C# AEP project should now be open in Visual Studio, as shown in
Figure 7-1.

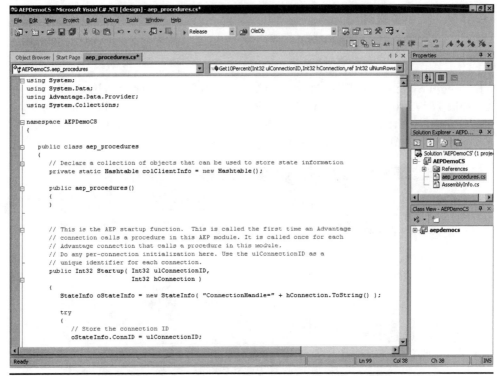

Figure 7-1 A new C# AEP project opened in Visual Studio .NET 2003

Renaming Your Stored Procedure

Like with the templates used to create AEPs in Delphi, the AEP template for C# creates a project that contains one stored procedure named MyProcedure. The following steps show you how to rename this procedure:

1. Locate the public method MyProcedure in the public aep_procedures class.

2. Change the name of the method from MyProcedure to **Get10Percent**.

NOTE

It is not necessary to change the name of the aep_procedures class, although you can do so if you like. Since the aep_procedures class is declared in the namespace associated with your project, it will be unique from any other aep_procedures classes that you create for other .NET AEPs, so long as they are defined in different namespaces. In Visual Studio, the project name defines the namespace, which is AEPDemoCS in this case.

Writing Your Stored Procedure

You are now ready to update and compile your AEP container as a .NET class library. Use the following steps:

1. Locate the Get10Percent method in the aep_procedures class.
2. Modify this method to look like that shown in Listing 7-2.
3. Select Build | Build AEPDemoCS.

Once you build, the file AEPDemoCS.dll will appear in the debug or release directory of your project's directory.

 ON THE CD

This listing is also located in listing7-2.txt, located on this book's CD-ROM (see Appendix B).

Listing 7-2

```
public Int32 Get10Percent( Int32 ulConnectionID,
  Int32 hConnection,
  ref Int32 ulNumRowsAffected )
{
  StateInfo         oStateInfo;
  IDbCommand        oCommand;
  IDataReader     oReader;

  AdsDataAdapter Adapter;
  DataSet DS;
  DataTable Table;
  Int32   custID;
  Int32 counter;
  Boolean oneOrMoreRows;

  lock( colClientInfo )
    oStateInfo = (StateInfo)(colClientInfo[ulConnectionID]);

  try
  {
    oCommand = oStateInfo.DataConn.CreateCommand();
    oCommand.CommandText = "SELECT * FROM __input";
    oReader = oCommand.ExecuteReader();
    oReader.Read();
```

```
    custID = oReader.GetInt32(0);
    //Close DataReader before connection can be reused
    oReader.Close();

    oCommand = oStateInfo.DataConn.CreateCommand();
    DS = new DataSet();
    Adapter = new AdsDataAdapter(
      "SELECT [Invoice No] FROM INVOICE " +
      "WHERE [Customer ID] = " + custID.ToString(),
      oStateInfo.DataConn);
    Adapter.Fill(DS, "INVOICES");
    Table = DS.Tables["INVOICES"];

    counter = 0;
    oneOrMoreRows = false;
    for (int i = 0; i<= (Table.Rows.Count-1)  ; i++)
    {
      counter++;
      if (counter == 10)
      {
        oCommand.CommandText =
          "INSERT INTO __output  VALUES ('"
          + Table.Rows[i].ItemArray[0].ToString() + "')";
        oCommand.ExecuteNonQuery();
        counter = 0;
        oneOrMoreRows = true;
      }
    }

    if (! oneOrMoreRows)
    {
      oCommand.CommandText = "INSERT INTO __error VALUES( 2500, '"+
        "Less than 10 records for "+custID.ToString()+"' )";
      oCommand.ExecuteNonQuery();
    }
  }
  catch( Exception e )
  {
    IDbCommand  oErrCommand = oStateInfo.DataConn.CreateCommand();
    oErrCommand.CommandText = "INSERT INTO __error VALUES( 1, '" +
      e.Message + "' )";
    oErrCommand.ExecuteNonQuery();
```

```
    }

    return 0;

}    // Get10Percent
```

Registering Your Stored Procedure

When you compile your project with Visual Studio, it registers your .NET class library in the Windows registry on your development machine. If your data dictionary is on this same machine, you are ready to install and test your AEP.

If you are running ADS as a remote server, and your data dictionary is on a machine other than the one where you compiled your .NET project, you must install the .NET class library before you can register the AEP in the data dictionary. This installation is performed using the regasm.exe utility, which is installed as part of the .NET framework. Since you cannot run the .NET class library without having installed the .NET framework, this utility should be on any machine on which you will run .NET AEPs.

NOTE

Depending on who is going to use your AEPs, and how you are going to distribute them, you may want to sign and strongly name your .NET assemblies. Refer to the .NET Framework SDK (software development kit) for more information on signing and strong names.

The following steps describe how to install your .NET class library:

1. Copy your .NET class library to the directory in which your data dictionary resides.

2. Open a command (CMD.EXE) window and navigate to the directory into which you copied your class library.

3. If regasm.exe is in a directory on your DOS path, you can register your library using a command similar to the following:

```
regasm AEPDemoCS.dll /codebase
```

4. If regasm is not on your DOS path, you must enter the fully qualified path to regasm. (If you do not know where regasm.exe is stored, use the Windows Explorer's searching capabilities to find it.) The command might look something like the following:

```
c:\Windows\Microsoft.NET\Framework\v1.1.4322\regasm
AEPDemoCS.dll /codebase
```

NOTE

The preceding command-line entry must be entered as a single command (in one line). It appears on two lines here because of the limited line space in this book.

The use of the /codebase command-line option is required here because you have not stored your AEP class library in the GAC (global assembly cache). If you did register your .NET executable in the GAC, you do not have to perform the preceding steps. While storing your class library in the GAC permits you to share it, sharing is really not an advantage in this case. Placing your AEP in the same directory as your data dictionary ensures that you do not introduce version control problems with AEPs that are used in more than one data dictionary.

Also, when you use the /codebase command-line option, unless you have signed your compiled library, you will see several lines of message warning you that you are registering an assembly that is not signed, and that does not use a strong name. Giving your assembly a strong name and signing it are options that you need to consider. Those topics, however, are beyond the scope of this book. For information on strongly named and signed assemblies, refer to the online documentation in Visual Studio .NET.

TIP

You can unregister a .NET class library using the same command line, replacing /codebase with /unregister as the command-line option. In fact, if you must update or replace an AEP container, it is strongly recommended that you first unregister the old version before registering the updated version. Otherwise, you may get multiple ProgID entries in your Windows registry.

Creating AEPs Using VB.NET

You create an AEP using VB.NET using the same steps as outlined in the previous section "Creating AEPs Using C# with Visual Studio .NET." There are only two differences:

▶ When the New Project dialog box is displayed, set Project Name to **AEPDemoVB7** instead of AEPDemoCS.

▶ Your AEP is implemented in VB.NET instead of C#. Implement your Get10Percent method using the code shown in Listing 7-3.

ON THE CD

This listing is also located in listing7-3.txt, located on this book's CD-ROM (see Appendix B).

Listing 7-3

```
Public Function Get10Percent(ByVal ulConnectionID As Int32, _
  ByVal hConnection As Int32, _
  ByRef ulNumRowsAffected As Int32) As Int32

  Dim oStateInfo As StateInfo
  Dim oCommand As IDbCommand
  Dim oReader As IDataReader
  Dim Adapter As AdsDataAdapter
  Dim DS As DataSet
  Dim Table As DataTable
  Dim custID As Int32
  Dim Counter As Int32
  Dim oneOrMoreRows As Boolean
  Try
    ' Get this client's state information before doing anything
    SyncLock colClientInfo
      oStateInfo = colClientInfo.Item(CStr(ulConnectionID))
    End SyncLock

    ' Create command object to use
    oCommand = oStateInfo.DataConnection.CreateCommand
    oCommand.CommandText = "SELECT * FROM __input"
    oReader = oCommand.ExecuteReader
    oReader.Read()
    custID = oReader.GetInt32(0)
    'Close DataReader before connection can be reused
    oReader.Close()

    oCommand = oStateInfo.DataConnection.CreateCommand
    DS = New DataSet
    Adapter = New AdsDataAdapter( _
      "SELECT [Invoice No] FROM invoice " + _
      "WHERE [Customer ID] = " + custID.ToString(), _
      oStateInfo.DataConnection)
    Adapter.Fill(DS, "invoices")
    Table = DS.Tables("invoices")

    Counter = 0
    oneOrMoreRows = False
    Dim i As Int32
    For i = 0 To (Table.Rows.Count - 1)
```

```
      Counter = Counter + 1
      If Counter = 10 Then
        oCommand.CommandText = _
          "INSERT INTO __output  VALUES ('" + _
          Table.Rows(i).ItemArray(0).ToString() + "')"
        oCommand.ExecuteNonQuery()
        Counter = 0
        oneOrMoreRows = True
      End If
    Next

    If Not oneOrMoreRows Then
      oCommand.CommandText = "INSERT INTO __error VALUES( " + _
        "2500, 'Less than 10 records for" + custID.ToString + "')"
      oCommand.ExecuteNonQuery()
    End If

  Catch Ex As Exception
    Dim oErrCommand As IDbCommand
    oErrCommand = oStateInfo.DataConnection.CreateCommand
    oErrCommand.CommandText = "INSERT INTO __error VALUES( 1, '" + _
      Ex.Message + "' )"
    oErrCommand.ExecuteNonQuery()
  Finally
    Get10Percent = 0
  End Try

End Function 'Get10Percent
```

Creating AEPs Using Visual Basic 6

Advantage provides a template for creating COM objects with Visual Basic 6. In
short, the process is very similar to the process you use when you implement a .NET
class library in VB.NET.

There is one very important difference between COM objects created with Visual
Basic 6 and those created with Visual Studio .NET, C#Builder, Delphi, Kylix, and
C++Builder. The COM objects that Visual Basic 6 produces create the COM object
in a single threaded apartment (STA). All calls made to stored procedures in an STA
are performed using the Windows message queue, which has the effect of serializing
these calls.

The fact that calls to Visual Basic 6–created COM objects are serialized dramatically reduces the value of these types of AEPs. Recall that stored procedures in an AEP are called from a thread on the Advantage Database Server. Many threads can be running concurrently, and if two or more threads need to call a stored procedure in a specific AEP at the same time, the execution of these calls normally proceeds concurrently.

This concurrent processing does not happen when the AEP is compiled as a COM object using Visual Basic 6. Instead, the first thread to call a stored procedure will begin executing it, and a second thread must wait until that execution is complete before being able to proceed with the stored procedure execution. As a result, Visual Basic 6 AEP COM objects represent a potentially serious performance bottleneck.

If you are a Visual Basic 6 developer, and your AEP is called only occasionally or by only one client, there is probably little harm in creating your AEP using Visual Basic 6. However, if your AEP is one that is called frequently from several different clients, you will be much better off creating your AEP using one of the other development environments, even if your client applications are written in Visual Basic 6.

Using AEPs

Once you have written your AEP, compiled it, and installed it on the machines from which it will be executed, you will need to add one stored procedure object to your data dictionary for each stored procedure function that you want to call. For example, if you have an AEP container with five stored procedure functions, and want to be able to call all of them from your client applications, you will need to create five stored procedure objects. Installing AEPs is discussed in the next section.

In addition to adding stored procedure objects, if your data dictionary is set up to require logins and check user rights, you will need to grant permissions to the groups and/or users who need to execute the stored procedures. Granting permissions to stored procedures is discussed later in this section.

Installing AEPs

Like all other objects in a data dictionary, you can install stored procedures using a number of techniques. For example, they can be installed using Advantage SQL and direct calls to the ACE (Advantage Client Engine) API. Typically, you use these techniques if you need to install an AEP at runtime.

Most of the time, however, installing an AEP is part of the overall design process of your data dictionary, which means that you do it at design time. In these cases, you install an AEP using the Advantage Data Architect.

Use the following steps to install your AEPs:

1. If the DemoDictionary data dictionary is not open in the Advantage Database Manager, open it.

2. From the Advantage Database Manager, right-click the STORED PROCS node in the tree view and select Add. The Advantage Database Manager responds by displaying the Advantage Extended Procedure dialog box, like that shown in Figure 7-2.

3. Set Object Name to the name you want to use to refer to your AEP. If you are installing one of the AEPs that you created by following the steps provided earlier in this chapter, set Object Name to **DelphiAEP**, **CSNetAEP**, or **VBNetAEP**, depending on which development tool you use to create the AEP.

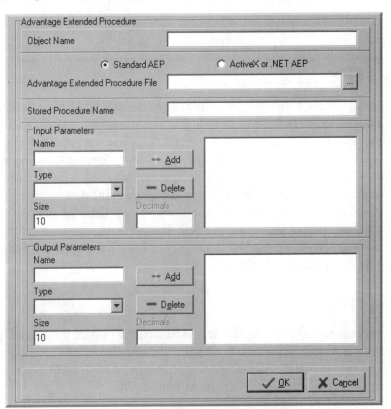

Figure 7-2   *The Advantage Extended Procedure dialog box*

4. If you are installing the Delphi AEP container (or any AEP container you created as a standard Windows DLL or shared object library), enable the Standard AEP radio button. If you created your AEP container as a COM server or a .NET class library, enable the ActiveX or .NET AEP radio button.

5. If you select Standard AEP, set the Advantage Extended Procedure File field to the AEP container filename. Most ADS developers prefer to store their DLLs (or shared object libraries) in the same directory in which they have stored their data dictionary. While this is the recommended approach, you can actually store your DLLs or shared object libraries in any directory on the same share as the data dictionary. If you do store the DLLs or shared object libraries in a directory other than the one in which your data dictionary is stored, we recommend that you refer to the libraries using a UNC (universal naming convention) path, rather than a DOS or Linux path.

If you select the ActiveX or .NET AEP radio button, set Advantage AEP Program ID (ProgID) to the ProgID of the COM server or managed assembly. The ProgID is a value registered under the HKEY_CLASSES_ROOT key of the Windows registry. So long as the COM server or .NET class library has been registered on the machine on which the Advantage Data Architect is running, you can click the ellipsis button to the right of the Advantage AEP Program ID (ProgID) field to see a list of the registered ProgIDs. Normally, the ProgID for a registered .NET class library is the combination of the .NET project name plus the AEP class name, separated by a period. For example, for the AEPDemoCS project, the ProgID is likely to be AEPDemoCS.aep_procedures.

6. Set the Stored Procedure Name field to the name of the stored procedure function that you are creating this stored procedure object for. If you are installing an AEP based on the steps provided earlier in this chapter, this name will be **Get10Percent**.

7. Use the Input Parameters section to define the optional input parameters for your stored procedure. For the Get10Percent function, set Name to **CustID**, and set Type to **INTEGER**. Click Add after defining the name and type to add the parameter to the input parameter list.

8. Use the Output Parameters section to define the optional output parameters of your AEP. For the Get10Percent function, set Name to **InvoiceNo**, set Type to **CHAR**, and set Size to **12**.

9. When you are done, click OK to save the stored procedure object.

10. If your data dictionary requires login and checks user rights, you need to grant execute privileges to each of the groups and users that need to be able to execute the stored procedure. For groups, right-click the node for the group in the Advantage Database Manager tree view and select Properties. Click the Procedure Rights button, and then enable the checkbox for each stored procedure that the group's members need to execute. Click OK to close the Permissions dialog box, and then click Save to save the new permissions.

    For each user who does not belong to a group from which they will inherit the rights to execute your stored procedures, right-click the user's node and select Properties. Click Procedure Rights and then check the checkbox next to each procedure that this user needs to be able to execute. Click OK to close the Permissions dialog box, and click Save to save your changes.

CAUTION

You cannot include spaces in either input parameter or output parameter names. If you attempt to define a parameter whose name includes at least one space, the stored procedure object cannot be created.

There are several points that need to be made concerning stored procedures. First, the input and output parameters that you define using the Advantage Extended Procedure dialog box are used to define the structures of the _ _input and _ _output tables that you work with in your stored procedure implementation. In particular, the order of the parameters defines the order of the resulting fields in the _ _input and _ _output tables. If the access mechanism that you are using references fields by their ordinal position, it is up to you to ensure that the order of the parameters in your stored procedure object definition matches the references you use in your stored procedure code.

Another point is that if you modify a stored procedure definition, all access rights to it are removed from your groups and users. Consequently, any time you update a stored procedure object, ensure that you also re-grant the necessary access rights to it. Of course, this is only necessary if you require login and check user rights for the data dictionary.

Testing AEPs

After you create your stored procedure objects, you will want to test them to make sure that they are doing what you want. One of the easiest ways to test a new stored procedure from the Advantage Data Architect is to execute it using the Native SQL Utility. The following steps show you how:

1. Select Tools | Native SQL Utility from the Advantage Data Architect main menu.

2. Set Connection Type to **Alias**, and set Alias to **DemoDD**. Click Connect. When the Native SQL Utility asks for the password, enter **password**. (If you find that you cannot open the Native SQL Utility, select the Query Options toolbar button on the Native SQL Utility, and verify that Connection Type is set correctly. The Native SQL Utility is discussed further in Chapter 9.)

3. Once connected, enter an EXECUTE PROCEDURE SQL statement in the SQL editor. You follow EXECUTE PROCEDURE with the name of the stored procedure object in your data dictionary, and enclose any input parameters in the parentheses that follow. For example, to execute the DelphiAEP object, enter the following SQL statement:

    ```
    EXECUTE PROCEDURE DelphiAEP(12037)
    ```

4. After entering the SQL statement, click the Execute SQL button. If the stored procedure returns data, the result set is displayed, as shown in Figure 7-3.

Debugging AEPs

You debug an AEP using the debugging features of your development environment. Most development environments permit you to set breakpoints in your code, and then cause an external host to load your compiled application. In Visual Studio .NET, the external application is referred to as the *calling application*, whereas in Borland products, it is called the *host application*.

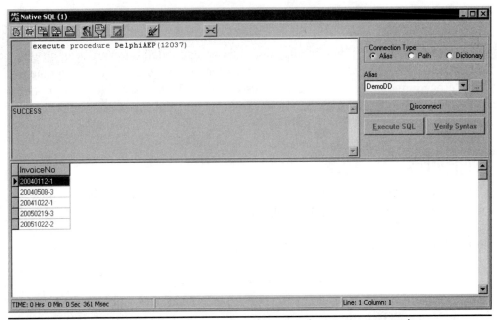

Figure 7-3   *The results of a stored procedure shown in the Native SQL Utility*

NOTE

Most developers debug their AEPs using ALS. However, beginning with ADS 7.0, the Windows NT/2000/2003 and Linux versions of the ADS server have an -exe command-line option, permitting ADS to be used during debugging. See the ADS documentation for more information on this feature.

When the external application calls your AEP and encounters the breakpoint, your application is loaded into the debugger. From that point, you can use the tools of your development environment's debugger to inspect variables, evaluate expressions, and step into or over individual instructions.

For specific information on debugging DLLs, shared object libraries, COM objects, and .NET class libraries, see the documentation for your particular development environment.

NOTE

In some cases you may need to adjust one or more properties of the project before it can be loaded by your development environment's debugger. For example, with a Delphi AEP, you must use the linker page of the Project Options dialog box to instruct the compiler to include TD32 debug info and include remote debug symbols. Once you are through debugging your AEP, be sure to turn off these settings before you deploy your AEP container.

Deploying AEPs

What steps you need to take when deploying an AEP container depend on the type of AEP container it is. The easiest AEP containers to deploy are those that are created as DLLs or shared object libraries, especially if you store them in the same directory as the data dictionary. Simply copy the DLL or shared object library to that directory. If you store your DLL or shared object library in a directory different from where your data dictionary files are, ensure that your stored procedure object definition includes the path to that library.

AEP containers deployed as COM objects or .NET class libraries are somewhat more complicated to deploy. Although your COM object or .NET assembly can be placed in any directory, it must be registered with the Windows registry. As you learned earlier in this chapter, you register it with regasm.exe, which ships with the .NET framework, and is therefore available on any machine on which the .NET framework has been deployed. The .NET framework must appear on any machine to which you deploy an AEP container created as a .NET-managed assembly.

NOTE

A number of development environments include an installation builder that can take responsibility for registering your COM objects and .NET class libraries.

There are several additional issues that apply to .NET assemblies that you want to deploy. Specifically, you may want to consider providing your deployed AEP assemblies with a strong name. Strongly naming an assembly prevents it from being spoofed, allowing unauthorized access to your database. In addition, you may want to sign your assemblies, which ensures your customers of the source of the executable. Refer to your .NET documentation for additional details about these issues.

Note that if you are deploying updated AEP containers that are either COM or .NET class libraries, it is a good idea to first unregister your older versions before replacing and registering the new versions. Failure to unregister older versions before replacing them may leave unwanted entries in that machine's Windows registry.

The problem of installation is magnified if you are using ALS instead of ADS. When you use ALS, the COM object or .NET-managed assembly must be installed on all client machines. Furthermore, the .NET framework must be present on all client machines as well.

In the next chapter, you will learn about Advantage triggers.

Defining Triggers

IN THIS CHAPTER:

A trigger is similar to a stored procedure in many respects. Like a stored procedure, a trigger is executable code that is installed on, and executes on, the server. However, unlike stored procedures, triggers are not executed by client applications. Instead, they are executed by the server in response to row-level data operations.

In this chapter, you will learn how to create and register triggers. We begin with a look at the types of triggers that are supported by the ADS (Advantage Database Server). Next, you will find examples of a trigger written in SQL, Delphi, C#, and Visual Basic .NET. Finally, you will learn how to register and configure triggers.

> **NOTE**
>
> *If you are unfamiliar with SQL, you may also want to refer to Chapters 9, 10, and 11 while reading this chapter.*

Overview of Triggers

Unlike a stored procedure, which is executed only when a client application includes a call to it, triggers are always invoked in response to an associated data event. For example, you can create a trigger that executes when a record is being inserted into your customer table. It doesn't matter whether you are inserting the record from the customer table using the Table Browser in the Data Architect or from a client application—the trigger will execute.

This is an important point, so let us repeat it in a slightly different way. There is no way to circumvent the execution of a trigger during a record-level operation on a table. By comparison, a given stored procedure is only executed when a client application specifically invokes it. Consequently, the operations embodied in a trigger are guaranteed to take place in response to an event, while those in a stored procedure are not.

You write triggers to perform validation or to perform additional tasks in response to a data operation. For example, a trigger can be used to generate a unique customer ID each time a new record is being inserted into the customer table. Likewise, a trigger can be used to write to a log table each time a change is made to a customer record. This type of operation is usually called an *audit trail*.

As with AEPs (Advantage Extended Procedures), you can write triggers using any development environment that can create Windows DLLs (dynamic link libraries), Linux SO (shared object) libraries, in-process COM (component object model) objects, or .NET class libraries (.NET managed assemblies). Because each of these libraries can have one or more triggers, they are referred to as *trigger containers* for convenience. You can also write triggers using SQL scripts. A SQL script is a series of one or more SQL statements. When a SQL script includes two or more SQL statements, they are separated by semicolons.

NOTE

The only triggers supported by ADS for NetWare are SQL triggers.

The fact that ADS can execute triggers written in languages other than SQL is significant. Most database servers only support SQL-based triggers. While those servers often can include some primitive control structures in the SQL triggers, this SQL is necessarily quite limited compared to most programming languages. As a result, when you write your triggers using DLLs, shared object libraries, COM objects, or .NET class libraries, your ADS triggers can be significantly more powerful than those you can create for most other database servers.

If you implement your trigger as a DLL, COM object, shared object library, or .NET class library, your triggers are passed seven parameters. The first parameter is a unique number that identifies the client connection whose actions are initiating the trigger.

The second parameter is a handle to a connection. You use this connection for two purposes. First, you can use it to access any tables, views, or stored procedures in the data dictionary with which your trigger is associated. Second, you use this connection to work with special temporary, in-memory tables that ADS creates with information about the trigger event. Because this connection is associated with the connection that initiated the trigger, if the initiating connection is currently in a transaction, any operations that you perform within your trigger are processed in that same transaction.

NOTE

These first two parameters are the same as the first two parameters passed to a stored procedure function.

The third parameter of a trigger is the trigger object's name, as defined in the data dictionary. The fourth parameter is the name of the table in the data dictionary with which the trigger is associated.

The fifth parameter identifies what trigger event is executing, and the sixth parameter is the type of trigger. Finally, the seventh parameter is the internal record number of the record being affected by the trigger.

As mentioned earlier, the connection handle passed in the second parameter provides you with access to one or more temporary in-memory tables. One of these is the error table, and that table has the name _ _*error* (this name is preceded by two underscore characters). The _ _error table has two fields: ERRORNO and MESSAGE. If you insert a record into the _ _error table, the trigger will fail, ADS will return an error, and the trigger event will not take place. For instance, if a BEFORE update trigger is executing, inserting a record into _ _error will prevent the record from being inserted (and any AFTER triggers will not fire either).

When you register your trigger into a data dictionary, it gives you the option to create additional temporary in-memory tables that can be accessed from the trigger. One option is to include value tables. For update triggers, these tables are named _ _*new* and _ _*old* (two underscore characters precede each of these names). The _ _old table c ontains the original values of the table's fields, and the _ _new table contains the data that needs to be updated. Insert event triggers only include the _ _new table, and delete event triggers can only access the _ _old table. Both of these tables contain exactly one record.

When you choose to include value tables for access by your triggers, you can optionally include memo and BLOB (binary large objects) data in the _ _old and _ _new tables. If your triggers do not need to work with memo or BLOB data, you can increase the performance of your trigger by omitting these types of fields.

Note that the _ _old, _ _new, and _ _error tables that you use in triggers are in-memory tables. Operations performed on in-memory tables are very fast.

The code that appears in a trigger is often used to write to one or more tables in a database. When a trigger writes to a table, there exists the possibility that the write operation itself will fire another trigger, which could then possibly write to another table, firing yet another trigger, and so on, and so on. To prevent an infinitely recursive trigger execution (which would ultimately stop when you run out of stack space), ADS will only permit trigger recursion to 64 levels.

ADS supports triggers on three types of events. These are record insertions, record updates, and record deletions. For each of these events, ADS provides three types of triggers. These are BEFORE triggers, INSTEAD OF triggers, and AFTER triggers. Each of these trigger types is discussed in the following sections.

BEFORE Triggers

A BEFORE trigger is one that is executed before the event takes place. For example, a BEFORE trigger for a delete event will execute prior to a record's deletion. From within this trigger, your code can evaluate the record that is being deleted and take an appropriate action. The action may be to do nothing, in which case the record will be deleted.

Alternatively, you can write an error message to the _ _error table, in which case no further action is taken by ADS, and the record will not be deleted. When you write to the _ _error table from within a trigger, no further triggers for that operation on that record will be fired. For example, if you write an error to the _ _error table from a BEFORE delete trigger, any AFTER triggers associated with deletions on that same record will be skipped for that data operation. (As is discussed in the next section, you cannot have a BEFORE trigger and an INSTEAD OF trigger on the same event type.)

BEFORE triggers permit you to implement many of the same types of validation that can be performed using field-level and record-level constraints. In most cases, if you have the choice to perform validation using either a trigger or constraints, it's nearly always preferable to use constraints. The reason for this is that constraints are easier to configure and manage, and they execute faster.

On the other hand, there are many types of validation that can be performed by a trigger that cannot be accomplished using constraints. For example, if validation can only be accomplished by verifying that data being written to a table is consistent with data values stored in other tables, and those relationships cannot be represented using referential integrity, triggers provide you with a reliable solution for validating the data.

While a BEFORE trigger can validate an operation for a table, at least with respect to insert and update triggers, a BEFORE trigger cannot be used to change the values of the record being affected. When you need to change the data that is being written to a table from within a trigger, use an INSTEAD OF trigger.

INSTEAD OF Triggers

INSTEAD OF triggers replace the event they are associated with. For example, if you create an INSTEAD OF insert trigger, ADS will not insert the associated record. If you want the record to be inserted, you do it yourself using the code in your trigger.

Before an INSTEAD OF trigger fires, ADS has already verified that the requested operation does not violate the table's field and record constraints. Note, however, that if the affected table is involved in one or more referential integrity relationships, those constraints are not applied unless the INSTEAD OF trigger completes without an error.

Using an INSTEAD OF trigger disables the execution of any AFTER triggers for the same event on the same table. If you add an INSTEAD OF trigger to a table event where there is already an AFTER trigger, move the AFTER trigger code to the INSTEAD OF trigger, and then delete the other trigger definitions.

INSTEAD OF triggers are a powerful tool for performing additional actions to coincide with an event. One of the more common uses is to insert a timestamp into a field that indicates the last time a record was updated. From within the INSTEAD OF trigger, you would update the existing table based on the data in the _ _new table, inserting the current date/time into the field reserved for the last access timestamp in the process.

Another example involves creating an audit trail. From the INSTEAD OF delete trigger you can write the values of the deleted record, as well as the time of deletion, to a special audit trail table. From the INSTEAD OF insert trigger, you can write the values of the fields being inserted, as well as the time of insertion, into the audit trail table. From the INSTEAD OF update trigger, you can write the values of the fields whose values have changed, as well as the time of the change, to the audit trail table. Importantly, so long as the trigger is being executed in a transaction, if for some reason the transaction must be rolled back, any changes written to the audit trail table in the trigger would also be rolled back. (An AFTER trigger can also be used for this purpose, but only if there is no INSTEAD OF trigger on the same event type.)

NOTE

If your INSTEAD OF trigger adds to, or modifies, the data while it is being written to the underlying table, it may be necessary for you to refresh that record in the client application if you want to use the new values, depending on the Advantage data access mechanism you are using.

AFTER Triggers

AFTER triggers execute following the successful insertion, deletion, or modification of a record. For example, you can use AFTER triggers to perform notifications. Imagine that you have a special table in your database where errors are logged. Imagine further that these error records have a field indicating the severity of the error. After an error is inserted into the error database, the trigger can inspect the severity of the error, and if severe enough, send an e-mail to the network administrator or the help desk.

If you want to implement notification, but your table already includes an INSTEAD OF trigger, perform the notification inside of the INSTEAD OF trigger, because an AFTER trigger will not be fired if an INSTEAD OF trigger exists.

Creating Triggers

If you are creating SQL-script triggers, you can write and configure your triggers entirely in the Advantage Data Architect. In fact, if you needed to, you could create your triggers at runtime using SQL. However, creating triggers, like AEPs, is often part of your overall database design process, which means that you are most likely to create and register your triggers at design time.

For any trigger other than SQL scripts, creating and registering the trigger requires two distinct steps. In the first step, you create the trigger container using your development environment of choice. You can then register the trigger for your data dictionary using the Advantage Data Architect, although this registration can also be performed programmatically at runtime, if necessary. If you are creating your triggers using SQL scripts, you define your SQL and configure the trigger all within the provided Triggers dialog box in the Advantage Data Architect.

Triggers and Transactions

As you learned earlier, triggers are commonly used to apply changes to one or more tables within your database. This is especially true with INSTEAD OF triggers, which take responsibility for applying the requested change.

When you register your trigger with a data dictionary, you are given the option to perform all changes within the trigger in an all-or-none fashion within a virtual transaction. When you do this, and your trigger returns an error code, all changes performed within the trigger prior to the error are rolled back.

This implicit transaction is distinct from any transaction that might be active on the connection through which the trigger is firing. Specifically, if a trigger is fired through a connection that is in a transaction, and the trigger returns an error, all changes made by the trigger are restored, but the transaction remains in force. It will be up to the client application to either commit or roll back the transaction, depending on the needs of the application.

It is also important to note that you cannot start a transaction on the connection passed to the trigger from within your trigger's code. Likewise, you cannot commit or roll back any transaction currently active on this connection.

You incur a performance penalty when you use this implicit transaction. Consequently, if data integrity is not as important as performance, you can disable implicit transactions using the Use implicit transactions to maintain data integrity option on the Triggers dialog box in the Advantage Data Architect.

ALS (Advantage Local Server) does not support transactions, nor does it support implicit transactions within triggers. As a result, if a trigger executed by ALS makes changes to more than one table, and an error occurs in the trigger, the changes already made to one or more tables within the trigger will remain.

Trigger Priority

When you define a trigger, you can assign a value to it that identifies the priority of the trigger. Trigger priority is used when you have two triggers of the same trigger type and event type on a given table. The trigger with a lower priority value gets executed before triggers with a higher priority value.

For example, imagine that you have two AFTER insert triggers on a particular table. If one of these triggers has a priority of 1, and the other has a priority of 2, the trigger with a priority of 1 will execute first, followed by the trigger with a priority of 2.

Trigger priority only applies to BEFORE and AFTER triggers. It does not apply to INSTEAD OF triggers. This is because you can have only one INSTEAD OF trigger for a given event type per table.

Triggers and Performance

Although triggers provide you with an important and creative way to ensure the integrity of your data, there are performance issues that you should consider. Specifically, triggers are executed once per row of data. For example, imagine that you have an INSTEAD OF delete trigger. If you execute a DELETE SQL query against the table that uses this trigger, and that query deletes 1,000 records, the trigger will execute 1,000 times. As a result, what might have been a fast query if no trigger was present may now be a time-consuming one.

The following are some guidelines for getting the most out of triggers:

▶ If a constraint can do the same task that you can perform from a trigger, use a constraint.

▶ When writing triggers, ensure that the code in your triggers is as efficient as possible.

▶ Avoid inherently slow operations from inside a trigger. For example, do not read from a file on the local file system within trigger code.

▶ If possible, only use the connection that is passed to your trigger to work with data. Obtaining a second connection is a relatively time-consuming operation.

Getting Started

As mentioned previously, you build your trigger either using a SQL script or using your development environment of choice. For all triggers other than SQL scripts, Advantage provides you with project templates for the most popular development environments, just as they do for AEPs. In most cases, you begin your trigger project by using the template, although you could also create your trigger project manually. If you decide to create your trigger project manually, it is a good idea to study the code created by the trigger template, so that you will implement your trigger project correctly for your particular development environment.

These templates include one function that provides you with a prototype for a trigger. This function can be used to create any type of trigger. For example, it could be used to create a BEFORE delete trigger, or an INSTEAD OF update trigger.

Normally, you will take this one function and change its name. For those environments, such as Delphi, where you must explicitly export your functions, you also need to change the name of the function that appears in the exports clause.

You will also likely make one or more copies of this trigger, providing each with a different name (and corresponding entry in the exports clause, if applicable). Each of these copies can be used to implement a different trigger. In other words, you can implement many different triggers in a single project.

The next section discusses how to create triggers for your DemoDictionary data dictionary.

Example Triggers

The following sections demonstrate how to create triggers for the DemoDictionary that we have been building throughout this book. Several of these triggers can be implemented using SQL scripts. In most cases, if your trigger is simple enough to implement in SQL, you probably want to use a SQL script.

Two of the triggers you need are too complex to implement in SQL. For triggers like these, you must resort to another development environment. Creating these triggers is demonstrated in Delphi, C#, and VB.NET. As in the preceding chapter, the steps that demonstrate how to create these trigger projects assume that you are already familiar with these development environments.

Unlike in the preceding chapter, creating triggers using Visual Basic 6 is not discussed in detail. As described in the preceding chapter, you are discouraged from creating AEPs using Visual Basic 6, except in very limited situations, due to potential performance bottlenecks that they can introduce. In short, because

Visual Basic 6–created AEPs make use of a single threaded apartment (STA), it is not possible for two threads on the Advantage Database Server to run the same Visual Basic 6–created AEP or AEPs located within the same AEP container concurrently.

With triggers, the issue is the same, but the problem is far more significant. Specifically, when a trigger container COM object is created using Visual Basic 6, the COM object uses an STA, and as a result, only one ADS thread at a time can invoke any of the trigger functions within a single trigger container. However, since triggers tend to execute far more often than AEPs, the performance bottleneck that these COM triggers would introduce makes it almost inconceivable to use them. As a result, Advantage does not provide a template for creating triggers using Visual Basic 6. If you are a Visual Basic 6 developer, please create your triggers using one of the other available options.

With respect to the examples provided in this section, we wanted to keep the trigger examples relatively simple, so you can concentrate more on what a trigger can do than on how to do it. Therefore, we are going to use four triggers to implement data archiving.

The first trigger will be associated with the EMPLOYEE table. With this trigger, each time an employee record is deleted, a copy of the record will be inserted into an archive table, named EMP_BAK.

The second, third, and fourth triggers are associated with archiving customer data. The second trigger will be more complicated than the one used to archive employee records. Specifically, when a customer record is being deleted, the trigger will first check to see if the customer has any outstanding invoices. If that customer has one or more invoice records in which the Date Payment Received field is empty, an error will be returned, and the record will remain in the CUSTOMER table. But if there are no outstanding invoices for this customer, the customer's record will be copied to the customer archive table, named CUST_BAK.ADT, and will be deleted from the CUSTOMER table.

The third trigger permits an archived customer record to be restored to the CUSTOMER table. This trigger, which will be attached to the CUST_BAK table, will trigger when a record is deleted from the CUST_BAK table. From within this trigger, a record being deleted from the CUST_BAK table will be reinserted into the CUSTOMER table, and then be removed from the CUST_BAK table. The effect of this second and third trigger is to make it impossible to ever lose a customer's record. It merely gets moved back and forth between CUSTOMER and CUST_BAK.

The fourth trigger is used to make sure that the customer IDs added to the CUSTOMER table do not conflict with customer IDs appearing in the CUST_BAK table. If that were to happen, an attempt to archive a customer to CUST_BAK could potentially fail due to a violation of the unique index order on the CUST_BAK table.

The first and third triggers described here are relatively simple, and can be implemented in SQL. The second and fourth triggers, with their more complicated logic, cannot be written in SQL. These triggers will be implemented using Delphi, C#, and VB.NET.

NOTE

If you ever wanted to permit client applications to write to the CUST_BAK table directly, you would need a fifth trigger. That trigger would be like the fourth trigger, in that it would verify that customer IDs being added to the CUST_BAK table do not currently exist in the CUSTOMER table. We are assuming with this sample database that CUST_BAK will never be used by client applications directly, making a fifth trigger unnecessary.

Before you can create these triggers, there are two additional tables that you need to add to your data dictionary. These tables are named CUST_BAK and EMP_BAK, and they are currently free tables that are located in the same directory as your data dictionary. The following steps show you how to make these additions to your data dictionary:

1. With the DemoDictionary data dictionary opened in the Advantage Data Architect, right-click the TABLES node and select Add Existing Table(s).

2. From the Open dialog box, keep the CTRL key depressed while you left-click CUST_BAK.ADT and then EMP_BAK.ADT. With both of these files selected, click Open. Your expanded TABLES node in the tree view in the Advantage Database Manager should now look like that shown in Figure 8-1.

Writing Triggers in SQL

Triggers that are implemented using SQL scripts are easy to create and maintain in your data dictionary, and do not require any additional tools to create them. From within a SQL script, you can write one or more SQL statements (with the statements being separated by semicolons). These SQL statements can reference the tables of your data dictionary, free tables, as well as tables in other data dictionaries for which your data dictionary has defined links.

Your SQL statements also are likely to make use of the _ _old table (for delete and update triggers) and the _ _new table (for insert and update triggers).

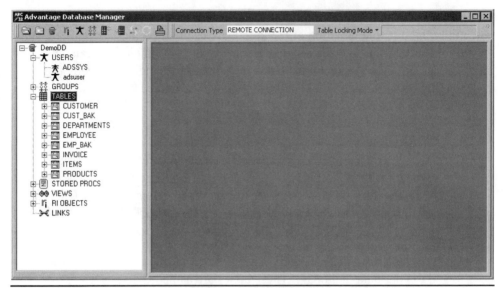

Figure 8-1   *The CUST_BAK and EMP_BAK tables have been added to the data dictionary.*

Use the following steps to create two triggers, one for archiving employee table records, and the other to restore archived customer records:

1. With the DemoDictionary data dictionary opened in the Advantage Database Manager, expand the TABLES node. Right-click the EMPLOYEE table and select Triggers. The Advantage Database Manager responds by displaying the Triggers dialog box shown in Figure 8-2.

2. Set Trigger Type to AFTER, and Event Type to DELETE. Leave Priority set to 1. Priority was discussed earlier in this chapter in the section "Trigger Priority."

3. In the Description field, enter **Trigger that archives deleted employee records**.

4. Enter the following SQL statement into the Script pane:

```
INSERT INTO EMP_BAK ("Employee Number", "First Name",
  "Last Name", Salary, "Department Code", "Date Archived")
  SELECT "Employee Number", "First Name",
    "Last Name", Salary, "Department Code", CurDate() FROM __old
```

At the Options section, leave the first two options checked, but uncheck Use Implicit Transactions To Maintain Data Integrity. There can be performance repercussions for enabling all three of these options, so you need to evaluate whether to enable them.

Since we will be using _ _old and/or _ _new tables, leave the Include Memo And Blob Data In VALUES Tables option checked. Unchecking this option can improve performance if your tables have large memo or BLOB fields and you will not be using this data in your triggers. ADS will build the _ _old and _ _new tables without including the memo or BLOB data in them. Since there are no memo or BLOB fields in the EMPLOYEE table, leaving this option checked does not affect performance.

The Use Implicit Transactions To Maintain Data Integrity option can be valuable when you are performing operations on two or more records from within the trigger. However, a transaction causes ADS to perform file I/O, which is costly, relatively speaking, when unnecessary. Since we are inserting a single record into the EMP_BAK table, the benefits of a transaction are not needed, and the performance benefits will be appreciated.

5. Click Save. The Trigger Name dialog box is displayed.

6. Set the trigger's name to **Archive Employee** and click OK.

7. Your Triggers dialog box should now look something like that shown in Figure 8-3. Click Close to close this dialog box.

8. Now right-click the CUST_BAK table and select Triggers.

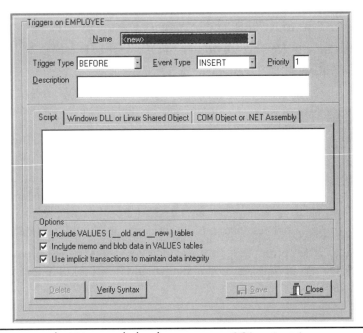

Figure 8-2   *You use the Triggers dialog box to create SQL script triggers.*

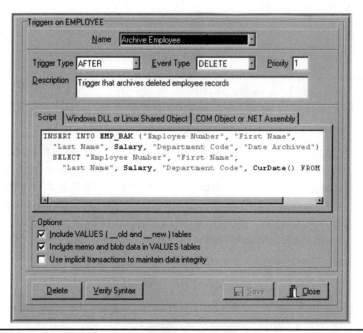

Figure 8-3   *The Archive Employee trigger in the Triggers dialog box*

9. Set Trigger Type to AFTER, and set Event Type to DELETE.

10. Set Description to **Restore customer to CUSTOMER table**.

11. Enter the following SQL statement in the Script pane:

```
INSERT INTO CUSTOMER ("Customer ID", "Last Name", "First Name",
   Address, City, State, "Zip Code", "Phone Number", Notes)
 SELECT "Customer ID", "Last Name", "First Name",
   Address, City, State, "Zip Code", "Phone Number", Notes
 FROM __old
```

12. Since the CUSTOMER table includes a MEMO field, it is essential that both the Include VALUES (__old and __new) Tables and Include Memo And Blob Data In VALUES Tables options are checked. For the same reason given for the previous trigger, uncheck Use implicit transactions to maintain data integrity.

13. Click Save. When prompted, set the trigger name to **Restore Customer** and click OK. Your Triggers dialog box should now look like that shown in Figure 8-4.

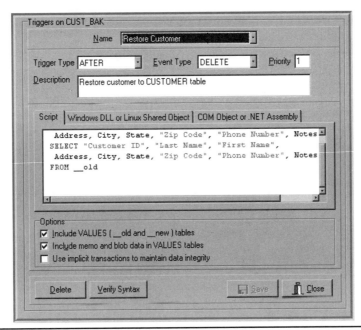

Figure 8-4   *The Restore Customer trigger in the Triggers dialog box*

These two triggers are now created and configured. If you want to test how they work, you can open the EMPLOYEE table in the Table Browser (right-click EMPLOYEE and select Open). Insert a new record and enter a unique employee number, and a first and last name. Click the Post edit button in the navigator to save the new record.

With your cursor on the newly inserted record, click the Delete button in the navigator. Two things happen. First, the record is deleted from the EMPLOYEE table. Second, this record is inserted into the EMP_BAK table, along with the date that the record was archived. You can see this by opening the EMP_BAK table in the Table Browser.

To view a previously created trigger, display the Triggers dialog box by either right-clicking the table to which the trigger applies in the Table Browser and selecting Open, or expanding the node of that table and clicking the Triggers node. Then select the trigger from the Name dropdown list.

Creating Triggers in Delphi

You create a Windows DLL when you create a trigger project in Delphi using the template provided by Advantage. This template is installed when you install the Advantage TDataSet Descendant. Templates are also available when you install the TDataSet Descendant for C++Builder and for Kylix. With Kylix, however, the template will create a shared object library.

Creating the Trigger Project

Use the following steps to create a trigger:

1. Select File | New | Other from Delphi's main menu to display the Object Repository.

2. Select the Projects tab from the Object Repository to display the Projects page.

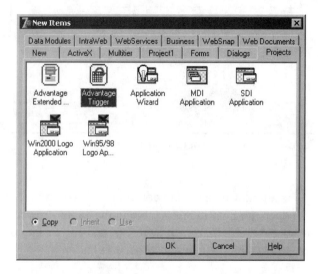

3. Select the Advantage Trigger template and click OK. When prompted, save this project to a directory where you want to store the source files.

Saving the Project Using a New Name

Delphi projects created from a project template are an exact copy of an existing project that has been added to the Object Repository. In case you ever plan to create more than one trigger project, it is a good idea to rename this project to something that is unique. The following steps show you how:

1. From Delphi's main menu, select File | Save Project As.

2. Using the Save dialog box, set File Name to **TriggerD**.

3. Click Save.

Changing the Trigger Function Name

The trigger project created from the template contains a function named MyFunction that you use as the basis for your trigger. One of the first things you need to do is create a second trigger by copying the one found in the template. Next, you will change the names of both of these triggers to something that better reflects what the triggers do. You must also change the exports clause, updating the name of the trigger function that appears there initially, as well as adding the name of the second trigger function.

Use the following steps to change the name of MyFunction:

1. Locate the MyFunction implementation in the editor. Select the entire function and copy it to the clipboard.

2. Move your cursor past the end of the first function, and paste the copy from the clipboard.

3. Change the name of the first function to **ArcCustomer**, and the name of the second function to **CheckCustArc**.

4. Locate the exports clause and change MyFunction to **ArcCustomer**, and add **CheckCustArc**. Your complete exports clause will look something like the following:

```
exports
  ArcCustomer,
  CheckCustArc;
```

Writing Your Trigger Functions

You are now ready to modify the two trigger functions and compile your project. Use the following steps:

1. Modify both of your trigger functions to look like those shown in Listing 8-1.

2. When you are done updating the functions, select Project | Compile TriggerD.dpr from the main menu.

You are now done. Your compiled DLL, named TriggerD.DLL, will be located in the directory where you saved your trigger project. While it is not required that you do so, we recommend that you copy TriggerD.DLL to the same directory where your DemoDictionary data dictionary is stored.

 ON THE CD

This listing is also located in listing8-1.txt on this book's CD-ROM (see Appendix B).

Listing 8-1

```
function ArcCustomer
(
  ulConnectionID : UNSIGNED32;
  hConnection    : ADSHANDLE;

  pcTriggerName  : PChar;
  pcTableName    : PChar;
  ulEventType    : UNSIGNED32;
  ulTriggerType  : UNSIGNED32;
  ulRecNo        : UNSIGNED32
) : UNSIGNED32;
{$IFDEF WIN32}stdcall;{$ENDIF}
{$IFDEF LINUX}cdecl;{$ENDIF}
var
  oConn  : TAdsConnection;
  InvQuery: TAdsQuery;
  ArcQuery: TAdsQuery;
begin
  Result := 0;

  oConn := TAdsConnection.CreateWithHandle( nil, hConnection );
  InvQuery := TAdsQuery.Create(nil);
  ArcQuery := TAdsQuery.Create(nil);

  try
    try
      oConn.Name := 'conn';
      InvQuery.DatabaseName := 'conn';
      ArcQuery.DatabaseName := 'conn';

      //Check for outstanding invoices
      InvQuery.SQL.Text :=
        'SELECT COUNT(*) as "num" FROM INVOICE '+
        'WHERE "Customer ID" IN '+
        '(SELECT "Customer ID" FROM __old) ' +
        'AND "Date Payment Received" IS NULL';
      InvQuery.Open;

      if InvQuery.Fields[0].AsInteger > 0 then
      begin
        SetError(oConn, 5500, 'Customer '+
```

```
                    ' has outstanding invoices. Cannot archive');
          Exit;
        end;

        //No outstanding invoices. Archive customer record
        ArcQuery.SQL.Text := 'INSERT INTO CUST_BAK ' +
          '("Customer ID", "Last Name", "First Name", "Address", '+
          'City, State, "Zip Code", "Phone Number", "Notes", '+
          '"Date Archived") SELECT "Customer ID", "Last Name", '+
          '"First Name", "Address", City, State, "Zip Code", '+
          '"Phone Number", "Notes", CURDATE() FROM __old';
        ArcQuery.ExecSQL;

        ArcQuery.SQL.Text := 'DELETE FROM CUSTOMER '+
          'WHERE "Customer ID" IN '+
          '(SELECT "Customer ID" FROM __old)';
        ArcQuery.ExecSQL;

    except
      on E : EADSDatabaseError do
        SetError( oConn, E.ACEErrorCode, E.message );
      on E : Exception do
        SetError( oConn, 0, E.message );
    end;

  finally
    InvQuery.Close;
    InvQuery.Free;
    ArcQuery.Free;
    oConn.Free;
  end;
end;

function CheckCustArc
(
  ulConnectionID : UNSIGNED32;
  hConnection    : ADSHANDLE;
  pcTriggerName  : PChar;
  pcTableName    : PChar;
  ulEventType    : UNSIGNED32;
  ulTriggerType  : UNSIGNED32;
  ulRecNo        : UNSIGNED32
) : UNSIGNED32;
```

```
{$IFDEF WIN32}stdcall;{$ENDIF}
{$IFDEF LINUX}cdecl;{$ENDIF}
var
  oConn  : TAdsConnection;
  ArcQuery: TAdsQuery;
begin
  Result := 0;

  oConn := TAdsConnection.CreateWithHandle( nil, hConnection );
  ArcQuery := TAdsQuery.Create(nil);

  try
    try
      oConn.Name := 'conn';
      ArcQuery.DatabaseName := 'conn';

      //Check for outstanding invoices
      ArcQuery.SQL.Text :=
        'SELECT COUNT(*) as "num" FROM CUST_BAK '+
        'WHERE "Customer ID" IN '+
        '(SELECT "Customer ID" FROM __new) ';
      ArcQuery.Open;

      if ArcQuery.Fields[0].AsInteger > 0 then
      begin
        SetError(oConn, 5501, 'A customer with that ID '+
          'already exists in CUST_BAK. Customer ID '+
          'must be unique');
        Exit;
      end;

    except
      on E : EADSDatabaseError do
        SetError( oConn, E.ACEErrorCode, E.message );
      on E : Exception do
        SetError( oConn, 0, E.message );
    end;

  finally
    ArcQuery.Close;
    ArcQuery.Free;
    oConn.Free;
  end;
end;
```

Creating Triggers in C# with Visual Studio .NET

When you create a trigger using C# with Visual Studio .NET, you begin with a template that is automatically installed when you install the Advantage .NET Data Provider.

NOTE

Advantage also provides a template for C#Builder developers. Using that template and the code provided in Listing 8-2, you can create this same project using C#Builder.

Creating the Trigger Project

Use the following steps to create a new trigger project in Visual Studio .NET using the trigger template installed with the Advantage .NET Data Provider:

1. Begin by selecting File | New | Project. Visual Studio responds by displaying the New Project dialog box.

2. In the Project Types tree view, select Visual C# Projects. The available templates are displayed in the Templates pane, which appears to the right of the Project Types tree view, shown here:

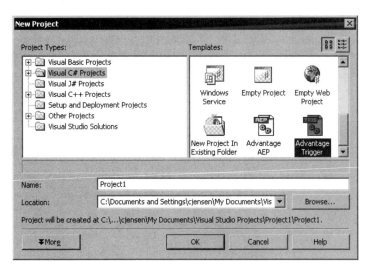

3. Scroll the Templates pane until you see the Advantage Trigger template. Select this template.

4. Set Project Name to **TriggerCS**.

5. Next, use the Browse button to choose the directory to which you want to save this project.

6. Click OK to continue.

7. Your new C# trigger project should now be open in Visual Studio, as shown in Figure 8-5.

Copying and Renaming Your Triggers

The trigger project created from the template contains a method named MyFunction that you use as the basis for your trigger. One of the first things you need to do is create a second trigger by copying the one found in the template. Next, you will change the names of both of these triggers to something that better reflects what the triggers do.

Use the following steps to copy the trigger method and assign new names to your two triggers:

1. Locate the MyFunction implementation in the editor. Select the entire method and copy it to the clipboard.

2. Move your cursor past the end of the first method, and paste the copy from the clipboard.

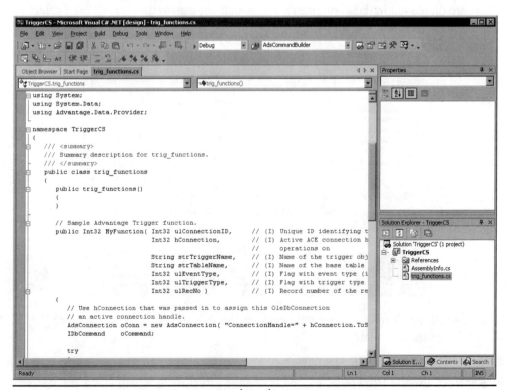

Figure 8-5 A new trigger project in Visual Studio .NET

3. Change the name of the first method to **ArcCustomer**, and the name of the second method to **CheckCustArc**.

Writing Your Triggers

You are now ready to modify the two trigger methods and compile your project. Use the following steps:

1. Modify both of your trigger methods to look like those shown in Listing 8-2.
2. When you are done updating the methods, select Build | Build TriggerCS from Visual Studio .NET's main menu.
3. If the project compiled correctly, set your Solutions Configuration to Release, and select Build | Build TriggerCS again.

   You are now done. Your compiled DLL, named TriggerCS.DLL, will be located in the bin\Release directory under where your project is located. While it is not required that you do so, we recommend that you copy TriggerCS.DLL to the same directory where your DemoDictionary data dictionary is stored.

ON THE CD

This listing is also located in listing8-2.txt on this book's CD-ROM (see Appendix B).

Listing 8-2

```
public Int32 ArcCustomer( Int32 ulConnectionID,
   Int32 hConnection,
   String strTriggerName,
   String strTableName,
   Int32 ulEventType,
   Int32 ulTriggerType,
   Int32 ulRecNo )
{
   // Use hConnection that was passed in to assign this
   //AdsConnection an active connection handle.
   AdsConnection oConn = new AdsConnection(
      "ConnectionHandle="+hConnection.ToString() );
   IDbCommand     oCommand;
   Int32 recCount;
   IDataReader    oReader;

   try
   {
```

```
   oConn.Open();
   oCommand = oConn.CreateCommand();
   oCommand.CommandText = "SELECT COUNT(*) as \"num\" "+
     "FROM INVOICE "+
     "WHERE [Customer ID] IN "+
     "(SELECT [Customer ID] FROM __old) " +
     "AND [Date Payment Received] IS NULL";
   oReader = oCommand.ExecuteReader();
   oReader.Read();
   recCount = oReader.GetInt32(0);
   oReader.Close();

   if (recCount > 0)
   {
     oCommand.CommandText = "INSERT INTO __error "+
       "VALUES( 5500, 'Customer has outstanding invoices. "+
       "Cannot archive' )";
     oCommand.ExecuteNonQuery();
     return 0;
   }

   oCommand.CommandText = "INSERT INTO CUST_BAK " +
     "([Customer ID], [Last Name], [First Name], Address, "+
     "City, State, [Zip Code], [Phone Number], Notes, "+
     "[Date Archived]) SELECT [Customer ID], [Last Name], "+
     "[First Name], Address, City, State, [Zip Code], "+
     "[Phone Number], Notes, CURDATE() FROM __old";
   oCommand.ExecuteNonQuery();

   oCommand.CommandText = "DELETE FROM CUSTOMER "+
     "WHERE [Customer ID] IN " +
     "(SELECT [Customer ID] FROM __old)";
   oCommand.ExecuteNonQuery();
 }
 catch( Exception e )
 {
   AdsCommand oErrCommand = oConn.CreateCommand();
   oErrCommand.CommandText = "INSERT INTO __error VALUES( 0, '"
     + e.Message + "' )";
   oErrCommand.ExecuteNonQuery();
 }
 return 0;
} // MyFunction
```

```
public Int32 CheckCustArc( Int32 ulConnectionID,
   Int32 hConnection,
   String strTriggerName,
   String strTableName,
   Int32 ulEventType,
   Int32 ulTriggerType,
   Int32 ulRecNo )
{
   AdsConnection oConn = new AdsConnection(
      "ConnectionHandle=" + hConnection.ToString() );
   IDbCommand      oCommand;
   Int32 recCount;
   IDataReader     oReader;

   try
   {
      oConn.Open();
      oCommand = oConn.CreateCommand();
      oCommand.CommandText = "SELECT COUNT(*) as [num] "+
         "FROM CUST_BAK WHERE [Customer ID] IN "+
         "(SELECT [Customer ID] FROM __new)";
      oReader = oCommand.ExecuteReader();
      oReader.Read();
      recCount = oReader.GetInt32(0);
      oReader.Close();

      if (recCount > 0) {
         oCommand.CommandText = "INSERT INTO __error "+
            "VALUES( 5501, 'A customer with that ID "+
            "already exists in CUST_BAK. Customer ID "+
            "must be unique')";
         oCommand.ExecuteNonQuery();
         return 0;
      }
   }
   catch( Exception e )
   {
      AdsCommand oErrCommand = oConn.CreateCommand();
      oErrCommand.CommandText = "INSERT INTO __error VALUES( 0, '"
         + e.Message + "' )";
      oErrCommand.ExecuteNonQuery();
   }
   return 0;
}  // CheckCustArc
```

Registering Your Trigger

When you compile your project with Visual Studio, it registers your .NET class library in the Windows registry on your development machine. If your data dictionary is on this same machine, you are ready to configure and test your trigger.

If you are running ADS as a remote server, and your data dictionary is on a machine other than the one where you compiled your .NET project, you must install the .NET class library before you can configure the trigger in the data dictionary. The same process must be used if you want to move your trigger executable from the directory to which the Visual Studio compiled it to the directory in which your data dictionary is stored, even if this is on the same machine.

This installation is performed using the regasm.exe utility, which is installed as part of the .NET framework. Since you cannot run the .NET class library without having installed the .NET framework, this utility should be on any machine on which you will run .NET triggers.

> **NOTE**
>
> *Depending on who is going to use your triggers, and how you are going to distribute them, you may want to sign and strongly name your .NET assemblies. Refer to the .NET Framework SDK (software development kit) for more information on signing and strong names.*

The following steps describe how to install your .NET class library:

1. Copy your .NET class library to the directory in which your data dictionary resides.

2. Open a command (CMD.EXE) window and navigate to the directory into which you copied your class library.

3. If regasm.exe is in a directory on your DOS path, you can register your library using a command similar to the following:

```
regasm TriggerCS.dll /codebase
```

4. If regasm is not on your DOS path, you must enter the fully qualified path to regasm. (If you do not know where regasm.exe is stored, use the Windows Explorer's searching capabilities to find it.) The command might look something like the following:

```
c:\Windows\Microsoft.NET\Framework\v1.1.4322\regasm
  TriggerCS.dll /codebase
```

> **NOTE**
>
> *The preceding command-line entry must be entered as a single command (on one line).*

The use of the /codebase command-line option is required here because you have not installed your trigger executable in the global assembly cache (GAC). If you did register your .NET executable in the GAC, you do not have to perform the preceding steps. While storing your class library in the GAC permits you to share it, sharing is really not an advantage in this case. Placing your trigger in the same directory as your data dictionary ensures that you do not introduce version control problems with triggers that are used in more than one data dictionary.

Also, when you use the /codebase command-line option, unless you have signed your compiled library, you will see several lines of message warning you that you are registering an assembly that is not signed, and that it does not use a strong name. Giving your assembly a strong name and signing it are options that you may want to consider. Those topics, however, are beyond the scope of this book.

TIP

You can unregister a .NET class library using the same command line, replacing /codebase with /unregister as the command-line option. In fact, if you must update or replace a trigger, it is strongly recommended that you first unregister the old version before registering the updated version. Otherwise you may end up with multiple entries in your Windows registry.

Creating Triggers in VB.NET with Visual Studio .NET

You create triggers in VB.NET using the same steps as outlined in the earlier section "Creating Triggers in C# with Visual Studio .NET." There are only two differences:

▶   When the New Project dialog box is displayed, set Project Name to **TriggerVB7** instead of TriggerCS.

▶   Your trigger methods are implemented in VB.NET instead of C#.

Modify both of your trigger methods to look like the code shown in Listing 8-3:

ON THE CD

This listing is also located in listing8-3.txt on this book's CD-ROM (see Appendix B).

Listing 8-3

```
Public Function ArcCustomer(ByVal ulConnectionID As Int32, _
    ByVal hConnection As Int32, _
    ByVal strTriggerName As String, _
    ByVal strTableName As String, _
    ByVal ulEventType As Int32, _
```

```
ByVal ulTriggerType As Int32, _
ByVal ulRecNo As Int32) As Int32

Dim oConn As AdsConnection
Dim oCommand As IDbCommand
Dim RecCount As Int32
Dim oReader As IDataReader

Try
  oConn = New AdsConnection( _
    "ConnectionHandle=" & hConnection)
  oConn.Open()

  oCommand = oConn.CreateCommand
  oCommand.CommandText = "SELECT COUNT(*) as [num]" + _
    "FROM INVOICE WHERE [Customer ID] IN " + _
    "(SELECT [Customer ID] FROM __old) " + _
    "AND [Date Payment Received] IS NULL"

  oReader = oCommand.ExecuteReader()
  oReader.Read()
  RecCount = oReader.GetInt32(0)
  oReader.Close()

  If RecCount > 0 Then
    Dim oErrCommand As AdsCommand
    oErrCommand = oConn.CreateCommand()
    oErrCommand.CommandText = "INSERT INTO __error " + _
      "VALUES( 5500, 'Customer has outstanding invoices. " + _
      "Cannot archive' )"
    oErrCommand.ExecuteNonQuery()
    ArcCustomer = 0
    Exit Function
  End If

  oCommand = oConn.CreateCommand()
  oCommand.CommandText = "INSERT INTO CUST_BAK " + _
    "([Customer ID], [Last Name], [First Name], Address, " + _
    "City, State, [Zip Code], [Phone Number], Notes, " + _
    "[Date Archived]) SELECT [Customer ID], [Last Name], " + _
    "[First Name], Address, City, State, [Zip Code], " + _
    "[Phone Number], Notes, CURDATE() FROM __old"
  oCommand.ExecuteNonQuery()

  oCommand = oConn.CreateCommand()
```

```
      oCommand.CommandText = "DELETE FROM CUSTOMER " + _
        "WHERE [Customer ID] IN " + _
        "(SELECT [Customer ID] FROM __old)"
      oCommand.ExecuteNonQuery()

    Catch Ex As Exception
      Dim oErrCommand As AdsCommand
      oErrCommand = oConn.CreateCommand
      oErrCommand.CommandText = "INSERT INTO __error " + _
        "VALUES( 0, '" & Ex.Message & "' )"
      oErrCommand.ExecuteNonQuery()
    Finally
      ArcCustomer = 0
    End Try

End Function 'ArcCustomer

Public Function CheckCustArc(ByVal ulConnectionID As Int32, _
    ByVal hConnection As Int32, _
    ByVal strTriggerName As String, _
    ByVal strTableName As String, _
    ByVal ulEventType As Int32, _
    ByVal ulTriggerType As Int32, _
    ByVal ulRecNo As Int32) As Int32

    Dim oConn As AdsConnection
    Dim oCommand As IDbCommand
    Dim RecCount As Int32
    Dim oReader As IDataReader

    Try
      oConn = New AdsConnection( _
        "ConnectionHandle=" & hConnection)
      oConn.Open()

      oCommand = oConn.CreateCommand
      oCommand.CommandText = "SELECT COUNT(*) as [num] " + _
        "FROM CUST_BAK WHERE [Customer ID] IN " + _
        "(SELECT [Customer ID] FROM __new)"
      oReader = oCommand.ExecuteReader()
      oReader.Read()
      RecCount = oReader.GetInt32(0)
      oReader.Close()

      If RecCount > 0 Then
```

```
       oCommand.CommandText = "INSERT INTO __error " + _
         "VALUES( 5501, 'A customer with that ID " + _
          "already exists in CUST_BAK. Customer ID " + _
          "must be unique' )"
       oCommand.ExecuteNonQuery()
       CheckCustArc = 0
       Exit Function
     End If

  Catch Ex As Exception
    Dim oErrCommand As AdsCommand
    oErrCommand = oConn.CreateCommand
    oErrCommand.CommandText = "INSERT INTO __error VALUES( 0, '" & _
       Ex.Message & "' )"
    oErrCommand.ExecuteNonQuery()
  Finally
    CheckCustArc = 0
  End Try

End Function 'CheckCustArc
```

Using Triggers

Triggers, like AEPs, can be registered with a data dictionary either using the Advantage Data Architect or programmatically by writing SQL or writing in your development language to the Advantage Client Engine API. Registering triggers programmatically is something you can do if you need to register a trigger with a data dictionary at runtime, but most developers only need to register their triggers at design time. As is the case with so many of the objects you work with in a data dictionary, the Advantage Data Architect is the preferred tool for registering triggers.

Unlike AEPs, which are invoked by a client, triggers are associated with a specific event for a specific table. As a result, you do not find a TRIGGERS node under your data dictionary node, like you do with stored procedures. Instead, you will find the node for working with triggers under each table in the TABLES branch of the Advantage Database Manager tree view.

Registering Triggers

You already registered the two SQL script-based triggers into your data dictionary. Use the following steps to register your compiled triggers:

1. Expand the CUSTOMER table node from the Advantage Database Manager tree view.

2. Click the Triggers node to display the Triggers dialog box.

3. Set Trigger Type to INSTEAD OF, and Event Type to DELETE.

4. Set Description to **Archive customer records with no outstanding invoices**.

5. If your trigger container is a DLL or a shared object file, click the Windows DLL or Linux Shared Object tab. The Triggers dialog box should look like that shown in Figure 8-6. Click the browse button to the right of the Container Path and Filename field, and use the displayed Open dialog box to select your trigger container. If you created the Delphi trigger earlier in this chapter, select TriggerD.dll and click Open.

   If your trigger container is a .NET class library, click the COM Object or .NET Assembly tab. When you do this, your Triggers dialog box will look like that shown in Figure 8-7. Click the browse button to the right of the Program ID (ProgID) field to display the Select ProgID dialog box, shown here:

   Use this dialog box to select the ProgID for your trigger container and then click OK. This ProgID should be the name of the project plus the name of the public class inside that class library, separated by a period. If you followed the steps given earlier in this chapter to create the class library using C#, your ProgID will be TriggerCS.trig_functions. If you created the Visual Basic .NET project, it will be TriggerVB7.trig_functions.

6. If you are registering a DLL trigger, set the Function Name in Container to the name of your exported trigger function. If you are registering a COM or .NET class library, you set the Method Name in Class field to the name of the method. If you created one of the projects described in this chapter, set this field to **ArcCustomer**.

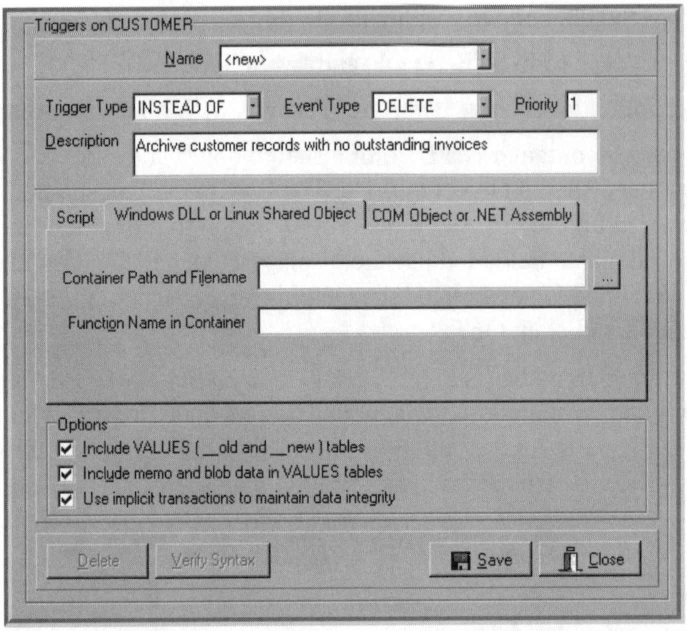

Figure 8-6   *Registering a DLL-based trigger*

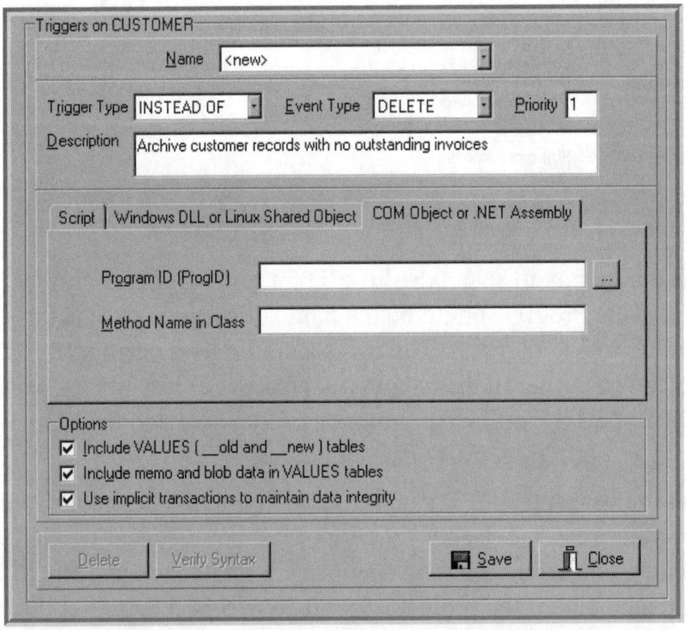

Figure 8-7   *Registering a COM or .NET class library trigger*

7. Leave the checkboxes in the Options section checked, meaning that your triggers will have access to the old and new values, will include BLOB data, and will operate within an implicit transaction (if you are running ADS).

8. Click Save to save your trigger. The Advantage Database Manager will respond by displaying the Trigger Name dialog box. Set the trigger name to **Archive Customers** and click OK.

9. We are now going to register the CheckCustArc trigger. This trigger needs to be configured to be used as both a BEFORE update and a BEFORE insert trigger. Let's begin with the BEFORE update trigger. With the Triggers dialog box for the CUSTOMER table still displayed, set Name to <new>.

10. Set Trigger Type to BEFORE and Event Type to UPDATE.

11. Set Description to **Verify unique ID before update**.

12. Select the pane you used in step 5. Select the library or ProgID for your trigger, and then set the Function Name or the Method Name to **CheckCustArc**.

13. Click Save. When prompted for the trigger name, enter **Verify ID Update**.

14. Set Name to <new> once more.

15. Set Trigger Type to BEFORE and Event Type to INSERT.

16. Set Description to **Verify unique ID before insert**.

17. Choose the same library and function/method name as you did for the Verify ID Update trigger.

18. Click Save. Save this trigger using the name **Verify ID Insert**. Click OK when you are done.

Updating and Deleting Triggers

You can update a trigger's description, as well as change which library and function/method to use for the trigger. To do this, open the Triggers dialog box, and then select the trigger you want to update. To delete the trigger, click Delete. After you are done, click the Save button to save your changes.

   If you change your trigger's library or function/method name, the new trigger will be used once the old trigger can be unloaded. With triggers implemented as DLLs, COM objects, and .NET class libraries, this will occur when the last user to use a trigger in the trigger's container drops their connection to ADS. With SQL scripts, this will occur as soon as the trigger stops executing.

Debugging Triggers

You cannot debug SQL script triggers. For all other trigger types, the process is nearly identical to that which you use when you debug an AEP. Specifically, while in your development environment, set up a host or calling application. Then, with your trigger project open and breakpoints set, start the debugger, which will automatically launch the host or calling application. See your development environment's documentation for details on how to do this.

Also, recall that most developers debug trigger containers using ALS, but with ADS 7.0 and later, you can use the -exe command-line option with the ads.exe host or calling application to debug triggers using ADS.

> ### NOTE
>
> *As is the case with Delphi AEPs, some development environments may require that you change your project options before you can successfully debug your project. For example, with triggers written in Delphi, you often have to enable debugger-related linker options. Remember to disable these options before you distribute your trigger libraries, as these options cause your projects to be very large.*

Deploying Triggers

Your triggers that are implemented as SQL scripts are stored in your data dictionary. There is nothing special that you need to do to deploy your SQL script triggers, other than deploy your updated data dictionary.

If your triggers are entirely SQL based, and you are adding triggers to an existing dictionary, it is not necessary to re-deploy that dictionary. Instead, you can write a simple SQL script that adds one or more triggers to your existing dictionary. If you decide to take this approach, you do not even have to write the SQL manually. You can use the Data Dictionary Differentiator to generate the SQL scripts that update your existing data dictionary.

For all other types of triggers, the issues of deployment are the same for triggers as they are for AEPs. Specifically, you will need to deploy your trigger containers to the machines on which they will be executed. Furthermore, for COM and .NET class libraries, you must register the library in order for ADS or ALS to load it. You might also want to consider signing and using strong names for .NET class libraries. If your development environment has an installer builder, you should be able to use it to register your .NET class libraries and COM objects.

Note that if you are deploying updated COM or .NET class library triggers, it is highly recommended that you first unregister your older versions before replacing and registering the new versions. Failure to unregister older versions before replacing them may leave unwanted entries in that machine's Windows registry.

Using Advantage SQL

ADS is a relational database server, and like all other sophisticated database servers, it permits you to access your data using the industry-standard SQL (structured query language). In Part II of this book, you find a detailed look at Advantage SQL, the dialect of SQL you use with ADS.

There are three chapters in this part, with each one playing a distinct role. In Chapter 9, you learn how to construct valid Advantage SQL statements. Topics discussed in this chapter include how to reference table and field names, literal values, the available operators, and Advantage SQL scalar functions in the queries that you write. This chapter also discusses parameterized queries, SQL scripts, live versus static cursors, and subqueries. This chapter concludes with a look at the various SQL-related tools provided by the Advantage Data Architect.

Chapter 10 demonstrates many of the essential SQL statements that you will use in your everyday applications. Filled with numerous examples of SQL statements that you can execute against the provided database, this chapter shows you how to create tables, select records, retrieve aggregate statistics, perform calculations, group records, sort results, and link tables. You will also learn how to delete, insert, and update data in your tables, all using Advantage SQL.

Chapter 11 concludes this exploration of Advantage SQL with a look at administrative tasks. This chapter begins with a discussion of the SQL statements that permit you to create databases and control access rights to data dictionary objects. Next you learn how to retrieve your data dictionary's metadata, the data that describes your data dictionary objects, users, groups, privileges, and more. Finally, you learn how to use a special collection of system stored procedures that permit you to perform those remaining tasks not support directly by Advantage SQL.

Introduction to Using Advantage SQL

IN THIS CHAPTER:

Overview of Advantage SQL Queries

Additional ADS SQL Topics

Advantage SQL Utilities

S QL (also pronounced *sequel,* which stands for structured query language) is an industry-standard language for describing operations that you want a database server to execute. Upon receiving the SQL instructions, the database server performs the requested operations, and if those operations return a result set, that result set is returned to the client who issued the instructions.

This chapter is the first of three designed to introduce you to using SQL with ADS (Advantage Database Server). This chapter begins with a look at the basic grammar of Advantage SQL, including keywords, references, operators, literals, SQL scalar functions, and parameters. It also describes the use of three query-related utilities: the Advantage Query Builder, the Native SQL Utility, and the ODBC SQL Utility.

Chapter 10 introduces you to the basic classes of SQL statements, and shows you some of the more common SQL queries that you can use in your applications. Chapter 11 discusses how to obtain metadata using SQL queries, as well as how to control data dictionaries and their objects.

If you are a seasoned SQL developer, you will probably want to quickly scan this chapter to learn the specifics of Advantage SQL and see the available SQL utilities. You may then want to skip to Chapter 11.

If you are new to SQL programming, these chapters will get you started. Note, however, that these chapters merely provide an introduction. A thorough discussion of SQL would take several volumes. Consequently, if you want to get the most out of SQL, you may want to consider picking up a good book on SQL, such as *SQL: The Complete Reference, Second Edition,* by James R. Groff and Paul N. Weinberg (McGraw-Hill/Osborne, 2002).

Overview of Advantage SQL Queries

Advantage SQL statements are text-based commands that you use to instruct ADS to perform some operation. Examples of operations that you can perform with Advantage SQL include creating and destroying (dropping) tables, adding or removing (dropping) indexes, inserting data into a table, deleting records from a table, updating data in one or more records in a table, adding permissions for users or groups, and selecting records to return to your client application, to name a few. These instructions are performed entirely on the server.

Many of the data access mechanisms for ADS provide alternative ways of requesting these same operations. For example, in Delphi, you can perform all of the preceding tasks using the Advantage TDataSet Descendant components.

Similarly, any development environment that can directly access the ACE (Advantage Client Engine) API—such as Visual Basic 6, Delphi, Visual C++, C++Builder, and the like—can perform these tasks through the functions of the ACE API. Refer to the ADS help for information on the ACE API.

While some data access mechanisms permit you to manipulate data using means other than SQL, Advantage SQL is the common denominator. Specifically, SQL can be used with every data access mechanism that ADS supports (except with the Advantage Clipper RDDs). For example, ODBC (open database connectivity) is a SQL-based standard for creating client/server applications. Any language that supports ODBC can be an effective tool for writing client applications that use ADS, even if that language cannot use the ACE API.

When used with ADS, Advantage SQL statements are executed on the remote database server. If you are using ALS (Advantage Local Server), the queries are executed on the client machine. To put this another way, only with ADS do you get the full benefits of distributed computing with SQL queries.

Although ALS does not provide a client application with the benefit of executing SQL statements on the server, there are still situations in which SQL is better suited or even required with ALS:

▶   With some of the ADS data access mechanisms, SQL provides the only mechanism for executing stored procedures.

▶   SQL provides a mechanism for joining tables from multiple data dictionaries with a single connection.

▶   SQL reduces the amount of coding required to perform some complex tasks, especially if tasks involve multiple tables.

▶   SQL makes code more portable to other RDBMS (relational database management systems).

SQL is a parsimonious language for performing many tasks. Even environments that support alternative ways of working with ADS data can exploit the powerful nature of Advantage SQL. For example, even though Delphi developers find the TAdsTable immensely useful, there are many times when using Advantage SQL through a TAdsQuery component performs a task more efficiently.

Advantage SQL queries consist of table references, field references, aliases, keywords, literals, operators, SQL scalar functions, comments, and parameters. Each of these is discussed in the following sections.

Field Names and Table Names

Almost every SQL statement refers to at least one table, and most refer to one or more fields. For example, consider the following statement:

```
SELECT Picture FROM PRODUCTS
```

Picture in this statement refers to the Picture field, and PRODUCTS refers to the PRODUCTS table.

Whether a reference is interpreted by ADS to be a field name or a table name depends on the location of the reference in the statement. In the preceding statement, Picture is interpreted to be the field name because field names, but not table names, can appear in this location of the SELECT statement. By the same token, PRODUCTS is interpreted to be the table name, since table names are expected in the FROM list of the SELECT statement.

When a field name or table name begins with a numeral, or contains characters other than 0–9 and A–Z, the name must be enclosed between either double quotes or square braces [ ]. For example, if you want to include the Product Name field in the preceding query, you enclose it in delimiters as follows:

```
SELECT Picture, "Product Name" FROM PRODUCTS
```

Likewise, the following query is equivalent:

```
SELECT Picture, [Product Name] FROM PRODUCTS
```

ADS does not care which delimiter pair you use. Which you choose to use will often depend on the development environment you are using. For example, in C#

you must escape double-quotation characters in string literals, preceding the double-quotation character with a backslash. Square braces, however, do not need to be escaped. Consequently, for readability, we prefer

```
oCommand.CommandText = "DELETE FROM CUSTOMER " +
  "WHERE [Customer ID] IN (SELECT [Customer ID] FROM __old)";
```

over

```
oCommand.CommandText = "DELETE FROM CUSTOMER " +
  "WHERE \"Customer ID\" IN (SELECT \"Customer ID\" FROM __old)";
```

Field Names and Table Aliases

It is not uncommon to reference field names from two or more tables in a single SQL statement. For example, consider the following query:

```
SELECT "Customer ID", "Employee ID", "Last Name"
  FROM INVOICE, EMPLOYEE
  WHERE "Employee ID" = "Employee Number"
```

This is a valid query because the field names in the SELECT list and the WHERE clause are unique to the tables listed in the FROM list. Nonetheless, this query is a bit more difficult to read unless you know for certain that Employee ID is a field of the INVOICE table and Employee Number is a field of the EMPLOYEE table.

If the field names are not unique, the problem is more serious. Consider the following query:

```
SELECT "Invoice No", "First Name", "Last Name"
  FROM INVOICE, CUSTOMER
  WHERE "Customer ID" = "Customer ID"
```

This is an invalid query, since the references to "Customer ID" in the WHERE clause are ambiguous. In cases like these, you have two options. The first is to use dot notation to qualify the field name with the table name. For example, the preceding query can be rewritten to look like the following:

```
SELECT INVOICE."Invoice No", CUSTOMER."First Name",
  CUSTOMER."Last Name"
  FROM INVOICE, CUSTOMER
  WHERE INVOICE."Customer ID" = CUSTOMER."Customer ID"
```

The drawback to this approach is that table names are often not short. As a result, using this technique may result in a lot of extra typing. Instead of using the entire table name, you can define aliases for the table name in the FROM clause of the query, and then qualify the field names using the aliases. This is demonstrated in the following query:

```
SELECT Inv."Invoice No", Cust."First Name", Cust."Last Name"
  FROM INVOICE Inv, CUSTOMER Cust
  WHERE Inv."Customer ID" = Cust."Customer ID"
```

Here, each table is associated with an alias, and that alias is used in dot notation to qualify the field references. As a result, there is no ambiguity, making this a valid query.

Now consider the following query:

```
SELECT Inv."Customer ID", Inv."Employee ID", Emp."Last Name"
  FROM INVOICE Inv, EMPLOYEE Emp
  WHERE Inv."Employee ID" = Emp."Employee Number"
```

While the aliases in the preceding query were not required, they produced a more readable query, one that will be easier to read, and hence, maintain, in the long run.

Keywords

Keywords are special words that are used to build the primary instructions embodied in a SQL statement. For example, consider the following SQL command:

```
SELECT Picture FROM PRODUCTS
```

The keywords in this SQL statements are SELECT and FROM. These words hold special meaning to ADS, and are used to drive the requested operations.

Keywords appear directly in your SQL statements, and are never enclosed within delimiters. Some SQL keywords are also reserved. As you learned in the preceding section, field names and table names that begin with a letter and that consist of only alphanumeric characters also do not require delimiters. However, if you have a field name or a table name that matches one of the reserved keywords, you must enclose that field name or table name in the double-quote or square brace delimiters. Doing so prevents ADS from confusing that field name or table name with the matching reserved keyword. For example, imagine that in the ITEMS table the Quantity field name was changed to Count. The following query would be invalid:

```
SELECT Count FROM ITEMS
```

When parsing this SQL statement, ADS will interpret Count to be the COUNT reserved keyword, which will cause an error because the keyword COUNT cannot be used like this. In order to distinguish between keywords and field or table names, use delimiters. If the ITEMS table had a field named Count, the following query would be parsed correctly:

```
SELECT "Count" FROM ITEMS
```

As is the case with field names that contain special characters, you can use square braces as the delimiters instead of double-quotation marks, as shown in the following query:

```
SELECT [Count] FROM ITEMS
```

The reserved keywords, as of the time of this writing, are listed in Table 9-1. ADS follows the ANSI (American National Standards Institute) SQL 92 standard when designating the reserved keywords. If a word is a keyword in the ANSI SQL 92 standard but not in the list of the reserved keywords shown in Table 9-1, it is still a good idea to enclose the keyword in double quotes or square braces. As ADS implements additional features, more keywords from the ANSI standard will be added to the list. Enclosing the words in double quotes or square braces will ensure that the SQL statement will work in future versions of ADS as well as other RDBMSs.

ADD	ALL	ALTER	AND	ANY
AS	ASC	AVG	BEGIN	BETWEEN
BY	CASE	COLUMN	COMMIT	CONSTRAINT
COUNT	CREATE	DEFAULT	DELETE	DESC
DISTINCT	DROP	ELSE	END	EXECUTE
EXISTS	FALSE	FROM	GRANT	GROUP
HAVING	IN	INDEX	INNER	INSERT
INTO	IS	JOIN	KEY	LEFT
LIKE	MAX	MIN	NOT	NULL
ON	OR	ORDER	OUTPUT	OUTER
PRIMARY	PROCEDURE	REVOKE	ROLLBACK	SELECT
SET	SQL	SUM	TABLE	THEN
TO	TRANSACTION	TRUE	UNION	UNIQUE
UPDATE	USER	VALUES	VIEW	WHEN
WHERE	WORK			

Table 9-1   *Reserved Keywords in Advantage SQL*

SQL Literals

Literals are explicit representations of data in expressions. They are used in SQL statements to represent data that does not change. How you specify a literal depends on the type of expression. String literals, for example, are enclosed in single quotation marks. Integer literals, by comparison, are numerals without delimiters. Consider the following statement:

```
SELECT * FROM INVOICE
  WHERE "Invoice Due Date" > "Invoice Date" + 60
```

In this query, all invoices where customers were given more than 60 days to pay are selected. The 60 in this query is a literal integer value.

The following is an example of a query with a string literal:

```
SELECT "Customer ID" FROM CUSTOMER
  WHERE State = 'CA'
```

This query selects the Customer ID field from the CUSTOMER table for all customers whose State field contains an exact match to the characters CA.

There are six literal types that you can use in Advantage SQL statements. These are Boolean, date, numeric, string, time, and timestamp. The rules for representing these literals are described in the following sections.

Boolean Literals

The Boolean value True is represented as 1 and a Boolean False is represented as 0. You can use the keywords TRUE instead of 1 and FALSE instead of 0.

Date Literals

Literal date values are enclosed in single quotes, and use the current date format setting (the default is mm/dd/ccyy) or the ANSI date format (ccyy-mm-dd), which will always work in ADS regardless of the current date format setting. Unless you use the default or ANSI setting, you set this format for your client applications programmatically using the ACE API AdsSetDateFormat function, or the Advantage TDataSet Descendant's TAdsSettings DateFormat property.

You can change the date format used for viewing data in the Advantage Data Architect by selecting Tools | Environment Settings from the main menu, which displays the ARC Env Settings dialog box. Note that this will not change the date format used in your applications. Look at a date field in the Table Browser to determine the current date format setting used for viewing dates within the Advantage Data Architect.

Note that you must represent the month and day with two digits (use a leading zero for single digits). For example, if the current date format is ccyy-mm-dd, the correct representation of January, 1, 2003, is '2003-01-01'. If your dates appear using the mm/dd/ccyy format, a valid date literal is '04/15/2005'. If dates appear using the ccyy.mm.dd format, you represent the same date using the '2005.04.15' literal.

Numeric Literals

Both integer and floating-point numbers are represented by numerals without delimiters. These numerals may be preceded by either a plus character (+) or a minus character (–) to denote sign. Floating-point values use a period to separate the whole number part from the decimal part. You cannot use a comma as a decimal point.

When the numbers you need to represent are very large, you can express numeric literals using exponential notation, sometimes referred to as scientific notation. Exponential notation specifies a number using two parts, the *mantissa* and the *exponent*. The mantissa is a number with one significant digit and some number of decimals. The exponent denotes the power of 10 to which the mantissa will be raised. Either the letter *e* or *E* separates the mantissa and the exponent.

If the exponent is a positive number, it indicates how many positions the decimal point of the mantissa should be shifted to the right; if the exponent is a negative number, it specifies how many decimal places the decimal point should be shifted to the left.

The following values are examples of numeric literals:

```
1
1.0
-3456.43
3454324.93783628
7.43e12
-4.087e6
```

String Literals

A string literal is a sequence of one or more characters enclosed in single quotation marks. Any printable character can appear in a string literal. However, if your string literal includes the single quotation mark character ('), you precede it with a single quotation mark. The following are examples of string literals:

```
'Robert "Bob" Jefferson'
'That''s the truth, the whole truth, and nothing but the truth'
'a'
'San Francisco'
```

With one exception, string literals are case sensitive. Specifically, the following three string literals are not equivalent: 'laser', 'Laser', and 'LASER'. The exception is string literals used with the CONTAINS scalar function on case-insensitive FTS (full text search) indexes.

In all other cases, if you want to perform a case-insensitive comparison between a string literal and another string value (either a string field reference, a string expression, or another string literal), you must use the UCASE or LCASE scalar functions to convert both parts of the comparison to a common case. SQL scalar functions are described later in this chapter.

Time Literals

Time literals are enclosed in single quotation marks, and use one of the following four formats: HH:MM, HH:MM AM (or PM), HH:MM:SS, or HH:MM:SS AM (or PM). If the AM (or PM) is missing from the literal, 24-hour time is assumed. The AM/PM part of time literals is not case sensitive. The following are valid time literals:

```
'19:10'
'4:43 AM'
'9:00:45 pm'
'22:19:59'
```

Timestamp Literals

A timestamp literal denotes a specific date and time, and can be accurate to the millisecond. Timestamp literals, like time literals, are enclosed in single quotation marks. The date part of a timestamp uses the date format as defined earlier in the "Date Literals" section. The time part of the timestamp literal uses the 24-hour HH:MM:SS time format, where seconds are required, but may optionally include milliseconds (HH:MM:SS.mmm). The date part and the time part are separated from each other using a single space. If your date format is mm/dd/ccyy, the following are valid stamp literals:

```
'7/6/2004 04:52:34'
'12/31/2006 23:59:59.999'
```

If your date format is ccyy/mm/dd, the following are valid timestamp literals:

```
'2004/7/6 04:52:34'
'2006/12/31 23:59:59.999'
```

The ANSI date format (ccyy-mm-dd) is always supported by ADS, regardless of the current date format setting. The following are valid timestamp literals regardless of current date format:

```
'2004-07-06 04:52:34'
'2006-12-31 23:59:59.999'
```

Other Literal Types

Not all data types can be represented literally in your SQL statements. For example, there is no raw literal. If you want to include a literal in your SQL statements, but there is no literal for the data you want to represent, you must convert one of the available literal types to the data type you need.

You perform data type conversions using the Convert SQL scalar function. When you invoke Convert, you pass two parameters. The first is a literal representation of your data using one of the available literal types, and the second is a SQL data type that you want that literal converted to. For example, the following is how you represent a literal raw value:

```
Convert ('{B54F3741-5B07-11cf-A4B0-00AA004A55E8}', SQL_BINARY)
```

Operators in SQL Statements

Operators are used to create or modify expressions. Unary operators, such as the integer – (negation) and the Boolean NOT (negation), modify an operand. Binary operators, such as the string + (concatenation) and the Boolean = (equals), create a new expression by combining two operands.

The process of applying an operator to an expression is referred to as *expression evaluation*, and the result is also an expression of some type. For example, the following is an expression:

```
1 + 1
```

In this case, two expressions, each a numeric literal, are combined through addition. The result is a single numeric expression with the value of 2.

Expression evaluation normally proceeds from left to right. Consider the following expression using the addition operator (+), in which 1 and 1 are added together to make 2, and then 2 is added to 5 to make 7:

```
1 + 1 + 5
```

But not all operators have the same precedence. Operations involving operators of a higher precedence are executed first, followed by operators of lower precedence. When two operators have the same precedence, the operators are evaluated from left to right. For example, the multiplication operator (*) has a higher precedence than the addition operator. Consider the following expression:

```
1 + 1 * 5
```

The result of this expression is 6. The multiplication is executed first, resulting in a value of 5. Next, the addition operator adds 1 to 5, resulting in 6.

You can control precedence by using parentheses. Operations within parentheses are always performed as a unit. For example, the following expression evaluates to 10. First, 1 is added to 1 to get 2. Next, 2 is multiplied by 5 to produce 10.

```
(1 + 1) * 5
```

The operators available in Advantage SQL are described in the following sections. These sections are divided by the type of expressions that the operators apply to. Within each section, the operators are further divided by operator type, ordered by operator type precedence.

Boolean Operators

There are three Boolean operator types. These are logical comparison operators, the logical complement operator, and logical operators.

Logical Comparison Operators   Logical comparison operators are binary operators that employee two logical operands, and that result in a Boolean expression. The logical comparison operators are = (equals), <> (not equals), IS NULL, and IS NOT NULL. For both IS NULL and IS NOT NULL, the first operand must be a field name reference.

Logical Complement Operator   The logical complement operator is NOT. Use it to convert a Boolean True to False, and a Boolean False to True.

Logical Operators   There are two logical operators—AND and OR—and both require two Boolean operands. An AND operation results in a Boolean True if, and only if, both operands are True, and results in False otherwise. An OR operation evaluates to a Boolean True if at least one of the operands is a Boolean True, and evaluates to False only if both operands are False.

Numeric Operators

There are three categories of numeric operators. These are numeric sign change operators, numeric arithmetic operators, and numeric comparison operators.

Numeric Sign Change Operators   Numeric sign change operators are unary operators, and there are two of them: – and +. In reality, only the – sign change operator has utility. Precede a numeric operand with a – to change the sign of the numeric expression.

Numeric Arithmetic Operators   There are four numeric arithmetic operators: * (multiplication), / (division), + (addition), – (subtraction). Each of these operators requires two numeric operands, and result in a numeric expression. If at least one of the operands is a floating-point expression, the result will be a floating-point expression. Within this type, * and / have higher precedence than + and –.

Numeric Comparison Operators   The numeric comparison operators are > (greater than), < (less than), >= (greater than or equal to), <= (less than or equal to), IN, NOT IN, BETWEEN, NOT BETWEEN, IS NULL, and IS NOT NULL. Numeric comparison operators require two numeric operands and evaluate to a Boolean expression.

String Operators

There are two types of string operators: the string concatenation operator and string comparison operators.

String Concatenation Operator   The string concatenation operator (|) is used to combine two string operands, producing a string expression. The resulting string expression contains all characters in the first operand plus all characters in the second operand.

String Comparison Operators   The string comparison operators are > (greater than), < (less than), >= (greater than or equal to), <= (less than or equal to), LIKE, NOT LIKE, IN, NOT IN, BETWEEN, NOT BETWEEN, IS NULL, and IS NOT NULL. These are binary operators that evaluate to a Boolean expression. The use of LIKE, IN, and BETWEEN is discussed in Chapter 10.

Date Operators

There are two types of date operators: date arithmetic operators and date comparison operators.

Date Arithmetic Operators   Date arithmetic operators are binary operators where one operand is a date expression and the other is an integer expression. Date arithmetic operators evaluate to a date expression. The date arithmetic operators are + (addition) and – (subtraction). Use the + operator to calculate a date some specified number of days in the future, and the – operator to calculate a date some specified number of days in the past.

Date Comparison Operators   Date comparison operators are binary operators that compare two date operands and evaluate to a Boolean expression. The valid date comparison operators are > (greater than), < (less than), >= (greater than or equal to), <= (less than or equal to), <> (not equal to), BETWEEN, NOT BETWEEN, IS NULL, and IS NOT NULL.

Time and Timestamp Operators

There is only one type of operator that applies to time and timestamp expressions. These are the time comparison operators.

Time Comparison Operators   Time comparison operators are binary operators that evaluate to a Boolean expression. The time operators are > (greater than), < (less than), >= (greater than or equal to), <= (less than or equal to), = (equal to), and <> (not equal to). The >, <, >=, <=, and <> operators require two time or timestamp operands.

Other Operators

Fixed-length and BLOB (binary large object) expressions can be used with comparison operators. Fixed-length binary expressions can employ the > (greater than), < (less than), >= (greater than or equal to), <= (less than or equal to), = (equal to), <> (not equal to), IN, NOT IN, IS NULL, and IS NOT NULL operators. These are binary operators that take two fixed-length binary operands and evaluate to a Boolean expression.

Variable-length binary (BLOB) fields support two comparison operators: IS NULL and IS NOT NULL. These unary operators take one BLOB field operand and evaluate to a Boolean expression.

SQL Scalar Functions

SQL scalar functions are built-in subroutines that can be used in your expressions. These functions permit you to write more flexible SQL statements by performing transformations on data or returning values that can only be determined at runtime.

NOTE

A scalar function is one that returns an expression.

For example, the following SQL statement uses the CURDATE() function, which returns the current date, based on your server's internal clock:

```
SELECT * FROM INVOICE
  WHERE "Invoice Due Date" > CURDATE() - 7
  AND "Invoice Due Date" < CURDATE() AND
  "Date Payment Received" IS NULL
```

This query will return all invoices that became due in the past week for which payment has not yet been received. Because of the use of the CURDATE() function, this query will always produce the past week's outstanding invoices, whether you execute it today, tomorrow, or two years from now.

The Advantage SQL scalar functions can be divided into four categories. These are date/time functions, math functions, string functions, and miscellaneous functions. Each of these is described briefly in the following sections. For a more detailed description of each function, including its syntax, refer to the ADS help.

Date/Time Functions

You use the Advantage date/time SQL scalar functions to determine or process date/time information. Table 9-2 contains a list of the supported date/time functions.

Math Functions

The Advantage math scalar functions provide you with a rich collection of arithmetic and trigonometric functions. Also included in this category are functions that round and truncate numbers, as well as a function that generates random numbers. The Advantage math SQL scalar functions are listed in Table 9-3.

String Functions

The Advantage string functions are used to process and convert string expressions. The Advantage string SQL scalar functions are listed in Table 9-4.

Miscellaneous Functions

The miscellaneous functions are those that do not fall into one of the other categories. Among other things, they can be used to return the name of the user whose connection the SQL query is being executed over, the name of the database being queried, several

CURDATE()	CURRENT_DATE()	CURRENT_TIME()
CURRENT_TIMESTAMP()	CURTIME()	DAYNAME()
DAYOFMONTH()	DAYOFWEEK()	DAYOFYEAR()
EXTRACT()	HOUR()	MINUTE()
MONTH()	MONTHNAME()	NOW()
QUARTER()	SECOND()	TIMESTAMPADD()
TIMESTAMPDIFF()	WEEK()	YEAR()

Table 9-2 *The Advantage Date/Time SQL Scalar Functions*

ABS()	ACOS()	ASIN()
ATAN()	ATAN2()	CEILING()
COS()	COT()	DEGREES()
EXP()	FLOOR()	LOG()
LOG10()	MOD()	PI()
POWER()	RADIANS()	RAND()
ROUND()	SIGN()	SIN()
SQRT()	TAN()	TRUNCATE()

Table 9-3   *The Advantage Math SQL Scalar Functions*

scalar conditional functions, IFNULL(), ISNULL(), and IIF(), as well as some functions that are used in conjunction with full text search. The Advantage miscellaneous SQL scalar functions are listed in Table 9-5.

Parameters in SQL Statements

A parameterized query is one that includes one or more parameters. A parameter is a placeholder for a value in the WHERE clause of SELECT, UPDATE, or DELETE queries. The value of a parameter does not need to be defined until just before the query is executed by the client application, permitting you to define the query at design time and then customize which records it will affect at runtime.

In addition to permitting you to create customizable query *templates*, parameterized queries offer potential performance benefits as well. Specifically, if you need to execute a parameterized query more than once, even when one or more of the parameter values change, the query will generally execute faster upon repeated execution.

There are two sources of this performance benefit. The first is that ADS need only parse and check the syntax of the query the first time it is executed. So long as the SQL statement being executed is unchanged, excluding the values of the parameters,

ASCII()	BIT_LENGTH()	CHAR()	CHAR_LENGTH()
CHARACTER_LENGTH()	CONCAT()	INSERT()	LCASE()
LEFT()	LENGTH()	LOCATE()	LOWER()
LTRIM()	OCTET_LENGTH()	POSITION()	REPEAT()
REPLACE()	RIGHT()	RTRIM()	SPACE()
SUBSTRING()	UCASE()	UPPER()	

Table 9-4   *The Advantage String SQL Scalar Functions*

CONVERT()	DATABASE()	DIFFERENCE()
SOUNDEX()	IFNULL()	ISNULL()
USER()	IIF()	CONTAINS()
SCORE()	SCOREDISTINCT()	

Table 9-5   *The Advantage Miscellaneous SQL Scalar Functions*

subsequent executions do not need parsing and syntax checking. Second, upon repeated execution of a parameterized query, only the parameter values need to be sent to the server. The remainder of the query does not, having already been sent during a previous execution.

There are two types of parameters that can appear in a parameterized query: named parameters and positional parameters. Named parameters are identified by placeholders that appear as a text label preceded by a colon. For instance, in the following SQL statement, the parameter is named custparam:

```
SELECT City, State FROM Customer
  WHERE [Customer ID] = :custparam
```

Positional parameters do not have labels. Instead, they are represented by a question mark (?). The following SQL statement is similar to the preceding one, except that it uses a positional parameter rather than a named parameter:

```
SELECT City, State FROM CUSTOMER
  WHERE [Customer ID] = ?
```

In order to execute a parameterized query, it is necessary to supply a value for each parameter prior to the execution of the query. How this is done depends on the development environment you are writing your client applications in. Using parameterized queries, and assigning values to parameters at runtime, is described for each of the ADS-supported data access mechanisms in the later chapters of this book. Refer to the chapter that discusses the data access mechanism you want to use for details.

Comments

You use comments in a SQL statement to document the statement's purpose as well as temporarily disable one or more parts of the statement. When ADS is executing the query, it ignores all comments. ADS supports three types of comments in SQL statements. Of these, two are single-line comments, and the third is a multiline comment.

A single-line comment instructs ADS to ignore all text to the right of the comment indicator. There are two single-line comment indicators: // (two consecutive forward slashes), and -- (two consecutive dashes). The following is an example of a SQL statement containing a single-line comment:

```
SELECT * FROM INVOICE //WHERE "Customer ID" IS NULL
```

In this example, the WHERE clause has been temporarily disabled. This type of comment can be useful while you are testing a SQL statement. Here is another example:

```
// Delete the customer records where the
// customer has already been processed
DELETE FROM CUSTOMER
  WHERE [Customer ID] IN
    (SELECT [Customer ID] FROM PROCESSED)
```

This time, the comment is designed to document what task the query is performing.
Multiline comments are enclosed between two delimiters. The comment begins with the /* (forward slash, asterisk) delimiter and concludes with the */ (asterisk, forward slash) delimiter. The following shows how this comment could have been used in the preceding query:

```
/* Delete the customer records where the
   customer has already been processed */
DELETE FROM CUSTOMER
  WHERE [Customer ID] IN
    (SELECT [Customer ID] FROM PROCESSED)
```

Unlike single-line comments, which comment out everything to the right of the comment indicator, a multiline comment can begin and conclude within a single line. For example, the following query will select only one field:

```
SELECT "Customer ID"/*, State*/ FROM CUSTOMER
```

In this query, the field name State has been commented out. This use of the multiline comment is quite valuable while you are testing your queries.

SQL Scripts

Since ADS 7.0 and later, you can use SQL scripts anywhere a simple SQL statement is expected, except within View definitions. A SQL script is two or more SQL statements separated by semicolons. SQL scripts permit you to package several SQL statements together when you send them to the server. They are particularly useful when you must communicate to the server over a slow connection, thereby reducing the number of round-trips required to complete a complicated task.

While SQL scripts permit you to send two or more queries to ADS in a single statement, they introduce a potential security risk that you must be aware of. Specifically, if you construct a query at runtime from data input by a user, you must check the user's input to prevent the unwanted introduction of semicolons. If a user enters a semicolon, and you subsequently concatenate that entry with your SQL query, ADS will interpret the semicolon as a SQL statement separator.

Initially, this might not sound like a security threat. After all, wouldn't the presence of the semicolon surely lead to a syntax error, causing ADS to return an error code? The answer is "It depends." A user aware of the use of semicolons to separate SQL statements, and knowledge of SQL, could exploit this feature to undermine your database.

Here's an example. Imagine that your client application includes a query that is constructed at runtime based on the user's entry of a Customer ID. The following is an example of how a query might be created from a user's input. This example is written in Delphi:

```
//Construct the query
AdsQuery1.SQL.Text := 'SELECT * FROM CUSTOMER ' +
  'WHERE [Customer ID] = ' + Edit1.Text;
//Execute the query
AdsQuery1.Open;
```

Here, the value entered into the input field named Edit1 is concatenated to the query being assigned to the SQL property of an AdsQuery. Now consider what would happen if the user enters the following data into the edit:

```
12037; DROP TABLE CUSTOMER; DROP TABLE ITEMS
```

The resulting query would actually be a SQL script, and would look like the following:

```
SELECT * FROM CUSTOMER
  WHERE [Customer ID] =12037; DROP TABLE CUSTOMER; DROP TABLE ITEMS
```

Obviously, if you were to execute this SQL script, it could seriously compromise your database.

The easiest way to prevent this from being a problem is to use parameterized queries where you bind the user's input to query parameters. Because of the way parameterized queries are executed, ADS will never confuse a semicolon in a parameter as a statement separator.

If it is not feasible to use parameterized queries when building SQL statements based on user input, you can do several things. First of all, limit the amount of text that the user can enter. If a Customer ID is never more than ten characters, don't accept more than ten characters. Similarly, if the input is necessarily an integer value, verify that the user entered an integer. Second, examine the contents of the user's input. If it contains a semicolon, or any other element that it should not, reject the entered data.

In the end, the most important point that you need to be aware of is that semicolons can be abused. You need to keep this in mind when working with user input that will contribute to a SQL statement.

Additional ADS SQL Topics

In addition to the topics covered earlier in this chapter, there are a couple of other topics that you should know before you continue onto Chapters 10 and 11. These are related to the limits of SQL statements, the difference between live and static cursors, and subqueries. These topics are discussed in the following sections.

SQL Statement Dimensions

There are limits to the length of individual SQL statements that you can pass to ADS. Fortunately, these limits are quite high and rarely, if ever, pose a problem.

For example, a single SQL statement cannot exceed 65,535 (64K) characters in length. Within that limit, individual string literals can be no longer than 1,024 characters. Table names and database names can be up to 256 characters in length, while column and index names can be up to 63 characters. For CREATE INDEX SQL statements, there can be no more than 15 column names in the index.

> **TIP**
>
> *If you need to use strings longer than the 1,024 character limit, use a parameterized query (described earlier) and assign the string literals to the parameter.*

Live Cursors Versus Static Cursors

You use SQL SELECT statements to retrieve data from the database server to your client application. When you execute a SELECT statement, ADS is going to produce one of two types of cursors: a live cursor or a static cursor. Which type of cursor is produced by a query has implications for both performance and features.

Creating Live Cursors

A live cursor is one that maps directly to an ADS table. If the live cursor does not include all records in the table being queried, the live cursor is produced by ADS by creating an AOF (Advantage Optimized Filter). (Selecting fewer than all records means that a WHERE clause is included in the SELECT statement.)

ADS will first attempt to build the AOF using existing indexes. If all of the necessary indexes already exist for the table, ADS is able to quickly build an AOF. These AOFs are referred to as *fully optimized AOFs*, and they are one of the primary sources of ADS's speed.

If the WHERE clause can make use of one or more indexes, and some, but not all, of the indexes that ADS requires are present, the AOFs will be partially optimized based on the existing indexes. These AOFs are referred to as *partially optimized filters*. ADS will then have to explicitly read the records that match the optimized part of the AOF to determine whether or not they match the nonoptimized part of the filter expression.

Imagine that you have a customer table that includes both Last Name and City fields. Imagine further that you have an index on Last Name, but not on City. If your filter expression is Last Name = "Green" and City = "Chicago", the AOF will be partially optimized. ADS will use the Last Name filter to quickly select all Greens, but then must read every one of these identified customers in order to determine whether or not they live in Chicago.

If no indexes currently exist to assist in satisfying the WHERE clause, the AOF is a *nonoptimized filter*. With a nonoptimized filter, ADS must read every record in the entire table to determine whether or not it passes the filter expression. As you can imagine, this results in the slowest performance of the three AOF types.

Once the AOF has been constructed, ADS begins returning records to the client. The number of records returned depends on the size of the result set, the size of individual records, the number of records requested by the application, and the requirements of the client. ADS will usually return to the client the number of records configured in the record cache setting (or a single record if the application requested only the first record in the result set). The default record cache setting is 10 or however many records fit into a transmission burst, whichever is smaller. A transmission burst is 22K bytes with IP, and 8K bytes with IPX.

NOTE

See the ADS help for information on changing the record cache size.

If the returned records do not satisfy the client's needs—for example, if the client application is attempting to populate a grid that can display more records than that received in the first transmission—another transmission, and then another, if necessary, is returned until the client is satisfied. This process is repeated each time the client navigates to another part of the result set, as well as each time the query is executed.

From a performance perspective, whether or not an optimized AOF can be created affects how quickly live cursors are returned. This is why it is important to create indexes on those expressions that will be used regularly to select data from your tables.

Using Live Cursors

The primary benefit of a live cursor is that it is a virtual view of a table. If another client changes the contents of the underlying table, that change is immediately reflected in the AOF. For example, newly inserted records that meet the WHERE clause become part of the live cursor, and will be received by the client the next time the client application requests data from the region of the AOF where the record was inserted. This may occur due to normal navigation, or be the result of an explicit refresh.

But there are two specific situations where live cursors based on AOFs do not have automatic access to newly posted data. With ALS, AOFs are not updated each time data changes. As a result, with ALS, an AOF may become obsolete on a client, returning data that no longer meets the WHERE clause. The second situation is when you are using compatibility locking to share DBF files with non-ADS applications. In these cases, ADS is not the sole application that is accessing those files, and once again, the AOF may become obsolete. For these situations, you need to reexecute the query to create a current AOF.

Creating Static Cursors

Static cursors are created automatically any time ADS cannot create a live cursor. This happens when the SELECT statement selects more than simple columns from a single table, contains the DISTINCT or TOP keyword or an aggregate function in the SELECT clause, contains a GROUP BY or HAVING clause, includes a subquery (discussed later in this section), or includes either a BLOB field or the LIKE operator in the WHERE clause. Another element that will prevent a live cursor is the use of any scalar function in an expression in the WHERE clause other than the functions listed in Table 9-6.

Even if your SELECT statement would not otherwise create a static cursor, you can specifically request a static cursor when you create your SQL statement. Simply include the {static} directive immediately following the SELECT keyword to request a static cursor. For example, the following query produces a static cursor, even though ADS would normally create a live cursor:

```
SELECT {static} * FROM INVOICE
```

ABS	BIT_LENGTH	CHAR	CHARACTER_LENGTH	CHAR_LENGTH
CONCAT	CONTAINS	CURDATE	CURRENT_DATE	CURRENT_TIME
CURTIME	IFNULL	IIF	ISNULL	LCASE
LEFT	LENGTH	LOCATE	LOWER	LTRIM
NOW	OCTET_LENGTH	PI	POSITION	POWER
RIGHT	RTRIM	SPACE	SUBSTRING	UCASE
UPPER				

Table 9-6   *SQL Scalar Functions That Can Be Used in Live Cursors*

While a live cursor is a filtered view of a table based on AOF, a static cursor is actually a new, temporary table constructed by (and managed by) the server. While this temporary table may take a while to create, ADS will begin returning records to the client before this temporary table is completely populated. As a result, there are rare situations where static cursors will make records available to the client faster than when live cursors are used. In most cases, using live cursors is faster because no temporary files will be created.

This behavior of static cursors—returning results before the temporary table is completely filled—is obvious if you first obtain a static cursor on a large result set and then attempt to navigate to the last record. Going to the last record is something that can only be accomplished once the static cursor is completely populated. Consequently, if you obtain a static cursor and then immediately attempt to move to the last record, there will often be a noticeable delay while ADS awaits the population of the temporary table prior to returning the last record.

SQL statements that cause a static cursor to be fully populated include the use of aggregate functions in your query, such as MIN, MAX, and COUNT, as well as including an ORDER BY clause.

This discussion is not meant to imply that static cursors are not optimized. Indeed, whenever possible, ADS will employ indexes and use other optimization techniques to identify the records that must be copied to the temporary table.

Using Static Cursors

From the standpoint of client applications, there are only two differences between using a live cursor and a static cursor. The first is that a static cursor is readonly. You cannot make changes to the result set created using a static cursor. (The exception is static, client-side cursors in ADO, which are updateable.) By comparison, you can insert, delete, and update records using a live cursor.

The second difference is that static cursors do not automatically reflect changes that have been posted to the underlying table. Recall that a static cursor actually points to a temporary table on the server. Consequently, if another client inserts a record into a table from which you selected a static cursor, the record is inserted into the destination table but not into the temporary table. If you want to see changes made to the underlying table, you have to reexecute the query, which causes ADS to rebuild the temporary table.

Using Subqueries

A subquery is a SQL SELECT query within another query. As discussed in more detail in Chapter 10, SELECT queries produce a result set of zero or more records. The values returned by the subquery are used to define which records are affected by the operation defined in the query that contains the subquery. For example, a subquery may select all customers who have a perfect record of payment. Those records can then be used to select the employee responsible for the greatest number of sales to that customer.

A subquery can appear in the values section of INSERT queries, the HAVING clause of SELECT queries, and the WHERE clause of DELETE, SELECT, and UPDATE queries. For example, the following query includes a subquery in the WHERE clause of a SELECT query:

```
SELECT * FROM EMPLOYEE
   WHERE "Employee Number" IN
      (SELECT Contact FROM DEPARTMENTS)
```

This SELECT query selects all fields for those records where the employee number appears in the Contact field of the DEPARTMENTS table. Assuming that the Contacts integer field contains the employee number of the department head, this query will select all employees who are department heads.

Here is a SQL script that employs a subquery, which assumes that an INV_BAK table (an archive table) exists:

```
INSERT INTO INV_BAK
   SELECT * FROM INVOICE
     WHERE "Date Payment Received" < CURDATE() - 365;
DELETE FROM INVOICE
   WHERE "Date Payment Received" < CURDATE() - 365
```

The first SQL statement in this script is an INSERT query that inserts records into the INV_BAK table from the INVOICE table where the payment was received more than one year ago. The second query then removes these records from the active INVOICE table.

In both of the subquery examples presented here, the subquery is one that can be optimized. Furthermore, because these subqueries do not include references to fields outside the table they are selecting from, ADS is able to execute the subquery once, and reuse that result for all operations performed by the query containing it.

Since subqueries can contain any valid statements that can appear in a SELECT statement, it is possible to include links to fields outside of the table the subquery is selecting from. These subqueries are referred to as *correlated subqueries*, and unless you have small tables that you are querying, they should probably be avoided for performance reasons. Consider the following query:

```
SELECT * FROM EMPLOYEE Emp WHERE "Employee Number" IN
   (SELECT "Employee ID" FROM INVOICE Inv
     WHERE Emp."Employee Number" = Inv."Employee ID"
     AND "Date Payment Received" IS NULL)
```

This query selects all fields from each employee record where that employee made a sale and the customer's payment was never entered. In this case, the WHERE clause in the subquery includes a Boolean comparison with a value from the outer query. Unlike the previous queries, this one requires the subquery to be executed repeatedly, once for each employee in the EMPLOYEE table. If the EMPLOYEE table has few records, this query will execute quickly. However, if the EMPLOYEE table is very large, this query could take a substantial amount of time to execute.

This discussion is not meant to dissuade you from using subqueries. Quite the opposite; subqueries are exceptionally powerful. However, if performance is an important element of your database design, you should consider what you are asking ADS to do in your subqueries, and balance the power of these queries with your performance requirements.

Advantage SQL Utilities

The Advantage Data Architect includes a number of useful and interesting utilities that you can use to build and test SQL statements. These include the Advantage Query Builder, the Native SQL Utility, and the ODBC SQL Utility. Each of these utilities is discussed in the following sections.

Advantage Query Builder

The Advantage Query Builder is a handy little utility for creating basic SQL SELECT statements. It provides a graphical user interface (GUI) that permits you to select fields and join tables visually. You can use this visual depiction to generate a SQL SELECT statement, which you can then test.

The following steps demonstrate how to use the Advantage Query Builder:

1. Select Tools | Advantage Query Builder from the Advantage Data Architect main menu. The Select Database dialog box is displayed:

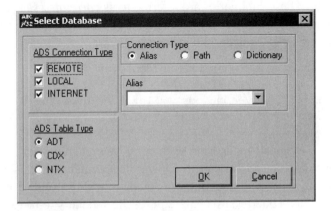

2. Use the Select Database dialog box to select the directory or data dictionary that contains the tables you want to include in your query. Click OK when you are done. If you are opening a data dictionary that requires you to log in, you will also need to enter the user name and password into the displayed dialog box and click OK to continue to the Advantage Query Builder, shown in Figure 9-1.

3. The Advantage Query Builder contains four sections. The table list in the right-hand pane contains all tables and views in your data dictionary. The bottom pane contains the work area where you will refine and display the query, the large section in the middle of the Advantage Query Builder contains the modeling area, and there is a toolbar along the top.

   Begin your query by dragging one or more tables or views into the modeling area. In this case, first drag the CUSTOMER table into the modeling area, and then drag the INVOICE table. Each table appears as a window in the modeling area. Each window contains an asterisk, as well as a row for each field in the table.

4. To select fields, click to the left of the * to select all fields from that table, or click to the left of individual field names to select specific fields. When a field

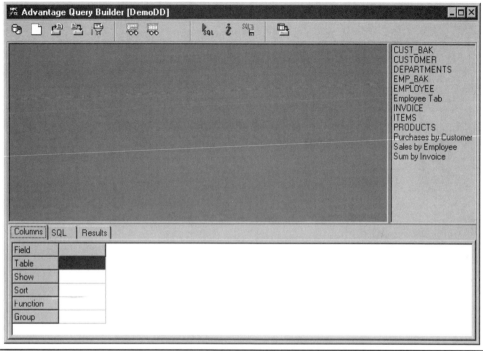

Figure 9-1   *The Advantage Query Builder*

is selected, a checkmark appears to the left of the field, and the field name appears in the Columns tab of the work area. Select the Customer ID, First Name, and Last Name fields from the CUSTOMER table, and the Invoice No, Employee ID, and Invoice Date fields from the INVOICE table.

5. If you have added two or more tables to the work area, you need to join them. To join two tables, drag from the field on which you want to link from one table, and drop it onto the corresponding field in the table to which you want to link. In this case, click the Customer ID field in the CUSTOMER table, and while keeping the mouse button depressed, drag to the Customer ID field of the INVOICE table, and then release the mouse button. A line will connect the two fields in the modeling area, as shown in Figure 9-2.

6. You perform the rest of the configuration, if needed, using the work area. If you want the query to sort by one or more fields, right-click the Sort row for those fields and select either Ascending or Descending, depending on which direction you want to sort by. In this case, right-click the Sort row for the Customer ID column, and select Ascending.

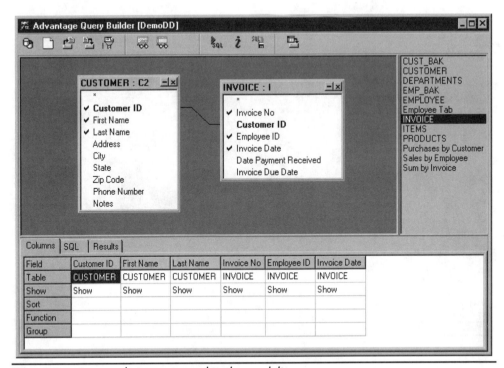

Figure 9-2   *A query being prepared in the modeling area*

7. If you want to calculate an aggregate statistic, right-click the Function row associated with the field you want to aggregate across, and select one of the available functions. If you use an aggregate function, you need to group by the fields across which you want the aggregate calculated. To group on fields, right-click on the Group row for the fields you want to group on, and select Group. In this example, we are not going to use aggregate functions or groups.

8. When you are ready to create your query, click the Generate SQL button in the Advantage Query Builder toolbar. The Advantage Query Builder examines your model, and then displays the generated SQL in the SQL pane of the work area, as shown in Figure 9-3.

9. You can use the generated SQL in the SQL pane as is, or you can make changes to it, if necessary. To test the query that appears in the SQL pane of the work

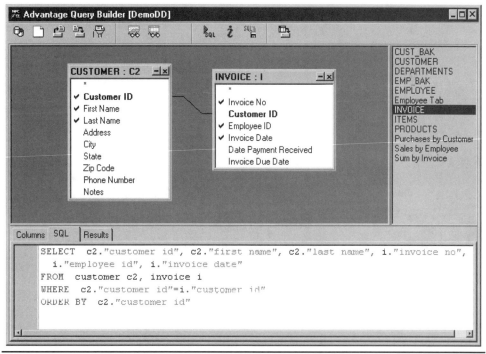

Figure 9-3   *Generated SQL appears in the SQL pane of the work area.*

area, click the Run Current SQL button in the toolbar. The query result will appear in the results pane of the work area, as shown in Figure 9-4.

NOTE

When you link tables, the join produced by the Advantage Query Builder is based on the left-to-right order of the tables in the modeling area.

If your model is a complicated one, and you want to work with it again later, you can click the Save Model button in the toolbar. To open a previously saved model, click the Open Model button in the toolbar.

If you want to save the SQL that appears in the SQL pane of the work area, click the Save SQL button in the toolbar. Alternatively, you can copy the SQL from the SQL pane to the clipboard, and paste it wherever you need it.

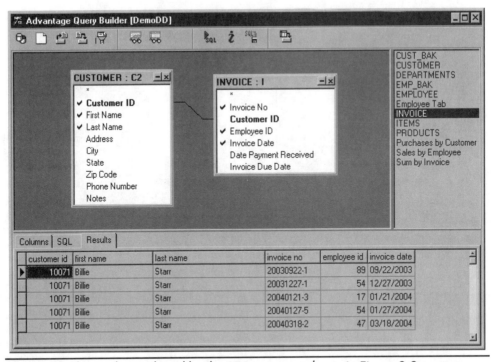

Figure 9-4 *The result set selected by the SQL statement shown in Figure 9-3.*

You can also save the query result to a new table (ADT or DBF) by selecting the Save Results button in the toolbar.

While the Advantage Query Builder is a nice little utility for creating simple SELECT statements, it is a limited tool with a few quirky behaviors. Consequently, in many cases, you will need to modify the SQL that the Advantage Query Builder generates, or build your queries manually instead.

Native SQL Utility

The Native SQL Utility, shown in Figure 9-5, is a valuable tool for testing SQL statements. To display the Native SQL Utility, select Tools | Native SQL Utility from the Advantage Data Architect main menu.

You must connect to a data dictionary or a directory before you can execute a SQL statement. To connect, select the Connection Type of Alias, Path, or Dictionary, and then specify the alias, path, or dictionary you want to connect to. Then click the Connect button. If you are connecting to a dictionary that requires login, you will also be prompted to enter your user name and password.

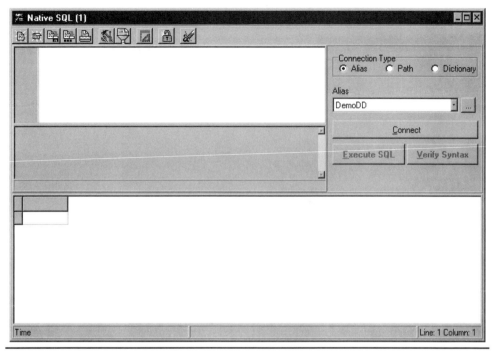

Figure 9-5   *The Native SQL Utility*

If you want to control exactly how you connect, click the Query Options dialog box in the Native SQL Utility toolbar to display the Options dialog box shown in Figure 9-6. Click OK after changing any settings in the Query Options dialog box.

> ### TIP
>
> *Use the Options dialog box prior to connecting to your database. If you use the Options dialog box to modify the settings used for a connection, but you are already connected to a database or a directory, disconnect and then reconnect to use the new settings.*

You use the Native SQL Utility by entering one or more SQL statements into the SQL pane, and then click the Execute SQL button. You can also control which statement or multiple statements to execute by highlighting it first before clicking Execute SQL. If your SQL statement or statements produce a result set, the returned records are shown in the results pane. In response to each SQL statement you execute, information about the query is displayed in the message area, which is located between the SQL editor and the results pane. Also, the length of time that ADS required to execute the query appears in the status bar, as shown in Figure 9-7.

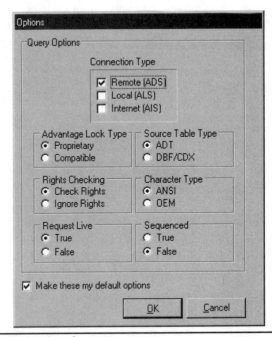

Figure 9-6   *Options dialog box for SQL queries*

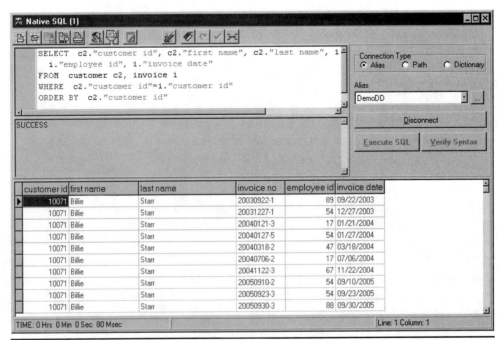

Figure 9-7   *The results of a query displayed in the results pane*

If a SQL query takes more than two seconds to complete, a progress bar showing the progress of the query execution is displayed. Click Cancel SQL if you want to cancel the execution of a query in progress. This is useful for queries that are taking a long time to execute and either you do not want to wait for it to finish execution, or you suspect that something is wrong with the query even though it is syntactically correct. You can check the syntax of your SQL statements before you execute them by clicking Verify Syntax.

The toolbar buttons in the Native SQL Utility provide a number of additional features. Open Script allows you to load text files containing SQL or to load previously saved SQL files into the SQL pane for testing. Close Script closes the current SQL file if one has been opened in the SQL pane. Save Current Script to File (CTRL-S) and Save Script As permit you to save the current SQL into a file (with a .sql extension). Click Print SQL Statements to print the statements in the SQL pane. Clear All SQL Statements clears the contents of the SQL pane.

Query Options displays the Query Options dialog box described earlier in this section. Editor Options allows you to configure the SQL editor using the Editor Options dialog box. Query Builder displays the Advantage Query Builder described earlier. Use the Table Passwords option to enter passwords for any encrypted free tables that are involved in your SQL statements.

Once you remotely connect to ADS from within the Native SQL Utility, the following toolbar buttons are displayed: Begin Transaction, Abort Transaction, and Commit Transaction allow you to run SQL queries within a transaction for a user account connected to ADS remotely. Finally, Data Dictionary Links displays the Active Links dialog box, which allows you to view active data dictionary links and to define data dictionary links, permitting you to execute queries involving multiple data dictionaries.

ODBC SQL Utility

The ODBC SQL Utility is a tool for testing queries using the Advantage ODBC driver. To display the ODBC SQL Utility, select Tools | ODBC SQL Utility from the Advantage Data Architect main menu. The ODBC SQL Utility is shown in Figure 9-8.

Before you can test SQL statements using the ODBC SQL Utility, you must connect to a data dictionary or a directory using the Advantage ODBC driver. If you are connecting to a data dictionary, make sure to check the Login Prompt checkbox. Once you click Connect, the ODBC SQL Utility will prompt you for a valid user name and password for the data dictionary.

Like with the Native SQL Utility, you can then enter SQL statements in the SQL pane, and then test them by clicking the Execute SQL button. Messages concerning

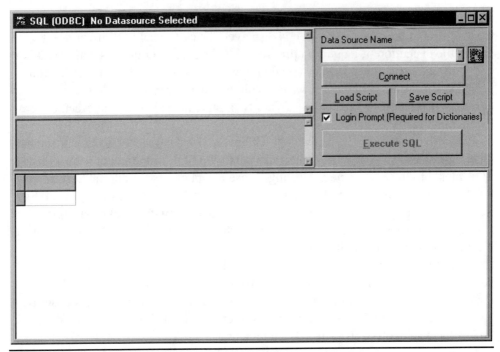

Figure 9-8 *The ODBC SQL Utility*

the SQL statement are displayed in the message area, which is located between the SQL pane and the results area, as shown in Figure 9-9.

Most developers prefer to use the Native SQL Utility over the ODBC SQL Utility. The Native SQL Utility provides more options than does the ODBC SQL Utility, and it also tells you how long ADS took to execute the query. The Native SQL Utility uses the ACE API to execute your queries, which is installed automatically when you install the Advantage Data Architect. With the ODBC SQL Utility, you must install the Advantage ODBC driver and configure a data source name before you can use the utility.

In the next chapter, you will learn how to use many of the more common SQL statements.

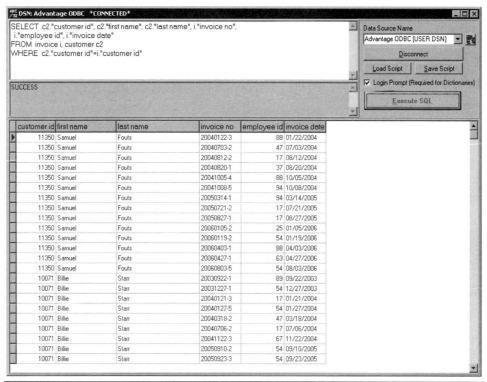

Figure 9-9   *A query has been executed from the ODBC SQL Utility.*

Using SQL to Perform Common Database Operations

IN THIS CHAPTER:

Creating and Modifying Objects

Selecting Data

Changing Data

Using Transactions

A s pointed out in the preceding chapter, SQL is the common denominator among all of the Advantage data access mechanisms. No matter how you connect to the Advantage Database Server (ADS), you can access your data and data dictionaries using the structured query language.

This chapter is designed to provide you with a large collection of examples of Advantage SQL statements. In selecting the examples presented here, we are driven by two concerns. First, we have chosen SQL statements that we feel are essential for common database-related tasks. Second, we want to provide you with a wide variety of examples that convey the breadth and power of Advantage SQL, given the limited space of a single chapter.

What we do not attempt to do with this chapter is provide the detailed syntax of the SQL statements that we cover. If we tried to do that, this chapter would be one big syntax statement. For a detailed description of the syntax of Advantage SQL, see the Advantage help.

The topics discussed in this chapter are primarily focused on tables, indexes, and data. Specifically, we do not discuss the larger issue of creating and managing data dictionaries, users, and groups within this chapter. Those topics are covered in Chapter 11, where you will also learn how to access and use metadata in your applications.

If you are already a seasoned SQL programmer, you can scan this chapter for anything that looks new or interesting. If you are new to SQL programming, we recommend that you try using each of these statements against the sample database included on this book's CD-ROM using the Native SQL Utility (discussed in Chapter 9).

However, before you begin working with these queries, we suggest that you make a duplicate of the data tables and your data dictionary, and use the Alias Configuration Utility to provide an alternative alias for this copy (see the ADS help for specific information on using the Alias Configuration Utility). You can then use this copy of the data dictionary and the tables without worrying about accidentally deleting or modifying data. Then, you can be creative with the copy of the database, modifying the presented queries to better understand what options you have when writing your own SQL. We are assuming that you are connecting to ADS remotely using the administrator account (ADSSYS).

ON THE CD

If you'd rather not manually type in the queries in this chapter, you can find all of them listed in this chapter in the file named ch10queries.sql on this book's CD-ROM. Each of the queries in this file has been commented out. To use a query in this file, copy the query text to the clipboard and insert it into in the Native SQL Utility or a querying tool of your choice, and then remove the comments before executing the query. Alternatively, open the ch10queries.sql file in the in the Native SQL Utility, remove comments for the desired query, and then execute it.

Creating and Modifying Objects

Which came first, the table or the data? The data, of course, which is why you need the table in the first place. But seriously, you can't have a database without one or more tables. Furthermore, tables are not much use if you do not have indexes for them. After that, views, stored procedures, triggers, and the like prove quite valuable.

This section covers three essential SQL statements: CREATE, ALTER, and DROP. You use CREATE to create tables and data dictionary objects, ALTER to modify the structure of an existing table, and DROP to destroy objects. Each of these statements is covered in the following sections.

Creating Tables and Indexes

You use the CREATE statement to create data dictionaries, tables, indexes, and views, and to register AEPs (Advantage Extended Procedures) and triggers. Creating tables and indexes is covered in the following sections.

Creating Tables

You create a table using the CREATE TABLE SQL statement. If your ADS connection is for a data dictionary, you must connect using the data dictionary administrator's user name (ADSSYS) and password. The created table will be bound to the data dictionary. If you are connected using a user account, or are not connected to a data dictionary, CREATE TABLE creates a free table.

When calling CREATE TABLE, you must supply a name for the table as well as the name and type of each field in the table, at a minimum. For example, the following statement creates a table named DEMO1 with four fields:

```
CREATE TABLE DEMO1 (
  "Full Name" CHAR(30),
  "Date of Birth" DATE,
  "Credit Limit" MONEY,
  Active LOGICAL)
```

The names that you use in SQL for the valid field types for ADT tables are shown in Table 10-1. For the valid field types for DBF tables, refer to the ADS help.

AUTOINC	BLOB	CHAR	CURDOUBLE	DATE
DOUBLE	INTEGER	LOGICAL	MEMO	MONEY
RAW	SHORT	TIME	TIMESTAMP	

Table 10-1   *Valid Field Types for ADT Tables*

Almost all tables will have at least one index, which is typically a unique, primary index. There are two ways to define a primary index. If the index is based on a single field, you can include the keywords PRIMARY KEY following the field type.

Alternatively, you can follow the field list with the keywords PRIMARY KEY followed by a list of one or more fields that will constitute the index key expression. If you want the index to sort in descending order, include the DESC keyword after each descending field.

The following CREATE TABLE statement creates a table named DEMO2 that includes a primary index named PrimeIdx:

```
CREATE TABLE DEMO2 (
  CustID INTEGER CONSTRAINT PrimeIdx PRIMARY KEY,
  [Full Name] CHAR(25),
  Date DATE)
```

The following statement performs the exact same task:

```
CREATE TABLE DEMO2 (
  CustID INTEGER,
  [Full Name] CHAR(25),
  Date DATE,
  CONSTRAINT PrimeIdx PRIMARY KEY (CustID))
```

In both of these statements, the CONSTRAINT PrimeIdx can be omitted, in which case ADS will assign the name PK_INDEX to the primary key index.

NOTE

You cannot define a primary key index for DBF tables.

You can also define field-level constraints when creating a table. This is demonstrated in the following CREATE TABLE statement:

```
CREATE TABLE DEMO3 (
  "Customer ID" INTEGER PRIMARY KEY,
  "Credit Limit" MONEY
    DEFAULT '0'
      CONSTRAINT MINIMUM '0'
      CONSTRAINT MAXIMUM '100000'
      CONSTRAINT NOT NULL
      CONSTRAINT ERROR MESSAGE 'Invalid credit limit',
  "Date Last Accessed" DATE)
```

NOTE

If you create a new table through the data dictionary administrator's account, and you have rights checking enabled for the data dictionary, you must specifically grant table access rights to the users and groups who need to work with it. Granting rights using SQL is discussed in Chapter 11.

TIP

Rather than writing a CREATE TABLE statement, you can use the Advantage Data Architect to create a table, after which you can select Tools | Export Table Structures as Code. Use the displayed dialog box to generate the CREATE TABLE SQL statement.

Using the SELECT statement, you can both create a table and populate it with data from an existing table. To do this, follow the SELECT list with the name of the table into which you want to place the selected records. For example, the following statement will create a new table based on the EMPLOYEE table. The resulting table has two fields, First Name and Last Name. This statement creates a free table and its files are written to the same path as the data dictionary in which the EMPLOYEE table is bound.

```
SELECT "First Name", "Last Name" INTO DEMO4 FROM EMPLOYEE
```

Creating Indexes

You create an index for a table using the CREATE INDEX SQL statement. If you are creating an index for a table in a data dictionary, you must be connected to the data dictionary using the administrative account (otherwise, the index will be temporary).

The following SQL script creates a new table, and then uses two CREATE INDEX statements to create indexes for it:

```
CREATE TABLE DEMO5 (
  CustID INTEGER,
  "Full Name" CHAR(30),
  Address CHAR(100),
  City CHAR(25),
  Phone CHAR(14),
  Notes MEMO);
CREATE UNIQUE INDEX UniqueIdx ON DEMO5 (CustID);
CREATE INDEX AddrIdx ON DEMO5 (Address, City);
```

Neither of these CREATE INDEX statements specifies an index file name. As a result, these index orders are created in the structural index file. If you want, you can create a new index file, in which case you can specify the filename and page size. This is shown in the following example:

```
CREATE INDEX NewIdx ON DEMO5 ("Full Name")
  IN FILE "newfile" PAGESIZE 1024
```

> **NOTE**
>
> *Page size can only be defined when creating the first index order in a given index file, and only applies to an ADI index file.*

You can also create FTS (full text search) indexes with CREATE INDEX. When creating an FTS index, you use the CONTENT keyword followed by one or more of the following keywords to define how the index is created and maintained: MIN WORD, MAX WORD, DELIMITERS, DROPCHARS, NOISE, CONDITIONALS, NOTMAINTAINED, CASESENSITIVE, KEEPSCORE, and PROTECTNUMBERS. The DELIMITERS, DROPCHARS, NOISE, and CONDITIONALS keywords can be preceded by the keyword NEW to define new values. When you omit the word NEW, the values are added to the default values for those parameters. (See Chapter 3 for a complete discussion of FTS indexes and their parameters.)

The following is an example of an FTS index on the Notes field of the DEMO5 table:

```
CREATE INDEX NotesIdx ON DEMO5 (Notes)
  CONTENT
  MIN WORD 3
  MAX WORD 15
  DELIMITERS ';:'
  KEEPSCORE
  CASESENSITIVE
```

Altering Tables

The ALTER TABLE statement can be used to change an existing table's definition. It permits you to add and remove fields from the table's structure, add or remove a primary index, and change field names and data types, as well as add, change, or drop field-level constraints.

If your table is bound to a data dictionary, you can only alter a table if you are connected using the data dictionary administrator's user name and password. In any case, you must also be able to obtain an exclusive lock on the table in order to alter it. The following is an example of an ALTER TABLE statement:

```
ALTER TABLE DEMO5
  ADD COLUMN State CHAR(40)
  ADD COLUMN Country CHAR(35)
  ALTER COLUMN Address Address CHAR(80)
  DROP COLUMN Phone
  ALTER COLUMN "Full Name" "Full Name" CHAR(30)
    CONSTRAINT NOT NULL
```

Advantage SQL does not support ALTER statements for indexes, views, stored procedures, or triggers. If you want to change one of these objects, you must use DROP to delete the object and then call CREATE to create a new version. Database properties can be modified using special stored procedures. These stored procedures are discussed in Chapter 11.

Dropping Objects

You use SQL DROP statements to destroy tables and objects within your data dictionary. DROP can be used with the following keywords: INDEX, PROCEDURE, TABLE, TRIGGER, and VIEW. For stored procedures, triggers, and views, as well as tables and index orders associated with a data dictionary, you must execute DROP using the data dictionary administrative connection.

To drop an index order, use dot notation to specify the table name and the index order name. For example, the following statement deletes the index named AddrIdx from the DEMO5 table:

```
DROP INDEX DEMO5.AddrIdx
```

The following example demonstrates how to destroy the DEMO5 table:

```
DROP TABLE DEMO5
```

DROP TABLE removes the specified table from the data dictionary (if it was bound to one) and deletes the files associated with the table. Dropping stored procedures, triggers, and views uses the same syntax as dropping a table. Simply provide the name of the object that you are dropping.

Selecting Data

The richest statement in SQL is the SELECT statement, and it is used to retrieve data from ADS to the client application. This section begins with a look at simple selections involving fields and expressions. Later, you will learn how to select specific records, as well as how to sort, group, and link data from two or more tables.

Selecting and Expressions

This section demonstrates how you populate one or more columns and zero or more rows of a result set using the SELECT statement.

Selecting Fields

In its simplest form, SELECT is used to unconditionally retrieve one or more fields from a table. For example, the following statement selects the First Name field from the EMPLOYEE table:

```
SELECT "First Name" FROM EMPLOYEE
```

If you have two or more fields to select from, you enter a comma-separated list of fields you want to select. For example, this query returns the First Name and Last Name fields:

```
SELECT "First Name", "Last Name" FROM EMPLOYEE
```

If you want to select all fields, you use the * (asterisk) character, like this:

```
SELECT * FROM EMPLOYEE
```

Selecting Using Expressions

You are not limited to simple field selection in the SELECT list. You can include expressions that make use of one or more of the following: field references, literals, SQL scalar functions, and operators. For example, the following query returns the concatenation of the First Name and Last Name fields:

```
SELECT "First Name" + ' ' + "Last Name" FROM EMPLOYEE
```

If you execute this query, you will notice something interesting, as shown in Figure 10-1. There is a large space between the first-name and last-name values, even though the query concatenates these values with a single space. This is because the First Name and Last Name fields include trailing blank spaces. To produce a more

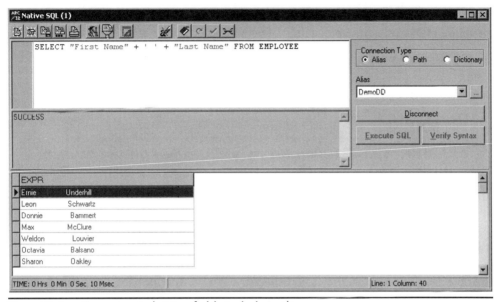

Figure 10-1   *Concatenated string fields include trailing spaces.*

normal looking full name, you need to trim these trailing values using the RTRIM function, as shown in the following query:

```
SELECT RTRIM("First Name") + ' ' + RTRIM("Last Name")
  FROM EMPLOYEE
```

Actually, your SELECT list doesn't need to include any field names at all. For example, the following query returns the value 1 for each record in the CUSTOMER table:

```
SELECT 1 FROM CUSTOMER
```

Normally, the result set returned from a SELECT query will use the names of the selected columns, or a temporary name, such as EXPR, EXPR_1, EXPR_2, and so forth, for the columns that are returned. Alternatively, you can provide specific names for the columns by following the expression with the AS keyword, followed by a column name. Just as you do with field names, if the new column name begins with a number or contains special characters, you must enclose it in either double-quotation marks or square brace delimiters, as shown here:

```
SELECT RTRIM("First Name") + ' ' + RTRIM("Last Name")
  AS "Full Name"
  FROM EMPLOYEE
```

NOTE

The use of expressions or scalar functions in the SELECT list always produces a static cursor.

Using CASE Statements

There is a special control structure, called CASE, that you can use to create conditional expressions in the SELECT clause. The CASE statement can evaluate two or more expressions, and always results in a single expression that will return a column in the result table.

There are two forms of the CASE statement. In the simplest form, CASE is followed by an expression that is evaluated by one or more WHEN clauses. Each WHEN clause compares a value to the CASE expression, and includes an expression following the THEN keyword that the CASE clause will evaluate to if the comparison returns a Boolean True.

If none of the WHEN clauses evaluate to True, you can include an optional ELSE clause, which returns the expression of the CASE clause. The CASE clause evaluates to the expression defined by the first WHEN clause that evaluates to True, or the value of the ELSE clause, if provided, when none of the WHEN clauses evaluate to True.

The following query demonstrates this form of the CASE statement. This example also shows connecting to a table bound to another data dictionary from within the current data dictionary, a topic described in Chapter 6, since SQL provides the only way to access tables from two or more data dictionaries with one connection:

```
SELECT "Customer ID", "First Name", "Last Name",
   CASE Active
     WHEN True THEN 'Account is active'
     WHEN False THEN 'Account is closed'
     ELSE 'Account status unknown' //if NULL
   END
  FROM Shared.CUST
```

This query produces the following result set:

Customer ID	First Name	Last Name	EXPR
12688	Frank	Jones	Account is active
18744	Peter	van Clive	Account is closed
15198	Juanita	Zapata	Account is active
22799	Jamie	Lutz	Account is active

The second form of the CASE statement permits you to evaluate two or more different expressions. In this form, the CASE statement is not followed by an expression. Instead, it is followed by one or more WHEN clauses, each of which evaluates an expression and includes the expression that the CASE statement will return if that WHEN clause evaluates to True.

Like the first form of CASE, there is also an optional ELSE clause, which includes the expression that the CASE statement will evaluate to if none of the WHEN clauses evaluate to True. The CASE statement evaluates to the expression associated with the first WHEN clause to evaluate to True; otherwise, it evaluates to the ELSE clause expression, if provided. The following is an example of this form of the CASE statement. As you can see, each of the WHEN clauses evaluates a different expression:

```
SELECT "Invoice No", "Customer ID", "Invoice Date",
  "Date Payment Received", "Invoice Due Date",
    CASE
      WHEN "Invoice Due Date" <= CURDATE()
        AND "Date Payment Received" IS NULL
        THEN 'Waiting for payment'
      WHEN "Invoice Due Date" > CURDATE()
        AND "Date Payment Received" IS NULL
        THEN 'Invoice is overdue'
      WHEN "Date Payment Received" > "Invoice Due Date"
        AND "Date Payment Received" IS NOT NULL
        THEN 'Invoice was paid late'
      ELSE 'Invoice was paid on time'
    END AS "Invoice Payment Status"
  FROM INVOICE
```

Using ROWID

You can also use the special ROWID identifier to retrieve the internal record identifier in a query. Unlike any other field in a table, the ROWID of a particular record never changes, making it the most reliable means by which you can access the same record repeatedly.

```
SELECT ROWID, "First Name", "Last Name" FROM CUSTOMER
```

Querying Free Tables and Other Dictionary Tables

In the FROM list of the preceding queries, the name of a table in the current data dictionary is listed. It is also possible to include both free tables as well as tables that are bound to another data dictionary in your SELECT statements.

If your free table is in the same directory as your data dictionary, simply include the table name as though it were bound to the data dictionary. So long as the CUST.ADT table that you created in Chapter 2 is still in the same directory as the DemoDictionary data dictionary, the following query should select all fields and all records from it:

```
SELECT * FROM CUST
```

If the free table is not in the same directory as the data dictionary, you can include a path (either a relative or a fully qualified path) to the table. For fully qualified paths, you are strongly encouraged to use UNC (universal naming convention) names. For example, if the CUST.ADT table is on the DATASERV computer in the directory named AppData in the C$ share, your SELECT statement might look something like the following:

```
SELECT * FROM "\\DATASERV\C$\AppData\cust.adt"
```

If the table you want to query is bound to another data dictionary, you have two alternative techniques that you can use to access that table. So long as the table is accessible in the other data dictionary to a user whose name and password you used to connect to your current data dictionary, you can qualify the table name with the name of the data dictionary, using dot notation. For example, if the CUST table is bound to the Share.ADD data dictionary, and Share.ADD is in the same directory as DemoDictionary, you can use the following statement:

```
SELECT * FROM "Share.ADD".CUST
```

If the Share.ADD data dictionary is not in the same directory, you still use dot notation but you must specify the path, as you did with a free table not in the same directory. For example, if Share.ADD is on the DATASERV computer in the directory named AppData in the C$ share, the following SELECT statement would access the CUST table:

```
SELECT * FROM "\\DATASERV\C$\AppData\Share.ADD".CUST
```

If the data dictionary to which the CUST.ADT table is bound does not include a user name and password that has rights to the CUST.ADT table, you must use the second alternative, which is to use a data dictionary link. For example, imagine that you have a data dictionary link named Shared in your current data dictionary, and this link specifies a user name and password in the data dictionary to which CUST.ADT is bound. You can access the CUST table from your current data dictionary using the link name in dot notation with the table name. This is shown in the following query:

```
SELECT * FROM Shared.CUST
```

If the link name includes special characters, you must enclose it in double quotation marks or square braces.

Data dictionary links are discussed in Chapter 6.

Conditional Selection

The preceding queries select all records, which is fine when your tables are small. However, in many instances, especially when you have a lot of data, you want to restrict your selections to a specific group of records. You use the WHERE clause in a SELECT statement to perform record selection. (The HAVING keyword can also influence record selection, but only when you are working with groups of records. HAVING is discussed later in this chapter.)

You follow the WHERE keyword with a Boolean expression. In most cases, this expression will include one or more field references. For example, the following query selects all fields from the ITEMS table where the Discount field contains the value 15 or higher:

```
SELECT * FROM ITEMS WHERE Discount >= 15
```

WHERE clauses often have many expressions combined using the AND and/or OR operators. For example, the following query selects these same records, but only where the Product Code field contains the value G54039:

```
SELECT * FROM ITEMS
  WHERE Discount >= 15 AND "Product Code" = 'G54039'
```

NOTE

The performance of queries that include WHERE clauses can be dramatically improved by the presence of one or more appropriate indexes. Also, if you use a MEMO or BLOB field in a WHERE clause, the query returns a static cursor.

SQL also supports several keywords that can be used in the WHERE clause. These include BETWEEN, IN, and LIKE. Each of these keywords is described in the following sections.

Using BETWEEN

Use BETWEEN to test whether an expression is within a range of values. If the value is in the range, BETWEEN evaluates to a Boolean True, and False otherwise. For example, the following query selects all invoices between May 7th and June 17th, 2005:

```
SELECT * FROM INVOICE
  WHERE "Invoice Date" BETWEEN '2005-05-07' AND '2005-06-17'
```

You can precede the BETWEEN keyword with the NOT keyword to select records that are not in the range.

Using IN

You use IN to compare an expression to either a list of values or a single-field subquery. (Subqueries are introduced in Chapter 9.) The expression evaluates to True if the expression on the left-hand side of the comparison is in the list or subquery on the right-hand side.

Assuming that employees in the Sales and Marketing and Administration departments can initiate invoices, and that these departments have the corresponding department codes 101 and 108, the following query returns the records for employees that can initiate invoices:

```
SELECT * FROM EMPLOYEE
WHERE "Department Code" IN (101, 108)
```

Although this same result could also be achieved using a series of WHERE clauses with OR operators, using IN is much simpler.

The following query performs the same task as the preceding one, but uses a subquery instead of a list of values:

```
SELECT * FROM EMPLOYEE
WHERE "Department Code" IN
  (SELECT "Department Code" FROM DEPARTMENTS
    WHERE "Department Name" = 'Administration' OR
      "Department Name" = 'Sales and Marketing')
```

Precede the IN keyword with the NOT keyword to return records that are not in the set.

NOTE

The use of a subquery with the IN operator in a WHERE clause always returns a static cursor.

Using LIKE

You use the LIKE operator to compare an expression to a pattern that includes one or more wildcard characters. The % (match any) wildcard character matches zero or more characters, and the _ (match one) wildcard character matches any one character. For example, the following query will return all customer records where the last name begins with the letter *S*:

```
SELECT * FROM CUSTOMER WHERE "Last Name" LIKE 'S%'
```

By comparison, the next query will return all customer records where the last name begins with *S* and is exactly five characters in length (there are four underscore characters following the *S*):

```
SELECT * FROM CUSTOMER WHERE "Last Name" LIKE 'S____'
```

NOTE

The use of trailing wildcard characters permits an appropriate index to be used for searching data, leading to faster queries. If you include a leading wildcard character (such as %s), indexes cannot be used, and ADS must search the physical records of the table. Also, the use of LIKE in a WHERE clause always produces a static cursor.

Sorting Data

Unless you specifically request that the records returned by the SELECT statement are sorted, a query will return records in the natural order of the table. As discussed in Chapter 3, this order is affected by the order in which records are entered, and has nothing to do with the data contained in those records.

To sort the results in a result set, add an ORDER BY clause to your SQL statement. ORDER BY clauses can be constructed in one of two ways. You can specify the ORDER BY columns either by name or by number. For example, the following SELECT statement will return the records of the PRODUCTS table ordered by the Description field:

```
SELECT * FROM PRODUCTS ORDER BY Description
```

If you want to sort by two or more fields, separate the field names with commas. Also, the default order direction is an ascending sort order, from lowest to highest.

You can follow your field name with DESC to sort in descending order, if you like. (You can also use the keyword ASC, but since ascending is the default order, this keyword has no effect.) The following query demonstrates a two-field sort where the Invoice Date field is sorted in descending order:

```
SELECT "Invoice No", "Employee ID",
  "Invoice Date", "Date Payment Received"
  FROM INVOICE
  ORDER BY "Employee ID", "Invoice Date" DESC
```

Actually, the ORDER BY clause can be any valid expression except those that use MEMO or BLOB fields. While the following example is obviously a meaningless sort order, it demonstrates the level of flexibility that you have when selecting which fields or expressions to order by:

```
SELECT "Invoice No", "Customer ID", "Invoice Date"
  FROM INVOICE
  ORDER BY 100 - "Employee ID"
```

Instead of using field names or expressions in the ORDER BY clause, if the fields or expressions that you want to sort by appear in the SELECT list, you can simply supply numerals that refer to the positions of the fields or expressions that you want to sort by. Just as you do when sorting by name, these numerals are separated by commas if you want to sort by more than one column, and can be followed by the DESC or ASC keywords. For example, the following query produces the same result set as did an earlier query in this section:

```
SELECT "Invoice No", "Employee ID",
  "Invoice Date", "Date Payment Received"
  FROM INVOICE
  ORDER BY 2, 3 DESC
```

You can even sort by position when using the * (select all) symbol, as shown here:

```
SELECT * FROM CUSTOMER ORDER BY 3, 2
```

NOTE

The performance of queries that include ORDER BY clauses can be dramatically improved by the presence of one or more appropriate indexes. Also, you cannot use MEMO or BLOB fields in an ORDER BY clause.

Grouping Data

Grouping data is necessary when you want to perform operations across one or more records. There are two primary types of operations that you perform across records. The first involves selecting the unique values, or combination of values, across all records in a table. The second involves calculating simple descriptive statistics.

Selecting Unique Values

You select unique values using the DISTINCT keyword. For example, if you want to know which employees are responsible for one or more sales appearing in the ITEMS table, you follow the SELECT keyword with the DISTINCT keyword, which you then follow with the list of fields or expressions you want unique values for. For example, consider the following query:

```
SELECT DISTINCT "Employee ID" FROM INVOICE
```

This query produces a table that has only one instance of each Employee ID that appears in the table, as shown here:

Employee ID
17
25
37
47
54
63
67
88
89
94

You can use DISTINCT with any combination of fields or expressions, in which case the result set will contain one column for each field or expression, and one record for each unique combination of those field values. For example, the following query selects each unique combination of the Employee ID and Customer ID fields:

```
SELECT DISTINCT "Employee ID", "Customer ID" FROM INVOICE
```

Of course, you can use WHERE clauses like those shown earlier in this chapter to select the distinct data from some subset of records from one or more tables.

NOTE

You cannot use MEMO or BLOB fields in the SELECT list of DISTINCT queries, although you can use them in the WHERE clause. Also, queries that use the DISTINCT keyword always return a static cursor.

Using TOP

The TOP keyword permits you to select some, but not all, of the records associated with the SELECT. You use TOP by immediately following the SELECT keyword by the TOP keyword. TOP is followed by an integer, which will either define the number of records you want returned or the percent of the overall number of records that you want returned. When selecting a percent of the records, follow the integer with the PERCENT keyword.

The following query returns only the first five of the records from the INVOICE table:

```
SELECT TOP 5 * FROM ITEMS
```

This next query returns the top five percent of the records from the ITEMS table:

```
SELECT TOP 5 PERCENT * FROM ITEMS
```

The TOP keyword is often associated with queries that calculate statistics across records (described next). For example, using TOP you can calculate which employees are responsible for the top ten percent of sales, or which five customers are responsible for the most purchases.

Calculating Simple Descriptive Statistics

Another operation that you can perform across records is the calculation of simple statistics. Advantage SQL, like most other SQL languages, supports five descriptive statistics: average (AVG), count (COUNT), maximum (MAX), minimum (MIN), and total (SUM).

Each of these statistical functions takes a single parameter, which can be any field or expression that can appear in the SELECT list. These functions return an expression appropriate for the function. For example, the following query returns a result set that calculates the sum of the Quantity field in the ITEMS table:

```
SELECT SUM(Quantity) FROM ITEMS
```

In this query, the sum of a single field was requested. However, there is no reason why you cannot perform the operation on an expression, as shown in the following query, which calculates the total value of items purchased in the ITEMS table:

```
SELECT SUM(Quantity * Price) FROM ITEMS
```

The COUNT function is slightly different from the other functions in that it can accept either a field or expression, or the * character. When passed the * character as an argument, COUNT calculates the number of records. For example, the following query returns the number of records in the INVOICE table:

```
SELECT COUNT(*) FROM INVOICE
```

NOTE

A query that includes one or more aggregate functions always returns a static cursor.

Using GROUP BY

Instead of calculating the preceding statistics across all records, you might want to calculate the statistic separately for groups of records. For example, rather than calculating the number of records in the invoice table, you might want to calculate the number of invoice records for each employee. In order to do this, you need to group by employee.

Defining groups within a table is performed using the GROUP BY keywords. You follow the GROUP BY keywords with a list of one or more fields or expressions. The statistic is then calculated once for each unique combination of the values within the group. For example, the following query returns the number of invoices associated with each employee:

```
SELECT COUNT(*) FROM INVOICE GROUP BY "Employee ID"
```

There is one problem with this query, however. As you can see from the result set that this query returns, although the statistics were calculated, there is no way to know for which employee each calculation applies:

EXPR
246
256
269
243
316
259
260
274
53
268

In order to display which employee each count is associated with, you need to include the "Employee ID" field in the SELECT list.

Another problem with this query is that the values that are calculated appear using a default name in the result set, which in this case is EXPR. As you learned earlier in this chapter, you can assign a name to a column returned in the result set using the AS keyword. Using AS to assign a meaningful name to calculated columns is especially important when you are calculating both statistics and expressions. The following is an improved version of the preceding query:

```
SELECT COUNT(*) AS "Count of Invoices", "Employee ID"
  FROM INVOICE
  GROUP BY "Employee ID"
```

This query produces the following result set:

Count of Invoices	Employee ID
246	17
256	25
269	37
243	47
316	54
259	63
260	67
274	88
53	89
268	94

When you include fields or expressions in the SELECT list, other than the statistical operator, you must also include those fields and expressions in the GROUP BY list. This requirement is obvious if you consider the following illegal SQL statement:

```
//The following query is illegal, and generates an error
SELECT COUNT(*) AS "Invoice Count", "Employee ID", "Customer ID"
  FROM INVOICE
  GROUP BY "Employee ID"
```

Consider what this query is asking. It is instructing ADS to calculate the number of invoices for each Employee ID, and to include the Customer ID in the result set. The problem is that each employee likely made sales to two or more customers. Since the result set will have only one record for each employee (by virtue of Employee ID being the only field in the GROUP BY clause), there isn't any way to include the one or more Customer IDs. If you want to see the customer that each employee made a sale to, you must also include the Customer ID field in the GROUP BY clause, as shown in the following query:

```
SELECT COUNT(*) AS "Invoice Count", "Employee ID", "Customer ID"
  FROM INVOICE
  GROUP BY "Employee ID", "Customer ID"
```

This query produces the following result set:

Invoice Count	Employee ID	Customer ID
4	17	10071
1	17	10238
1	17	10335
3	17	11350
1	17	12001
1	17	12035
11	17	12037
1	17	12058

Similar to ORDER BY, you can also use the column ordinal numbers instead of column names in the GROUP BY clause:

```
SELECT COUNT(*) AS "Invoice Count", "Employee ID", "Customer ID"
  FROM INVOICE
  GROUP BY 2, 3
```

NOTE

You cannot use MEMO or BLOB fields in the GROUP BY clause, although you can use them in the WHERE clause. Also, queries that include GROUP BY always return a static cursor.

All of the preceding examples calculate the resulting statistic based on all of the records in the table. If you want to calculate the statistic across some, but not all of the records, you have two options. One option is to use a WHERE clause.

As you learned earlier in this chapter, WHERE clauses limit the SELECT operation to those records for which the WHERE Boolean expression evaluates to True. For example, the following query counts the number of invoices entered between January 1st and December 31st, 2004, assuming that your date format is set to mm/dd/ccyy:

```
SELECT COUNT(*) FROM INVOICE
  WHERE "Invoice Date" BETWEEN '1/1/2004' AND '12/31/2004'
```

Using HAVING

Another way to limit which records are considered is to use a HAVING clause. Unlike a WHERE clause, which is used to select records based on values and expressions related to individual records, you use a HAVING clause to base the selection on statistics calculated across records, as defined by the GROUP BY clause. For example, consider the following query:

```
SELECT Count("Invoice No") AS "Count of Invoices", "Employee ID"
  FROM INVOICE
  GROUP BY "Employee ID"
  HAVING COUNT("Invoice No") > 10
```

This query calculates the total number of invoices associated with each employee, but only for those employees responsible for ten or more invoices. Employees with ten or fewer sales are ignored.

NOTE

Queries that employ a HAVING clause always return a static cursor.

Multitable Queries

The queries covered so far in this chapter have all involved a single table. However, in the world of relational databases, your data is typically distributed across two or more related tables. Queries that include two or more tables make use of joins or unions. When data in two or more tables is compared, the query is called a *join*. When data in two or more results sets is combined, the query is called a *union*. The following sections describe joins and unions.

NOTE

Any time you execute a query that contains a join of any type, the result is a static cursor.

Creating Table Joins in the WHERE Clause

The simplest mechanism for defining a join is to define the relationship between two or more fields in two or more tables in the WHERE clause. For example, consider the following query:

```
SELECT Count(INVOICE."Invoice No") AS "Count of Invoices",
  INVOICE."Employee ID",
  RTRIM(EMPLOYEE."First Name") + ' ' + RTRIM(EMPLOYEE."Last Name")
  FROM INVOICE, EMPLOYEE
  WHERE INVOICE."Employee ID" = EMPLOYEE."Employee Number"
  GROUP BY 2, 3
```

This query joins records in the EMPLOYEE table to those in the INVOICE table based on the fields that uniquely identify the employee. Those fields are the Employee ID field in the INVOICE table and the Employee Number field in the EMPLOYEE table. By selecting those records where these fields match in the WHERE clause, we effectively produce a join. The following is the result set produced by this query:

Count of Invoices	Employee ID	EXPR
246	17	Weldon Louvier
256	25	Butch Harbour
269	37	Carey Breedlove
243	47	Letha Varner
316	54	Donnie Bammert
259	63	Shawn Brunton
260	67	Max McClure
274	88	Logan Beauchamp
53	89	Octavia Balsano
268	94	Sharon Oakley

This type of join is called an *inner join*. With an inner join, the result set only includes records for which the same values appear in both tables for those fields involved in the join. With respect to this query, it means that only employees associated with at least one invoice in the INVOICE table, and whose Employee Number appears in the EMPLOYEE table, will be selected to the result set. Any employee whose number does not appear in the INVOICE table will not appear in the result set, nor will employees whose Employee ID appears in the INVOICE table, but whose Employee ID does not appear in the Employee Number field of the EMPLOYEE table.

NOTE

Any time you join data from two or more tables using either the WHERE clause or the JOIN keyword (described next), appropriate indexes can have a dramatic impact on query performance.

Using JOIN

In addition to using a WHERE clause to produce an inner join, you can join data from two or more tables in records of your result using the JOIN keyword. With JOIN, you can create both inner and outer joins.

You create an inner join by preceding the JOIN keyword by the keyword INNER, followed by a table that you want to JOIN, and then listing the field associations following the ON keyword. For example, the following query creates the same inner join as that shown in the preceding query using a WHERE clause:

```
SELECT Count(INVOICE."Invoice No") AS "Count of Invoices",
  INVOICE."Employee ID",
  RTRIM(EMPLOYEE."First Name") + ' ' + RTRIM(EMPLOYEE."Last Name")
  FROM INVOICE
  INNER JOIN EMPLOYEE ON
    INVOICE."Employee ID" = EMPLOYEE."Employee Number"
  GROUP BY INVOICE."Employee ID",
    RTRIM(EMPLOYEE."First Name") + ' ' + RTRIM(EMPLOYEE."Last Name")
```

Because inner joins defined in the WHERE clause tend to be shorter in length, those queries tend to be used more often than those that employ the INNER JOIN keywords. By comparison, outer joins cannot be accomplished using the WHERE clause. Instead, you use the OUTER JOIN keywords.

When you define an outer join, all records from the left-side table of the ON clause are included in the result set, even if no corresponding records appear in the table listed on the right side of the ON clause. Consider the following query:

```
SELECT Count(INVOICE."Invoice No") AS "Count of Invoices",
   EMPLOYEE."Employee Number",
   RTRIM(EMPLOYEE."First Name") + ' ' + RTRIM(EMPLOYEE."Last Name")
   FROM EMPLOYEE
   LEFT OUTER JOIN
      INVOICE ON INVOICE."Employee ID" = EMPLOYEE."Employee Number"
   GROUP BY EMPLOYEE."Employee Number",
      RTRIM(EMPLOYEE."First Name") + ' ' + RTRIM(EMPLOYEE."Last Name")
```

This query counts the number of invoices found in the INVOICE table for all employees, not just those employees whose employee numbers appear in the INVOICE table. A count of 0 is returned for those employees listed in the EMPLOYEE table for whom no corresponding records appear in the INVOICE table, as seen in the following result set:

Count of Invoices	Employee Number	EXPR
246	17	Weldon Louvier
0	23	Ernie Underhill
256	25	Butch Harbour
0	30	Elisabeth Owens
269	37	Carey Breedlove
0	43	Leon Schwartz
243	47	Letha Varner
316	54	Donnie Bammert
259	63	Shawn Brunton
0	65	Neal Adams

Using UNION

You use UNION to combine records from two result sets with a similar structure (same number of fields and similar data types at the corresponding fields) into one result set. Each result set is produced by a SELECT statement that may be from one or more tables. When using UNION, only distinct records are retrieved to the result set. If you use UNION ALL, duplicate records are not suppressed. Consider the following query:

```
SELECT "Employee ID",
  'Has Sales' AS "Sales Status"
  FROM INVOICE
  UNION SELECT "Employee Number",
      'No Sales' AS "Sales Status"
    FROM EMPLOYEE
    WHERE "Employee Number" NOT IN
      (SELECT "Employee ID" FROM INVOICE)
```

This query will return the employee identification number from both the INVOICE and the EMPLOYEE tables. Those employees associated with at least one invoice in the INVOICE table will have the string "Has Sales" associated with their records in the result set, while those without corresponding entries in the INVOICE table will display the string "No Sales." The following is the result set returned by this query:

Employee ID	Sales Status
17	Has Sales
23	No Sales
25	Has Sales
30	No Sales
37	Has Sales
43	No Sales
47	Has Sales
54	Has Sales
63	Has Sales
65	No Sales

NOTE

You cannot use MEMO or BLOB fields in queries that use the UNION keyword, except in the case of UNION ALL.

Full Text Search Queries

Full text search (FTS) was added to ADS in version 7.0. With this capability, you can search string and BLOB (binary large object) fields for specific strings and patterns.

Queries that perform full text searches make use of either the CONTAINS scalar function, the SCORE or SCOREDISTINCT scalar functions, or both.

Using CONTAINS

You use the CONTAINS scalar function in the WHERE clause of your query. CONTAINS is passed two parameters, and evaluates to a Boolean expression.

CONTAINS returns True for each record where the search criteria is found in the index or fields being searched, and False otherwise.

The first parameter of CONTAINS is either the name of a field or * (asterisk). If you pass the name of the field in the first parameter, only the named field will be searched. Depending on the size of the table, this search can be significantly improved if the field already has an FTS index. If you pass * in the first parameter, CONTAINS will search all of the available FTS indexes for the table being queried for the search criteria.

The second parameter is a string containing the search criteria. The search criteria can include one or more strings, and can include the AND, OR, NOT, and NEAR operators. For example, the following query selects all records for which the Notes FTS index contains the word "birthday":

```
SELECT * FROM CUSTOMER
   WHERE CONTAINS(Notes, 'birthday')
```

> **NOTE**
>
> *These queries assume that you created an FTS index on the Notes field in the CUSTOMER table, as described in Chapter 3.*

The following query returns all records where any of the FTS indexes (though there is only one FTS index on the CUSTOMER table) contain either the word "birthday" or the word "card":

```
SELECT * FROM CUSTOMER
   WHERE CONTAINS(Notes, 'birthday OR card')
```

The next example returns all records from the CUSTOMER table where the Notes index contains the words "birthday" and "card," but only if they are located in close proximity to one another using the NEAR*(x)* operator where *x* specifies the number of words. If you do not include *(x)*, the default for NEAR is eight words.

```
SELECT * FROM CUSTOMER
   WHERE CONTAINS(Notes, 'birthday NEAR card')
```

Using SCORE and SCOREDISTINCT

You use the SCORE and SCOREDISTINCT integer functions in the SELECT list, WHERE clause, or ORDER BY clause of a query. These functions return the number of matches to the search criteria located during the search.

There are two syntax options for both SCORE and SCOREDISTINCT functions. The first option accepts the same parameters as does the CONTAINS scalar function. SCORE will return the total number of matches to the values specified in the search criteria, and SCOREDISTINCT returns the number of unique matches.

For example, consider the following query:

```
SELECT RTRIM("First Name") + ' ' + RTRIM("Last Name")
   AS "Full Name",
  SCORE(Notes, 'birthday OR card') AS "Count"
FROM CUSTOMER
WHERE CONTAINS(Notes, 'birthday OR card')
```

This query will return the customer name as well as the total number of instances of either birthday or card in the Notes field. By comparison, the following query, which uses the SCOREDISTINCT function, will return a count of either 1 or 2. When you use SCOREDISTINCT, multiple instances of either birthday or card will be counted only once.

```
SELECT RTRIM("First Name") + ' ' + RTRIM("Last Name")
   AS "Full Name",
  SCOREDISTINCT(Notes, 'birthday OR card') AS "Count"
FROM CUSTOMER
WHERE CONTAINS(Notes, 'birthday OR card')
```

Instead of passing the same parameters to SCORE and SCOREDISTINCT as you would to CONTAINS, you can pass a single integer parameter. When you pass an integer, that integer refers to one of the CONTAINS functions in the same query. If you pass 1, SCORE or SCOREDISTINCT will use the parameters of the first CONTAINS function call, while passing 2 means that there are at least two CONTAINS function calls, and SCORE or SCOREDISTINCT should use the arguments of the second instance.

For example, the following query returns the same result set at the preceding one:

```
SELECT RTRIM("First Name") + ' ' + RTRIM("Last Name")
   AS "Full Name",
  SCOREDISTINCT(1) AS "Count"
FROM CUSTOMER
WHERE CONTAINS(Notes, 'birthday OR card')
```

Changing Data

There are three primary statements that you use to change data in existing tables. These are INSERT, UPDATE, and DELETE. Unlike the SELECT statement demonstrated in the preceding section, these statements do not return a result set.

INSERT, UPDATE, and DELETE are discussed in the following sections.

Inserting Records

You insert data into a table using the INSERT SQL statement. At a minimum, you must specify which table data is being inserted into, as well as the values to insert into fields of the table, in order of the table's structure. For example, consider the following SQL script:

```
CREATE TABLE TEMP1 (
  "Full Name" CHAR(30),
  "Number of Visits" SHORT,
  "Credit Limit" MONEY,
  Active LOGICAL);
INSERT INTO TEMP1 VALUES ('Bob Smith', 1, 1000, True);
```

The first statement creates a table named TEMP1. The INSERT statement then inserts a single record into this table.

Using this syntax, you must supply a value for each field in the table. If you want to leave a particular field blank, use the NULL keyword. To insert default values into fields (when default values are defined for those fields in the data dictionary), use the DEFAULT keyword. This is shown in the following statements:

```
INSERT INTO TEMP1 VALUES ('Julie Jones', NULL, NULL, NULL);
INSERT INTO TEMP1 VALUES ('Lee Singh', DEFAULT, DEFAULT, DEFAULT);
```

If you want to insert data into only specific fields, you can follow the table name with a comma-separated list of the fields into which you want to insert data. This list of field names must be enclosed in parentheses. For example, the following query inserts data into the Full Name and Active fields:

```
INSERT INTO TEMP1 ("Full Name", Active)
  VALUES ('Jose Luiz', True)
```

If the data you want to insert can be found in another table, you can replace the VALUES list with a subquery. For example, the following query inserts data from the EMPLOYEE table into TEMP1:

```
INSERT INTO TEMP1 ("Full Name", Active)
  SELECT RTRIM("First Name") + ' ' + RTRIM("Last Name"), True
    FROM EMPLOYEE
      WHERE EMPLOYEE."Department Code" = 108
```

If the fields in the SELECT list match the type, order, and number of fields in the structure of the table you are inserting into, you omit the list of fields being inserted into. This is demonstrated in the following query:

```
INSERT INTO TEMP1
  SELECT RTRIM("First Name") + ' ' + RTRIM("Last Name"),
    1, 1000, True
    FROM EMPLOYEE
      WHERE EMPLOYEE."Department Code" = 104
```

> **NOTE**
>
> *You can both create and insert records in a single SELECT statement, as discussed earlier in this chapter in the section "Creating Tables."*

Updating Records

You update records in a table using the UPDATE statement. When you use UPDATE, you must specify the name of the table whose records are being updated, as well as which fields you want to update. For example, the following query updates TEMP1, setting the credit limit field to 500 for all records:

```
UPDATE TEMP1 SET "Credit Limit" = 500
```

The preceding statement updates all records in the table. In most cases, however, you will want to update only specific records. To specify which records to update, use a WHERE clause. For example, the following statement sets the Active field to False for those records where the Active field has not been assigned a value:

```
UPDATE TEMP1 SET Active = False
  WHERE Active IS NULL
```

Here is another example:

```
UPDATE TEMP1 SET "Credit Limit" = 0
  WHERE Active = False
```

The UPDATE statement also supports a FROM clause. You use FROM if you are using fields and expressions involving another table to perform the update. For example, the following UPDATE statement changes the Credit Limit field to 10000 for all records in TEMP1 where the full name is associated with an employee record, and that employee's department code is 108:

```
UPDATE TEMP1 SET TEMP1."Credit Limit" = 10000
  FROM EMPLOYEE Emp INNER JOIN TEMP1 ON
    TEMP1."Full Name" =
      RTRIM(Emp."First Name") + ' ' + RTRIM(Emp."Last Name")
  WHERE Emp."Department Code" = 108
```

Deleting Records

You delete records from a table using the DELETE statement. With DELETE, you use the optional WHERE clause to define which records to delete. If you omit the WHERE clause, all records are deleted from the table.

For example, the following query will remove all records from the TEMP1 table where the Active field contains the value False:

```
DELETE FROM TEMP1
  WHERE Active = False
```

You can use a subquery to delete records from a table based on values in another table. For example, the following DELETE statement removes all records from TEMP1 where the Full Name field is associated with an employee whose department code is 104:

```
DELETE FROM TEMP1
  WHERE "Full Name" IN
    (SELECT RTRIM(Emp."First Name") + ' ' + RTRIM(Emp."Last Name")
      FROM EMPLOYEE Emp
        WHERE Emp."Department Code" = 104)
```

Using Transactions

You use transactions with ADS to guarantee that changes that you want to apply to two or more records are performed in an all or none fashion. You begin a transaction using the BEGIN TRAN or BEGIN TRANSACTION keywords. Once the transaction has been started, you execute one or more queries to make changes to the data in your tables.

> ### NOTE
>
> *The Advantage Local Server (ALS) ignores transaction-related instructions. In order to use transactions, you must use ADS.*

If the changes can be applied successfully, you issue the COMMIT WORK statement to make those changes permanent and to end the transaction. If at least one of the SQL statements failed, you issue a ROLLBACK WORK statement. ROLLBACK WORK restores any changes made during the transaction and ends the transaction.

From the perspective of ADS, it does not matter whether the transaction is controlled using SQL or calls to the Advantage Client Engine (ACE) API—both are equivalent. For example, you can begin a transaction using BEGIN TRAN, and end a transaction by calling the AdsCommitTransaction function of the ACE API.

For most developers, there are two approaches that you can take when using transactions in SQL. The first is to use a single SQL script, and the other is to use multiple SQL statements, executed one after the other.

When using a single SQL script, you begin the transaction, perform one or more queries, and then commit the work. The following is an example of how a script like this might look:

```
BEGIN TRAN;
INSERT INTO TEMP1 VALUES('Gordon Hall', NULL, 1000, True);
INSERT INTO TEMP1 VALUES('Marti Schultz', NULL, 1000, True);
COMMIT WORK;
```

So long as the transaction is begun within the SQL script, if an error occurs within the script, the transaction is automatically rolled back. If no errors occur, the COMMIT WORK statement completes the transaction.

If you do not use a SQL script where the work is performed under a transaction and committed, it is the responsibility of your client application to test whether each of your individual SQL statements work, and to explicitly commit or roll back the transaction, depending on whether or not an error is encountered.

For example, in Delphi, Visual Basic.NET, or C#, you trap for any exceptions raised during the attempt to execute SQL statements after initiating a transaction. If an exception is caught, your code should send a ROLLBACK WORK SQL command to ADS. This looks like the following:

```
ROLLBACK WORK
```

If none of the queries that you execute following the beginning of the transaction raise an exception, your code needs to submit a COMMIT WORK instruction, as shown here:

```
COMMIT WORK
```

You can use SET TRAN or SET TRANSACTION to automatically start a transaction whenever an INSERT, UPDATE, or DELETE statement is sent in the transaction. You follow SET TRAN with one of three autocommit settings: AUTOCOMMIT_ON (automatically begins transaction and commits completed transaction), AUTOCOMMIT_OFF (automatically begins transaction, but you must then commit or roll back the transaction), and EXPLICT (returns SET TRAN to default state in which you must explicitly begin and commit transactions). For example:

```
SET TRAN AUTOCOMMIT_ON;
INSERT INTO TEMP1 VALUES('Sue Alan', NULL, 1000, True);
```

There are a couple of important points to note about transactions. First, you cannot initiate a transaction on the data dictionary administrator's connection (ADSSYS). Attempting to initiate a transaction from the administrative connection will cause an error.

Second, ADS permits only one transaction per connection. In other words, once you begin a transaction you must commit it or roll it back before you can initiate another transaction.

Finally, it is important to keep in mind that transactions should be kept brief. Never wait for user input after beginning a transaction. If you need user input, get it before you initiate the transaction, so that your code can start the transaction, apply changes, and commit or roll back as quickly as possible.

In the next chapter you will learn how to access metadata, as well as perform maintenance tasks on your data dictionary using SQL.

Using SQL to Access Metadata and Managed Data Dictionaries

IN THIS CHAPTER:

System Tables

Dictionary-Related SQL Statements

System Stored Procedures

his chapter concludes the discussion of Advantage SQL with a look at the SQL statements and stored procedures that permit you to create and manage data dictionaries and their related objects. This discussion begins with a look at the system tables—special result sets that permit you to quickly obtain information about your data dictionary. Next, our attention turns to SQL statements that you use to create, destroy, and manage access rights to data dictionaries and their objects. These include the CREATE, DROP, GRANT, and REVOKE statements.

Finally, this chapter discusses a collection of system stored procedures that exist in both ADS (Advantage Database Server) and ALS (Advantage Local Server). You use these system stored procedures to manage data dictionaries and the objects they contain. Importantly, these system stored procedures provide you with capabilities that are not supported by other SQL statements.

This chapter also contains a number of tables that list values that are used in the system tables and system stored procedures. These tables are based on the values that apply to ADS 7.0. If you are working with a version of ADS later than 7.0, there may be additional valid values for the listed value categories.

Also, some of these tables associate a name with each code. These names are very similar to those used when you program to the ACE (Advantage Client Engine) API. In those cases, names are variable names that are defined in the header file, VB module, or Delphi unit that you add to your programming project when using the ACE API. See the appropriate source file (ace.h, ace32.bas, ace.pas, and so on) that comes with ADS for a complete list of variable names and values.

System Tables

Both ADS and ALS provide 16 system tables that you can query to retrieve metadata about your data dictionaries and the objects they contain. These tables are available when you are connected to ADS or ALS using a data dictionary.

You use system tables to discover the properties of the data dictionary you are connected to, the names of tables bound to that data dictionary, individual table structures, index file names, index order names, constraints, views, and stored procedures. If you are connected to a data dictionary using the administrative account (ADSSYS), you can also get information about referential integrity constraints, users, groups, and access permissions.

In order to ensure that system table names are unique and identifiable, all system tables are qualified using dot notation with the "system" schema. For example, you use the system.columns table to obtain information about the individual columns available in your database tables, and the system.users table to retrieve information about the data dictionary's users.

You access system tables by querying them. For example, the following query returns information about the stored procedures in the data dictionary to which you are connected:

```
SELECT * FROM system.storedprocedures
```

System tables are often used to automate the management of your data dictionary from your client applications. For example, if your client application creates a new table that must be available to all users, you can use information in the system.users and system.usergroupmembers system tables to determine which groups and users need to have access rights granted to them.

The actual granting of the rights is something that your client application can do using the SQL GRANT statement (described later in this chapter). Note, however, that creating automated operations like these requires that the client application connect to the data dictionary using the administrative user name, ADSSYS.

NOTE

Client applications should not use the administrative connection for normal data processing. However, when a client application needs to perform some administrative function, such as granting access rights, it is perfectly acceptable to establish a second, temporary connection using the data dictionary administrative account, which you close once the administrative operation is complete.

In order to protect confidential information, the information that is returned in a system table query is sensitive to the rights of the user whose connection is used for the query. When queried using the data dictionary administrative connection, all information contained in the data dictionary is available. By comparison, user connections are limited as to what information can be retrieved. The system table may not be accessible, or the system table retrieved contains less information.

The following sections are divided into related topics, where one or more system tables are discussed in each section. Each discussion includes the primary purpose of the table or tables. In many cases, individual fields in the returned result sets are introduced, and some example queries are given. However, no attempt is made to list the structures of the tables begin examined. That information is available in the ADS help. Also, additional fields will likely be added to these tables in future versions of ADS. You can easily discover the column names of each of these tables by executing a simple SELECT * FROM query.

Getting Dictionary Information

You retrieve the properties of your data dictionary using the system.dictionary table. This table has one record, which contains one field for each property of the data dictionary to which you are connected. The following is how a query of this system table looks:

```
SELECT * FROM system.dictionary
```

If you are connected to the data dictionary using the administrator's account, every column in this record is populated with the associated property value. If you are connected on any other account, only the Version_major and Version_minor columns of this table are populated—all other columns contain NULL values.

Getting Table-Related Information

There are five system tables that provide you with information about your dictionary-bound tables: system.tables, system.columns, system.indexes, system.indexfiles, and system.triggers. The table system.tables contains one record for each table in your data dictionary. (Views are not listed in this table. You can get view information from the system.views table.) Columns in this table contain information about a table's name, physical location on disk, encryption, permissions level, primary key, and record-level constraint, to name a few.

The following query retrieves information about all nonsystem tables in the data dictionary:

```
SELECT * FROM system.tables
```

The next query returns one record with information about the PRODUCTS table:

```
SELECT * FROM system.tables WHERE UCASE(Name) = 'PRODUCTS'
```

> **NOTE**
>
> *The Name field in the preceding query, which holds the names of the tables in the data dictionary, is converted to uppercase using the UCASE SQL scalar function. String values are case sensitive, and this conversion ensures that you will retrieve the record for the PRODUCTS table, regardless of the case of this name in the system.tables result set.*

The system.columns table contains one record for every field in every table in your data dictionary. Fields in this table include the name of the field, the name of the table to which the field belongs, the ordinal position of the field in its table structure, column type, constraints, and so forth.

The values in the Field_type column are integer codes. Table 11-1 contains the values for these codes.

The following query demonstrates how to retrieve the column names for the EMPLOYEE table:

```
SELECT Name FROM system.columns WHERE UCASE(Parent) = 'EMPLOYEE'
```

The system.indexes table returns one record for each index order in the data dictionary. Columns in this table include the name of the index order, the table it is associated with, the index file it is associated with, and the type of index, as well as FTS (full text search) options such as noise words, delimiters, and drop characters. The index options field contains an integer, which consists of the sum of the index options shown in Table 11-2. For example, a unique, compound ascending index, with no other options, has the index option value of 3, which is the sum of ADS_ ASCENDING, ADS_UNIQUE, and ADS_COMPOUND.

Type	Value
ADS_UNKNOWN	0
ADS_LOGICAL	1
ADS_NUMERIC	2
ADS_DATE	3
ADS_STRING	4
ADS_MEMO	5
ADS_BINARY	6
ADS_IMAGE	7
ADS_VARCHAR	8
ADS_COMPACTDATE	9
ADS_DOUBLE	10
ADS_INTEGER	11
ADS_SHORTINT	12
ADS_TIME	13
ADS_TIMESTAMP	14
ADS_AUTOINC	15
ADS_RAW	16
ADS_CURDOUBLE	17
ADS_MONEY	18
ADS_LONGLONG	19

Table 11-1   *Field Type Codes*

Type	Value
ADS_ASCENDING	0
ADS_UNIQUE	1
ADS_COMPOUND	2
ADS_CUSTOM	4
ADS_DESCENDING	8
ADS_USER_DEFINED	16
ADS_FTS_INDEX	32
ADS_FTS_FIXED	64
ADS_CASE_SENSITIVE	128
ADS_FTS_KEEP_SCORE	256
ADS_FTS_PROTECT_NUMBERS	512

Table 11-2   *Index Option Codes*

The following query returns a list of all index orders in the structural index of the ITEMS table:

```
SELECT * FROM system.indexes
  WHERE UCASE(Parent) = 'ITEMS' AND
    UCASE(Index_File_Name) = 'ITEMS.ADI'
```

You use the system.indexfiles table to return one record for each index file in the data dictionary. The columns of this table include the index filename, the table it is associated with, the path to the file, and the index file page size.

The system.triggers table returns one record for each registered trigger in the data dictionary. Columns returned by this table include the trigger name, the table it is associated with, trigger type, trigger event type, trigger container type, the trigger's SQL (where appropriate), the function name (for trigger containers), trigger priority, and trigger options. The values for the trigger type, trigger event type, container type, and trigger options are integer codes. These codes are listed in Table 11-3, Table 11-4, Table 11-5, and Table 11-6, respectively.

Type	Value
ADS_TRIGEVENT_INSERT	1
ADS_TRIGEVENT_UPDATE	2
ADS_TRIGEVENT_DELETE	3

Table 11-3   *Trigger Type Codes*

Type	Value
ADS_TRIGTYPE_BEFORE	1
ADS_TRIGTYPE_INSTEADOF	2
ADS_TRIGTYPE_AFTER	4

Table 11-4   *Trigger Event Type Codes*

Type	Value
ADS_TRIG_WIN32DLL	1
ADS_TRIG_COM	2
ADS_TRIG_SCRIPT	3

Table 11-5   *Trigger Container Type Codes*

Type	Value
ADS_TRIGOPTIONS_NO_VALUES	0
ADS_TRIGOPTIONS_WANT_VALUES	1
ADS_TRIGOPTIONS_WANT_MEMOS_AND_BLOBS	2
ADS_TRIGOPTIONS_DEFAULT	3
ADS_TRIGOPTIONS_NO_TRANSACTION	4

Table 11-6   *Trigger Option Codes*

Getting User and Group Information

There are four tables that contain information about users, groups, and permissions: system.users, system.usergroups, system.usergroupmembers, and system.permissions. With the exception of the system.permissions table, you must be connected to the data dictionary using the ADSSYS administrative account to access this information.

You use the system.users table to retrieve one record for each user defined in the data dictionary. The columns in this table provide you with the user's name, description, and whether or not the user is enabled for Internet access. (ADSSYS is not included in this table.) The following query returns the names of the users defined for the connected dictionary:

```
SELECT Name FROM system.users
```

The system.usergroups table contains one record for each group defined for your data dictionary. Columns returned in this result set include the group name and description. The following query demonstrates how to retrieve the names of your data dictionary's groups:

```
SELECT Name FROM system.usergroups
```

To discover which groups your data dictionary's users are assigned to, you query the system.usergroupmembers table. This table has one record for each group to which each user belongs. (Recall that a given user may be a member of zero or more groups.) There are only two fields in this group: Name and Group_Name.

You use the system.permissions table to discover the names of objects, object type, name of user or group with access rights, object parent (when applicable), rights conveyed, and whether or not the rights are inherited. The values for the object type field in this table are codes. These codes are shown in Table 11-7.

All information is available from an administrative account connection. The system.permissions table access from an administrative connection will include the access rights assigned for each specific user and group to each object in the data dictionary.

Type	Value
ADS_DD_UNKNOWN_OBJECT	0
ADS_DD_TABLE_OBJECT	1
ADS_DD_RELATION_OBJECT	2
ADS_DD_INDEX_FILE_OBJECT	3
ADS_DD_FIELD_OBJECT	4
ADS_DD_COLUMN_OBJECT	4
ADS_DD_INDEX_OBJECT	5
ADS_DD_VIEW_OBJECT	6
ADS_DD_VIEW_OR_TABLE_OBJECT	7
ADS_DD_USER_OBJECT	8
ADS_DD_USER_GROUP_OBJECT	9
ADS_DD_PROCEDURE_OBJECT	10
ADS_DD_DATABASE_OBJECT	11
ADS_DD_LINK_OBJECT	12
ADS_DD_TABLE_VIEW_OR_LINK_OBJECT	13
ADS_DD_TRIGGER_OBJECT	14

Table 11-7 *Data Dictionary Object Type Codes*

From a user connection, all objects in the data dictionary are shown in this table, but only that user's access rights information is displayed. The user's access rights displayed are the cumulative rights assigned to the user and those rights inherited from any groups to which that user also belongs.

Getting Other Object Information

There are four additional system tables that you use to retrieve information about data dictionary objects. The system.relations table can only be queried from the administrative account. The system.links, system.storedprocedures, and system.views tables can be accessed using either the administrative or a user account, although some column values in the result set may be NULL when queried from the user account.

You use system.relations to return one record for each referential integrity relationship defined in your data dictionary. Columns returned in this result set include RI name, parent table, child table, parent table primary index order name, child table foreign key index order name, update rule, delete rule, and related error messages. The update and delete rule values are codes. The values for these codes are listed in Table 11-8.

You use the system.links table to retrieve one record for each available data dictionary link. Data returned in this result set includes the link name, path to the linked dictionary, link options, and user name associated with the link. Link options are represented by an integer value. The value that appears in the system.links table is the sum of the link options listed in Table 11-9.

The system.storedprocedures table returns one record for each visible, registered stored procedure. Columns returned in this result set include the name of the stored procedure object, the AEP container name, input parameters, output parameters, and the name of the function in the AEP container.

You query the system.views table to retrieve one record for each visible view. Fields returned by this query include view name, length of the SQL statement that defines the view, and the view's SQL statement.

Type	Value
ADS_DD_RI_CASCADE	1
ADS_DD_RI_RESTRICT	2
ADS_DD_RI_SETNULL	3
ADS_DD_RI_SETDEFAULT	4

Table 11-8   *Update and Delete RI Rule Codes*

Type	Value
ADS_LINK_GLOBAL	1
ADS_LINK_AUTH_ACTIVE_USER	2
ADS_LINK_PATH_IS_STATIC	4

Table 11-9   *Data Dictionary Link Option Codes*

Other System Tables

There are two final system tables that do not fall into any of the preceding categories. These tables, system.objects and system.iota, can be accessed using either the administrative or a user connection.

The system.objects table returns information about the structure of each system table, with the exception of system.objects and system.iota. Each record includes a system table name (minus the system schema qualification), the parent table (where appropriate), the fields on which the table is sorted, and the primary key of the table.

The system.iota table is a trivial table that contains one field, named iota, and one record with the NULL value in the iota field. (Iota, the ninth letter in the Greek alphabet, is also a term that means "infinitesimally small.") This table permits you to execute queries that select from SQL scalar functions and other expressions with a minimum of overhead. For example, consider the following query:

```
SELECT USER() FROM system.iota
```

This query returns the name of the user over whose connection the query is executed. Here are some more examples, along with comments, to give some ideas about how you can use this system table:

```
//Returns a random integer
SELECT RAND() FROM system.iota;
//Returns the qualified data dictionary file name
SELECT DATABASE() FROM system.iota;
//Returns an integer reflecting the current day of the week
SELECT DAYOFWEEK(CURDATE()) FROM system.iota
```

Dictionary-Related SQL Statements

SQL statements used to grant and revoke rights to data dictionary objects are described in this section.

Creating a Data Dictionary

You create a data dictionary using the CREATE DATABASE statement. At a minimum, you must supply the name of the data dictionary you are creating. For example, the following statement creates a data dictionary named NEW.ADD:

```
CREATE DATABASE "NEW.ADD"
```

This statement created the data dictionary in the directory associated with the connection over which this query is executed. If you are connected to a data dictionary, this will be the data dictionary's default directory. If you are using a free table connection, it will be the directory associated with those free tables.

To specify where the data dictionary is created, qualify the data dictionary name with a valid path. For example, if you want to create NEW.ADD on the DATASERV computer in the directory named AppData in the C$ share, your CREATE DATABASE statement might look something like the following:

```
CREATE DATABASE "\\DATASERV\C$\AppData\NEW.ADD"
```

CREATE DATABASE supports three options when creating a new database. You can assign a password to the ADSSYS user name, you can attach a description to the data dictionary, and you can choose to encrypt the data dictionary. The following statement demonstrates the use of these three options:

```
CREATE DATABASE "\\DATASERV\C$\AppData\NEW.ADD"
  PASSWORD 'password'
  DESCRIPTION 'A data dictionary created using SQL'
  ENCRYPT True
```

There is no SQL DROP statement for destroying a data dictionary. If you need to destroy a data dictionary, you need to use your client application development environment's capabilities to delete the data dictionary's .ADD, .AI, and .AM files. However, if there are tables bound to that data dictionary that you want to keep, be sure to release those tables prior to deleting the data dictionary's files.

NOTE

You do not need an administrative connection to create a data dictionary.

Granting Rights

If you configure your data dictionary to check user rights, any new objects that you add to your data dictionary must have rights granted to the groups and users who need to work with those objects. With Advantage SQL, you grant rights to objects using the SQL GRANT statement. You must be connected to your data dictionary through the administrative account in order to grant rights.

You follow the GRANT keyword with the type of rights you want to convey. The type of rights is followed by the ON keyword, which you follow with the object to which you are granting the rights. You complete the GRANT statement using the TO keyword followed by the name of the user or group to whom you are granting the rights.

NOTE

All rights can be granted to either users or groups, with the exception of INHERIT. INHERIT can only be granted to a user.

For example, if you have a table named TEMP and you want to convey SELECT and INSERT rights to the ALL group, but not UPDATE and DELETE rights, you could execute the following SQL script:

```
GRANT INSERT ON TEMP TO [ALL];
GRANT SELECT ON TEMP TO [ALL]
```

NOTE

The group named ALL is enclosed in delimiters since ALL is an Advantage SQL reserved keyword.

Similarly, if you have a table named DEMO1 in your data dictionary, and you want to grant all rights to the adsuser user, use the following statement:

```
GRANT ALL ON DEMO1 TO adsuser
```

Granting rights to a table explicitly grants those same rights to every field in the table as well.

Rights can be granted for tables, table columns, stored procedures, views, and data dictionary links. Which rights can be granted depends on the object to which rights are being conveyed. Table 11-10 lists the type of rights and the objects to which those rights can be granted.

As you can see in Table 11-10, you can grant INSERT, SELECT, and UPDATE rights to individual columns of a table. When you do so, the syntax of the GRANT statement is slightly different. You follow the INSERT, SELECT, or UPDATE keyword with the name of the column to which you are granting rights in parentheses. For example, the following statement grants SELECT rights to the Full Name

Type	Applies To
ALL	Any object
ACCESS	Data Dictionary Link
DELETE	Table or View
EXECUTE	Stored Procedure
INHERIT	Table, Stored Procedure, View, or Link (users only)
INSERT	Table, Table Column, or View
SELECT	Table, Table Column, or View
UPDATE	Table, Table Column, or View

Table 11-10   *Object Rights*

column in the DEMO1 table (although this field already has SELECT rights since ALL rights were granted to DEMO1 in the previous statement):

```
GRANT SELECT("Full Name") ON DEMO1 TO adsuser
```

As you learned in Chapter 4, when no field-level rights have been explicitly granted, your groups' and users' rights to the individual fields of a table are the same as the rights conveyed to the table itself. This situation changes once you explicitly grant rights to one or more fields. Specifically, if you grant explicit access rights to one or more fields of a table, users and groups can access only those fields of the table for which rights have been explicitly granted. As you learned earlier in this section, when you execute a GRANT SQL statement for a table, those same rights are explicitly granted to every field in that table. By comparison, granting rights to a table in the Advantage Data Architect has no effect whatsoever on individual field-level rights.

> **TIP**
>
> As mentioned in Chapter 4, if you have one or more fields in a table that you do not want users or groups to have access to, you can provide access to a view that does not include those fields you want to protect.

Revoking Rights

The syntax of the REVOKE SQL statement is nearly identical to the GRANT statement. The only differences are that you use the REVOKE keyword in place of

GRANT, and FROM in place of TO. All other aspects of this statement are identical, including the use and applicability of the rights and object to which they apply that appear in Table 11-10.

For example, to revoke the adsuser's SELECT rights from the Full Name field of the DEMO1 table, you can use the following statement:

```
REVOKE SELECT("Full Name") ON DEMO1 FROM adsuser
```

NOTE

If the SELECT rights to the Full Name field was the only field-level rights granted to the DEMO1 table, revoking those rights would restore to adsuser the access rights granted to the DEMO1 table, based on adsuser's table-level access rights to DEMO1, including those inherited from the ALL group to which adsuser belongs. Field-level rights only apply when rights have been explicitly granted to one or more of the table's fields.

To remove access rights to the DEMO1 table from the adsuser user altogether, you use the following statement:

```
REVOKE ALL ON DEMO1 FROM adsuser
```

System Stored Procedures

While you can create a data dictionary, as well as many of the objects they contain, with Advantage SQL, there are limits to what you can do. For example, you can create a data dictionary, and you can create a table in a data dictionary, but there are no commands in Advantage SQL to add a free table to a data dictionary.

The reason for this relates to standards. For the most part, Advantage SQL is designed to conform to most of the ANSI (American National Standards Institute) SQL/92 standard. No database vendor complies 100 percent with this standard, but all try to support most of it, and Advantage is no different.

The problem with conforming to standards is that they discourage customization, such as the introduction of new base keywords. While CREATE, GRANT, and INVOKE are part of the SQL/92 specification, there are no base keywords such as ADD and REMOVE.

In order to maintain a close conformance with ANSI SQL/92 and still be able to handle the many necessary data dictionary maintenance tasks through SQL, Advantage chose to implement these tasks by using stored procedures built into ADS and ALS. In ADS version 7.0, there are 17 data dictionary–related system stored procedures. The names of these system stored procedures are listed in Table 11-11.

sp_AddIndexFileToDatabase	sp_AddTableToDatabase
sp_AddUserToGroup	sp_CreateGroup
sp_CreateLink	sp_CreateReferentialIntegrity
sp_CreateUser	sp_DropGroup
sp_DropLink	sp_DropReferentialIntegrity
sp_DropUser	sp_ModifyDatabase
sp_ModifyFieldProperty	sp_ModifyGroupProperty
sp_ModifyTableProperty	sp_ModifyUserProperty
sp_RemoveUserFromGroup	

Table 11-11   *Supported System Stored Procedures*

Each of these stored procedures requires one or more input parameters, and can only be executed from an administrative (ADSSYS) connection (with the exception of sp_ModifyUserProperty, which can also be executed from a user connection). The operations performed by these stored procedures are applied to the data dictionary that the administrative account is connected to.

The following sections describe how to use the stored procedures listed in Table 11-11. These sections are divided into six functional areas, including changing database properties, adding free tables and indexes to a data dictionary, creating and dropping referential integrity definitions, creating and dropping links, changing table and field properties, and creating and modifying users and groups.

In addition, many of these sections contain tables that list the valid values that you can pass to one or more of the stored procedures. These tables and values are based on ADS 7.0, although later versions of ADS may include additional valid values. If you are working with a later version of the server, and you cannot find a value that you expect to find, refer to the ADS documentation.

Note also that no attempt is made in these sections to describe the features being affected by the stored procedures. For example, while the section on creating and dropping data dictionary links describes how to perform those tasks, it does not describe what a data dictionary link is, nor does it go into detail about the various link options. ADS features affected by these stored procedures are described elsewhere in this book. For details on the features being described, please refer to the appropriate chapter of this book.

But first, let's discuss how to create a well-formed stored procedure invocation using SQL.

Executing Stored Procedures

You execute system stored procedures using the SQL EXECUTE PROCEDURE keywords. You follow these keywords with the name of the stored procedure, and the stored procedure's input parameters enclosed in parentheses. For example, the following query sets the password of the data dictionary's administrative account to **password**:

```
EXECUTE PROCEDURE sp_ModifyDatabase('ADMIN_PASSWORD', 'password')
```

If a stored procedure includes an input parameter, but supplying a value for that parameter is optional, you can simply pass the value NULL. This is demonstrated in the following stored procedure invocation, which creates a new group but does not set the group's description:

```
EXECUTE PROCEDURE sp_CreateGroup('accounting', NULL)
```

Changing Database Properties

The CREATE DATABASE SQL statement permits you to create a new data dictionary, as well as set several of its properties, including administrative password, encryption, and description. If you want to set any of the other properties, or modify one of the properties other than data dictionary encryption, you call the sp_ModifyDatabase system stored procedure. The following is the syntax of this stored procedure:

```
sp_ModifyDatabase( Property char(200), Value memo )
```

The first parameter is a string that identifies the property that you want to change. The valid values for this parameter are listed in Table 11-12.

In the second parameter, you pass the value you want to set for the property identified in the first parameter. This value will always be a string expression, even

ADMIN_PASSWORD	COMMENT
DEFAULT_TABLE_PATH	ENABLE_INTERNET
ENCRYPT_NEW_TABLE	ENCRYPT_TABLE_PASSWORD
INTERNET_SECURITY_LEVEL	LOG_IN_REQUIRED
MAX_FAILED_ATTEMPTS	TEMP_TABLE_PATH
VERIFY_ACCESS_RIGHTS	VERSION_MAJOR
VERSION_MINOR	

Table 11-12   *Data Dictionary Properties*

though the value you are setting may be a Boolean or integer value. For example, the following statement enables Internet access for the connected data dictionary:

```
EXECUTE PROCEDURE sp_ModifyDatabase('ENABLE_INTERNET', 'True')
```

Similarly, the next statement sets the data dictionary's major version number to **2**:

```
EXECUTE PROCEDURE sp_ModifyDatabase('VERSION_MAJOR', '2')
```

Adding Free Tables and Indexes

ADS provides a system stored procedure for adding a free table to a data dictionary. It also provides a procedure to add a nonstructural index to a data dictionary–bound table, which makes that index an auto-open index. These system stored procedures are described in this section.

Adding Free Tables

You use the sp_AddTableToDatabase stored procedure to add a free table to the connected data dictionary. The following is the syntax of this procedure:

```
sp_AddTableToDatabase( TableName  char(200),
  TablePath char(260), TableType integer, CharType integer,
  IndexFiles memo, Comment memo )
```

The first parameter is the name of the table using any valid SQL table reference. This name does not have to match the name of the table, though most developers prefer that it match. The second parameter is the table's filename. If you omit the path, the default path of the data dictionary will be assumed.

The third parameter is an integer that identifies the type of table, and the fourth parameter is an integer that identifies the type of character set. The valid integers for TableType and CharType are listed in Tables 11-13 and 11-14, respectively.

The fifth parameter is a semicolon-separated list of any nonstructural index files that should be added to the data dictionary along with the table. You should include

Type	Value
ADS_NTX	1
ADS_CDX	2
ADS_ADT	3

Table 11-13 *The Valid Table Type Integers*

Type	Value
ADS_ANSI	1
ADS_OEM	2

Table 11-14   *The Valid Character Set Type Values*

the index file paths if the files are not in the data dictionary's default directory. The final parameter is an optional description for the table.

The following is an example call to sp_AddTableToDatabase. In this example, the CUST.ADT table is assumed to be a free table located in the data dictionary's default directory, and no additional index files are added:

```
EXECUTE PROCEDURE sp_AddTableToDatabase( 'CUST', 'CUST.ADT',
  3, 1, NULL, 'A sample temporary table' )
```

NOTE

If you execute this stored procedure, you can remove CUST.ADT from your data dictionary by first right-clicking CUST under the TABLES node in the Advantage Database Manager's tree view, then select Remove. If you do not see CUST under the TABLES node, click the Refresh button in the Advantage Database Manager toolbar.

Adding Nonstructural Indexes to Tables

You use the sp_AddIndexFileToDatabase stored procedure to add an existing, nonstructural index file to a data dictionary–bound table. The following is the syntax of this procedure:

```
sp_AddIndexFileToDatabase( TableName char(200),
  IndexFilePath char(515), Comment memo )
```

The first parameter is the name of the table to which you want to add the nonstructural index file as it appears in the Advantage Database Manager's tree view. The second parameter is the name of the index file, which should include path information if it is not located in the data dictionary's default directory. The third parameter is an optional description of the index.

The following example demonstrates how you can add the index file named TEMPIDX.ADI to the data dictionary, associating it with the table named TEMP. Since this file does not exist, you cannot actually run this example unless you create a free table named TEMP, as well as a nonstructural index for TEMP named TEMPIDX.ADI:

```
EXECUTE PROCEDURE sp_AddIndexFileToDatabase( 'TEMP',
  'TEMPIDX.ADI', NULL )
```

Creating and Dropping RI Definitions

There are two system stored procedures that you can use to create and drop referential integrity definitions. These stored procedures are discussed in this section.

Creating RI Definitions

You call the sp_CreateReferentialIntegrity stored procedure to create a new referential integrity definition. The following is the syntax of this procedure:

```
sp_CreateReferentialIntegrity( Name char(200),
  PrimaryTable char(200), ForeignTable char(200),
  ForeignKey char(200), UpdateRule shortint,
  DeleteRule shortint, FailTable char(515),
  PrimaryKeyError memo, CascadeError memo )
```

The first parameter of this stored procedure is the name of the RI definition. The second and third parameters are the names of tables bound to the connected data dictionary—the parent and child table names, respectively.

The fourth parameter is the name of the child table's foreign key index order. Note that you do not pass the name of the parent table's primary key index order. ADS uses the primary key index property of the parent table to determine this value.

The fifth and sixth parameters define the update rule and the delete rule, respectively. The valid values for these parameters are listed in Table 11-15.

The seventh parameter is the name of the optional fail table. If you provide a fail table name, the named fail table is created, overwriting a previous table of that name, if it existed, and the violating records are written to the table. If you pass a value of NULL in this parameter, violating records are deleted.

The eighth and ninth parameters are the optional error messages that you can associate with primary key and cascading errors.

In order to execute this stored procedure, ADS must be able to temporarily obtain exclusive access to all tables involved in this definition. If any of these tables are already open by another user, sp_CreateReferentialIntegrity will fail.

Type	Value
RI_CASCADE	1
RI_RESTRICT	2
RI_SETNULL	3
RI_SETDEFAULT	4

Table 11-15   *Valid Values for Update and Delete Rule Parameters*

The following statement demonstrates how to replicate the Employee Sales RI definition described in Chapter 5. If you want to test this stored procedure against your DemoDictionary database, you need to first manually delete the Employee Sales RI definition, or execute the sp_DropReferentialIntegrity stored procedure, passing to it the string 'Employee Sales'. (An example of how to drop this definition using sp_DropReferentialIntegrity is shown in the next section.)

```
EXECUTE PROCEDURE sp_CreateReferentialIntegrity('Employee Sales',
  'EMPLOYEE', 'INVOICE', 'Employee ID', 1, 2,
  'c:\Program Files\Extended Systems\Advantage\ADSbook\RIFAIL.ADT',
  'You must provide an Employee ID', NULL)
```

NOTE

The preceding stored procedure example assumes that the Employee Number index order has been designated as the primary key of the EMPLOYEE table, and the Employee ID index order (a foreign key index order) has been added to the INVOICE table. Performing these steps is described in Chapter 5.

Dropping RI Definitions

You drop an RI definition by calling sp_DropReferentialIntegrity, passing to it the name of the RI definition you want to drop. The following is the syntax of this stored procedure:

```
sp_DropReferentialIntegrity( Name char(200) )
```

In order to execute this stored procedure, ADS must be able to temporarily obtain exclusive access to all tables involved in this definition. If any of these tables are already open by another user, sp_DropReferentialIntegrity will fail.

The following statement demonstrates how to drop the Employee Sales RI definition. If you actually drop this definition, please be sure to restore it, either manually using the Advantage Data Architect or by executing the sp_CreateReferentialIntegrity statement provided in the preceding section.

```
EXECUTE PROCEDURE sp_DropReferentialIntegrity( 'Employee Sales' )
```

Creating and Dropping Links

ADS provides two system stored procedures for working with data dictionary links. The first permits you to create links and the second permits you to drop links. These procedures are covered in this section.

Creating a Data Dictionary Link

You create a data dictionary link by calling the sp_CreateLink stored procedure. This procedure has the following syntax:

```
sp_CreateLink( Name char(200), Dictionary char(515),
  Global logical, StaticPath logical, AuthenticateActiveUser
  logical, UserName char(50), Password char(20) )
```

The first parameter is the name of the link you are creating, and the second parameter is the name of the data dictionary that the link refers to. If the data dictionary is not in the current data dictionary's default directory, provide the path to the link dictionary.

If you want this link definition to remain in the data dictionary, making it potentially available to all users (so long as they are granted access rights to the link), set the third parameter, Global, to True. If you pass a Boolean False in the third parameter, the link is temporary and can only be used by the connection that created it.

If you want to use the connected user's user name and password to authenticate to the linked data dictionary, pass a Boolean True in the fourth parameter. If you pass a Boolean False in this fourth parameter, you must set a value to the fifth and sixth parameters, which hold the user name and password to authenticate with, respectively. If you pass a Boolean False in the fourth parameter, pass NULL in the fifth and sixth parameters. The following example demonstrates how to add a data dictionary link to the connected data dictionary:

```
EXECUTE PROCEDURE sp_CreateLink('NEWLink', 'DATA\GENERAL.ADD',
  True, False, True, NULL, NULL)
```

In this example, a link is created to a data dictionary named GENERAL.ADD, which is located in the DATA directory beneath the default directory of the connected data dictionary (a relative path was given here). This link is a global link that does not use a static path, and which authenticates with the user name and password of the current connection.

Dropping a Data Dictionary Link

You drop a link using the sp_DropLink stored procedure. The following is the syntax of this procedure:

```
sp_DropLink(NameOrPath char(200), Global logical)
```

This stored procedure requires two parameters. The first parameter is either the name of the link or a path to which the link refers. If you enter a path, and more than one link is associated with that path, the first link that is found will be dropped. If the link being dropped is a global link, set the second parameter to True. The following is an example of a call to drop the link created in the preceding example:

```
EXECUTE PROCEDURE sp_DropLink ('NEWLink', True)
```

Changing Table and Field Properties

ADS provides you with two system stored procedures for setting or modifying table properties, one for the table-level properties and the other to modify properties of the table's fields.

Modifying Table Properties

You set or modify the properties of a table using the sp_ModifyTableProperty stored procedure. The following is the syntax of this procedure:

```
sp_ModifyTableProperty(TableName char(200), Property char(200),
  Value memo, ValidationOption char(25), FailTable char(515))
```

The first parameter of this stored procedure is the name of the table and the second parameter is the property that you want to set or modify. Table 11-16 contains a list of the valid table property strings.

Use the third parameter to assign a value to the property you specify in the second parameter. Always pass this value as a string. ADS will convert the string to the appropriate data type.

If you are changing the table's record-level constraint (TABLE_VALIDATION_ EXPR), use the fourth parameter to specify how ADS validates the data. The valid validation option codes are listed in Table 11-17.

If you are changing the table's record-level constraint, and you pass the string APPEND_FAIL or WRITE_FAIL in the fourth parameter, supply the name of the fail table in the fifth parameter. The following example demonstrates how to set the auto-create property of the table named ITEMS to True:

```
EXECUTE PROCEDURE sp_ModifyTableProperty( 'ITEMS',
  'TABLE_AUTO_CREATE',  'True', NULL, NULL)
```

COMMENT	TABLE_AUTO_CREATE
TABLE_DEFAULT_INDEX	TABLE_MEMO_BLOCK_SIZE
TABLE_PERMISSION_LEVEL	TABLE_PRIMARY_KEY
TABLE_VALIDATION_EXPR	TABLE_VALIDATION_MSG

Table 11-16 *Valid Table Property Values*

APPEND_FAIL	NO_SAVE
NO_VALIDATE	RETURN_ERROR
WRITE_FAIL	

Table 11-17   *Valid Validation Option Codes*

Modifying Field Properties

You use the stored procedure named sp_ModifyFieldProperty to change properties for individual fields in a table. This procedure has the following syntax:

```
sp_ModifyFieldProperty(TableName char(200),
  FieldName char(200), Property char(200), Value memo,
  ValidationOption char(25), FailTable char(515))
```

The first parameter of this stored procedure is the name of the table to which the field belongs, and the second is the name of the field whose property you want to change. The third parameter is the name of the property. The valid field property codes are listed in Table 11-18.

The fourth parameter is the value that you want to assign to the property specified in the third parameter. You always pass this value as a string, regardless of the data type of the property you are modifying.

If you are changing the table's FIELD_CAN_BE_NULL, FIELD_MIN_VALUE, or FIELD_MAX_VALUE properties, you must use the fifth parameter to define what you want ADS to do if data currently in the table fails the validation. The values that you can use in this parameter are listed in Table 11-17. Just as you do with table properties, if you need to set the fifth parameter to APPEND_FAIL or WRITE_FAIL, you must supply a fail table name in the sixth parameter.

The following SQL statement demonstrates how you can set the FIELD_CAN_BE_NULL property for the Invoice No field of the INVOICE table:

```
EXECUTE PROCEDURE sp_ModifyFieldProperty( 'INVOICE', 'Invoice No',
  'FIELD_CAN_BE_NULL', 'False', 'WRITE_FAIL', 'FAILTAB.ADT')
```

COMMENT	FIELD_CAN_BE_NULL
FIELD_DEFAULT_VALUE	FIELD_MAX_VALUE
FIELD_MIN_VALUE	FIELD_VALIDATION_MSG

Table 11-18   *Valid Field Property Codes*

Creating and Modifying Users and Groups

There are eight system stored procedures that you use to create, modify, and drop users and groups. These stored procedures are discussed in this section.

Creating Groups

You create a group in a data dictionary using the sp_CreateGroup stored procedure. This stored procedure has the following syntax:

```
sp_CreateGroup(GroupName char(100), Comment memo)
```

This stored procedure takes two parameters. Pass the name of the group you are creating in the first parameter and an optional group description in the second parameter. The following example demonstrates the creation of a group named POWERUSER:

```
EXECUTE PROCEDURE sp_CreateGroup( 'POWERUSER',
  'Group given power user privileges')
```

Creating Users

You create a new user account by calling the sp_CreateUser stored procedure. The syntax of this procedure is shown here:

```
sp_CreateUser(UserName char(50), Password char(20), Comment memo)
```

As you can see, this stored procedure takes three parameters. You pass the new user name in the first parameter, and pass the user's password in the second parameter. Note that the password is case sensitive. You pass an optional description of the user in the third parameter. The following example demonstrates the creation of a new user named SARAH:

```
EXECUTE PROCEDURE sp_CreateUser( 'SARAH', 'password',
  'Sarah is a power user')
```

Adding a User to a Group

You invoke the sp_AddUserToGroup stored procedure to add a user to a group. The following is the syntax of sp_AddUserToGroup:

```
sp_AddUserToGroup(UserName char(50), GroupName char(100))
```

This simple procedure takes two parameters, the user you are adding to the group and the name of the group. The following statement demonstrates how to add the user SARAH to the group POWERUSER:

```
EXECUTE PROCEDURE sp_AddUserToGroup( 'SARAH', 'POWERUSER')
```

Modifying Group Properties

You call the sp_ModifyGroupProperty stored procedure to change a property of a group. This procedure has the following syntax:

```
sp_ModifyGroupProperty(GroupName char(100), Property char(200),
  Value memo)
```

The first parameter of this stored procedure is the name of the group, the second is the property you want to change, and the third is the value you want to assign to this property. Groups have only one property, COMMENT. The following example demonstrates how to change the COMMENT property for the group POWERUSER:

```
EXECUTE PROCEDURE sp_ModifyGroupProperty( 'POWERUSER',
  'COMMENT', 'The power user group')
```

Modifying User Properties

Call the sp_ModifyUserProperty stored procedure to change a property for a user. The syntax of the procedure is shown here:

```
sp_ModifyUserProperty(UserName char(50), Property char(200),
  Value memo)
```

Like sp_ModifyGroupProperty, this stored procedure takes three parameters, the user whose property you want to change, the property being changed, and the value you are setting the property to. The valid values for the second parameter, Property, are listed in Table 11-19. The value you pass in the third parameter is a string, even when setting the Boolean ENABLE_INTERNET property.

The following statement sets the password for the user SARAH:

```
EXECUTE PROCEDURE sp_ModifyUserProperty( 'SARAH', 'USER_PASSWORD',
  'password')
```

There is only one property, USER_PASSWORD, that you can change with this stored procedure for the ADSSYS administrative account. From a user account, you can invoke sp_ModifyUserProperty to change that user's password.

COMMENT	ENABLE_INTERNET	USER_PASSWORD

Table 11-19   *Valid User Property Values*

Removing a User from a Group

Call sp_RemoveUserFromGroup to remove a user from a group. As shown in the following syntax listing, this stored procedure takes two parameters; the user name and the group this user should be removed from:

```
sp_RemoveUserFromGroup(UserName char(50), GroupName char(100))
```

The following example demonstrates how to remove the user SARAH from the POWERUSER group:

```
EXECUTE PROCEDURE sp_RemoveUserFromGroup('SARAH', 'POWERUSER')
```

Removing Users

Remove a user from the data dictionary to which you are connected using the sp_DropUser stored procedure. This procedure takes a single parameter: the name of the user to remove. Following is the syntax of this procedure:

```
sp_DropUser(UserName char(50))
```

If you drop a user while that user is connected, that user will remain connected until their connection terminates. After that, the user will no longer be able to log in with that user name.

If the data dictionary to which this user belonged does not check user rights, a connected, removed user will continue to have access to data dictionary objects. If the data dictionary does check user rights, a connected, removed user is prevented from performing any data access operations that require rights be checked.

Removing Groups

You remove a group from a data dictionary using the sp_DropGroup procedure, which takes the name of the group to drop as its sole parameter. The following is the syntax of this stored procedure:

```
sp_DropGroup(GroupName char(100))
```

Any users belonging to a group that is dropped are removed from that group, and any additional rights conveyed by that group are revoked. The following statement removes the POWERUSER group from the connected data dictionary:

```
EXECUTE PROCEDURE sp_DropGroup('POWERUSER')
```

The next five chapters describe how to work with the Advantage Database Server from various development environments.

Accessing ADS Data

Part III of this book brings it all together by showing you how to access ADS data from many of your favorite development tools. By design, each of these chapters is similar in structure to one another. Once you have read one chapter, you will be able to quickly absorb the remaining chapters that you are interested in.

Each chapter begins with an introduction to a specific data access mechanism supported by ADS. This discussion includes any special features of the data access mechanism under consideration. Next, each chapter takes a look at a project that implements a number of common tasks that you will find in many client applications. These tasks include connecting to a server, executing a query, and binding data to query parameters, to name a few.

Next, each chapter takes a look at the navigational features supported by the data access mechanism of focus. While every data access mechanism supports forward navigation, at a minimum, some support much more than that. This is the section that is most different among the various chapters.

Finally, each chapter concludes with a look at tasks that you might include in a client application in order to perform basic data dictionary administrative operations, including adding a table to a data dictionary, granting rights to a newly added table, and permitting a user to change their password. Only in Chapter 16, where the Advantage PHP Extension is used to build a dynamic Web site, are these operations absent (administrative tasks are normally inappropriate for Web server extensions).

Chapter 12 discusses the Advantage TDataSet Descendant, and how it is used in Delphi applications (as well as in Kylix and C++Builder applications). Java and the Advantage JDBC Driver is the focus of Chapter 13, and in Chapter 14 you learn how to access ADS data from Visual Basic 6.0. Microsoft's .NET Framework Class Library and the Advantage .NET Data Provider is the focus of the C# project found in Chapter 15. Finally, Chapter 16 gives you insight into using the Advantage ODBC Driver, the Advantage PHP Extension, and the Advantage DBI Driver.

CHAPTER 2

Using ADS from Delphi

Without a doubt, Delphi developers have the richest choice of options for accessing ADS. In addition to being able to use ACE (Advantage Client Engine), Delphi developers can use the Advantage ODBC Driver, the Advantage OLE DB Provider, and the Advantage .NET Data Provider. But there is one data access mechanism that beats them all—the Advantage TDataSet Descendant. Using the TDataSet descendant classes, Delphi developers, as well as Kylix and C++Builder developers, can utilize almost every feature available in ADS. Only ACE provides access to more capabilities, but at the expense of being significantly more complicated to use.

NOTE

If you are using C++Builder or Kylix, install the Advantage TDataSet Descendant for either C++Builder or Kylix, respectively. The TDataSet descendant classes are identical to those described in this chapter. The Kylix code is identical to the Delphi code with few exceptions, all due to working in Linux. For C++Builder code, the methods and properties are the same, but the syntax of C++ is different.

This chapter provides you with examples of using the Advantage TDataSet Descendant classes to perform a wide range of common data-related tasks using Delphi. As is the case with the other chapters in Part III, this discussion assumes that you are already familiar with the development environment being described. Instead, the focus is on code that works with the data dictionary you have been using throughout this book.

NOTE

If you are using Borland's Delphi for .NET solution, you will want to use the Advantage .NET Data Provider. See Chapter 15 for information on the Advantage .NET Data Provider.

ADS and Delphi

Delphi has been the development environment of choice for ADS developers for some time. While we anticipate that other languages, such as C#, will be the choice of a growing number of ADS developers due to the availability of the Advantage .NET Data Provider, Delphi will continue to be an excellent tool for working with ADS.

There are two primary reasons why ADS and Delphi go so well together. The first is the abundance of ADS features that are available through the Advantage TDataSet

Descendant classes. Using these components, it is extremely easy to access, change, and manage your ADS data.

The second reason is that the data access model supported by the BDE (Borland Database Engine), and encapsulated in the TDataSet abstract class of the VCL (visual component library), fits beautifully with the navigational model that ADS's ISAM architecture permits. This reason is actually closely related to the first. The ease with which Delphi developers can use ADS is a direct result of the nearly seamless way in which the TDataSet interface and the ADS API (application programming interface) interact.

But there is more. The ADS components that descend from TDataSet do much more than simply conform to much of the TDataSet interface. In addition, they also expose a large number of functions in the ACE API. For example, you can call AdsStmtSetTablePassword on an AdsQuery to submit a free table's encryption password before attempting to query it. This method is not part of the TDataSet interface, but is exposed by this component to simplify your work with ADS without having to deal directly with ACE.

An interesting piece of evidence for this near perfect fit between ADS and Delphi is that the Advantage Data Architect is written in Delphi. In fact, when you install the Advantage Data Architect, the Delphi source files and packages that are used to build the Advantage Data Architect are included. Indeed, these Delphi units can be a fascinating source of ideas if you need to perform some task that is out of the ordinary.

Understanding the TDataSet Descendants

The name TDataSet descendant is actually something of a misnomer. While the TAdsTable, TAdsQuery, and TAdsStoredProc components do indeed descend from the TDataSet class, there are several other classes on the Advantage page of the Component Palette in Delphi that do not. These include the TAdsConnection, TAdsDictionary, and TAdsSettings classes. Nonetheless, these components, which are shown here, are generically referred to as *TDataSet descendants*.

That TAdsTable, TAdsQuery, and TAdsStoredProc all descend from TDataSet means that they share a common programming interface with all other standard Delphi data access components. This interface is largely navigational, although it also supports the entire range of set-based operations of Advantage SQL through the TAdsQuery class.

Because the TDataSet descendants share a common interface with other Delphi data access components, such as TTable, TSQLDataSet, TIBQuery, TClientDataSet, among others, converting an existing Delphi application to use ADS is pretty straightforward. In fact, now that Borland has officially deprecated the BDE, ADS is an almost unbeatable option when choosing an alternative data access mechanism, especially if your application already uses the navigational model.

The remainder of this chapter shows you how to access ADS using Delphi. This discussion is divided into three parts. The first part describes common basic tasks, such as connecting to ADS and accessing data. The second shows you how to leverage the navigational model with Delphi and ADS. The third part demonstrates several basic administrative tasks, such as creating tables and granting rights to them.

ON THE CD

The Delphi project Delphi_TDataSet.dpr can be found on this book's CD-ROM (see Appendix B). This project was created using Delphi 7, but is compatible with Delphi versions 5 and later.

All of the examples presented here can be found in a Delphi project named Delphi_TDataSet. Figure 12-1 shows the main form of this project in Delphi.

A final comment about this project is in order. Many of the operations performed in this project make use of the AdsTable component, which is pretty common for Delphi applications. Many of these same operations can be performed using a SQL query executed through an AdsQuery. For examples of possible SQL alternatives, refer to Chapters 13–16.

Performing Basic Tasks with ADS and Delphi

This section describes some of the more common tasks that you can perform with Delphi. These include connecting to a data dictionary, opening a table, executing a query, using a parameterized query, and executing a stored procedure.

Connecting to Data

You connect to a data dictionary or a directory in which free tables are located using an AdsConnection component. (AdsConnection is very similar to the VCL's Database component, located on the BDE page of the Component Palette.) At a minimum, you

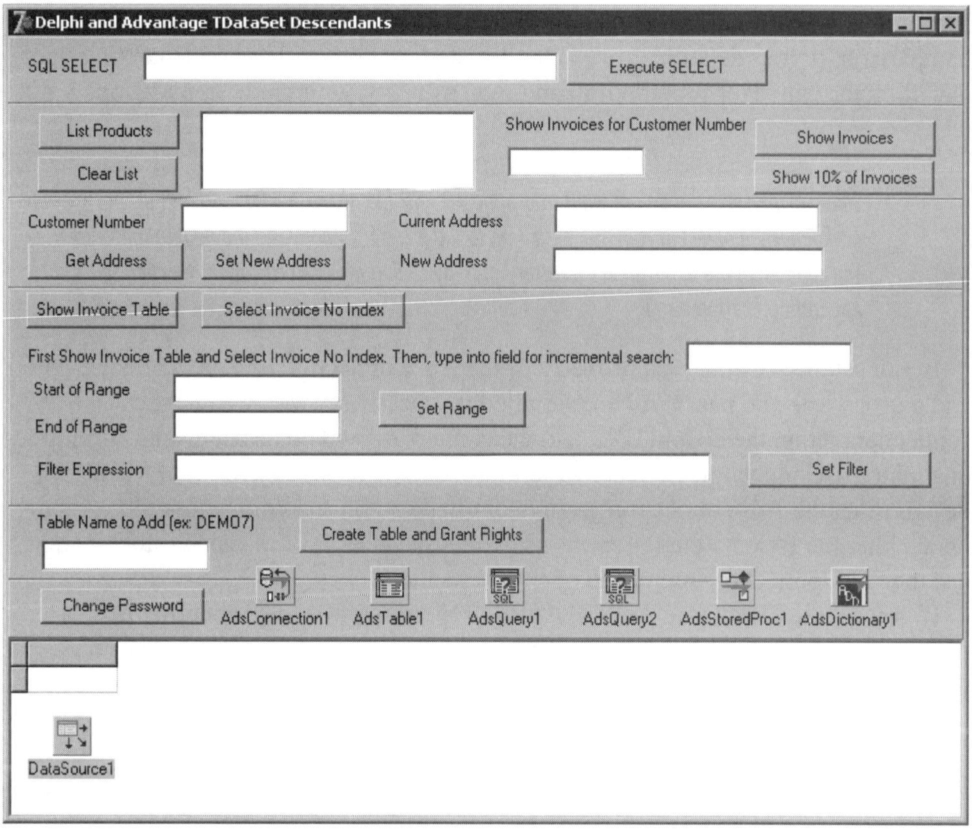

Figure 12-1   *The Delphi_TDataSet project's main form*

must set a property of this component to describe where the data dictionary or free tables are located, after which you set the IsConnected property to True. If you are connecting to a data dictionary that requires a login, and you do not want the user to have to enter their user name, you must also set the Username and Password properties of this component.

There are two ways to indicate the location of your data. The easiest way, if you have an alias defined for your data dictionary or data directory, is to set the Alias name property of the AdsConnection to a defined alias. Aliases are defined in the ADS.INI file, which can be stored in the same directory as your client application (under Windows), or anywhere on your search path.

Alternatively, you can set the ConnectPath of the AdsConnection to a path, preferably a UNC path. The benefit of using an ADS.INI file is that you can change the directory in which ADS looks for your data by changing an entry in the ADS.INI file. By comparison, if your data directory is hard-coded in your application, changing your data directory involves recompiling and redistributing your client application.

> ### TIP
>
> *Some developers who do not want to use the ADS.INI file assign the ConnectPath property of the AdsConnection object at runtime, assigning to it a directory relative to the application's directory. You can obtain the application's directory path by calling the ExtractFilePath function, passing Application.ExeName to it.*

If you set the IsConnected property of the AdsConnection to True at design time, and a user name and password are supplied (if necessary), you will have an active connection within the Delphi IDE, and the connection will be reestablished at runtime once the AdsConnection is created and initialized. If IsConnected is set to False at design time, the AdsConnection component will establish a connection at runtime once either the IsConnected property is explicitly set to True or any TDataSets that use the AdsConnection attempt to open or execute.

If you set the Username and Password properties prior to connecting an AdsConnection, set the LoginPrompt property to False. If LoginPrompt is True, the user will be prompted for their user name and password.

> ### TIP
>
> *If LoginPrompt is set to True, but no login dialog box is displayed, you must add the DBLogDlg unit to your unit's uses clause.*

In the Delphi_TDataSet project, the Alias property of the AdsConnection is set to DemoDD (the alias you defined for the DemoDictionary data dictionary in Chapter 4), the user name is set to **adsuser**, the password is set to **password**, and the LoginPrompt is set to False. With these settings in place, you will not be prompted for a user name or password when connecting to the data dictionary.

> ### NOTE
>
> *If you have difficulty connecting, it might be because you have other client applications, such as the Advantage Data Architect, connected using a local connection. Ensure that all clients on the same machine use the same type of connection. You control the type of connections attempted by an AdsConnection using the AdsServerTypes property.*

Accessing an ADS Table

The easiest way to access data is with an AdsTable component. At a minimum, you must set the AdsTable's DatabaseName property to an AdsConnection (this is often done at design time), its TableName property to the name of a table or view you want to access, and the Active property to True. Calling the AdsTable's Open method sets the AdsTable's Active property to True.

This is demonstrated in the following event handler, which is associated with the Show Invoice Table button (shown in Figure 12-1):

```
procedure TForm1.ShowInvoiceBtnClick(Sender: TObject);
begin
  if AdsTable1.Active then AdsTable1.Close;
  AdsTable1.TableName := 'INVOICE';
  AdsTable1.Open;
  DataSource1.DataSet := AdsTable1;
end;
```

Reading and Writing Data

You access individual records in a TDataSet using its Fields property or its FieldByName method. Fields is a collection property, and you must pass it an index that identifies which field you want to read from or write to, based on its zero-based ordinal position in the table's structure. When you invoke FieldByName, you pass a string containing the name of the field you want to work with. This approach works for any AdsTable, AdsQuery, or AdsStoredProc component that returns a result set.

The following event handler, associated with the Get Address button (shown in Figure 12-1), demonstrates how to read a field:

```
procedureC TForm1.GetAddressBtnClick(Sender: TObject);
begin
  if AdsTable1.Active then AdsTable1.Close;
  AdsTable1.TableName := 'CUSTOMER';
  AdsTable1.IndexName := 'Customer ID';
  AdsTable1.Open;
  if AdsTable1.FindKey([CustNoText.Text]) then
    OldAddressText.Text :=
      AdsTable1.FieldByName('Address').AsString
  else
    ShowMessage('Customer ID ' + CustNoText.Text + ' not found');
  DataSource1.DataSet := AdsTable1;
end;
```

The following event handler, associated with the Set New Address button (shown in Figure 12-1), demonstrates writing to a field:

```
procedure TForm1.SetAddressBtnClick(Sender: TObject);
begin
  if AdsTable1.Active then AdsTable1.Close;
  AdsTable1.TableName := 'CUSTOMER';
  AdsTable1.IndexName := 'Customer ID';
  AdsTable1.Open;
  if AdsTable1.FindKey([CustNoText.Text]) then
  begin
    AdsTable1.Edit;
    AdsTable1.FieldByName('Address').AsString :=
      NewAddressText.Text;
    AdsTable1.Post;
  end
  else
    ShowMessage('Customer ID ' + CustNoText.Text + ' not found');
  DataSource1.DataSet := AdsTable1;
end;
```

Executing a Query

You define a query by assigning the SQL statement you want to execute to the SQL StringList property of an AdsQuery. If the query returns a result set, you execute it by calling its Open method or by setting its Active property to True. If the query does not return a result set, execute it by calling its ExecSQL method.

By default, you cannot edit the result set returned by an AdsQuery. If your query produces a live cursor, setting the AdsQuery's RequestLive property to True permits you to edit the data in the result set.

The following code demonstrates the execution of a query entered by the user. It is associated with the Execute SELECT button (shown in Figure 12-1):

```
procedure TForm1.DoSelectClick(Sender: TObject);
begin
  if AdsQuery1.Active then AdsQuery1.Close;
  AdsQuery1.SQL.Text := SELECTText.Text;
  AdsQuery1.Open;
  DataSource1.DataSet := AdsQuery1;
end;
```

Using a Parameterized Query

The AdsQuery component supports both named and positional parameters. You must bind data to every parameter of a parameterized query prior to executing it. You can do this either using the Params property, which is a collection property indexed by parameter position, or the ParamByName method, which takes a parameter name as an argument. Both of these approaches return a TParam, which you use to assign a value to the parameter.

The AdsQuery2 component on this project's main form has the following SQL statement assigned to its SQL property:

```
SELECT * FROM INVOICE WHERE [Customer ID] = :cust
```

The parameter, named cust, is bound and the query executed from the event handler shown in the following code segment. This event handler is associated with the Show Invoices button (shown in Figure 12-1):

```
procedure TForm1.ShowInvoicesBtnClick(Sender: TObject);
begin
  if AdsQuery2.Active then AdsQuery2.Close;
  if ParamText.Text = '' then
  begin
    ShowMessage('Please enter a customer number');
    Exit;
  end;
  AdsQuery2.Params[0].AsInteger := StrToInt(ParamText.Text);
  AdsQuery2.Open;
  DataSource1.DataSet := AdsQuery2;
end;
```

Calling a Stored Procedure

Stored procedures are invoked using SQL EXECUTE PROCEDURE statements in most of the Advantage data access mechanisms, and you can use an AdsQuery in Delphi to do the same. But Delphi developers have an alternative solution, being able to invoke a stored procedure using the AdsStoredProc component.

There are several advantages to invoking a stored procedure using an AdsStoredProc. The first is that you can use the Params property of the stored procedure to configure and assign the stored procedure's input parameters. After configuring a stored procedure in the Delphi IDE, you can select the Params property editor of the stored procedure to view the names and data types of each parameter. You can even assign a default value for each of your stored procedure's input parameters using this property editor.

Another advantage of AdsStoredProc is realized when the stored procedure returns a result set. Specifically, stored procedures that return a result set can be treated exactly the same as AdsTables and AdsQueries that return a result set. They can be assigned to the DataSet property of a DataSource so that the returned data can be associated with data-aware controls. The AdsStoredProc also populates any output parameters, which can be read individually using the Params property or ParamByName method.

At a minimum, you must set the DatabaseName and the StoredProcName properties of the stored procedure. Also, you must assign values to all input parameters, if present, prior to executing the stored procedure. Set the AdsStoredProc component's ParamBindMode property to pbByName or pbByNumber based on whether you want to bind parameters by name or position, respectively.

If your stored procedure returns a result set, you execute it by calling its Open method, or by setting its Active property to True. If your stored procedure does not return a result set, you execute it by calling its ExecProc method.

If you want to execute a given stored procedure more than once, and with different values passed to its input parameters, you must first close the stored procedure before changing any input parameters. This is not necessary for a stored procedure that does not return a result set.

The use of a stored procedure is demonstrated by the following code associated with the OnClick event handler for the Show 10% of Invoices button (shown in Figure 12-1): The stored procedure referenced in this code is the Delphi AEP (Advantage Extended Procedure) created in Chapter 7. If you did not create this AEP, but created one of the other AEPs described in that chapter, substitute the name of the stored procedure object in your data dictionary in the EXECUTE PROCEDURE string or StoredProcName property, like this:

```
procedure TForm1.CallStoredProcBtnClick(Sender: TObject);
begin
  if AdsStoredProc1.Active then AdsStoredProc1.Close;
  if ParamText.Text = '' then
  begin
    ShowMessage('Please enter a customer number');
    Exit;
  end;
  AdsStoredProc1.Params[0].Value := ParamText.Text;
  try
    AdsStoredProc1.Open;
  except
```

```
   on e: Exception do
     ShowMessage(e.Message);
 end;
 DataSource1.DataSet := AdsStoredProc1;
end;
```

To view the stored procedure's parameters, select AdsStoredProc1 on the main form, and then using the Object Inspector, select the Params property and click the ellipsis button that appears. Delphi displays the parameters in the Params collection editor:

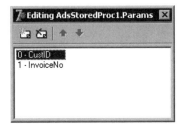

If you select one of the available parameters in the Params collection editor, you can view and edit the parameters properties using the Object Inspector shown here:

Navigational Actions with ADS and Delphi

The TDataSet class of the VCL supports a wide range of navigational actions. While all of these actions apply to AdsTables, many of them are also supported by the AdsQuery and AdsStoredProc components when they return a result set.

Setting an Index

If you are connected to a data dictionary, and you have designated a default index for a table, that index will automatically be used when you open that table using an AdsTable. If you do not have a default index, or want to switch to some other index, you set the IndexName property of the AdsTable to the name of the index you want to use. This is demonstrated in the following code segment, which is associated with the Select Invoice No Index button (shown in Figure 12-1):

```
procedure TForm1.SetIndexBtnClick(Sender: TObject);
begin
  if (AdsTable1.TableName <> 'INVOICE') and
    (AdsTable1.Active) then
    AdsTable1.Close;
  AdsTable1.IndexName := 'Invoice No';
end;
```

Finding a Record Based on Data

TDataSets support a number of methods for locating records based on their contents. These include FindKey, FindNearest, and Locate, in addition to the brute-force method of scanning through every record in the table. Of these techniques, FindKey and FindNearest are the fastest and easiest to use, locating a record using the currently selected index.

Both of these methods take a single parameter consisting of a constant array. You represent a constant array by enclosing one or more values within parentheses, separating the values using commas when there is more than one value. Both of these methods search for the first element of the array in the first field of the current index, then search the second value, if present, in the second field of the current index, and so on.

FindKey is a Boolean function that returns True if a matching record is found. If FindKey returns True, the located record is made the current record. FindNearest is a procedure. It always repositions the current record to the closest match to the search criteria.

The use of FindNearest is demonstrated in the following event handler. This event handler is associated with the OnChange event of the Edit named SearchText. After clicking the Show Invoice Table and the Set Invoice No Index buttons, this code permits an incremental search through the INVOICE table.

```
procedure TForm1.SearchTextChange(Sender: TObject);
begin
  if (not AdsTable1.Active) or
    (AdsTable1.TableName <> 'INVOICE') or
    (AdsTable1.IndexName <> 'Invoice No') then
    begin
      ShowMessage('Click Show Invoice Table and Select Invoice '+
        'No Index before performing an incremental search');
      Exit;
    end;
  AdsTable1.FindNearest([SearchText.Text]);
end;
```

NOTE

Unlike the BDE, ADS employs indexes with the Locate and Lookup methods whenever appropriate indexes are available, and creates AOFs (Advantage Optimized Filters) when they are not. As a result, these methods are much faster than their BDE counterparts. However, Locate and Lookup are more complicated to use than FindKey and FindNearest. For information on using Locate and Lookup, refer to the ADS help.

Setting a Range

Delphi uses the term *range* instead of *scope*, but they mean the same thing. A range defines a subset of records to view in a table, based on an index.

You set a range in Delphi by calling SetRange. This method takes two parameters, both of which are constant arrays. The first constant array contains the beginning values of the range, where the first value defines the beginning of the range based on the first field of the current index, the second value, if present, defines the beginning of the range on the second field of the index, and so on. The second constant array contains the ending values of the range, again on a field-by-field basis, based on the current index.

The following code, which is associated with the OnClick event handler of the Set Range button, demonstrates how to apply a range. An example of a range set on the INVOICE table is shown in Figure 12-2. Notice that there are only 3 records, out of more than 2,000 records, in this range:

```
procedure TForm1.SetRangeBtnClick(Sender: TObject);
begin
  if (not AdsTable1.Active) or
    (AdsTable1.TableName <> 'INVOICE') or
```

```
  (AdsTable1.IndexName <> 'Invoice No') then
  begin
    ShowMessage('Click Show Invoice Table and Select Invoice '+
      'No Index before setting a range');
    Exit;
  end;
AdsTable1.SetRange([StartRange.Text], [EndRange.Text]);
end;
```

Setting a Filter

A filter is similar to a range in that it can limit a table to a subset of records.
Unlike a range, however, a filter does not rely on the current index.

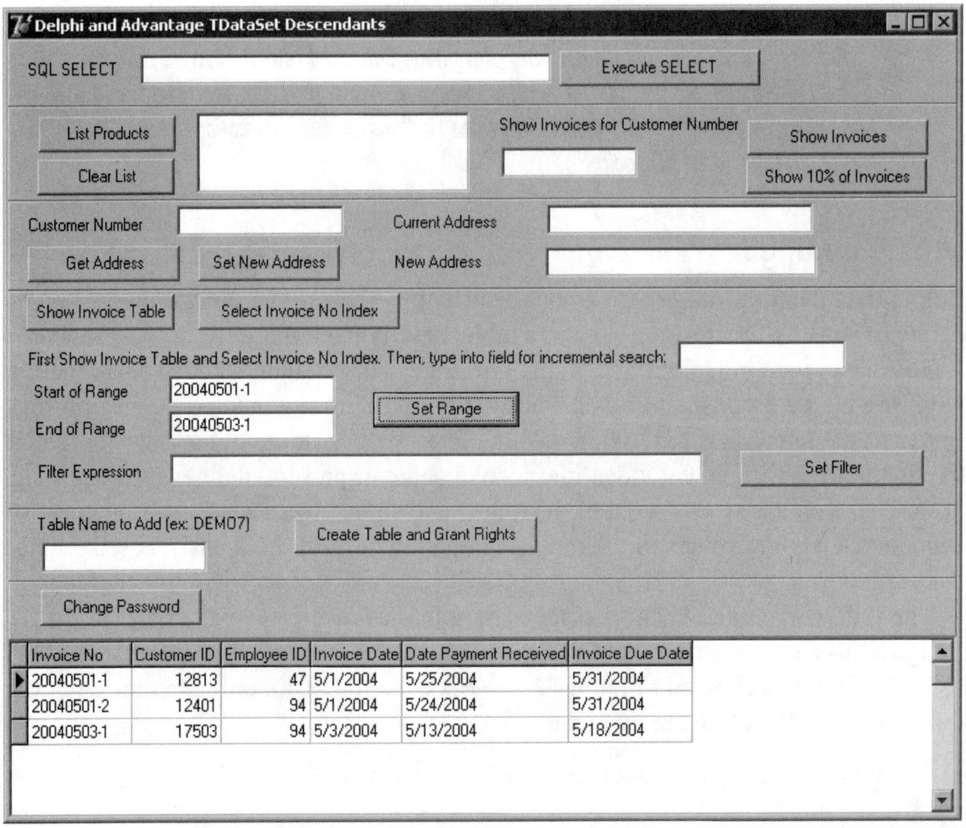

Figure 12-2   *A range limits the records available in a table.*

You set a filter by assigning a filter expression to an AdsTable's Filter property, and then setting the Filtered property to True. You drop a filter by setting the Filter property to an empty string or by setting Filtered to False (or both). Setting and dropping a filter is demonstrated in the following code, which is located in the OnClick event handler for the Set Filter button (shown in Figure 12-1):

```
procedure TForm1.FilterBtnClick(Sender: TObject);
begin
if FilterBtn.Caption = 'Drop Filter' then
  begin
    AdsTable1.Filtered := False;
    FilterBtn.Caption := 'Set Filter';
  end
  else
  begin
    if (not AdsTable1.Active) or
      ( not (DataSource1.DataSet is TAdsTable)) then
      begin
        ShowMessage('Please open a table before '+
          'setting a filter');
        Exit;
      end;
    AdsTable1.Filter := FilterText.Text;
    AdsTable1.Filtered := True;
    FilterBtn.Caption := 'Drop Filter';
  end;
end;
```

If you run this project, click Show the Invoice Table button, and then enter the following filter expression, the DBGrid at the bottom of the form will display only two records if you click the Set Filter button:

```
Customer ID = 12037 and Employee ID = 89
```

NOTE

Although a filter does not rely on the current index, the speed with which a filter can be applied is directly related to the available indexes on the table. Specifically, filters use AOFs (AOFs are described in Chapter 3). As a result, filters can be applied quickly when the expressions in the filter expression map to available indexes on the underlying table. By comparison, filters applied when you use the BDE do not use indexes, making filters under ADS significantly faster than the corresponding filters under the BDE.

Scanning a Result Set

Scanning is the process of sequentially reading every record in a result set or table, or every record in the range and/or filtered view of the result set or table if either a filter or a range, or both, are active. In most cases, scanning involves an initial navigation to the first record of the result set or table, followed by repeated calls to advance one record, until all of the records have been visited.

Although scanning is a common task, it is important to note that it necessarily requires the client application to retrieve all of the records in the result set. This is not a problem when few records are involved, but if a large number of records are being scanned, network resources may be taxed.

TIP

If you are using ADS, and you must scan a large number of records, implement the operation using an AEP as described in Chapter 7. Scanning from an AEP installed on ADS requires no network resources.

The following code demonstrates the scanning of an AdsTable. This code, associated with the OnClick event handler of the List Products button (shown in Figure 12-1), navigates the entire PRODUCTS table, assigning data from each record to the ProductList list box:

```
procedure TForm1.ListProductsBtnClick(Sender: TObject);
begin
  DataSource1.DataSet := nil;
  if AdsTable1.Active then AdsTable1.Close;
  AdsTable1.TableName := 'PRODUCTS';
  AdsTable1.Open;
  AdsTable1.First;
  while not AdsTable1.EOF do
  begin
    ProductList.Items.Add(AdsTable1.Fields[0].AsString +
      '      ' + AdsTable1.Fields[1].AsString);
    AdsTable1.Next;
  end;
  AdsTable1.Close;
end;
```

Administrative Operations with ADS and Delphi

While ADS requires little in the way of periodic maintenance to keep it running smoothly, many applications need to provide administrative functionality related to the management of users, groups, and objects.

This section is designed to provide you with insight into exposing administrative functions in your client applications. Two related, yet different, operations are demonstrated here. In the first, a new table is added to the database and all groups are granted access rights to it. This operation requires that you establish an administrative connection. The second operation involves permitting individual users to modify their own passwords. Especially in the security-conscious world of modern database management, this feature is often considered an essential step to protecting data.

Like many of the other operations described in this chapter, Delphi provides a variety of different means for implementing these features. An obvious solution is to use SQL queries to perform these tasks. This approach is demonstrated in other chapters in this part of the book, and in many of those cases represents the only mechanism available.

Since the SQL approach is shown elsewhere, the following sections demonstrate how to implement these operations using methods of the AdsTable, AdsConnection, and AdsDictionary components. While this approach is sometimes more involved than the SQL approach, it is nonetheless valuable in that it demonstrates the utility of the various TDataSet descendant components. If you prefer to use the SQL approach in your Delphi applications, refer to the SQL statements used in Chapters 13–16.

Creating a Table and Granting Rights to It

The Delphi_TDataSet project permits a user to enter the name of a table that will be created in the data dictionary, after which all groups will be granted rights to the table. This operation is demonstrated in the following event handler, which is associated with the OnClick event of the Create Table and Grant Rights button (shown in Figure 12-1). Unlike most of the code shown in this chapter, several comment lines are retained here, due to its complexity:

```
procedure TForm1.CreateTableBtnClick(Sender: TObject);
var
  AdminConnection: TAdsConnection;
  AdminTable: TAdsTable;
```

```
    Strings: TStringList;
    i: Integer;
begin
  if TableNameText.Text = '' then
  begin
    ShowMessage('Please enter the name of the table to create');
    Exit;
  end;
  //Create Connection and Table objects
  AdminConnection := TAdsConnection.Create(nil);
  AdminConnection.Name := 'Admin';
  AdminTable := TAdsTable.Create(AdminConnection);
  AdminTable.DatabaseName := AdminConnection.Name;
  Strings := TStringList.Create;
  try
    //Configure Connection and Table objects
    AdminConnection.AliasName := AdsConnection1.AliasName;
    AdminConnection.AdsServerTypes :=
      AdsConnection1.AdsServerTypes;
    AdminConnection.Username := 'adssys';
    AdminConnection.Password := 'password';
    AdminConnection.LoginPrompt := False;
    AdminConnection.IsConnected := True;
    AdminConnection.GetTableNames(Strings, TableNameText.Text);
    for i := 0 to Pred(Strings.Count) do
      if AnsiCompareText(Strings.Strings[i],
        TableNameText.Text) = 0 then
      begin
        ShowMessage('This table already exists. Cannot create');
        Exit;
      end;
    //Define new table structure and create it
    with AdminTable.FieldDefs do
    begin
      Add('Full Name', ftString, 30);
      Add('Date of Birth', ftDate);
      with AddFieldDef do
      begin
        Name := 'Credit Limit';
        DataType := ftBCD;
        Precision := 20;
        Size := 4;
      end;
```

```
    Add('Active', ftBoolean);
  end;
  AdminTable.TableType := ttAdsADT;
  AdminTable.TableName := TableNameText.Text;
  AdminTable.CreateTable;
  //Configure and connect the AdsDictionary object
  AdsDictionary1.AliasName := AdminConnection.AliasName;
  AdsDictionary1.AdsServerTypes :=
    AdminConnection.AdsServerTypes;
  AdsDictionary1.UserName := AdminConnection.Username;
  AdsDictionary1.Password := AdminConnection.Password;
  AdsDictionary1.LoginPrompt := False;
  AdsDictionary1.Connect;
  Strings.Clear;
  AdsDictionary1.GetGroupNames(Strings);
  if Strings.Count = 0 then
  begin
    ShowMessage('No groups to grant rights to');
    Exit;
  end;
  //Grant access rights to all groups
  for i := 0 to Pred(Strings.Count) do
    AdsDictionary1.SetObjectAccessRights(TableNameText.Text,
      Strings.Strings[i], 'RW');
  //cleanup
finally
  AdsDictionary1.Disconnect;
  Strings.Free;
  AdminTable.Free;
  AdminConnection.IsConnected := False;
  AdminConnection.Free;
end;
ShowMessage('The ' + TableNameText.Text + ' table has been ' +
  'created, with rights granted to all groups');
end;
```

This event handler demonstrates a number of interesting techniques. First, while it uses an AdsDictionary component that was placed at design time onto the main form (shown in Figure 12-1), the AdsConnection and AdsTable used by the administrative connection are created and then discarded at runtime. This approach is always valid, and could have been used by many of the other event handlers listed in this chapter. In most cases, however, components that are placed and configured at design time are easier to maintain.

After verifying that the requested table does not already exist in the data dictionary, the administrative connection is configured and opened, and a new AdsTable is configured to use it. Next, the table's structure is defined (using both the Add and AddFieldDefs methods of the AdsTable), and the table is created with a call to CreateTable.

> **NOTE**
>
> *The administrative user name and passwords are represented by string literals in this code segment. This was done for convenience, but in a real application, either you would ask for this information from the user or you would scramble this data to prevent its discovery.*

After creating the table, the AdsDictionary component is configured and opened. Finally, the list of groups is retrieved and used to grant read and write access to the table.

Changing a User Password

A user can change the password on their own connection, if you permit this. In most cases, only when every user has a distinct user name would you expose this functionality in a client application. When multiple users share a user name, this operation is usually reserved for an application administrator.

As was done in the preceding section, this code demonstrates changing a user password using an AdsDictionary component. For an example of changing a password using the sp_ModifyUserProperty stored procedure, refer to Chapter 13, 14, or 15.

```
procedure TForm1.ChangePasswordBtnClick(Sender: TObject);
var
  UserName: String;
  OldPass: String;
  NewPass1: String;
  NewPass2: String;
  {$HINTS OFF}
  function CheckPass(UName, UPass: String): Boolean;
  var
    TempConnection: TAdsConnection;
  begin
    result := False;
    TempConnection := TAdsConnection.Create(nil);
    try
      TempConnection.AliasName := AdsConnection1.AliasName;
      TempConnection.AdsServerTypes :=
        AdsConnection1.AdsServerTypes;
```

```
      TempConnection.Username := UName;
      TempConnection.Password := UPass;
      TempConnection.LoginPrompt := False;
      try
        TempConnection.IsConnected := True;
      except
        result := False;
      end;
      result := True;
    finally
      TempConnection.IsConnected := False;
      TempConnection.Free;
    end;
  end; //CheckPass
  {$HINTS ON}

begin
  UserName := AdsConnection1.Username;
  OldPass := '';
  InputBox('Password', 'Enter your current password', OldPass);
  if OldPass = '' then Exit;
  if not CheckPass(UserName, OldPass) then
  begin
    ShowMessage('Cannot validate your current password. ' +
      'Cannot change password');
    Exit;
  end;
  NewPass1 := '';
  NewPass2 := '';
  InputBox('Password', 'Enter your new password', NewPass1);
  if NewPass1 = '' then
  begin
    ShowMessage('Password cannot be blank. ' +
      'Cannot change password');
    Exit;
  end;
  InputBox('Password', 'Confirm your new password', NewPass2);
  if NewPass1 <> NewPass2 then
  begin
    ShowMessage('Passwords did not match. ' +
      'Cannot change password');
    Exit;
  end;
```

```
//Connect AdsDictionary1 and change password
AdsDictionary1.AliasName := AdsConnection1.AliasName;
AdsDictionary1.AdsServerTypes :=
  AdsConnection1.AdsServerTypes;
AdsDictionary1.UserName := AdsConnection1.Username;
AdsDictionary1.Password := AdsConnection1.Password;
AdsDictionary1.LoginPrompt := False;
AdsDictionary1.Connect;
AdsDictionary1.SetUserProperty(AdsConnection1.Username,
  ADS_DD_USER_PASSWORD, PChar(NewPass1),
  (StrLen(PChar(NewPass1)) + 1));
AdsDictionary1.Disconnect;
ShowMessage('Password successfully changed. ' +
  'New password will be valid next time you connect');
end;
```

This code segment is a bit simpler than the preceding one. After verifying
that the user knows the current password with which they are connected, they
are prompted for their new password twice, for confirmation purposes. Next, the
AdsDictionary component is configured to connect with the user account, after
which its SetUserProperty method is invoked to change the user's password. As
the final dialog box displayed by this event handler indicates, this password will
be valid once the user terminates all connections on this user account.

NOTE

*If you run this code, and change the password of the adsuser account, you should use the
Advantage Data Architect to change the password back to **password**. Otherwise, you will
not be able to run this project again, since the password is assigned to the Password property
of the AdsConnection component.*

CHAPTER 3

Using ADS from Java

J ava developers have long been able to work with ADS using the JDBC-ODBC bridge, a class 1 JDBC (Java database connectivity) driver. The JDBC-ODBC bridge, however, is not convenient to use, and is even more difficult to deploy since it requires the additional installation and deployment of an appropriate ODBC (open database connectivity) driver. With the Advantage JDBC Driver, a class 4 JDBC driver first released in ADS version 7.0, working with ADS from Java is a breeze.

This chapter provides you with examples of using the Advantage JDBC Driver with the JDBC classes to perform a wide range of common data-related tasks—using the Java language in general, and Borland's JBuilder in particular. As is the case with the other chapters in Part III, this discussion assumes that you are already familiar with Java programming.

ADS and Java

JDBC (Java database connectivity) is the core technology for accessing data from Java applications, applets, and servlets. Furthermore, using the JDBC Connector, available from Sun Microsystems, you can use this JDBC driver with any J2EE-compliant server. The Advantage JDBC Driver, named ADSDriver, is located in the com.extendedsystems.jdbc.advantage namespace. Once you have registered this driver and obtained a connection from the DriverManager, you access your ADS data using the classes and interfaces of the java.sql namespace.

The Advantage JDBC Driver is a class 4 JDBC driver. Unlike class 1, class 2, and class 3 JDBC drivers, a class 4 driver requires no additional libraries, beyond the Java driver itself, to connect to the underlying data. With the Advantage JDBC Driver, the connection to ADS is accomplished using sockets. Unlike the other Advantage data access mechanisms, the Advantage JDBC Driver does not require the services of the Advantage Client Engine (ace32.dll and libace.so are the ACE libraries for Windows and Linux, respectively).

The Advantage JDBC Driver communicates with ADS using TCP/IP port 6262 by default. If you need to communicate with ADS using a different port number on the server, you must change the server configuration. See the ADS help for information on how to configure your TCP/IP (transmission control protocol/Internet protocol) port number for the version of the ADS server that you are using.

Before you can use the Advantage JDBC Driver, you must install the adsjdbc.jar file and add it to your CLASSPATH environment variable. Java uses CLASSPATH to locate Java classes and other resources at runtime. The Advantage JDBC Driver installation will automatically install the JAR file. Depending on which environment you install the driver on, you may have to add the JAR file location to your CLASSPATH variable manually.

This chapter shows you how to access ADS using the Advantage JDBC Driver. This discussion is divided into four major sections. The first section describes common basic tasks, such as connecting to ADS, executing queries, and calling stored procedures.

NOTE

You cannot access ALS (Advantage Local Server) using the Advantage JDBC Driver. You must use ADS.

The second section shows you how to perform basic navigation with JDBC, and the third section demonstrates several basic administrative tasks, such as creating tables and granting rights to them. In the fourth and final section, you will find a brief discussion of using the Advantage JDBC Driver with JBuilder's DataExpress components.

The use of the Advantage JDBC Driver is demonstrated in this chapter using Borland's JBuilder, the most popular Java IDE (integrated development environment). Figure 13-1 shows the AdsJava.jpx project opened in JBuilder 9, with the public JFrame class, named MainFrame, displayed in the JBuilder designer.

 ### ON THE CD

The sample code in this chapter can be found in the JBuilder project named AdsJava.jpx, available on this book's CD-ROM (see Appendix B).

Even if you do not have a copy of JBuilder, you can still explore this project using the JDK (Java Development Kit) available from Sun Microsystems. Simply compile the two Java source files named Application1.java and MainFrame.java using javac.exe, the Java compiler. Once you have compiled these java files into byte-code class files, launch the application by running the Application1.class file using java.exe, the Java runtime launcher. The Application1 class contains the public, static main method entry point.

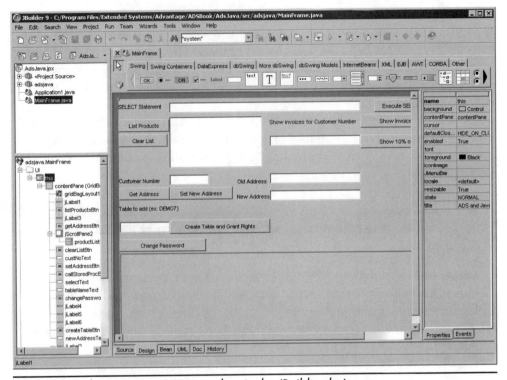

Figure 13-1   *The MainFrame JFrame class in the JBuilder designer*

Performing Basic Tasks with ADS and Java

This section describes some of the more common tasks that you can perform with Java and the Advantage JDBC Driver. These include connecting to a data dictionary, opening a table, executing a query, using a parameterized query, and executing a stored procedure.

Connecting to Data

You connect to a data dictionary or to a directory in which free tables are located by calling the getConnection method of the DriverManager. The getConnection method takes a connection string, which must be prefaced by the driver manager class that you want to get the connection for. For a connection to ADS, this prefix is jdbc:extendedsystems:advantage:.

Prior to calling getConnection, you must have instantiated the Advantage JDBC Driver. This is done by calling the forClass method of the Class class, passing the name of the Advantage JDBC Driver as an argument.

Because numerous event handlers associated with the MainFrame class use this connection, a variable of type Connection (a JDBC class) is declared in the MainFrame's class declaration, which places this variable in scope of all event handlers that need it. This variable declaration, as well as several additional JDBC class variables that are used in two or more event handlers in this project, are shown here:

```
public class MainFrame extends JFrame {
  Connection conn;
  Statement stmt;
  PreparedStatement prepStmt;
//additional declarations
```

The Connection variable (conn) in the preceding segment is assigned a connection from a private method that is called from the MainFrame class constructor. This method, databaseInit, is shown in the following code segment:

```
private void databaseInit() throws Exception{
  Class.forName("com.extendedsystems.jdbc.advantage.ADSDriver");
  conn = DriverManager.getConnection("jdbc:extendedsystems:" +
    "advantage://server:6262/share/program files/" +
    "extended systems/advantage/adsbook/"+
    "demodictionary.add;user=adsuser;password=password");
  stmt = conn.createStatement();
  prepStmt = conn.prepareStatement("SELECT * FROM INVOICE "+
    "WHERE [customer id] = ?" );
}
```

As you can see from the preceding method, forName is passed the name of the class of the Advantage JDBC Driver, which instantiates the driver. When the getConnection method of the DriverManager is called, it locates the instantiated driver by means of the prefix in the connection string.

In addition to containing the prefix for the Advantage JDBC Driver, this connection includes a URL (uniform resource locator) that points to the TCP/IP port on the machine named *server* where the data is located. This URL also includes an optional data location, identified by a share on that server (named *share* in this instance), and a qualified path to the data dictionary. Two additional parameters, the user name and password, are passed in this connection string as well.

> **NOTE**
>
> *If an exception is raised when you attempt to connect, verify that your URL is correct and try again. You should also ensure that all clients on the same machine use a remote connection (since the Java driver only uses remote).*

Because this connection string refers to the DemoDictionary data dictionary, and this dictionary requires logins, this particular connection string contains all of the essential parameters needed to connect to this database. Additional parameters could have been passed in this connection string as name/value pairs, where an equal sign separates the name and value. As you can see in the preceding connection string, when the connection string contains two or more name/value pairs, semicolons separate them. The full list of the optional connection string parameters is shown in Table 13-1.

Executing a Query

You can execute a query against ADS by calling any one of a number of methods of a java.sql.Statement instance, including execute, executeQuery, and executeUpdate. The execute method returns True if the statement returns a result, False if it does not,

Parameter	Description
Catalog	If the data directory or data dictionary path is not provided in the connection URL, set it to the qualified name of the data dictionary or the file location on the specified server where the free tables are located.
CharType	Identifies the character set used by the server. Can be set to **ansi** or **oem**. The default is ansi.
LockType	Identifies the type of locking to be used by ADS. Can be set to **compatibility** or **proprietary**. The default is proprietary.
Password	If the data dictionary requires logins, use this parameter to submit the user's password.
ShowDeleted	Set to **true** to include deleted records in DBF files, or set to **false** to suppress deleted records. The default is false.
TableType	Used to identify the type of table when connecting to free tables. This parameter can be set to **adt**, **cdx**, or **ntx**. The default is adt. This property is not used when you connect to a data dictionary.
User	If the data dictionary requires login, use this parameter to submit the user's user name.

Table 13-1   *The Optional Connection String Parameters*

and throws an exception if the statement fails. The execute method is best when you do not know ahead of time if the statement returns a result set. Call executeQuery when you know that a result set will be returned, and executeUpdate when you know that one will not be returned.

The following event handler demonstrates the execution of a query that returns a result set. This event handler is associated with the Execute SELECT button (shown in Figure 13-1):

```
void executeSelect_actionPerformed(ActionEvent e) {
  try {
    ResultSet rs = stmt.executeQuery(selectText.getText());
    if (isRSEmpty(rs)) {
      JOptionPane.showMessageDialog(this,
        "No records in result set");
      return;
    }
    jTable1.setModel(new ResultTableModel(rs));
  }
  catch (Exception e1) {
    System.err.println( e1.getMessage());
  }
}
```

Since this is the first event handler from this project that we've inspected, there are two characteristics that need to be introduced—specifically, the isRSEmpty method and the use of the ResultTableModel class. Both of these are declared in the MainFrame.java file.

The isRSEmpty method is called by many of the event handlers in this application to determine whether or not there are records in the ResultSet returned by executeQuery. This method was added to the MainFrame class declaration as a public static method. The following is the implementation of this method:

```
public static boolean isRSEmpty(ResultSet rs) {
  try {
    return ! rs.first();
  }
  catch (Exception e1) {
    System.err.println( e1.getMessage());
    return false;
  }
}
```

The second item of interest is the class ResultTableModel. This class extends the abstract class AbtractTableModel, and it is used to create a model that can be used by the JTable class to display the contents of the result set. (Java swing classes employ a model-view architecture. The view is supplied by the visual component, and the model is responsible for handling the data.) At a minimum, ResultTableModel must override getColumnCount, getRowCount, and getValueAt. In this case, getColumnName is also overridden.

The following code implements the ResultTableModel class:

```
class ResultTableModel
   extends javax.swing.table.AbstractTableModel {
   Object obj [] [];
   int rows, columns;
   ResultSetMetaData rsMeta;

   public ResultTableModel (ResultSet rs) {
     try {
       if (rs == null) {
         rows = 0;
         columns = 0;
         obj = new Object[0][0];
         return;
       }
       rsMeta = rs.getMetaData();
       //get column count
       columns = rsMeta.getColumnCount();
       //calculate number of rows
       rows = 0;
       rs.first();
       do {
         rows++;
       } while (rs.next());
       //set array dimension
       obj = new Object [rows][columns];
       //load data
       rs.first();
       rows = 0;
       do {
         for (int j = 0; j <= (columns-1); j++) {
           obj[rows][j] = rs.getString(j+1);
         }
         rows++;
```

```
      } while (rs.next());
   } catch (Exception e1) {
   System.out.println(e1.getMessage());
   }
}

   public int getColumnCount() {
         return columns;
   }

     public int getRowCount() {
         return rows;
     }

     public String getColumnName(int col)  {
        String res = "";
        if (rsMeta == null) {
          return res;
        }
        try {
          res = rsMeta.getColumnName(col+1);
        }
        catch (Exception e1) {
          System.out.println(e1.getMessage());
        }
        return res;
     }

     public Object getValueAt(int row, int col) {
         return obj[row][col];
     }
} //ResultTableModel class
```

As you can see in this code, the constructor of ResultTableModel is passed the
ResultSet. This ResultSet is used to obtain a ResultSetMetaData object, which is
then used to determine the number of columns in the ResultSet. This ResultSetMetaData
object is also used to obtain the column names from within the getColumnName method.

Next, the ResultSet is navigated in order to count how many records the ResultSet
contains. Finally, a two-dimensional array of Object is declared and populated with
the rows and columns of the ResultSet.

Admittedly, this code is somewhat inefficient, in that it necessitates the retrieval
of all of the records in the ResultSet, which is a time-consuming task when many

records are involved. Consequently, this is not the type of TableModel that would be appropriate for every application. But for this sample Java project, it works just fine.

ResultTableModel is used to populate the JTable instance, a grid control, that appears in the JFrame. Figure 13-2 shows this JTable populated with the results of a SQL SELECT statement.

Using a Parameterized Query

Instead of using a Statement object, you use a PreparedStatement object when you need to execute a parameterized query. You can create a PreparedStatement object by calling the prepareStatement method of a Connection object, passing the parameterized query as an argument.

Before executing the PreparedStatement, you must call one of its setter methods for each parameter in the query. Which setter method you call depends on the data type of the parameter. If the parameter is a String, you call setString. On the other hand, if the parameter is an Integer, you call setInt.

The PreparedStatement was created in the databaseInit method shown earlier in this chapter. Data is bound to the single parameter, and the query is executed, from

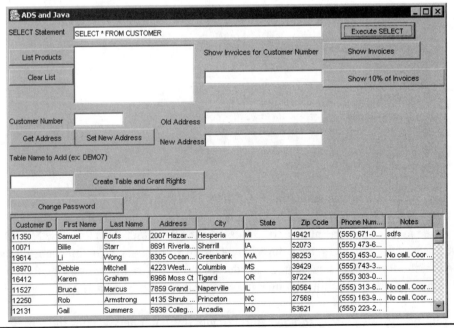

Figure 13-2   *The JTable obtains its data from ResultTableModel.*

the following event handler, which is associated with the Show Invoices button (shown in Figure 13-1):

```
void showInvoiceBtn_actionPerformed(ActionEvent e) {
  try{
    prepStmt.setInt( 1, Integer.parseInt(paramText.getText()));
    ResultSet rs = prepStmt.executeQuery();
    if (isRSEmpty(rs)) {
      JOptionPane.showMessageDialog(this,
        "No records in result set");
      return;
    }
    jTable1.setModel(new ResultTableModel(rs));
  }
  catch (Exception e1) {
    System.err.println( e1.getMessage());
  }
}
```

Reading and Writing Data

You access individual columns in a ResultSet by calling one of its getter methods. All ResultSet getter methods are overloaded. You can identify a column either by ordinal position or by name.

Which getter method you call depends on the data type of the column you are reading. For example, you call getString in order to read a column containing text, and getBoolean to read a logical column.

If the result set is based on a live (dynamic) cursor, you can change its data and apply the change to the underlying ADS table. You write to a column of a ResultSet by calling one of its setter methods. Like getter methods, ResultSet setter methods are overloaded, taking either the ordinal position of a field or the field name, in addition to the value you are writing to the field.

Once you have written to one or more fields of an updatable ResultSet record, you apply the changes to the underlying table by calling the ResultSet's updateRow method.

The following event handler, associated with the Get Address button (shown in Figure 13-1), demonstrates how to read a field from a ResultSet:

```
void getAddressBtn_actionPerformed(ActionEvent e) {
  PreparedStatement getCustStmt;
  if (custNoText.getText() == "") {
    System.out.println("Enter a customer ID");
```

```
      return;
    }
    try {
      getCustStmt = conn.prepareStatement(
        "SELECT * FROM CUSTOMER WHERE [customer id] = ?" );
      getCustStmt.setInt( 1,
        Integer.parseInt(custNoText.getText()));
      ResultSet rs = getCustStmt.executeQuery();
      if (isRSEmpty(rs)) {
        JOptionPane.showMessageDialog(this,
         "No records in result set");
        jTable1.setModel(new ResultTableModel(null));
        return;
      }
      oldAddressText.setText(rs.getString("Address"));
      jTable1.setModel(new ResultTableModel(rs));
    }
    catch (Exception e1) {
      System.err.println( e1.getMessage());
    }
  }
```

The next event handler, associated with the Set New Address button (shown in Figure 13-1), demonstrates writing to a field and saving the change to ADS:

```
void setAddressBtn_actionPerformed(ActionEvent e) {
  PreparedStatement getCustStmt;
  if (custNoText.getText() == "") {
    System.out.println("Enter a customer ID");
    return;
  }
  try {
    getCustStmt = conn.prepareStatement(
      "SELECT * FROM CUSTOMER WHERE [customer id] = ?" );
    getCustStmt.setInt( 1,
      Integer.parseInt(custNoText.getText()));
    ResultSet rs = getCustStmt.executeQuery();
    if (isRSEmpty(rs)) {
      JOptionPane.showMessageDialog(this,
       "No records in result set");
      return;
    }
    rs.updateString("Address", newAddressText.getText());
```

```
      rs.updateRow();
  }
  catch (Exception e1) {
    System.err.println( e1.getMessage());
  }
}
```

Calling a Stored Procedure

Calling a stored procedure is no different than executing any other query. If your stored procedure does not require input parameters, you use a Statement instance. You use a PreparedStatement instance if there are one or more input parameters. If the stored procedure returns one or more records, you invoke the executeQuery method of the Statement or PreparedStatement object, and the execute or executeUpdate methods when the stored procedure does not return records.

Invoking a stored procedure that takes one input parameter is demonstrated by the following code associated with the actionPerformed event handler for the Show 10% of Invoices button (shown in Figure 13-1). The stored procedure referenced in this code is the Delphi AEP (Advantage Extended Procedure) created in Chapter 7. If you did not create this AEP, but created one of the other AEPs described in that chapter, substitute the name of the stored procedure object in your data dictionary in the EXECUTE PROCEDURE string, like this:

```
void callStoredProcBtn_actionPerformed(ActionEvent e) {
  PreparedStatement getCustStmt;
  if (custNoText.getText() == "") {
    System.out.println("Enter a customer ID");
    return;
  }
  try {
    getCustStmt = conn.prepareStatement(
      "EXECUTE PROCEDURE DelphiAEP( ? )" );
    getCustStmt.setInt( 1,
      Integer.parseInt(paramText.getText()));
    ResultSet rs = getCustStmt.executeQuery();
    if (isRSEmpty(rs)) {
      jTable1.setModel(new ResultTableModel(null));
      JOptionPane.showMessageDialog(this,
        "No records in result set");
      return;
    }
```

```
    jTable1.setModel(new ResultTableModel(rs));
  }
  catch (Exception e1) {
    JOptionPane.showMessageDialog(this,
      e1.getMessage());
  }
}
```

Navigational Actions with ADS and Java

Unlike Delphi and ADO-based ADS applications, which support a wide range of
navigational operations, JDBC supports only simple navigation. Specifically, the
ResultSet class permits you to navigate forward through the records of the result set,
and if the cursor is bidirectional, you can move forward and backward, using methods
with names such as first, next, last, and previous. The use of simple forward navigation
is demonstrated in the following section.

NOTE

Some classes in Borland's DataExpress in JBuilder support additional navigational capabilities,
such as filtering. These classes, however, are not native to JDBC.

Scanning a Result Set

Scanning is the process of sequentially reading every record in a result set.
Although scanning is a common task, it is important to note that it necessarily
requires the client application to retrieve all of the records in the result set. This
is not a problem when few records are involved, but if a large number of records
are being scanned, network resources may be taxed.

TIP

If you must scan a large number of records, implement the operation using an AEP. Scanning from
an AEP installed on ADS requires no network resources.

The following code demonstrates scanning. It is associated with the actionPerformed
event handler of the List Products button (shown in Figure 13-1), and it navigates the
entire PRODUCTS table, assigning data from each record to the ProductList JListBox:

```
void listProductsBtn_actionPerformed(ActionEvent e) {
  DefaultListModel listModel = new javax.swing.DefaultListModel();
  try {
```

```
    ResultSet rs = stmt.executeQuery("SELECT * FROM PRODUCTS");
    rs.first();
    do {
      listModel.addElement(rs.getString(1) + "      " +
        rs.getString(2));
    } while (rs.next());
    productList.setModel(listModel);
  }
  catch (Exception e1) {
    System.err.println( e1.getMessage());
  }
}
```

Note that the do-while loop in the preceding event handler could also have been written as follows:

```
while (rs.next()) do {
  listModel.addElement(rs.getString(1) + "      " +
    rs.getString(2));
}
```

While the behavior of these two control structures is equivalent, there is a potential drawback to the second version, the while-do loop. Specifically, if the ResultSet has been navigated in any way prior to the while-do loop, the first record will be skipped. The do-while statement preceded by a call to the first method, by comparison, always processes every record in the ResultSet, whether or not the ResultSet has been navigated previously.

Administrative Operations with ADS and Java

While ADS requires little in the way of periodic maintenance to keep it running smoothly, many applications need to provide administrative functionality related to the management of users, groups, and other objects.

This section is designed to provide you with insight into exposing administrative functions in your client applications. Two related, yet different, operations are demonstrated here. In the first, a new table is added to the database and all groups are granted access rights to it. This operation requires that you establish an administrative connection. The second operation involves permitting individual users to modify their own passwords. Especially in the security-conscious world of modern database management, this feature is often considered an essential step to protecting data.

Creating a Table and Granting Rights to It

The AdsJava project permits a user to enter the name of a table that will be created in the data dictionary, after which all groups will be granted rights to the table. This operation is demonstrated in the following event handler, which is associated with the actionPerformed event of the Create Table and Grant Rights button (shown in Figure 13-1):

```java
void createTableBtn_actionPerformed(ActionEvent e) {
  boolean found = false;
  Connection adminconn;
  Statement adminstmt;
  Statement grantstmt;
  ResultSet rs;
  String tn = tableNameText.getText();
  //Check for semicolon hack
  if (! (tn.indexOf(";") == -1)) {
    JOptionPane.showMessageDialog(this,
      "Table name may not contain a semicolon");
    return;
  }
  if (tableNameText.getText().equals("")) {
    JOptionPane.showMessageDialog(this,
      "Please enter a table name");
    return;
  }
  try {
    adminconn = DriverManager.getConnection(
      "jdbc:extendedsystems:advantage://server:6262/share"+
      "/program files/extended systems/advantage/adsbook/" +
      "demodictionary.add;user=adssys;password=password");
    adminstmt = adminconn.createStatement();
    rs =
      adminstmt.executeQuery("SELECT NAME FROM system.tables");
    String tabName;
    if (! isRSEmpty(rs)) {
      rs.first();
      do {
        tabName = rs.getString("Name");
        if (tabName.equalsIgnoreCase(tn)) {
          found = true;
```

```
      break;
      }
    } while (rs.next());
  }
  if (found) {
    JOptionPane.showMessageDialog(this,
      "Table already exists. Cannot create");
    return;
  }
  adminstmt.executeUpdate("CREATE TABLE " + tn +
    "([Full Name] CHAR(30)," +
    "[Date of Birth] DATE," +
    "[Credit Limit] MONEY, " +
    "Active LOGICAL)");
  rs = adminstmt.executeQuery("SELECT * FROM system.usergroups");
  if (isRSEmpty(rs)) {
    JOptionPane.showMessageDialog(this,
      "No groups to grant rights to");
    return;
  }
  grantstmt = adminconn.createStatement();
  rs.first();
  do {
    grantstmt.executeUpdate("GRANT ALL ON [" + tn + "]" +
      " TO [" +  rs.getString("Name") + "]");
  } while (rs.next());
  JOptionPane.showMessageDialog(this, "The " + tn + " table " +
    "has been created, with rights granted to all groups");
} catch (Exception e1) {
  System.out.println(e1.getMessage());
}
}
```

This event handler begins by verifying that the table name does not include a semicolon, which could be used to convert the subsequent GRANT SQL statement into a SQL script. Since this value represents a table name, using a parameterized query is not an option.

Next, this code verifies that the table does not already exist in the data dictionary. Once that is done, a new connection is created using the data dictionary administrative account. This connection is then used to call CREATE TABLE to create the table, and then to call GRANT for each group returned in the system.usergroups table.

> ### *NOTE*
>
> *The administrative user name and passwords are represented by string literals in this code segment. This was done for convenience, but in a real application, either you would ask for this information from the user, or you would obfuscate this information so that it could not be retrieved.*

Changing a User Password

A user can change the password on their own connection, if you permit this. In most cases, only when every user has a distinct user name would you expose this functionality in a client application. When multiple users share a user name, this operation is usually reserved for an application administrator.

The following event handler, associated with the Change Password button (shown in Figure 13-1), demonstrates how you can permit a user to change their password from a client application:

```
void changePasswordBtn_actionPerformed(ActionEvent e) {
  String userName;
  String oldPass;
  String newPass1;
  String newPass2;
  try {
    ResultSet rs = stmt.executeQuery("SELECT USER() as Name " +
                                     "FROM system.iota");
    rs.first();
    userName = rs.getString("Name");
    oldPass = JOptionPane.showInputDialog(this,
      "Enter your current password");
    if (oldPass.equals("")) {
      return;
    }
    try {
      Connection tempcon =
          DriverManager.getConnection(
          "jdbc:extendedsystems:advantage://server:6262/share" +
          "/program files/extended systems/advantage/adsbook/" +
          "demodictionary.add;user=" + userName +
          ";password=" + oldPass);
    }
    catch (Exception e1) {
      JOptionPane.showMessageDialog(this,
```

```
           "Invalid password. Cannot change password");
      return;
    }
    //Check for semicolon hack
    newPass1 = JOptionPane.showInputDialog(this,
      "Enter your new password");
    if (! (newPass1.indexOf(";") == -1)) {
    JOptionPane.showMessageDialog(this,
        "Password may not contain a semicolon");
      return;
    }
    newPass2 = JOptionPane.showInputDialog(this,
      "Confirm your new password");
    if (!newPass1.equals(newPass2)) {
    JOptionPane.showMessageDialog(this,
          "Passwords did not match. Cannot change password");
      return;
    }
    stmt.executeUpdate("EXECUTE PROCEDURE sp_ModifyUserProperty('" +
      userName + "', 'USER_PASSWORD', '" + newPass1 + "')");
    JOptionPane.showMessageDialog(this,
      "Password successfully changed. " +
        "New password will be valid next time you connect");
  } catch (Exception e1) {
    System.out.println(e1.getMessage());
  }
}
```

A number of interesting tricks are used in this code. First, the user name is obtained by requesting the USER scalar function from the system.iota table. USER returns the user name on the connection through which the query is executed. Next, the user is asked for their current password, and the user name and password are used to attempt a new connection, which, if successful, confirms that the user is valid.

Finally, the user is asked for their new password twice (for confirmation). If all is well, the sp_ModifyUserProperty stored procedure is called to change the user's password. As the final dialog box displayed by this event handler indicates, this password will be valid once the user terminates all connections on this user account.

NOTE

If you run this code, and change the password of the adsuser account, you should use the Advantage Data Architect to change the password back to **password**. *Otherwise, you will not be able to run this project again, since the password is hard-coded into the connection string.*

The Advantage JDBC Driver and JBuilder's DataExpress

DataExpress is a set of Java classes from Borland's JBuilder. With DataExpress, you get design time configuration of data access components, design time data views, direct binding to data-aware swing controls, a sophisticated SQL query builder, and much more.

One of the most important features of DataExpress is that it works with any JDBC driver, and the Advantage JDBC Driver is no exception. As a result, if you are a JBuilder developer, you can enjoy the benefits and ease of development afforded by DataExpress with your existing data.

A detailed discussion of DataExpress is well beyond the scope of this book. All you really need to know is that when you place a Database component into your project, you use its Connection property editor to reference the Advantage JDBC Driver, as shown in Figure 13-3. From that point forward, you build your DataExpress application as you would using any other JDBC driver.

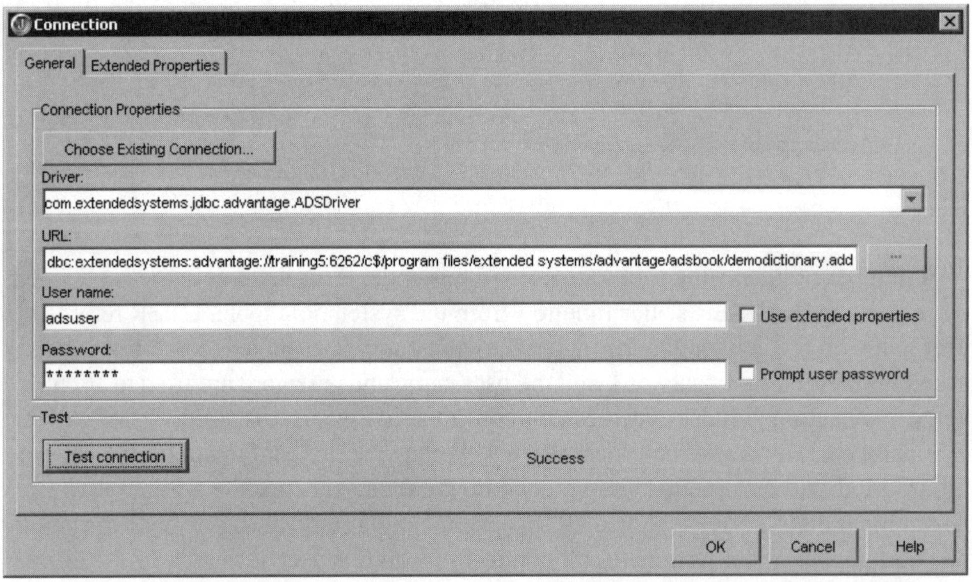

Figure 13-3   *Use the Connection property editor to reference the Advantage JDBC Driver.*

Using ADS from Visual Basic and ADO

IN THIS CHAPTER:

MDAC, OLE DB, ADO, and ADS

Performing Basic Tasks with ADS and ADO

Navigational Actions with ADS and ADO

Administrative Operations with ADS and ADO

ADO (ActiveX data objects) provides the API part of MDAC (Microsoft Data Access Components). MDAC is the implementation of Microsoft's Universal Data Access strategy, which is aimed at providing a high-performance, language-independent data access layer in the Windows operating system.

This chapter provides you with an introduction to MDAC, and ADO in particular. Because ADO is language neutral, the examples presented in this chapter could have been produced using any one of a wide variety of programming languages. Due to its popularity, and heavy reliance on ADO for data access, we have chosen Visual Basic.

This chapter begins with a high-level introduction to ADO and OLE DB. It then continues by showing you how to access your ADS data using ADO.

MDAC, OLE DB, ADO, and ADS

There are three layers to Universal Data Access, Microsoft's ambitious initiative to build a data access layer into the Windows operating system. At the lowest layer are data-providing applications and services. In most cases, such as with ADS, these are client/server database servers. But in practice, they can be almost any type of application imaginable. Nonetheless, the one characteristic that all data providers and services share is that they provide access to information.

Above this lowest layer is OLE DB, which consists of a series of COM (component object model) interfaces. OLE DB provides a layer of abstraction between the data providers and the data consumers, which are your client applications in the traditional client/server architecture.

COM interfaces are simply API templates, which by themselves are useless unless they are implemented by objects. This is where OLE DB providers come in. OLE DB providers are the objects that implement the OLE DB interfaces, and which perform the physical communication with the data-providing applications and services. In the MDAC scheme of things, both OLE DB and OLE DB providers reside in this middle layer.

While it is conceivable for an application developer to program directly to the OLE DB API, doing so would be both time-consuming and complicated. This is because OLE DB, being a low-level interface, was not designed as a developer API. And this is where the third and highest layer comes in, ADO.

ADO consists of a collection of ActiveX data objects that encapsulate calls to OLE DB. By comparison to OLE DB, the ADO API is simple, providing client application developers with convenient access to the data supplied by the data providers and services.

MDAC is normally available on all 32-bit Windows machines (only Windows 95, which is no longer supported by Microsoft, did not come with MDAC already installed). Furthermore, the latest version of MDAC can be freely downloaded from Microsoft's Web site at http://www.microsoft.com/data. The licensing for MDAC specifically permits you to distribute it with your applications, but that is rarely necessary (unless you are installing your applications on obsolete machines).

MDAC consists of all of the ActiveX data objects, as well as a collection of OLE DB providers. The standard providers include the Microsoft Jet 4.0 OLE DB Provider, the Microsoft OLE DB Provider for SQL Server, the Microsoft OLE DB Provider for Oracle, and the Microsoft OLE DB Provider for ODBC, just to name a few.

There are two critical characteristics of Microsoft's Universal Data Access that make this an appealing data access solution. First, regardless of which OLE DB provider you want to use, you access it through the one set of ActiveX data objects. They provide the common API.

The second is that you are not limited to using just the standard OLE DB providers that ship with MDAC. Any COM objects that correctly implement the necessary OLE DB interfaces can be installed on a Windows computer and executed through ADO. The Advantage OLE DB Provider is an example of such an implementation. After installing the Advantage OLE DB Provider, which automatically registers this provider with COM, you can use ADO to access your ADS data.

There is one final issue that deserves mention before turning our attention to using ADS through ADO: client-side cursors versus server-side cursors. In ADO, when you execute a command that returns a result set, you specify where the result set will reside using the CursorLocation property of a Connection or Recordset object. If you set CursorLocation to adUseClient, all records from the result set are downloaded from the server and stored in-memory on the client workstation. By comparison, if you set CursorLocation to adUseServer, the Advantage OLE DB Provider manages the access of data using ADS, retrieving to the client only those records required by your application. The default value of the CursorLocation property of Connection and Recordset objects is adUseServer.

When you load your data into a client-side cursor, operations such as sorting, finding, filtering, and the like are performed by the ADO client cursor engine, and do not involve ADS until you are ready to write changes back to the server. By comparison, when you use server-side cursors, you are leveraging the power and performance of ADS in operations that involve filters, indexes, seeks, and navigation. As a result, the examples discussed in this chapter make use of server-side cursors. If you are interested in learning more about client-side cursors and their features, refer to a book on ADO.

NOTE

Because client-side cursors require that all records be downloaded from the server into memory on your workstation before you can work with your data, you may experience significant delays when loading large result sets using client-side cursors. In most cases, you will achieve excellent performance with ADS and server-side cursors, making them a better solution—particularly when your result sets are large.

The remainder of this chapter shows you how to access ADS using Visual Basic 6. These discussions are divided into three parts. The first part describes common tasks, such as connecting to ADS and accessing data. The second part shows you how to perform simple navigation using ADO. The third and final part demonstrates several basic administrative tasks, such as creating tables and granting rights to them.

ON THE CD

The VB project VB_ADS.vbp can be found on this book's CD_ROM (see Appendix B).

All of the examples presented here can be found in the VB_ADO.vbp Visual Basic project. Figure 14-1 shows the main form of this project in Visual Studio.

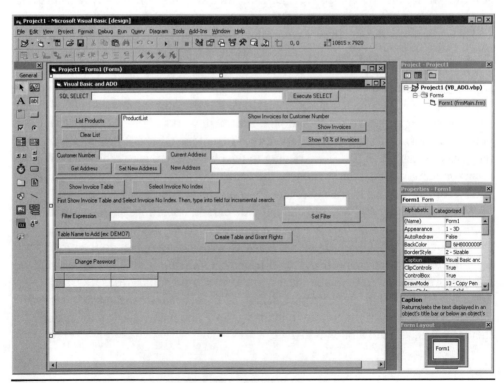

Figure 14-1   *The VB_ADO project in Visual Studio*

NOTE

The VB_ADO project on the code disk was compiled with MDAC 2.8, the latest version of MDAC at the time of this writing. If you are not using MDAC 2.8, you will get an error when you first try to run this project. If this happens, select Project | References. Use the displayed dialog box to uncheck the Microsoft ActiveX Data Objects Library 2.8 (if necessary). Then, scroll to find the version of the Microsoft ActiveX Data Objects Library that you want to use (this must be version 2.1 or later), and add a check mark to it. Click OK when you are done.

As is the case with all data access mechanisms described in Part III, the following discussion of ADS programming with Visual Basic touches on just a few of the available techniques. For a more comprehensive discussion of ADO programming, you may want to pick up a book on ADO programming.

If you are creating a new project that uses ADO, you must add a reference to the Microsoft Data Access Objects library before you can use the Advantage OLE DB Provider with Visual Studio. To do this, use the following steps:

1. From Visual Studio, select Projects | References. Visual Studio displays the References dialog box.

2. Scroll the Available References list until you see Microsoft ActiveX Data Objects Library. Place a check mark next to the version with the highest major and minor version, like this:

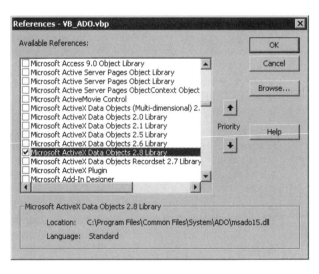

3. Click OK to close the References dialog box.

Performing Basic Tasks with ADS and ADO

This section describes some of the more common tasks that you can perform with ADO. These include connecting to a data dictionary, executing a query, using a parameterized query, retrieving and editing data, and executing a stored procedure.

Connecting to Data

You connect to a data dictionary or a directory in which free tables are located using a Connection object found in the ADODB namespace. At a minimum, you must provide the Connection object with sufficient information to locate your data and configure how the data should be accessed. This can be done either with the Parameters collection property or the ConnectionString property. Both of these properties accept name/value pairs using the parameters listed in Table 14-1. If you use the ConnectionString property, and use more than one name/value pair, separate them with semicolons.

Parameter	Description
CharType	Set to the character set type for DBF files. Valid values are ADS_ANSI and ADS_OEM. The default value is ADS_ANSI.
Compression	Set to ALWAYS, INTERNET, NEVER, or empty. If left empty (the default), the ADS.INI file will control the compression setting. This parameter is not used by ALS.
Data Source	The path to your free tables or data dictionary. If you are using a data dictionary, you must include the data dictionary filename in this path. It is recommended that this path be a UNC path. Data Source is a required parameter.
DbfsUseNulls	Set to TRUE to return empty fields from DBF files as NULL values. If set to FALSE, empty fields are returned as empty data values. The default is FALSE.
EncryptionPassword	Set to an optional password to use for accessing encrypted free tables. If using less than a 20-letter password, a semicolon should be included directly after the password so the Advantage OLE DB Provider knows when the password ends. This parameter is ignored for data dictionary connections.
FilterOptions	Set to IGNORE_WHEN_COUNTING or RESPECT_WHEN_COUNTING. When set to IGNORE_WHEN_COUNTING, the RecordCount property of a Recordset may not accurately reflect the number of records in a result set. Set to RESPECT_WHEN_COUNTING for accurate record counts. Requesting accurate record counts can reduce performance significantly, and should be used only if accurate counts are needed. The default is IGNORE_WHEN_COUNTING.

Table 14-1   *Parameters for Connecting with ADO*

Parameter	Description
IncrementUsercount	Set to TRUE to increment the user count when the connection is made, or FALSE to make a connection without incrementing the user count. The default is FALSE.
Initial Catalog	Optional name of a data dictionary if the data dictionary is not specified in the Data Source parameter.
LockMode	Set to ADS_PROPRIETARY_LOCKING or ADS_COMPATIBLE_LOCKING to define the locking mechanism used for DBF tables. Use ADS_COMPATIBLE_LOCKING when your connection must share data with non-ADS applications. The default is ADS_PROPRIETARY_LOCKING.
Password	When connecting to a data dictionary that requires logins, set to the user's password.
Provider	This required parameter must be set to either Advantage OLE DB Provider or Advantage.OLEDB.1.
SecurityMode	Set to ADS_CHECKRIGHTS to observe the user's network access rights before opening files, or ADS_IGNORERIGHTS to access files regardless of the user's network rights. The default is ADS_CHECKRIGHTS. This property applies only to free table connections.
ServerType	Set to the type of ADS server you want to connect to. Use ADS_LOCAL_SERVER, ADS_REMOTE_SERVER, or ADS_INTERNET_SERVER. To attempt to connect to two or more types, separate the server types using a vertical bar (|). This is demonstrated in the ConnectionString shown later in this chapter.
ShowDeleted	Set to TRUE to include deleted records in DBF files, or FALSE to suppress deleted records. The default is FALSE.
StoredProcedure Connection	Set to TRUE if connecting from within a stored procedure. When set to TRUE, the connection does not increment the user count. The default is FALSE.
TableType	Set to ADS_ADT, ADS_CDX, or ADS_NTX to define the default table type. The default is ADS_ADT. This parameter is ignored for data dictionary connections.
TrimTrailingSpaces	Set to TRUE to trim trailing spaces from character fields, or FALSE to preserve trailing spaces. The default is FALSE.
User ID	If connecting to a data dictionary that requires logins, set to the user's user name.

Table 14-1   *Parameters for Connecting with ADO* (continued)

For any of the optional connection string parameters that you fail to provide, ADO will automatically insert the default parameters. Furthermore, instead of supplying a connection string with your connection information, you can set the connection string to the following pattern:

```
FILE NAME=path\filename.udl
```

where *path* is the physical or UNC path to a directory in which a file with the .udl file extension resides, and *filename* is the name of a UDL (universal data link) file. UDL files are INI-style files that contain ADO connection information. Under the most recent versions of Windows, UDL files are stored in

```
C:\Program Files\Common Files\System\Ole DB\Data Links
```

You do not even need to know how a UDL file is structured to create one. Simply create a new empty file in the preceding directory using the UDL file extension. Then, using the Windows Explorer, right-click this filename and select Properties. Use the displayed properties dialog box, shown in Figure 14-2, to configure the connection information. At runtime, when ADO processes the connection string containing FILE NAME=*path\filename*.udl, it will expand the connection string, populating it with the definitions located in the UDL file.

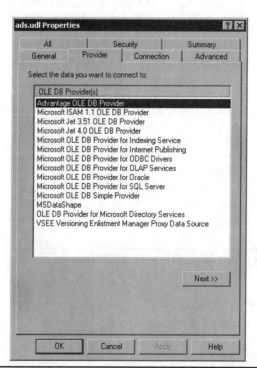

Figure 14-2   *Setting the connection properties of an empty UDL file*

Because the Connection object that is used by this project must be used by a number of subprocedures, the AdsConnection variable and several other variables that must be repeatedly referenced are declared global to the project. The following is this global declaration. Note also that the location of the data source location of the data dictionary is declared as a global constant.

```
'Require explicit variable declarations
Option Explicit
Dim AdsConnection As ADODB.Connection
Dim AdsCommand As ADODB.Command
Dim AdsRecordset As ADODB.Recordset
Dim AdsParamQueryCommand As ADODB.Command
Dim AdsParamQueryRecordset As ADODB.Recordset
Dim AdsParameter As ADODB.Parameter
Dim AdminConnection As ADODB.Connection
Dim AdminCommand As ADODB.Command
Const DataPath = "\\server\share\Program Files\Extended Systems" + _
  "\Advantage\ADSBook\DemoDictionary.add"
```

This Connection, named AdsConnection, is created, configured, and opened from the Load event of the form, along with several other Command, Recordset, and Connection objects. The relevant portion of this subprocedure is shown in the following code:

```
Private Sub Form_Load()
  On Error GoTo ErrorHandler
  Set AdsConnection = New ADODB.Connection
  Set AdsCommand = New ADODB.Command
  Set AdsRecordset = New ADODB.Recordset
  Set AdminConnection = New ADODB.Connection
  Set AdminCommand = New ADODB.Command
  'Setup the connection
  AdsConnection.ConnectionString = _
    "Provider=Advantage OLE DB Provider;" + _
    "Data Source=" + DataPath + ";user ID=adsuser;" + _
    "password=password;" + _
    "ServerType=ADS_LOCAL_SERVER | ADS_REMOTE_SERVER;" + _
    "FilterOptions=RESPECT_WHEN_COUNTING;TrimTrailingSpaces=True"

  AdsConnection.Open

  Set AdsCommand.ActiveConnection = AdsConnection
  'Additional code not shown follows
  Exit Sub
```

```
ErrorHandler:
    MsgBox "Error: " & Err.Number & vbCrLf & _
        "Description: " & Err.Description
    Exit Sub
End Sub
```

As you inspect this code, you will notice that all errors are handled by displaying the error code and message of the error. This type of error handler is present in every subprocedure in this Visual Basic project. In order to reduce redundancy in this chapter, the error handling block, as well as the subprocedure declaration, is omitted from the remaining subprocedure listings in this chapter.

> **NOTE**
>
> *If you have difficulty connecting, it might be because you have other client applications, such as the Advantage Data Architect, connected using a local connection. Ensure that all clients on the same machine use the same type of connection.*

Executing a Query

You execute a query that returns a result set by calling the Open procedure of a Recordset. This procedure has five optional parameters. The first is the command you want to execute. This can be either a Command object, the name of a table or stored procedure, or (as in the case in the following code segment) the actual text of the query. The second parameter is the connection over which the query will be executed.

The third parameter identities the type of cursor that you want returned, and the fourth specifies the type of record locking you want. The fifth and final parameter identifies what kind of command you pass in the first parameter. If you pass a table name in the first parameter, you can pass the value adCmdTable in this fifth parameter, and a SELECT * FROM query will be generated. If you pass the name of a stored procedure that takes no input parameters in the first parameter, an EXECUTE PROCEDURE statement is generated if adCmdStoredProc is given as the fifth parameter.

The following code demonstrates the execution of a query entered by the user into the TextBox named SELECTText. This subprocedure is associated with the Execute SELECT button (shown in Figure 14-1):

```
If AdsRecordset.State = adStateOpen Then
    AdsRecordset.Close
End If
```

```
AdsRecordset.Open SELECTText.Text, AdsConnection, adOpenDynamic, _
  adLockPessimistic, adCmdText
Set DataGrid1.DataSource = AdsRecordset
```

This code begins by verifying that the Recordset is not currently open, by checking its State property. Next, the query is executed and the returned records are assigned to the Recordset. Finally, the Recordset is assigned to the DataSource property of the DataGrid. The effects of executing this code are shown in Figure 14-3.

If you need to execute a query that does not return a Recordset, use a Command object. The use of a Command object to execute a query that does not return a Recordset is demonstrated later in this chapter.

Using a Parameterized Query

Parameterized queries are defined using a Command object. This command object can then be executed directly, so long as the query does not return a result set. If the parameterized query returns one or more records, you can execute it using the Open method of a Recordset, just as you can with a query that takes no parameters.

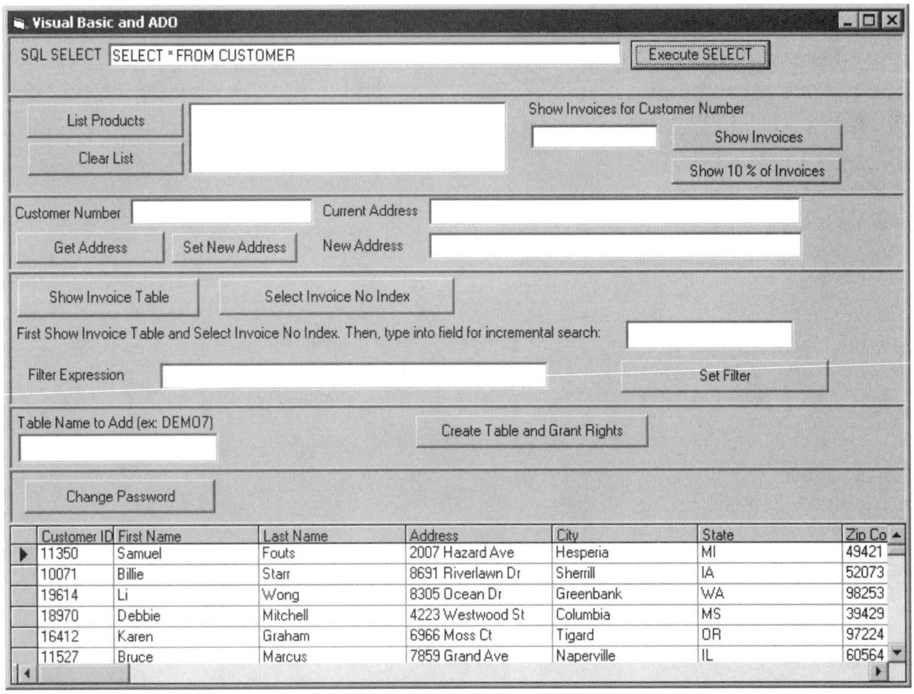

Figure 14-3   *Records returned from a query are displayed in a data grid.*

Before you can invoke a parameterized query, you must create one Parameter object for each of the query's parameters, and then associate each Parameter with the Command holding the parameterized query.

The definition of a parameterized query, including the creation and configuration of a parameter, is shown in the following code segment. This code segment is part of the Load event for the form object, and was omitted from the code listing shown earlier (in the section "Connecting to Data"):

```
'Set up the parameterized query that will be reused
Set AdsParamQueryCommand = New ADODB.Command
Set AdsParamQueryRecordset = New ADODB.Recordset
Set AdsParamQueryCommand.ActiveConnection = AdsConnection
AdsParamQueryCommand.CommandText = _
   "SELECT * FROM INVOICE WHERE [Customer ID] = ?"
Set AdsParameter = AdsParamQueryCommand.CreateParameter
AdsParamQueryCommand.Prepared = True
AdsParamQueryCommand.NamedParameters = False
AdsParameter.Type = adInteger
AdsParamQueryCommand.Parameters.Append AdsParameter
```

Once a Parameter has been created, configured, and associated with the Command holding the parameterized query statement, there is only one more step necessary before the query can be executed. You must bind data to each parameter. This is shown in the following click event of the DoParamQuery button (the button labeled Show Invoices in Figure 14-1):

```
If IsNumeric(ParamText.Text) = False Then
   MsgBox "Invalid customer number"
   Exit Sub
End If
If AdsParamQueryRecordset.State = adStateOpen Then
   AdsParamQueryRecordset.Close
End If
AdsParameter.Value = CInt(ParamText.Text)
AdsParamQueryRecordset.Open AdsParamQueryCommand, , adOpenDynamic, _
   adLockPessimistic, adCmdText
If AdsParamQueryRecordset.BOF And _
   AdsParamQueryRecordset.EOF Then
   MsgBox "No invoices for customer ID"
   Set DataGrid1.DataSource = Nothing
Else
```

```
Set DataGrid1.DataSource = AdsParamQueryRecordset
End If
```

As you can see from this code, after verifying that a numeric value has been entered into the customer ID field, the entered data is assigned to the Value property of the parameter and the query is executed.

This example is actually a classic example of how parameterized queries are used. Specifically, the query text is defined only once, but can be executed repeatedly. And by changing only the value of the parameter, a different result set can be returned upon each execution.

Reading and Writing Data

You read data from fields of a Recordset by using the Recordset's Fields property, which is a collection property. The Fields property takes a single parameter that identifies which field's value you want to read. This value can either be an integer identifying the ordinal position of the field in the table's structure (this value is zero-based) or it can be a string identifying the field's name. The Value property of the identified field holds the field's data.

Reading data from a Recordset is demonstrated in the following Click subprocedure associated with the Get Address button (shown in Figure 14-1):

```
Dim AdsGetCustCommand As ADODB.Command
Dim AdsGetCustRecordset As ADODB.Recordset
Dim AdsGetCustParameter As ADODB.Parameter

If CustNoText.Text = "" Or Not IsNumeric(CustNoText.Text) Then
  MsgBox "Please supply a valid customer ID number"
  Exit Sub
End If
Set AdsGetCustCommand = New ADODB.Command
Set AdsGetCustRecordset = New ADODB.Recordset
Set AdsGetCustCommand.ActiveConnection = AdsConnection
AdsGetCustCommand.CommandText = _
  "SELECT * FROM CUSTOMER WHERE [Customer ID] = ?"
Set AdsGetCustParameter = AdsGetCustCommand.CreateParameter
AdsGetCustCommand.Prepared = True
AdsGetCustCommand.NamedParameters = False
AdsGetCustParameter.Type = adInteger
AdsGetCustCommand.Parameters.Append AdsGetCustParameter
AdsGetCustParameter.Value = CInt(CustNoText.Text)
```

```
AdsGetCustRecordset.Open AdsGetCustCommand, , adOpenDynamic, _
   adLockPessimistic, adCmdText
If AdsGetCustRecordset.BOF And _
   AdsGetCustRecordset.EOF Then
   MsgBox "No records for customer ID"
   Set DataGrid1.DataSource = Nothing
Else
   Set DataGrid1.DataSource = AdsGetCustRecordset
   OldAddressText.Text = _
     AdsGetCustRecordset.Fields("Address").Value
End If
```

So long as your Recordset contains a dynamic (live) cursor, you can make changes to a Recordset by assigning data to one or more of the Recordset's Fields Value properties, where you identify the field you are writing to using the same technique that you use to read from a field. After changing one or more fields, you call the Update method of the Recordset to write those changes to ADS. Alternatively, you can call the Recordset's Update, passing to it either a field name/value pair or
an array of field name/value pairs. This second approach writes one or more updated fields to ADS in a single command.

The following code demonstrates one way to update a Recordset. This code can be found for the click procedure associated with the button labeled Set New Address in Figure 14-1:

```
If CustNoText.Text = "" Or Not IsNumeric(CustNoText.Text) Then
   MsgBox "Please supply a valid customer ID number"
   Exit Sub
End If
If InStr(1, TableNameText.Text, ";", vbTextCompare) <> 0 Then
   MsgBox "Customer ID may not contain a semicolon"
   Exit Sub
End If
Dim AdsGetCustRecordset As ADODB.Recordset
Set AdsGetCustRecordset = New ADODB.Recordset
AdsGetCustRecordset.Open "SELECT Address FROM CUSTOMER " + _
   "WHERE [Customer ID] = " + CustNoText.Text, AdsConnection, _
   adOpenDynamic, adLockPessimistic, adCmdText
If AdsGetCustRecordset.BOF And _
   AdsGetCustRecordset.EOF Then
   MsgBox "Customer ID not found"
Else
```

```
  AdsGetCustRecordset.Fields("Address").Value = _
    NewAddressText.Text
  AdsGetCustRecordset.Update
End If
MsgBox "Address for customer " + CustNoText.Text + " " + _
  "has been updated"
Exit Sub
```

Of course, a SQL UPDATE query can also be used to achieve a similar result.

Calling a Stored Procedure

Calling a stored procedure is no different than executing any other query. If your stored procedure does not require input parameters, you can define the query text using a Command object or by passing the call to EXECUTE PROCEDURE in the first parameter of a Recordset Open invocation. Alternatively, you simply pass the name of the stored procedure object in the CommandText, and set the CommandType property (of a Command object) or CommandType parameter (of the Resultset's Open method) to adCmdStoredProc (this second technique is demonstrated in the following example). Typically, you use a Command object—executing it directly—when the stored procedure does not return records, and use the Open method of a Recordset when your stored procedure returns one or more records.

Invoking a stored procedure that takes one input parameter is demonstrated by the following code associated with the click event for the Show 10% of Invoices button (shown in Figure 14-1). The DelphiAEP stored procedure referenced in this code is the Delphi AEP (Advantage Extended Procedure) created in Chapter 7. If you did not create this AEP, but created one of the other AEPs described in that chapter, substitute the name of the stored procedure object in your data dictionary in the CommandText property of the Command object.

```
Dim AdsSPCommand As ADODB.Command
Dim AdsSPRecordset As ADODB.Recordset
Dim AdsSPParameter As ADODB.Parameter

If ParamText.Text = "" Or Not IsNumeric(ParamText.Text) Then
  MsgBox "Please supply a valid customer ID number"
  Exit Sub
End If
Set AdsSPCommand = New ADODB.Command
Set AdsSPRecordset = New ADODB.Recordset
Set AdsSPCommand.ActiveConnection = AdsConnection
```

```
AdsSPCommand.CommandText = "DelphiAEP"
Set AdsSPParameter = AdsSPCommand.CreateParameter
AdsSPCommand.Prepared = True
AdsSPCommand.NamedParameters = False
AdsSPParameter.Type = adInteger
AdsSPCommand.Parameters.Append AdsSPParameter
AdsSPParameter.Value = CInt(ParamText.Text)
AdsSPRecordset.Open AdsSPCommand, , adOpenDynamic, _
  adLockPessimistic, adCmdStoredProc
Set DataGrid1.DataSource = AdsSPRecordset
Exit Sub
```

Navigational Actions with ADS and ADO

ADO supports a number of navigational operations on populated Recordsets, and is second only to Delphi's capabilities in this area. In fact, the only navigational operation supported by Delphi but not by ADO is setting a range (though you can explicitly set a range by calling into the ACE API using Visual Basic, but this is not an ADO issue).

This section describes the navigational options made available through server-side cursors. These operations can be performed on any SQL result set that returns a live cursor or any table opened directly.

Unlike most remote relational database servers, ADS also supports a non-SQL technique for working with a server-side cursor. It involves opening a table directly. When you open a table directly, the Advantage OLE DB Provider obtains a table handle, which permits ADS to use its high-performance indexes, Advantage Optimized Filters, and read-ahead record caching to supply data to your client application. Fortunately, with live cursors, ADS also uses these high-performance features.

You open a table directly by setting the CommandText property of a Command object or the Source parameter of a Recordset's Open method to the table name. You then set the CommandType property of the Command, or the Options parameter of the Recordset's Open method, to adCmdTableDirect. This is shown in the following code segment, which is taken from the ShowInvoiceBtn click event:

```
If AdsRecordset.State = adStateOpen Then
  AdsRecordset.Close
End If
AdsRecordset.Open "INVOICE", AdsConnection, _
  adOpenDynamic, adLockPessimistic, adCmdTableDirect
Set DataGrid1.DataSource = AdsRecordset
```

It's worth noting that there are some similarities, but also some significant differences between using a CommandType of adCmdTable and adCmdTableDirect. Just as you do when you set CommandType (or Options) to adCmdTableDirect, when you use adCmdTable, you assign the name of the table to the CommandText property of a Command object, or pass the table name in the Source parameter of a Recordset's Open method. In response, the Command or Recordset object generates a SELECT * FROM query. Queries like these return a live, server-side cursor (so long as you did not specifically request a client-side cursor), which enables the use of the table's indexes for searching, filtering, and the like.

By comparison, when you set CommandType (or Options) to adCmdTableDirect, the Advantage SQL engine is bypassed altogether, instead opening the table using an OLE DB Rowset object. Opening a table this way enables additional capabilities, including being able to obtain an exclusive lock on the table, which cannot be done through a SQL SELECT statement.

Performing navigational actions on server-side cursors is described in the following sections.

NOTE

The Advantage OLE DB Provider also supports high-performance bookmarks on server-side cursors. For information on using bookmarks, see the ADS help.

Setting an Index

From within an ADO application, you select an available index for one of two reasons. Either you want to sort the records in your Recordset based on the index expression, or you want to use the index to enable high-speed searches using a Recordset.

Fortunately, selecting an index that you have defined in a table's index file is straightforward. You assign the name of an index order to the Index property of a Recordset that returns either a dynamic (live) cursor or a table that is opened directly using the adCmdTableDirect command type. If you are connected to a data dictionary, the index order name can be in any of your table's auto-open indexes.

You return to the natural index order by setting the Index property of the Recordset to an empty string. Setting an index is demonstrated in the following code segment, which is associated with the Select Invoice No Index button (shown in Figure 14-1):

```
If AdsRecordset.State <> adStateOpen Then
    MsgBox "Please open Invoice table before setting index"
    Exit Sub
  End If
AdsRecordset.Index = "Invoice No"
```

Note that you cannot set an index if the Recordset is already actively employing a filter. However, you can apply a filter on a Recordset that is using an index.

Finding a Record Based on Data

ADO supports two methods for searching for data in a Recordset. One of these, Find, performs a record-by-record search for data. When used with server-side cursors, these sequential reads are performed by ADS, but nonetheless the sequential nature of this operation means that it is often relatively slow—especially when the result set is large.

The second method, Seek, is only supported in server-side cursors by OLE DB providers that also support indexes, and fortunately, the Advantage OLE DB Provider is one of them. Unlike Find, Seek uses ADS indexes on server-side cursors to quickly locate records. Compared to Find, Seek is typically much faster at finding records with server-side cursors.

Before you can call Seek on a Recordset, you must set an index that you will use to find the record you are looking for. Once the index is set, you call Seek, passing either a single value or an array of values. If you pass a single value, ADS will search the current index for that value in the first field of the index.

You pass an array of values to Seek when you want to search on more than one expression of a multisegment index order (a multisegment index order is based on two or more fields or expressions). In this case, Seek searches for the first array element in the first field or expression of the current index, then searches the second array element, if present, in the second field or expression of the current index, and so on.

The second, optional parameter, SeekOption, defines how the Seek is performed. Valid values for this second parameter include adSeekAfter, adSeekAfterEQ, adSeekBefore, adSeekBeforeEQ, adSeekFirstEQ, and adSeekLastEQ. The default value is adSeekFirstEQ.

If a matching record is found, based on the SeekOption, the record associated with the value or values is made the current record. If the value or values are not found, the Recordset will point to the end-of-file marker.

The use of Seek is demonstrated in the following code segment. This code is associated with the change event of the TextBox named SearchText. After clicking the Show Invoice Table and Set Invoice No Index buttons, this code permits an incremental search through the INVOICE table:

```
If AdsRecordset.State <> adStateOpen Then
  MsgBox "Please open Invoice table before setting index"
  Exit Sub
End If
If AdsRecordset.Index <> "Invoice No" Then
  MsgBox "You must set the Invoice No index before searching"
```

```
  Exit Sub
End If
AdsRecordset.Seek SearchText.Text, adSeekAfterEQ
If AdsRecordset.EOF Then
  MsgBox "End of file"
End If
```

Setting a Filter

You use a filter to limit a Recordset to a subset of records. When executed on a server-side Recordset, ADS produces an AOF (Advantage Optimized Filter), after which it repopulates the Recordset based on the filtered view.

You set a filter by assigning a filter expression to a Recordset's Filter property. You drop a filter by setting the Filter property to an empty string.

Although the filter expressions that you can assign to the Filter property of a Recordset are similar to those that you can set to ADS using other mechanisms (such as using the Advantage Data Architect or the Advantage TDataSet Descendant), there is one important difference. If you include a field name that contains embedded spaces, you must enclose the field name in square brace delimiters.

Setting and dropping a filter is demonstrated in the following code, which is located in the click subprocedure for the Set Filter button (shown in Figure 14-1):

```
If AdsRecordset.State <> adStateOpen Then
  MsgBox "Please open Invoice table before setting index"
  Exit Sub
End If
If FilterBtn.Caption = "Drop Filter" Then
  AdsRecordset.Filter = ""
  FilterBtn.Caption = "Set Filter"
Else
  AdsRecordset.Filter = FilterText.Text
  FilterBtn.Caption = "Drop Filter"
End If
Set DataGrid1.DataSource = AdsRecordset
```

If you run this project, click the Show Invoice Table button and then enter the following filter expression:

```
[Customer ID] = 12037 and [Employee ID] = 89
```

Once you click the Set Filter button, the DataGrid at the bottom of the form will display only two records, as shown in Figure 14-4.

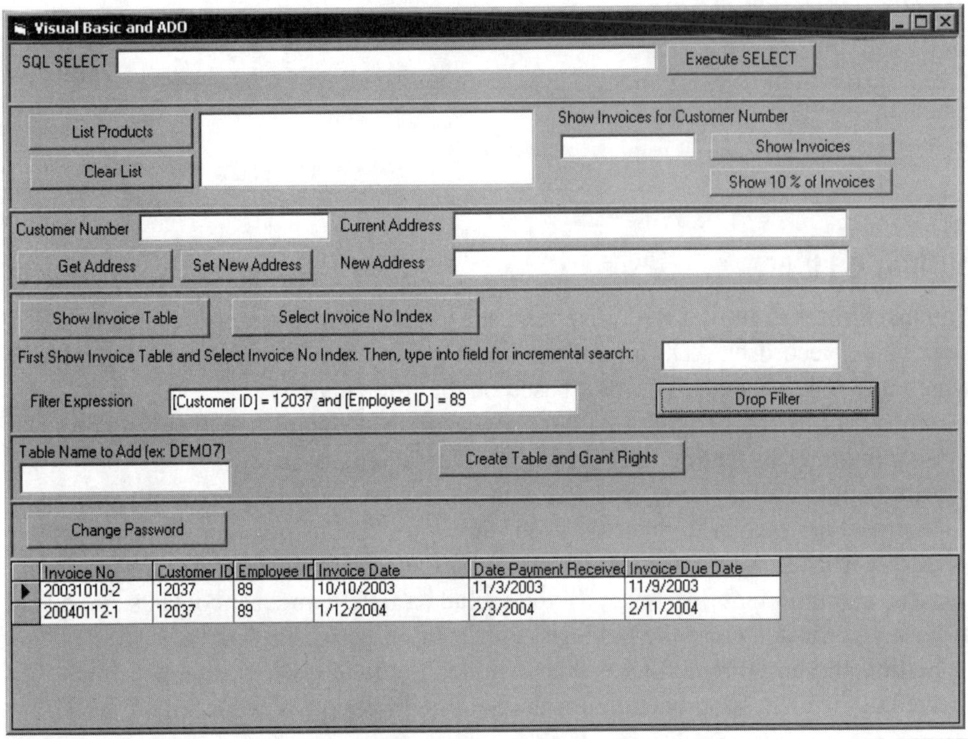

Figure 14-4 *A filter has been applied to a Recordset.*

NOTE

Although a filter does not rely on the current index, the speed with which a filter can be applied is directly related to the available indexes on the table. Specifically, filters can be applied quickly when the expressions in the filter expression map to available indexes on the underlying table.

Scanning a Result Set

Scanning is the process of sequentially reading every record in a result set, or every record in the filtered view of the result set if a filter is active. In most cases, scanning involves an initial navigation to the first record of the result set, followed by repeated calls to advance one record until all of the records have been visited.

Although scanning is a common task, it is important to note that it necessarily requires the client application to retrieve all of the records in the result set.

When using a client-side cursor, all records must be retrieved to the client before any action can be taken. However, once retrieved, the scanning process itself is very fast. By comparison, when using a server-side cursor, the records are read to the client during the scanning process. Consequently, scanning can initiate faster but may take longer when using a server-side cursor.

TIP

If you are using ADS, and you must scan a large number of records, implement the operation using an AEP as described in Chapter 7. Scanning from an AEP installed on ADS requires no network resources.

The following code demonstrates scanning records in a Recordset. This code, associated with the click subprocedure of the List Products button (shown in Figure 14-1), navigates the entire PRODUCTS table, assigning data from each record to the ProductList list box:

```
If AdsRecordset.State = adStateOpen Then
   AdsRecordset.Close
End If
AdsRecordset.Open "SELECT * FROM PRODUCTS", AdsConnection, _
   adOpenDynamic, adLockPessimistic, adCmdText
ProductList.Clear
AdsRecordset.MoveFirst
While Not AdsRecordset.EOF
   ProductList.AddItem (AdsRecordset.Fields(0).Value & _
     vbTab & AdsRecordset.Fields(1).Value)
   AdsRecordset.MoveNext
Wend
AdsRecordset.Close
```

Administrative Operations with ADS and ADO

While ADS requires little in the way of periodic maintenance to keep it running smoothly, many applications need to provide administrative functionality related to the management of users, groups, and objects.

This section is designed to provide you with insight into exposing administrative functions in your client applications. Two related, yet different, operations are demonstrated here. In the first, a new table is added to the database and all groups are granted access rights to it. This operation requires that you establish an administrative connection. The second operation involves permitting individual users to modify their own passwords. Especially in the security-conscious world of modern database management, this feature is often considered an essential step to protecting data.

Creating a Table and Granting Rights to It

The VB_ADO.vbp project permits a user to enter the name of a table that will be created in the data dictionary, after which all groups will be granted rights to the table. This operation is demonstrated in the following subprocedure, which is associated with the click event of the Create Table and Grant Rights button (shown in Figure 14-1):

```
Dim Found As Boolean

If TableNameText.Text = "" Then
  MsgBox "Please enter the name of the table to create"
  Exit Sub
End If
'Check for semicolon hack
If InStr(1, TableNameText.Text, ";", vbTextCompare) <> 0 Then
  MsgBox "Table name may not contain a semicolon"
  Exit Sub
End If
If AdsRecordset.State = adStateOpen Then
  AdsRecordset.Close
End If
AdminConnection.ConnectionString = _
  "Provider=Advantage OLE DB Provider;" + _
  "Data Source=" + DataPath + ";user ID=adssys;" + _
  "password=password;" + _
  "ServerType=ADS_LOCAL_SERVER | ADS_REMOTE_SERVER;" + _
  "FilterOptions=RESPECT_WHEN_COUNTING;TrimTrailingSpaces=True"
AdminConnection.Open
Set AdminCommand.ActiveConnection = AdminConnection
AdsRecordset.Open "SELECT * FROM system.tables", _
  AdminConnection, adOpenDynamic, adLockPessimistic, adCmdText
AdsRecordset.MoveFirst
Found = False
Do While Not AdsRecordset.EOF
  If UCase(AdsRecordset.Fields(0).Value) = _
    UCase(TableNameText.Text) Then
    Found = True
    Exit Do
  End If
```

```
    AdsRecordset.MoveNext
Loop
If Found Then
  MsgBox "This table already exists. Cannot create"
  Exit Sub
End If
AdminCommand.CommandText = "CREATE TABLE " + TableNameText.Text + _
  "([Full Name] CHAR(30)," + _
  "[Date of Birth] DATE," + _
  "[Credit Limit] MONEY, " + _
  "Active LOGICAL)"
AdminCommand.Execute
AdsRecordset.Close
AdsRecordset.Open "SELECT * FROM system.usergroups", _
  AdminConnection, adOpenDynamic, adLockPessimistic, adCmdText
If AdsRecordset.BOF And AdsRecordset.EOF Then
  MsgBox "No groups to grant rights to"
  Exit Sub
End If
AdsRecordset.MoveFirst
While Not AdsRecordset.EOF
  AdminCommand.CommandText = "GRANT ALL ON " + _
    TableNameText.Text + " TO """ + _
    AdsRecordset.Fields(0).Value + """"
  AdminCommand.Execute
  AdsRecordset.MoveNext
Wend
AdminConnection.Close
MsgBox "The " + TableNameText.Text + " table has been " + _
  "created, with rights granted to all groups"
```

This subprocedure begins by verifying that the table name does not include a semicolon, which could be used to convert the subsequent GRANT SQL statement into a SQL script. Since this value represents a table name, a parameterized query is not an option.

Next, this code verifies that the table does not already exist in the data dictionary. Once that is done, a new connection is created using the data dictionary administrative account. This connection is then used to call CREATE TABLE to create the table, and then to call GRANT for each group returned in the system.usergroups table.

NOTE

The administrative user name and passwords are represented by string literals in this code segment. This was done for convenience, but in a real application, either you would ask for this information from the user or you would scramble this information so that it could not be retrieved from the executable.

Changing a User Password

A user can change the password on their own connection, if you permit this. In most cases, only when every user has a distinct user name would you expose this functionality in a client application. When multiple users share a user name, this operation is usually reserved for an application administrator.

The following subprocedure, associated with the Change Password button (shown in Figure 14-1), demonstrates how you can permit a user to change their password from a client application:

```
Dim UserName As String
Dim OldPass As String
Dim NewPass1 As String
Dim NewPass2 As String
If AdsRecordset.State = adStateOpen Then
  AdsRecordset.Close
End If
AdsRecordset.Open "SELECT USER() FROM system.iota", _
  AdsConnection, adOpenDynamic, adLockPessimistic, adCmdText
UserName = AdsRecordset.Fields(0).Value
AdsRecordset.Close
OldPass = InputBox("Enter your current password")
If OldPass = "" Then Exit Sub
If Not CheckPass(UserName, OldPass) Then
  MsgBox "Cannot validate your current password. " + _
    "Cannot change password"
  Exit Sub
End If
'Get new password
NewPass1 = InputBox("Enter your new password")
If NewPass1 = "" Then
  MsgBox "Password cannot be blank. Cannot change password"
  Exit Sub
End If
'Check for semicolon hack
If InStr(1, NewPass1, ";", vbTextCompare) <> 0 Then
```

```
  MsgBox "Password may not contain a semicolon"
  Exit Sub
End If
NewPass2 = InputBox("Confirm your new password")
If NewPass1 <> NewPass2 Then
  MsgBox "Passwords did not match. Cannot change password"
  Exit Sub
End If
'Green light to change password
AdsCommand.CommandText = _
  "EXECUTE PROCEDURE sp_ModifyUserProperty('" + UserName + _
  "', 'USER_PASSWORD', '" + NewPass1 + "')"
AdsCommand.Execute
MsgBox "Password successfully changed. " + _
  "New password will be valid next time you connect"
```

A number of interesting tricks are used in this code. First, the user name is obtained by requesting the USER scalar function from the system.iota table. USER returns the user name on the connection through which the query is executed. Next, the user is asked for their current password, and the user name and password are used to attempt a new connection, which, if successful, confirms that the user is valid. This validation occurs in a subfunction named CheckPass. The following code is found in this function:

```
Private Function CheckPass(UName As String, _
  Pass As String) As Boolean
  Dim TempConnection As ADODB.Connection
  On Error GoTo ErrorHandler
  'Try to make a new connection using this password
  Set TempConnection = New ADODB.Connection
  TempConnection.ConnectionString = _
    "Provider=Advantage OLE DB Provider;" + _
    "Data Source=" + DataPath + ";user ID=" + UName + ";" + _
    "password=" + Pass + ";" + _
    "ServerType=ADS_LOCAL_SERVER | ADS_REMOTE_SERVER;"
  TempConnection.Open
  'Password must be ok. Close TempConnection
  TempConnection.Close
  CheckPass = True
  Exit Function
ErrorHandler:
  CheckPass = False
End Function
```

Finally, the user is asked for their new password twice (for confirmation). If all is well, the sp_ModifyUserProperty stored procedure is called to change the user's password. This password will be valid once the user terminates all connections on this user account.

NOTE

If you run this code, and change the password of the adsuser account, you should use the Advantage Data Architect to change the password back to ***password****; otherwise, you will not be able to run this project again since the password is hard-coded into the connection string.*

Using the Advantage .NET Data Provider

IN THIS CHAPTER:

ADS and ADO.NET

Performing Basic Tasks with ADS and ADO.NET

Navigational Actions with ADS and ADO.NET

Administrative Operations with ADS and ADO.NET

Things change, and in the computer software industry things seem to change even faster. But one thing that hasn't changed is your need to access data. It's the way you access data that's changed, in this case.

The most recent data access mechanism, at least for now, is ADO.NET, the data access layer of the .NET FCL (framework class library). This technology is significant, and sooner or later you'll probably be using it. And when you do, you'll be comforted to find that ADS is there with you.

This chapter provides you with an introduction to data access using the .NET FCL, specifically ADO.NET. It begins with an overview of ADO.NET and the Advantage .NET Data Provider. It continues with a look at accessing your ADS data using ADS and ADO.NET.

In keeping with the language-agnostic nature of ADS, data access is demonstrated in this chapter using C#, one of the newest object-oriented languages. Keep in mind, however, that .NET classes are .NET classes, regardless of which .NET-enabled language you use. Consequently, all the data access techniques demonstrated in this chapter can be used from any .NET language, including VB.NET, C#Builder, Delphi for .NET, and Visual J#.NET, to name a few.

ADS and ADO.NET

ADO.NET is the common name for the classes and interfaces of the System.Data second-level namespace of the FCL. Conceptually, ADO.NET can be divided into two distinct parts: the data access layer and the data storage system.

The classes associated with the data storage system are stand-alone classes that you can employ in any ADO.NET application. These classes include DataColumn, DataRelation, DataRow, DataSet, DataTable, and DataView. Of these, the most central class is DataSet.

Unlike the storage mechanism, which is defined around classes, the data access layer is formally defined using interfaces (abstract application programming interface definitions). Concrete classes—that is, classes that can be instantiated—associated with a particular data access mechanism implement these interfaces.

There are five data access mechanisms native to the version 1.1 FCL, which is also to say that Microsoft provides them. These are associated with the System.Data.SqlClient, System.Data.OleDb, System.Data.Odbc, System.Data.SqlServerCE, and System.Data.OracleClient third-level namespaces.

As is the case with ADO and OLE DB providers, database vendors are permitted, and warmly encouraged, to create their own data access classes that implement these same interfaces. Advantage calls their implementation the Advantage .NET Data Provider, and it can be found in the Advantage.Data.Provider namespace.

The primary responsibility of the Advantage .NET Data Provider classes is the same as that of the native implementations—supply data to the data storage system, and in particular, insert data into DataTables. DataTables are the individual data stores that reside in a DataSet.

The second, and obviously crucial, role of data providers is to permit direct manipulation of a data source. This, too, is deftly handled by the Advantage .NET Data Provider.

There is one final point concerning ADO.NET that you should be aware of. For the most part, ADO.NET relies heavily on the client-side caching of records. Specifically, much of what you do with data in ADO.NET involves the manipulation of records that are stored in one or more DataSets, which are in-memory data stores.

While this style of data management is particularly well-suited for distributed computing, most developers take a while to get accustomed to it. For example, in ADO.NET, there are never pessimistic locks on records. You discover whether your changes can be applied to the underlying database or not when you finally attempt to apply the one or more changes in the cache.

This discussion is not meant to discourage you from ADO.NET. There's a lot to like about it. However, due to ADO.NET's reliance on features exposed by the DataSet and other related classes, you are less able to exploit all of ADS's strengths compared with ADS's other data access mechanisms. But, this is true with respect to ADO.NET and any other database server.

As is the case with all data access mechanisms described in this part of this book, the following discussion of ADS programming with ADO.NET touches on just a few of the available techniques, particularly those that apply to ADS. Unlike some of the other data access mechanisms covered in this part of this book, the native .NET classes provide a significant amount of standard database functionality, such as filtering, sorting, and seeking. Consequently, these topics are not ADS specific, and are not covered in this chapter. For a comprehensive discussion of ADO.NET programming, you may want to pick up a good book, such as *ADO.NET, The Complete Reference*, by Otey and Otey (McGraw-Hill/Osborne, 2003).

 ON THE CD

The examples provided in this chapter can be found in the C# project CS_ADONET on this book's CD-ROM (see Appendix B). This project was written in Visual Studio .NET 2003. If you are working with an older version of Visual Studio .NET, project format incompatibilities will prevent you from compiling the project as is. Nonetheless, the same classes and methods demonstrated in this project can be used in earlier .NET environments.

The main form of the CS_ADONET C# project used in the examples in this chapter is shown in Figure 15-1.

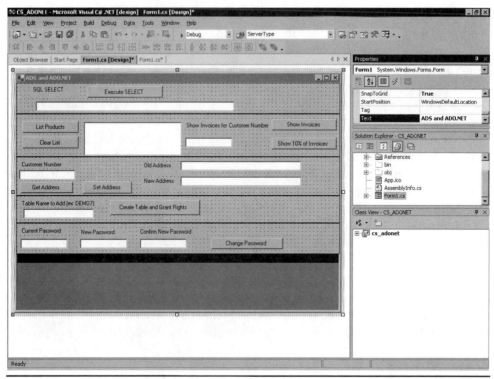

Figure 15-1 *The CS_ADONET project in Visual Studio*

Note that before you can use ADS with Visual Studio for .NET, you must add a reference to the Advantage.Data.Provider namespace. To do this, use the following steps:

1. From Visual Studio .NET, select Projects | Add Reference. Visual Studio displays the Add Reference dialog box.

2. Select Advantage.Data.Provider and click Select.

3. Click OK to close the Add Reference dialog box.

Performing Basic Tasks with ADS and ADO.NET

This section describes some of the more common tasks that you can perform with the Advantage .NET Data Provider. These include connecting to a data dictionary, executing a query, using a parameterized query, retrieving and editing data, and executing a stored procedure.

Connecting to Data

You connect to a data dictionary or a directory in which free tables are located using an AdsConnection object found in the Advantage.Data.Provider namespace. At a minimum, you must provide the AdsConnection object with sufficient information to locate your data and configure how the data should be accessed. This is done using the ConnectionString property. This property accepts name/value pairs using the parameters listed in Table 15-1. If you use more than one name/value pair, separate them with semicolons.

Parameter	Description
CharType	Set to the character set type for DBF files. Valid values are ADS_ANSI and ADS_OEM. The default value is ADS_ANSI.
Compression	Set to ALWAYS, INTERNET, NEVER, or empty. If left empty (the default), the ADS.INI file will control the compression setting. This parameter is not used by ALS.
Connection Lifetime	The number of seconds after which a connection will be destroyed after being returned to the connection pool. The default is 0.
Data Source	The path to your free tables or data dictionary. If you are using a data dictionary, you must include the data dictionary filename in this path. It is recommended that this path be a UNC path. Data Source is a required parameter.
DbfsUseNulls	Set to TRUE to return empty fields from DBF files as NULL values. If set to FALSE, empty fields are returned as empty data values. The default is FALSE.
EncryptionPassword	Set to an optional password to use for accessing encrypted free tables. This parameter is ignored for data dictionary connections.
IncrementUsercount	Set to TRUE to increment the user count when the connection is made, or FALSE to make a connection without incrementing the user count. The default is FALSE.
Initial Catalog	Optional name of a data dictionary if the data dictionary is not specified in the Data Source parameter.
LockMode	Set to ADS_PROPRIETARY_LOCKING or ADS_COMPATIBLE _LOCKING to define the locking mechanism used for DBF tables. Use ADS_COMPATIBLE_LOCKING when your connection must share data with non-ADS applications. The default is ADS_PROPRIETARY_LOCKING.
Max Pool Size	The maximum number of connections to maintain in the connection pool. The default is 100.
Min Pool Size	The minimum number of connections to maintain in the connection pool. The default is 0.

Table 15-1   *Parameters for Connecting with the Advantage .NET Data Provider*

Parameter	Description
Password	When connecting to a data dictionary that requires logins, set to the user's password.
Pooling	Set to TRUE to enable connection pooling, and FALSE to disable it. The default is TRUE.
ReadOnly	Set to TRUE to open tables readonly, or FALSE to open tables as editable (read-write). This setting applies to all CommandType values. The default is FALSE.
SecurityMode	Set to ADS_CHECKRIGHTS to observe the user's network access rights before opening files, or ADS_IGNORERIGHTS to access files regardless of the user's network rights. The default is ADS_CHECKRIGHTS. This property applies only to free table connections.
ServerType	Set to the type of ADS server you want to connect to. Use ADS_LOCAL_SERVER, ADS_REMOTE_SERVER, or ADS_INTERNET_SERVER. To attempt to connect to two or more types, separate the server types using a vertical bar (|). This is demonstrated in the ConnectionString shown later in this chapter.
Shared	Set to TRUE to open tables shared, or FALSE to open tables exclusively. This setting only applies to CommandType.TableDirect. The default is TRUE.
ShowDeleted	Set to TRUE to include deleted records in DBF files, or FALSE to suppress deleted records. The default is FALSE.
StoredProcedureConnection	Set to TRUE if connecting from within a stored procedure. When set to TRUE, the connection does not increment the user count. The default is FALSE.
TableType	Set to ADS_ADT, ADS_CDX, or ADS_NTX to define the default table type. The default is ADS_ADT. This parameter is ignored for data dictionary connections.
TrimTrailingSpaces	Set to TRUE to trim trailing spaces from character fields, or FALSE to preserve trailing spaces. The default is FALSE.
User ID	If connecting to a data dictionary that requires logins, set to the user's user name.

Table 15-1   *Parameters for Connecting with the Advantage .NET Data Provider (continued)*

With the Advantage .NET Data Provider, the connection string property values can be enclosed in either double or single quotes, if necessary. For example, if the password contains a semicolon (the connection string parameter delimiter), it would be necessary to enclose it in single or double quotes.

For any of the optional connection string parameters that you fail to provide, the Advantage .NET Data Provider will automatically employ the default parameters.

Because the AdsConnection object that is used by this project must be used by a number of methods, the AdsConnection variable and several other variables that must be repeatedly referenced are declared private members of the Form class. The following is this declaration:

```
private AdsConnection connection;
private IDbCommand command;
private AdsCommand paramCommand;
private IDataReader dataReader;
```

The data source location of the data dictionary is also declared as a constant member of this class. This constant refers to a share named "share," on a server named "server," as shown in the following declaration:

```
private const String DataPath = "\\\\server\\share\\program files" +
  "\\extended systems\\advantage\\adsbook\\DemoDictionary.add;";
```

This connection, named AdsConnection, is created, configured, and opened from the InitializeDataComponents method of the form, along with several other objects. InitializeDataComponents is called from the Form's constructor. The relevant portion of this custom private method is shown in the following code:

```
private void InitalizeDataComponents() {
  connection = new AdsConnection();
  connection.ConnectionString = "Data Source=" + DataPath +
    ";user ID=adsuser;password=password;"+
    "ServerType=ADS_LOCAL_SERVER | ADS_REMOTE_SERVER;" +
    "FilterOptions=RESPECT_WHEN_COUNTING;TrimTrailingSpaces=True";
  connection.Open();
  command = new AdsCommand();
  command = connection.CreateCommand();
//additional statements follow
```

NOTE

If you have difficulty connecting, it might be because you have other client applications, such as the Advantage Data Architect, connected using a local connection. Ensure that all clients on the same machine use the same type of connection.

Executing a Query

You execute a query that returns a result set using an AdsCommand. There are numerous overloaded methods for doing this. The following code segment demonstrates one of these, where a query string and an open connection are passed as parameters to an AdsDataAdapter's constructor. Within this constructor, the query string is assigned to an internally created AdsCommand object that is associated with the SelectCommand property of the AdsDataAdapter, which performs the query execution. The Fill method is then invoked on this AdsDataAdapter, which causes the result set to be loaded into a DataTable of a DataSet.

This DataTable is then used to display the resulting data in a DataGrid, as shown in Figure 15-2. The following code demonstrates the execution of a query entered by the user into the TextBox named selectText. This method is associated with the Execute SELECT button (shown in Figure 15-1):

```
private void executeSELECTBtn_Click(object sender,
  System.EventArgs e) {
  IDataAdapter adapter ;
  adapter = new AdsDataAdapter(selectText.Text, connection);
  DataSet ds = new DataSet();
  adapter.Fill(ds);
  DataTable dt = ds.Tables[0];
  dataGrid1.DataSource = dt;
}
```

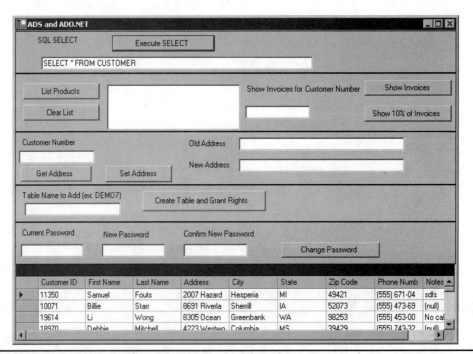

Figure 15-2 *The results of a SELECT query displayed in a DataGrid*

Notice that the AdsDataAdapter that is created is assigned to a variable of type IDataAdapter. IDataAdapter is the interface that all data adapters implement. While we could have just as well assigned this object to a variable of type AdsDataAdapter, assigning it to an interface variable makes our code more portable, since any IDataAdapter implementing class can be assigned to this variable. This technique is used extensively in this chapter, wherever no Advantage .NET Data Provider functionality is specifically needed.

If you need to execute a query that does not return a record set, call the ExecuteNonQuery method of an AdsCommand object. The use of an AdsCommand object to execute a query that does not return a recordset is demonstrated later in this chapter.

Using a Parameterized Query

Parameterized queries are defined using an AdsCommand object. Before you can invoke a parameterized query, you must create one AdsParameter object for each of the query's parameters. You can create an AdsParameter instance by calling the Add method of the AdsCommand object's Parameters property.

The definition of a parameterized query, including the creation of a parameter, is shown in the following code segment, which is part of the private InitializeDataComponents method shown earlier:

```
paramCommand = new AdsCommand("SELECT * FROM INVOICE " +
  "WHERE [Customer ID] = ?", connection);
paramCommand.Parameters.Add(1,System.Data.DbType.Int32);
```

Before you can execute an AdsCommand that contains a parameterized query, you must bind data to each of its parameters. This is shown in the following method, which is called by the Show Invoices button (shown in Figure 15-1):

```
private void doParamQuery_Click(object sender,
  System.EventArgs e) {
  IDataAdapter dataAdapter;
  DataSet ds = new DataSet();
  DataTable dt;
  if (paramText.Text.Equals("")) {
    MessageBox.Show(this,
      "You must supply a customer ID");
    return;
  }
  paramCommand.Parameters[0].Value = Int32.Parse(paramText.Text);
```

```
    dataAdapter = new AdsDataAdapter(paramCommand);
    dataAdapter.Fill(ds);
    dt = ds.Tables[0];
    if (dt.Rows.Count == 0)
    {
      MessageBox.Show(this,
        "No invoices for customer ID");
      return;
    }
    dataGrid1.DataSource = dt;
}
```

As you can see from this code, after verifying that a value has been entered into the customer ID field, the entered data is assigned to the Value property of the AdsParameter. The AdsCommand object that holds the parameter is passed as an argument to an AdsDataAdapter, which then executes the query and assigns the result set to a DataTable. Note that it was not necessary to pass a connection object to the AdsDataAdapter constructor, since the AdsCommand object itself was constructed based on a connection.

This example is actually a classic example of how parameterized queries are used. Specifically, the query text is defined only once, but can be executed repeatedly. And by changing only the value of the parameter, a different result set can be returned upon each execution.

Reading and Writing Data

You read data from the fields of a table using either an AdsDataReader or a DataColumn, depending on how you are working with your data. Reading a field is demonstrated in this section using a DataColumn. Using an AdsDataReader is discussed later in this chapter.

You can use a DataColumn to read and write data from a field of a record. You obtain a DataColumn from the Items property of a DataRow. You obtain a DataRow through the Rows property of a DataTable.

Once you have a reference to a DataColumn, you can execute its ToString method to read its data. This technique is demonstrated in the following method associated with the Get Address button (shown in Figure 15-1):

```
private void getAddressBtn_Click(object sender,
  System.EventArgs e) {
  AdsCommand getCustCommand;
  IDataAdapter dataAdapter;
```

```
String custNo;
custNo = custNoText.Text;
if (custNo.Equals(""))
{
   MessageBox.Show(this, "You must supply a customer ID");
 return;
}
getCustCommand = new AdsCommand(
  "SELECT * FROM CUSTOMER WHERE [Customer ID] = ?",
  connection);
getCustCommand.Parameters.Add(1,System.Data.DbType.Int32);
getCustCommand.Parameters[0].Value =
  Int32.Parse(custNo);
dataAdapter = new AdsDataAdapter(getCustCommand);
DataSet ds = new DataSet();
dataAdapter.Fill(ds);
DataTable dt = ds.Tables[0];
DataRow dr = dt.Rows[0];
oldAddressText.Text = dr.["Address"].ToString();
}
```

You can also use a DataColumn to write data back to ADS. This process, however, is somewhat involved.

In ADO.NET, data is always written to the underlying provider using SQL queries. These queries are associated with the DeleteCommand, InsertCommand, and UpdateCommand AdsCommand properties of an AdsDataAdapter. In order for the applicable change to be submitted to ADS, the corresponding property of the AdsDataAdapter must have an AdsCommand object assigned to it. For example, in order to insert a new record into an ADS table, the AdsDataAdapter must have an appropriate INSERT query assigned to the AdsCommand referenced by the InsertCommand property.

The queries associated with the DeleteCommand and UpdateCommand AdsCommands are parameterized, including a WHERE clause that identifies the record that is being deleted or updated, respectively. The values for these parameters are automatically bound by the AdsDataAdapter prior to the execution of the associated query.

Although you can create the AdsCommand objects manually, doing so is not necessary if the query returns a live cursor. Instead, you merely need to call the constructor of an AdsCommandBuilder, passing the AdsDataAdapter as an argument. The AdsCommandBuilder will examine the query associated with the SelectCommand property of the AdsDataAdapter, and will then generate the appropriate AdsCommand objects and will assign them to the proper AdsCommand properties of the AdsDataAdapter.

If your query returns a static cursor, or if you want to have complete control over the query, you must build the delete, insert, and update Command objects manually. You must then assign these Command objects to the appropriate properties of your AdsDataAdapter before you can call Update.

After making changes to one or more columns of one or more records of a DataTable, you call the Update method of the AdsDataAdapter, passing the corresponding DataSet as an argument. The AdsDataAdapter responds by applying the changes from the DataSet. The following code, associated with the Set Address button (shown in Figure 15-1), demonstrates this operation:

```
private void setAddressBtn_Click(object sender,
 System.EventArgs e) {
  AdsCommand updateCustCommand;
  IDataAdapter dataAdapter;
  String custNo;
  AdsCommandBuilder commandBuilder;
  custNo = custNoText.Text;
  if (custNo.Equals(""))
  {
     MessageBox.Show(this, "You must supply a customer ID");
   return;
  }
  updateCustCommand = new AdsCommand(
    "SELECT * FROM CUSTOMER WHERE [Customer ID] = ?",
    connection);
  updateCustCommand.Parameters.Add(1,
    System.Data.DbType.Int32);
  updateCustCommand.Parameters[0].Value =
   Int32.Parse(custNo);
  dataAdapter = new AdsDataAdapter(updateCustCommand);
  commandBuilder =
    new AdsCommandBuilder((AdsDataAdapter)dataAdapter));
  DataSet ds = new DataSet();
  dataAdapter.Fill(ds);
  DataTable dt = ds.Tables[0];
  DataRow dr = dt.Rows[0];
  dr["Address"] = newAddressText.Text;
  dataAdapter.Update(ds);
}
```

Of course, you can write a SQL UPDATE query and execute it using an AdsCommand to achieve a similar result. While this approach is more efficient at runtime than using a CommandBuilder, since the CommandBuilder will require a number of round trips to the server to collect the metadata that it needs to construct the DELETE, INSERT, and UPDATE commands, each manually created SQL query introduces one more thing about your code that must be maintained—the queries themselves. You can decide yourself which approach is best for your applications.

Calling a Stored Procedure

Calling a stored procedure is no different than executing any other query. You can define a SQL EXECUTE PROCEDURE statement and assign it to the CommandText property of an AdsCommand object. Alternatively, you can assign the name of the stored procedure to the CommandText property of the AdsCommand object, and then set the CommandType property to CommandType.StoredProcedure.

You create an AdsCommand object explicitly or permit an AdsDataAdapter to create one for you. If the stored procedure returns a result set, you will either call the ExecuteReader method of the AdsCommand, or an appropriate method of an AdsDataAdapter. Otherwise, you can execute the stored procedure by calling the ExecuteNonQuery method of the AdsCommand.

Invoking a stored procedure that takes one input parameter is demonstrated by the following code associated with the Show 10% of Invoices button (shown in Figure 15-1). The stored procedure referenced in this code is the Delphi AEP created in Chapter 7. If you did not create this AEP, but created one of the other AEPs described in that chapter, substitute the name of the stored procedure object in your data dictionary in the first parameter in the AdsCommand constructor.

```
private void callStoredProc_Click_1(object sender,
  System.EventArgs e) {
  AdsCommand storedProcCommand;
  IDataAdapter dataAdapter;
  DataSet ds = new DataSet();
  DataTable dt;
  if (paramText.Text.Equals(""))
  {
    MessageBox.Show(this, "You must supply a customer ID");
   return;
  }
  storedProcCommand = new AdsCommand("DelphiAEP", connection);
  storedProcCommand.CommandType = CommandType.StoredProcedure;
```

```
  storedProcCommand.Parameters.Add(1,System.Data.DbType.Int32);
  storedProcCommand.Parameters[0].Value = Int32.Parse(paramText.Text);
  dataAdapter = new AdsDataAdapter(storedProcCommand);
  dataAdapter.Fill(ds);
  dt = ds.Tables[0];
  if (dt.Rows.Count == 0)
  {
    MessageBox.Show(this, "No invoices for customer ID");
    return;
  }
  dataGrid1.DataSource = dt;
}
```

Navigational Actions with ADS and ADO.NET

Most of the navigational features that you can access with other data access mechanisms, such as ADO and TDataSet, are implemented in the ADO.NET DataSet class. For example, indexing, sorting, filtering, and seeking are all operations that are performed on a DataSet's cached records. In other words, these operations do not involve ADS, other than using ADS as the original source of the data that is manipulated in memory.

There is, in fact, only one ADO.NET navigational operation that involves ADS—scanning. Specifically, using an AdsDataReader, you can perform a record-by-record navigation of data. This operation is demonstrated in the following section.

Scanning a Result Set

Scanning is the process of sequentially reading every record in a result, or every record in the filtered view of the result set if a filter is active. In ADO.NET, scanning is performed using an AdsDataReader, which you obtain from an AdsCommand object that contains a SQL SELECT statement.

You obtain an AdsDataReader from an AdsCommand object by calling its ExecuteReader method. You then invoke the AdsDataReader's Read method to access the first record in the result set. Repeated calls to Read fetch additional records, until the entire result set has been traversed. When no records remain in the result set, Read evaluates to a Boolean False.

After successfully fetching a record through an AdsReader's Read method, you can read individual fields of the fetched record by calling an appropriate AdsReader getter method. For example, you call GetString to read a string field, and call GetInt32 to read an integer field. When you call a getter method, you indicate which field you want to read by passing either the ordinal position of that field in the table's structure, or a string that identifies the field.

If you are using ADS, and you must scan a large number of records, consider implementing the operation using an AEP (Advantage Extended Procedure) as described in Chapter 7. Scanning from an AEP installed on ADS requires no network resources.

The following code demonstrates scanning using an AdsDataReader. This code is associated with the List Products button (shown in Figure 15-1):

```
private void listProductsBtn_Click(object sender,
  System.EventArgs e) {
  command.CommandText = "SELECT * FROM PRODUCTS";
  dataReader = command.ExecuteReader();
  while (dataReader.Read()) {
    productList.Items.Add(dataReader.GetString(0) + "   " +
      dataReader.GetString(1));
  }
  dataReader.Close();
}
```

NOTE

In addition to the Read method, the AdsDataReader supports ReadPrevious. Also, it is possible that future versions of AdsDataReader will support additional navigational methods. See the ADS help for more information.

Administrative Operations with ADS and ADO.NET

While ADS requires little in the way of periodic maintenance to keep it running smoothly, many applications need to provide administrative functionality related to the management of users, groups, and objects.

This section is designed to provide you with insight into exposing administrative functions in your client applications. Two related, yet different, operations are demonstrated here. In the first, a new table is added to the database and all groups are granted access rights to it. This operation requires that you establish an administrative connection. The second operation involves permitting individual users to modify their own passwords. Especially in the security-conscious world of modern database management, this feature is often considered an essential step to protecting data.

Creating a Table and Granting Rights to It

The CS_ADONET project permits a user to enter the name of a table that will be created in the data dictionary, after which all groups will be granted rights to the table. This operation is demonstrated in the following method, which is associated with the Create Table and Grant Rights button (shown in Figure 15-1):

```
private void addTableBtn_Click(object sender,
  System.EventArgs e)
  {
  AdsConnection adminConnection;
  IDbCommand adminCommand;
  AdsDataAdapter adminAdapter;
  DataSet ds;
  DataTable dt;
  DataRow dr;
  String tabName;

  tabName = tableNameText.Text;
  if (tabName.Equals(""))
  {
    MessageBox.Show(this,
      "Please enter the name of the table to create");
   return;
  }
  //Check for semicolon hack
  if ((tabName.IndexOf(";") >= 0))
  {
    MessageBox.Show(this,
      "Table name may not contain a semicolon");
   return;
  }
  try
  {
   adminConnection = new AdsConnection(
    "Data Source=" + DataPath + ";user ID=adssys;" +
    "password=password;" +
    "ServerType=ADS_LOCAL_SERVER | ADS_REMOTE_SERVER;" +
    "FilterOptions=RESPECT_WHEN_COUNTING;" +
    "TrimTrailingSpaces=True");
  adminConnection.Open();
  adminAdapter = new AdsDataAdapter("SELECT Name FROM " +
```

```
    "system.tables " +
    "WHERE UCase(Name) = '" + tabName.ToUpper() + "'",
    adminConnection);
ds = new DataSet();
adminAdapter.Fill(ds);
dt = ds.Tables[0];
if (dt.Rows.Count != 0)
{
  MessageBox.Show(this,
    "This table already exists. Cannot create");
  return;
}
adminCommand = new AdsCommand("CREATE TABLE [" +
  tabName + "] " +
  "([Full Name] CHAR(30), [Date of Birth] DATE," +
  "[Credit Limit] MONEY, Active LOGICAL)", adminConnection);
adminCommand.ExecuteNonQuery();
adminAdapter = new AdsDataAdapter("SELECT Name FROM " +
  "system.usergroups", adminConnection);
ds = new DataSet();
adminAdapter.Fill(ds);
dt = ds.Tables[0];
if (dt.Rows.Count == 0)
{
  MessageBox.Show(this, "No groups to grant rights to");
  return;
}
adminCommand = adminConnection.CreateCommand();
for (int i=0; i <= dt.Rows.Count - 1 ; i++)
{
  dr = dt.Rows[i];
  adminCommand.CommandText = "GRANT ALL ON " +
    tabName + " TO \"" + dr[0].ToString() + "\"";
  adminCommand.ExecuteNonQuery();
 }
}
catch (System.Exception ex)
{
  Console.WriteLine("Exception", ex);
  throw(ex);
}
MessageBox.Show(this,
  "The " + tabName + " table has been " +
```

```
      "created, with rights granted to all groups");
    return;
  }
```

This method begins by verifying that the table name does not include a semicolon, which could be used to convert the subsequent GRANT SQL statement into a SQL script. Since this value represents a table name, a parameterized query is not an option.

Next, this code verifies that the table does not already exist in the data dictionary. Once that is done, a new connection is created using the data dictionary administrative account. This connection is then used to call CREATE TABLE to create the table, and then to call GRANT for each group returned in the system.usergroups table.

NOTE

The administrative user name and passwords are represented by string literals in this code segment. This was done for convenience, but in a real application you would either ask for this information from the user or you would obfuscate this information so that it could not be retrieved.

Changing a User Password

A user can change the password on their own connection, if you permit this. In most cases, only when every user has a distinct user name would you expose this functionality in a client application. When multiple users share a user name, this operation is usually reserved for an application administrator.

The following method, associated with the Change Password button (shown in Figure 15-1), demonstrates how you can permit a user to change their password from a client application:

```
private void changePasswordBtn_Click(object sender,
    System.EventArgs e)
{
    IDataReader dataReader;
    String userName;
    String oldPass, newPass, confirmPass;
    oldPass = oldPassText.Text;
    if (oldPass.Equals(""))
    {
     MessageBox.Show(this,
       "Please enter your current password");
     return;
    }
    newPass = newPassText.Text;
```

```
if (newPass.Equals(""))
{
 MessageBox.Show(this,
  "Please enter your new password");
 return;
}
confirmPass = confirmPassText.Text;
if (confirmPass.Equals(""))
{
 MessageBox.Show(this,
  "Please confirm your new password");
 return;
}
if (! newPass.Equals(confirmPass))
{
 MessageBox.Show(this,
  "New passwords do not match");
 return;
}
if ((newPass.IndexOf(";") >= 0))
{
 MessageBox.Show(this,
  "Password may not contain a semicolon");
 return;
}
//Get user name
command = connection.CreateCommand();
command.CommandText = "SELECT USER() FROM system.iota";
dataReader = command.ExecuteReader();
dataReader.Read();
userName = dataReader.GetString(0);
dataReader.Close();
//Verify current password
if (! CheckPassword(userName, oldPass))
{
 MessageBox.Show("Cannot validate your current password. " +
  "Cannot change password");
 return;
}
try
{
 command.CommandText =  "EXECUTE PROCEDURE sp_ModifyUserProperty('"
  + userName + "', 'USER_PASSWORD', '" + newPass + "')";
```

```
  command.ExecuteNonQuery();
  }
  catch (Exception ex)
  {
   MessageBox.Show(ex.Message);
   return;
  }
  MessageBox.Show("Password successfully changed. " +
   "New password will be valid next time you connect");
}
```

A number of interesting tricks are used in this code. First, the user name is obtained by requesting the USER scalar function from the system.iota table. USER returns the user name on the connection through which the query is executed. Next, the user is asked for their current password, and the user name and password is used to attempt a new connection, which if successful confirms that the user is valid. This password validation is performed using the custom CheckPassword method. The following is the implementation of this method:

```
private Boolean CheckPassword(String uName, String pass)
{
  //Verify the current password
  AdsConnection tempConnection;
  tempConnection = new AdsConnection(
    "Data Source=" + DataPath + ";user ID=" + uName + ";" +
    "password=" + pass + ";" +
    "ServerType=ADS_LOCAL_SERVER | ADS_REMOTE_SERVER;" +
    "FilterOptions=RESPECT_WHEN_COUNTING;" +
    "TrimTrailingSpaces=True");
  try
  {
    tempConnection.Open();
    tempConnection.Close();
    return true;
  }
  catch (Exception)
  {
    return false;
  }
} //CheckPassword
```

Finally, the user is asked for their new password twice (for confirmation). If all is well, the sp_ModifyUserProperty stored procedure is called to change the user's password. This password will be valid once the user terminates all connections on this user account.

NOTE

If you run this code, and change the password of the adsuser account, you should use the Advantage Data Architect to change the password back to **password***. Otherwise, you will not be able to run this project again since the password is hard-coded into the connection string.*

CHAPTER 6

Using ADS with ODBC, PHP, and DBI/Perl

IN THIS CHAPTER:

E ach of the preceding chapters in this section describes building client applications using an IDE (integrated development environment) such as Delphi, JBuilder, Visual Studio, or Visual Studio .NET. This final chapter introduces you to a collection of related data access mechanisms that are not associated with a particular IDE, or even a specific operating system. These are the Advantage ODBC (open database connectivity) Driver, the Advantage PHP Extension, and the Advantage DBI Driver (for Perl).

As in the previous chapters on writing ADS client applications, this chapter is not intended to show you how to program in the environments supporting the covered drivers, focusing instead on how to connect to and use ADS. For information on developing in the languages covered in this chapter, refer to the documentation or a good book on the subject.

Accessing ADS Using the Advantage ODBC Driver

ODBC (open database connectivity) is based on the Open SQL CLI (call-level interface), a SQL-based standard for accessing data. Advantage supplies ODBC drivers for both Windows and Linux.

ODBC is an API (application programming interface). However, most developers who use ODBC to access their data do not make direct ODBC calls. Instead, they use an IDE that supports ODBC.

A good example of this can be found in the Borland products that use the BDE (Borland Database Engine). The BDE provides three mechanisms for accessing data, including direct local table access to Paradox and dBase file formats, and Borland SQL Links for Windows—native SQL drivers that support a number of remote database servers, such as MS SQL Server and Oracle. The third data access mechanism supported by the BDE makes use of the ODBC API, through which you can use any installed ODBC driver. However, developers who use ODBC through the BDE rarely make direct ODBC calls. Instead, they use the TDataSet interface of the VCL (visual component library). The TBDEDataSet classes that implement the TDataSet interface encapsulate calls to ODBC.

While ODBC is an older standard, compared with ADO (ActiveX data objects) and ADO.NET, ODBC is easily the most widely supported data access mechanism for Windows and Linux. Nearly every database currently available is supported by at least one, and in some cases many, ODBC drivers. Consequently, every development environment for Windows and Linux that we are aware of provides some support for ODBC. Even Java, with its JDBC-ODBC bridge class 1 driver (Java database connectivity/open database connectivity), and .NET, with its classes in the System .Data.Odbc third-level namespace of the FCL (framework class library), provide support for ODBC.

The Advantage ODBC Driver is compliant with the core API and level 1 API for ODBC 2.0. In addition, it supports most of the level 2 API functions. For a complete list of ODBC functions and information on Advantage's ODBC conformance level, see the ADS help.

Who Should Use the Advantage ODBC Driver

There are two groups of users who should use the Advantage ODBC Driver. The first group consists of those developers who are using a development environment for which there are no alternative drivers. For example, if you are using a proprietary development environment that does not support the ACE (Advantage Client Engine) API, Java, .NET, or VCL, the Advantage ODBC Driver is your fallback solution.

For those developers for whom there is an alternative to ODBC, ODBC is usually a poor choice for connecting to ADS. This is because the alternative solutions offer more options than does ODBC. In short, ODBC is the lowest common denominator for data access. All other data access solutions, including the two others covered in this chapter, provide a more extensive API than that supplied by ODBC alone.

The second group of developers who will use ODBC to access ADS are those that use the Advantage PHP Extension or the Advantage DBI Driver. Both of these drivers, which are used by Web developers through the PHP and Perl languages, respectively, connect to ADS through the ODBC driver. However, these drivers supply additional support beyond that provided by plain ODBC.

Connecting to ADS Using the Advantage ODBC Driver

Before you can execute SQL statements against ADS, you must obtain a connection to ADS through the ODBC driver. ADS supports two ODBC API functions for obtaining a connection. These are SQLConnect and SQLDriverConnect.

You use SQLConnect when there is a DSN (data source name) for the directory or data dictionary that you want to connect to. SQLDriverConnect, by comparison, does not require a DSN. Instead, the connection request is passed to SQLDriverConnect in its connection string. How you connect using these functions is described in the following sections.

Connecting Through ODBC Using a Data Source Name

A DSN is a definition that is stored on the workstation, and can be used to connect to data using an ODBC driver. Under the Windows operating system, DSN definitions are stored in the Windows registry, while in Linux these definitions appear in a configuration file named odbc.ini.

Windows users typically do not add the Windows registry entries for a DSN manually. Instead, they use an applet found in either the Control Panel (for older Windows installations), or the Administrative Tools page of the Control Panel. The name of this applet depends on which operating system you are using, but it always includes the letters ODBC. In Windows 2000 and Windows XP, for example, it is called Data Sources (ODBC).

To define a DSN manually, run this utility after you have installed the Advantage ODBC Driver on the workstation. If your client application is going to run under an end users account, you can add a user DSN. If your application is going to run under some other account, such as IUSER_MACHINE (used by Microsoft's Internet Information Server), add a system DSN.

Once you have decided to add either a user or system DSN (by selecting either the User or System tabs of this applet), click the Add button. Windows responds by displaying the Create New Data Source dialog box. Select Advantage StreamlineSQL ODBC from this list, then click Finish.

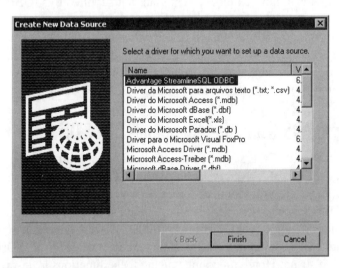

You will then see the Advantage StreamlineSQL ODBC Driver Setup dialog box, shown in Figure 16-1. You use this dialog box to configure the DSN.

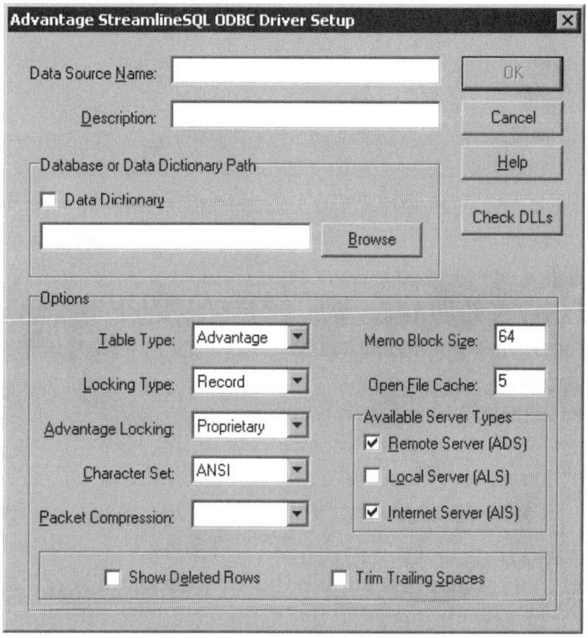

Figure 16-1   *The Advantage StreamlineSQL ODBC Driver Setup dialog box*

Set Data Source Name to the name you will use to refer to this DSN, and provide an optional description for the Description field.

If you will use this DSN to connect to a data dictionary, check the Data Dictionary checkbox and enter the full path to the data dictionary in the provided field. If you will use this DSN to connect to free tables, enter the data directory path here. In most cases you will want to use a UNC (universal naming convention) path in this field.

Use the Table Type, Locking Type, Advantage Locking, Character Set, and Packet Compression dropdown lists to define what data you are connecting to and how. To configure the size of memo blocks created by ODBC, or to adjust the number of tables to cache, set the corresponding fields. Also, you can configure the ODBC driver to show deleted rows for DBF tables, as well as trim trailing spaces from character fields.

When you are done configuring your DSN, click the OK button to save the DSN definition in the registry.

It is also possible to create a DSN by writing to the Windows registry programmatically. This approach is useful if you want to create an automated setup for your client applications, rather than having to enter the DSN information manually on every machine. Note, however, that you should extensively test any code that writes to the Windows registry, after making a backup of the registry, as inappropriate changes to the Windows registry can render a computer unstable or even unusable.

> **TIP**
>
> *For guidance on creating registry entries programmatically, start by adding a DSN using the Data Sources (ODBC) applet. Then, inspect the entries that this applet added to the registry for the keys, values, and data that you need to insert. You will find these entries in HKEY_CURRENT_USER\ SOFTWARE\ODBC\ODBC.INI for user DSNs, and HKEY_LOCAL_MACHINE\SOFTWARE\ODBC\ ODBC.INI for system DSNs. You can also find information on creating DSNs at http://www .msdn.Microsoft.com.*

In Linux, you create a DSN by adding entries to the odbc.ini file. Refer to the ADS help for information on working with the odbc.ini file.

Once you have created the DSN that you are going to use, you will be able to call the SQLConnect function of the ODBC API. This function takes seven parameters. The first parameter is a connection handle that you previously allocated by calling SQLAllocHandle. The remaining parameters are string and integer pairs, where you pass the DSN name, user name, and password in the second, fourth, and sixth parameters, respectively; and the length of these strings in the third, fifth, and seventh parameters.

Connecting Through ODBC Using a Connection String

The primary drawback to using a DSN is that you must define the DSN on each workstation, which increases the complexity of your client installations. Fortunately, ODBC provides an alternative to using a DSN. This second mechanism employs a connection string.

The ODBC API includes two functions that accept a connection string: SQLDriverConnect and SQLBrowseConnect. ADS only supports SQLDriverConnect.

SQLDriverConnect takes eight parameters. The first parameter is a connection handle, which you obtain by calling SQLAllocHandle, and the second is the Windows handle of your client application. The third and fifth parameters are used for the input connection string and the completed connection string, respectively. (The completed connection string is the version of the connection string used by ODBC to connect to the database. It includes any parameters that have been expanded by ODBC, as well as any default values not included in the input connection string.) The fourth parameter is the size of the input connection string, and the sixth parameter is the size of the buffer that you have allocated for the completed connection string.

The seventh parameter is the size of the completed connection string that was written to the buffer referenced in the fifth parameter, and the eighth parameter permits you to configure whether or not the ODBC driver manager should prompt the user for additional connection information, if needed. For example, if you pass empty strings in place of the user name and password parameters, and a user name and password is required to connect, you can instruct SQLDriverConnect to prompt the user for this information at runtime.

The connection string itself consists of zero or more parameters that you use to connect to ADS in the form of name/value pairs. The name and value parts are separated by an equal sign (=), and individual name/value pairs are separated by semicolons. Table 16-1 shows a complete list of the connection string parameters and the values that you can assign to them.

Parameter	Description
AdvantageLocking	Set to ON to use Advantage proprietary locking, or OFF to use compatibility locking. The default value is ON.
CharSet	Set to either ANSI or OEM. The default is ANSI.
Compression	Set to ALWAYS, INTERNET, NEVER, or empty. If left empty (the default), the ADS.INI file will control the compression setting. This parameter is not used by ALS.
DataDirectory	The path to your free tables or data dictionary. If you are using a data dictionary, you must include the data dictionary filename in this path. It is recommended that this path be a UNC path. This is a required parameter.
DefaultType	Set to FoxPro, Advantage, or Clipper. This parameter is ignored for data dictionary connections, but is required for free tables. The default is Advantage.
Description	This parameter is not used.
MaxTableCloseCache	Set this parameter to the number of underlying tables to hold in cache when cursors are opened and closed. The default value is 25.
MemoBlockSize	Use this parameter to define the block size that ODBC will use for memo fields. This value is always 512 for Clipper-compatible DBF tables (DBF/DBT). The default is 64 for FoxPro-compatible DBF tables (DBF/FPT), and 8 for Advantage proprietary tables (ADT/ADM).
PWD	When connecting to a data dictionary that requires logins, set to the user's password.

Table 16-1   *Connection String Parameters*

Parameter	Description
RightsChecking	Set to OFF to ignore client rights, or ON to respect them. The default is ON.
Rows	Set to TRUE to display deleted records in DBF files, or FALSE to suppress them. The default is FALSE.
ServerTypes	Set to an integer between 1 and 7 to define the server types the ODBC driver should attempt to connect to. Set to 1 for ALS, 2 for ADS, and 4 for Internet. To attempt to connect to more than one server type, set this parameter to the sum of the values. For example, to attempt to connect to ADS and then to ALS if the ADS connection fails, set ServerType to 3.
TrimTrailingSpaces	Set to TRUE to trim trailing spaces from character fields, or FALSE to preserve trailing spaces.
UID	If connecting to a data dictionary that requires logins, set to the user's user name.

Table 16-1   *Connection String Parameters* (continued)

Examples of ODBC connections strings are provided in the following discussion of PHP.

Accessing ADS Using the Advantage PHP Extension

PHP, the PHP: Hypertext Preprocessor language, is an open source scripting language that can be embedded into HTML documents in order to generate dynamic content for the World Wide Web. PHP can be used with any Web server that supports the PHP scripting engine. Most PHP development is done with Apache server for Linux, but other Web servers, such as Microsoft's IIS (Internet Information Server), can be configured to support PHP.

When a properly configured Web server reads a text file containing PHP commands, it runs the PHP scripting engine to execute those commands. The Web server then replaces the PHP commands with whatever output the scripting instructions call for. In most cases, the scripting commands are replaced either by simple text, HTML, or both.

Unlike client-side scripting, such as browser-executed JavaScript (or JScript or VBScript), all of the PHP commands are processed on the server—the client browser never receives them. As a result, end users cannot discover the PHP commands that you include in your PHP files.

ads_autocommit	ads_binmode	ads_close
ads_close_all	ads_columnprivileges	ads_columns
ads_commit	ads_connect	ads_cursor
ads_do	ads_error	ads_errormsg
ads_exec	ads_execute	ads_fetch_array
ads_fetch_into	ads_fetch_object	ads_fetch_row
ads_field_len	ads_field_name	ads_field_num
ads_field_precision	ads_field_scale	ads_field_type
ads_foreignkeys	ads_free_result	ads_gettypeinfo
ads_longreadlen	ads_next_result	ads_num_fields
ads_num_rows	ads_pconnect	ads_prepare
ads_primarykeys	ads_procedurecolumns	ads_procedures
ads_result	ads_result_all	ads_rollback
ads_setoption	ads_specialcolumns	ads_statistics
ads_tableprivileges	ads_tables	

Table 16-2   *The Advantage Extended Functions for PHP*

After installing the Advantage PHP Extension, you will need to configure your Web server to load the PHP extension. Refer to your Web server documentation or your PHP add-on documentation for information on how to configure your Web server to use the Advantage PHP Extension.

Once you have enabled the Advantage PHP Extension, you can call any of the ADS extended functions from within your PHP files. Table 16-2 contains a list of these available functions.

If you want to see a list of all of the functions supported by the Advantage PHP Extension, create and retrieve the following PHP file from a PHP-enabled Web server (or alternatively, add these commands to a file and pass the filename as a command-line parameter to the php.exe executable):

```
<html><body>
<?$functions = get_extension_funcs('advantage');
echo "Functions available in the Advantage PHP Extension:<P>";
foreach($functions as $func)
   echo $func."<br>";
echo "<br>"; ?>
</body>
</html>
```

The following sections demonstrate how to perform a number of essential tasks with ADS and PHP. Unlike many of the examples of ADS access presented in the preceding chapters, these examples do not include administrative operations such as granting rights to a newly created table. While there is nothing to stop you from opening an administrative connection with PHP, these types of operations are rarely performed via a browser interface, as they represent a potential security risk. If you find that you do need to perform administrative tasks using PHP, extrapolate one or more of the examples given in earlier chapters using the PHP extended functions.

NOTE

In order to run the examples provided in the following section, you must have a PHP-enabled Web browser, and have correctly configured a Web server–accessible directory to hold these PHP executable files. See the documentation for performing these tasks, or visit http://www.php.net for further information.

A Sample PHP Web Site

In order to demonstrate the basic use of ADS using PHP, we have provided you with a simple PHP-based Web site on this book's CD-ROM . The main page of this site is named index.htm, and it produces the page shown in Figure 16-2 when rendered in a Web browser.

 ### ON THE CD

The examples in this chapter can be found in the PHP directory on this book's CD-ROM (see Appendix B).

This Web page contains five different HTML forms, each of which submits an HTTP (Hypertext Transfer Protocol) GET request to an associated PHP file. The following is the contents of this HTML file:

```
<html>
<head>
<title>Advantage Database Server</title>
</head>
<body>
<form method="GET" action="getcustomer.php" name="getcustomer">
  <h1 align="center">
   Advantage Database Server: The Official Guide</h1>
  <h2 align="center">PHP Demonstration</h2>
```

```
   <p align="center">
   <img border="0" src="advantage_logo.gif"></p>
   Get a customer record<br>
   Customer Number
      <input type="text" name="custnumber" size="7"><br>
   <input type="submit" value="Submit" name-"B1">
      <input type="reset" value="Reset" name="B2"><br>
</form>
<form method="GET" action="storedproc.php" name="storedproc">
   <hr>
   Execute a stored procedure<br>
   Return 10% of invoices for Customer Number
      <input type="text" name="custnumber" size="7"><br>
   <input type="submit" value="Submit" name="B1">
      <input type="reset" value="Reset" name="B2"><br>
</form>
<form method="GET" action="changeaddress.php" name="changeaddress">
   <hr>
   Change an address in the customer table <br>
   Customer Number
      <input type="text" name="custnumber" size="7"><br>
   New Address <input type="text" name="newaddress" size="50"><br>
   <input type="submit" value="Submit" name="UpdateAddress">
      <input type="reset" value="Reset" name="B1"><br>
</form>
<form method="GET" action="showproducts.php">
   <hr>
   Build product selection page<br>
   <input type="submit" value="Submit" name="B1"><br>
</form>
<form method="GET" action="showtables.php" name="showtables">
   <hr>
   Show table names<br>
   <input type="submit" value="Submit" name="B1"><br>
</form>
</body>
</html>
```

NOTE

These forms were submitted using the HTTP GET method so that you can see any submitted data in the URL displayed in your Web browser. Many Web developers prefer to submit forms using the POST method.

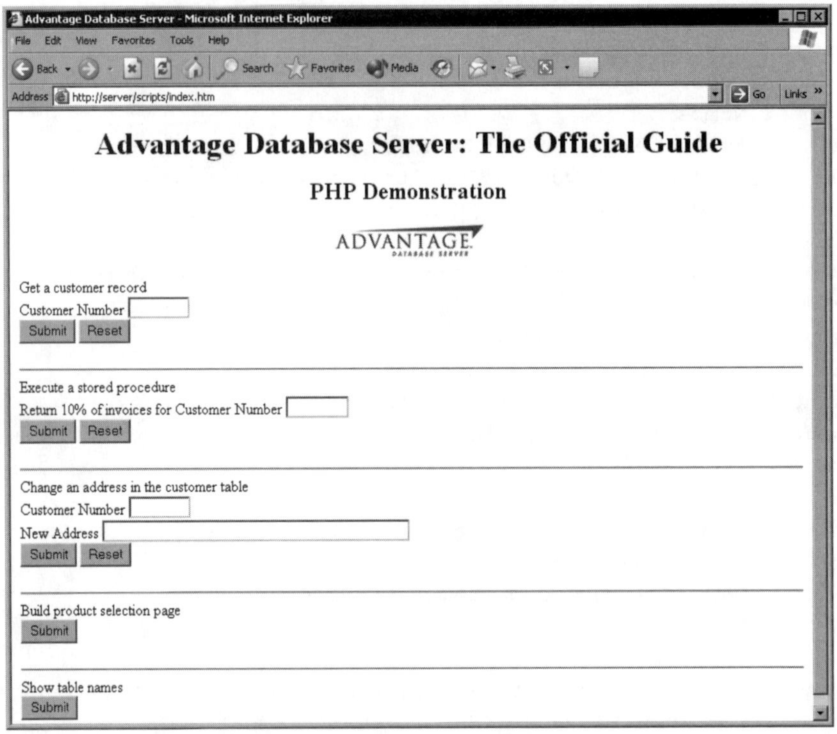

Figure 16-2   *The home page for the PHP Web site*

There is another characteristic of these examples that is worth noting. Several of these example PHP files expect user input, which is then incorporated into SQL queries. Parameterized queries are used when user input is incorporated into the SQL queries in these examples. As you learned in Chapter 9, since ADS version 7.0 you can execute SQL scripts that contain two or more SQL statements, separated by semicolons. While this is convenient, it exposes a potential security risk if you do not use parameterized queries. Because all user input is incorporated into queries using parameters, this security risk is eliminated.

Connecting to ADS Using PHP

You connect to ADS from PHP by calling the function ads_connect. This function takes either three or four arguments and returns a connection resource. The first argument is an ODBC connection string. The PHP driver connects through the ODBC API by invoking SQLDriverConnect, to which it passes this connection string. See Table 16-1 for the required and valid connection string parameters.

The second and third parameters are the user name and password to use for the connection, and the optional fourth parameter is used to define what type of cursor you want returned. The valid values for this fourth parameter are 0 (SQL_CURSOR_FORWARD_ONLY), 1 (SQL_CURSOR_DYNAMIC), and 2 (SQL_CURSOR_KEYSET_DRIVEN). If you omit this parameter, a live (dynamic) cursor is returned.

The following is an example of a call to ads_connect:

```
$rConn = ads_connect("DataDirectory=\\\\server\\share\\".
  "program files\\extended systems\\advantage\\adsbook\\".
  "DemoDictionary.add;ServerTypes=2;", "adsuser", "password");
```

The connection string in this command attempts to connect to the DemoDictionary data dictionary located on a share named *share* on a server named *server*. In addition, this connection string specifies that it wants to connect to ADS (the license for ALS does not permit you to connect to ALS from a Web server). As is the case with ODBC connections, all parameters not included in the connection string will be expanded using the default parameter values.

Once you are through with the connection, you must close it. You do this by invoking ads_close, passing the connection resource obtained from the call to ads_connect. The following is a simple example of this function call:

```
ads_close( $rConn );
```

Using Parameterized Queries in PHP

Once you have established a connection, you invoke the ads_prepare function to prepare a parameterized query. This function takes two parameters. The first parameter is the connection resource obtained by calling ads_connect, and the second is a string containing the parameterized query.

Once you have prepared your parameterized query, you bind the parameters and execute the query by calling ads_execute. This function takes two parameters: the handle of the prepared statement returned from the ads_prepare function, and an array of values to bind to the parameters, based on their ordinal position within the query.

The execution of a parameterized query is demonstrated in the following listing, which contains the PHP statements from the getcustomer.php file:

```
<?
$rConn = ads_connect( "DataDirectory=\\\\server\\share\\".
  "program files\\extended systems\\advantage\\adsbook\\".
  "DemoDictionary.add;ServerTypes=2;", "adsuser", "password" );
```

```
$rStmt = ads_prepare( $rConn, "SELECT * FROM customer ".
  "WHERE [Customer ID] = ?" );
$aParams = array( 1 => $_GET[ "custnumber" ] );
$rResult = ads_execute( $rStmt, $aParams );
if ( ads_fetch_row( $rStmt ) )
   {
   $strFirstName = ads_result( $rStmt, "First Name" );
   $strLastName = ads_result( $rStmt, "Last Name" );
   $strAddress = ads_result( $rStmt, "Address" );
   echo "Name: " . $strFirstName . " " . $strLastName . "<br>";
   echo "Address: " . $strAddress . "<br>";
   }
else
   {
   echo "Invalid Customer Number! <br>";
   }

ads_close( $rConn );
?>
```

As you can see, once the connection is established, and the parameterized query is prepared, a single element array is constructed from the custnumber value passed in the query string of this HTTP GET request (if you used a POST action, you would have read this value using the $_POST PHP function). The query is then executed.

Following the execution of the query, ads_fetch_row is called to retrieve one record from the result set. Individual fields of this record are read using the ads_result function.

If you enter customer number 12037 in the Customer Number field of the Get a customer record HTML form of index.htm and click Submit, your browser will display the following page:

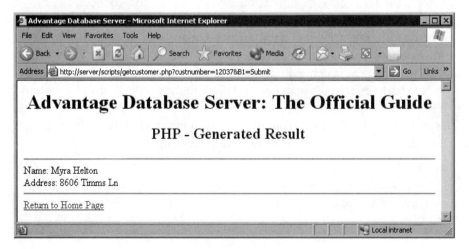

Getting Tables from Result Sets Using PHP

After executing a query, you can easily display the entire result set by calling ads_result_all. This function takes the handle returned from a call to ads_execute in its first parameter, and an optional string containing HTML table element attributes in the second, and returns a string containing a complete HTML <TABLE> definition that includes one row for each record in the result set. This function is only used when you execute a query that returns one or more records.

The use of ads_result_all is demonstrated in the showtables.php script. The PHP statements from this file are shown in the following listing. When this script is rendered, it produces the Web page shown in Figure 16-3:

```
<?
$rConn = ads_connect( "DataDirectory=\\\\server\\share\\".
  "program files\\extended systems\\advantage\\adsbook\\".
  "DemoDictionary.add;ServerTypes=2;", "adsuser", "password" );
$rStmt = ads_prepare( $rConn, "SELECT Name FROM system.tables" );
$rResult = ads_execute( $rStmt );
ads_result_all( $rStmt );
ads_close( $rConn );
?>
```

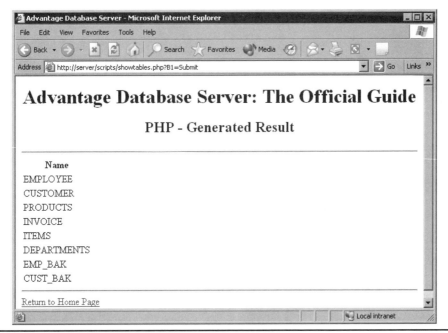

Figure 16-3   *The Web page returned by showtables.php*

As mentioned earlier, the ads_result_all function can accept a second, optional parameter. You use this parameter to pass a string that will be incorporated into the <TABLE> element. Normally you use this parameter to pass one or more table attributes that will be used to control the table's format and behavior, such as bgcolor, border, onclick, style, id, and width, to name a few.

Editing Data

Since PHP uses ODBC, and ODBC uses SQL to edit data, you change data from a PHP script by executing a SQL UPDATE statement. This is demonstrated in the following PHP statements from the script named changeaddress.php. This script expects two values, a customer ID and a string containing a new address, to be passed in the HTTP GET query string. These values are used to execute a parameterized UPDATE query statement. Once the update has been executed, this script performs a SQL SELECT to read the newly updated address from the CUSTOMER table:

```
<?
$rConn = ads_connect( "DataDirectory=\\\\server\\share\\".
  "program files\\extended systems\\advantage\\adsbook\\".
  "DemoDictionary.add;ServerTypes=2;", "adsuser", "password" );
$rStmt = ads_prepare( $rConn, "UPDATE customer ".
  "SET Address = ? WHERE [Customer ID] = ?" );
$aUpdateParams = array( 1 => $_GET[ "newaddress" ],
                        2 => $_GET[ "custnumber" ] );
$rResult = ads_execute( $rStmt, $aUpdateParams );
$iRowsAffected = ads_num_rows( $rStmt );
if ( $iRowsAffected == 0 )
    {
    echo "Invalid customer ID!<br><br>\n";
    }
$rStmt = ads_prepare( $rConn, "SELECT * FROM customer ".
  "WHERE [Customer ID] = ?" );
$aSelectParams = array( 1 => $_GET[ "custnumber" ] );
$rResult = ads_execute( $rStmt, $aSelectParams );
if ( ads_fetch_row( $rStmt ) )
    {
    $strFirstName = ads_result( $rStmt, "First Name" );
    $strLastName = ads_result( $rStmt, "Last Name" );
    $strAddress = ads_result( $rStmt, "Address" );
    echo "Address successfully changed!<br><br>";
    echo "The new address is: " . $strAddress . "<br>";
```

```
    }
ads_close( $rConn );
?>
```

Scanning Result Sets

Scanning involves the sequential navigation of the records in a result set. Scanning is often done when you want to manually insert HTML based on your result set into the stream that is inserted in place of the PHP commands.

The following PHP commands are located in the showproducts.php script. These commands produce an HTML form that includes one radio button for each product found in the PRODUCT table. Because of the action attribute of the HTML form, the product code of the selected product name will be appended to the query string part of the HTTP GET command that will be submitted to the showselection.php script.

```
<?
$rConn = ads_connect( "DataDirectory=\\\\server\\share\\".
  "program files\\extended systems\\advantage\\adsbook\\".
  "DemoDictionary.add;ServerTypes=2;", "adsuser", "password" );
$rStmt = ads_prepare( $rConn, "SELECT [Product Name], ".
  "[Product Code] FROM Products" );
$rResult = ads_execute( $rStmt );
while ( ads_fetch_row( $rStmt ) )
    {
    $strProductName = ads_result( $rStmt, "Product Name" );
    $strProductCode = ads_result( $rStmt, "Product Code" );
    echo "<INPUT Type = \"radio\" Name = \"rb\" Value = \"" .
        trim( $strProductCode ) .  "\" > " .
        $strProductName . "<br>\n";
    }
ads_close( $rConn );
?>
```

When this PHP file is processed, it produces the Web page shown in Figure 16-4.

Calling a Stored Procedure

This final example demonstrates the execution of a stored procedure using PHP. Actually, as you can see from these statements, executing a stored procedure is no different than any other type of parameterized query. After a call to ads_prepare, an array is created to hold the parameter values, after which it is passed as an argument

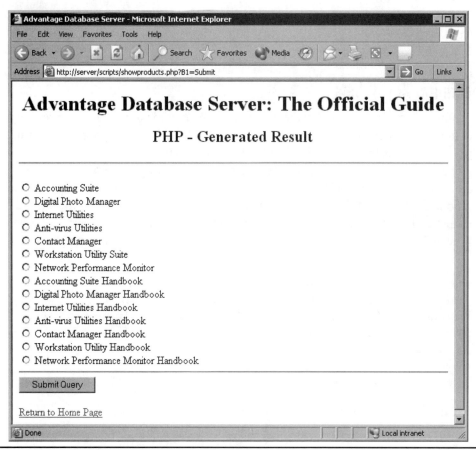

Figure 16-4   *The output from showproducts.php*

to ads_execute. Once again, the ads_result_all function is used to render an HTML table from the query result set.

```
<?
$rConn = ads_connect( "DataDirectory=\\\\server\\share\\".
  "program files\\extended systems\\advantage\\adsbook\\".
  "DemoDictionary.add;ServerTypes=2;", "adsuser", "password" );
$rStmt = ads_prepare( $rConn,
  "EXECUTE PROCEDURE DelphiAEP ( ? )" );
$aParams = array( 1 => $_GET[ "custnumber" ] );
$rResult = ads_execute( $rStmt, $aParams );
```

```
if ( $rResult == FALSE )
   {
   echo ads_errormsg( $rConn ) . "<br>\n";
   }
else
   {
   ads_result_all( $rStmt );
   }
ads_close( $rConn );
?>
```

Accessing Data Using the Advantage DBI Driver (for Perl)

Accessing data using the Advantage DBI Driver (for Perl) is very similar to that for PHP, since both drivers rely on the Advantage ODBC Driver, but there are important differences. Besides the language difference, there are four primary differences between the Advantage PHP Extension and the Advantage DBI Driver.

The first is associated with the connection string that the DBI driver will send to the ODBC API. This connection string always begins with the dbi:Advantage: string. Everything that follows this string is identical to the parameters listed in Table 16-1 that you use for both the Advantage ODBC Driver and the Advantage PHP Extension.

The following is an example of a connection string that makes a connection similar to that shown in the PHP examples:

```
use DBI;
$dbh = DBI->connect( 'dbi:Advantage:DataDirectory=\\server\share' .
   '\program files\extended systems\advantage\adsbook\' .
   'DemoDictionary.add;ServerTypes=2;', 'adsuser', 'password' );
```

The second difference, which you may have already noticed if you examined the preceding example, is that the extended functions for the DBI driver are similar in name, but not identical, to those used by the PHP Extension. Specifically, while the number and type of parameters are the same, the functions do not use the "ads_" prefix. For example, in PHP you connect to ADS by calling the ads_connect function, but in Perl you call the connect method of the DBI object.

The third difference is that data access in Perl uses a different paradigm from PHP. This approach to data access should be familiar to any seasoned Perl developer.

And the fourth difference is that the Advantage DBI Driver can only produce a forward-scrolling cursor. In most Web applications, this is inconsequential since most CGI applications don't need to perform any navigation other than forward navigation.

For more information about the Advantage DBI Driver, see the Advantage help files, which can be accessed through perldoc, the integrated Perl help system.

Appendixes

ADS Installation and Other Setup Issues

IN THIS CHAPTER:

Installation

Running ADS Without a Network

Getting Information About Advantage
Error Codes

The Error Table

Exclusive Locks and Cursor Caching

This appendix provides you with a brief discussion of installing the Advantage Database Server (ADS) and its associated client drivers and utilities. It also provides you with a few tips for using and troubleshooting ADS.

Installation

In short, ADS and its utilities are easy to install. Installation is simply a matter of responding to a few options from the installation program's dialog boxes.

While most installations are quite simple, there is one point to keep in mind: Servers, and some of the utilities, require you to specify the collation sequence or OEM character set that you want to use. It is critical that the server and all clients that will access it use the same collation sequence or OEM character set. Mixing collation sequences or OEM character sets can result in incompatible clients.

At the end of each installation, you are given a chance to view the README file associated with that installation. We recommend that you read this README file. If you want to read it at a later time, you can find the associated README file in the directory in which the server, driver, or utility is installed.

Normally, we suggest that you install the server first. However, if you already have a licensed version of ADS version 7.0 or later, there is no need to install the server.

If you do not have a copy of ADS 7.0 or later already installed on your machine or on a server on your network, you have two options. The first is to install the single-user license version of ADS 7.0 located on this book's CD-ROM. This server is designed to permit you to test all of ADS's features described in this book. This server license does not expire. However, this server is designed for testing client applications, and the license does not permit you to deploy this server.

To install the single-user version of Advantage Database Server (applies to Windows operating systems), do this:

1. Insert the CD and wait for the initial splash screen for the Advantage Database Server: The Official Guide CD dialog box to display.

2. Click the servers button located on the left side of the dialog box. You will see a list of the Advantage Database Server installations. Select the version of the server you want to install, then click the install button. Follow the instructions, as applicable.

ır development environments by clicking
the dialog box. Follow the instructions,
mplete, you can then install the sample
this book, as described in Appendix B.

ge Database Server for Linux, execute
the CD-ROM. This launches a splash
Official Guide CD. From here, the
lvantage Database Server for Linux

ıctories under Advantage on your hard disk;
t the servers, clients, or utilities in that directory.

of the Advantage Database
·user trial button) provided on
Se   ɔn program. Alternatively, visit
the   the links to download a trial 5-user
http   ı to access ADS simultaneously
lice   a trial copy, and the license expires
fror   st purchase an appropriate license,
30 c   :he single-user license available on
use
the (

Wnether you choose to install the single-user version or the 5-user trial version
should be influenced by how you plan to use this book. If you've never used ADS
before, and want to take your time working through the examples in this book, we
recommend that you install the single-user version. Since this version does not expire,
you don't have to worry about having to reinstall after 30 days. Once you are ready
to test multiple machines using ADS, you can always download and install the 5-user
trial version of ADS or purchase a multiuser license.

On the other hand, if you are going to work through the examples in this book
relatively quickly, and want to be able to experience ADS's superior performance in
a multiuser environment, you can begin by downloading and installing the 5-user
trial version of ADS. As mentioned earlier, if this copy does expire, you can always
purchase a license, use ALS, or install the single-user version located on this book's
CD-ROM.

Regardless of which version of ADS you install, the Advantage client installation
programs install the Advantage Local Server (only the Advantage JDBC Driver does

not install ALS, as this driver requires ADS). As discussed in Chapter 1, ALS is a 5-user, local engine version of ADS, sporting the same API as ADS, making it a great platform for developing your applications. However, some features available in ADS, such as transactions and Java connectivity, are unavailable when you are using ALS.

Running ADS Without a Network

ADS is a remote database server. Consequently, you will almost always be running on some type of network, such as a standard file-server based network, a peer-to-peer network, an intranet, or the Internet.

Some developers, however, need to run ADS without a network present—for example, you may want to work with ADS from your laptop while on an airplane traveling to a client site. In a situation like this, your laptop is probably not connected to a network.

When you are not connected to a network, ADS will sometimes be unavailable. This is particularly true of machines running Windows operating systems. Specifically, unless a computer has been configured to do otherwise, a Windows machine will not load the IP stack when it is booting without a network present. The IP stack is required to communicate with ADS.

There are several solutions to this problem. The first solution is to simply use ALS when you are not connected to a network. Since ALS and ADS have the exact same API, you can use ALS to build applications that will be deployed using ADS. As mentioned earlier in this appendix, the only difference is that with ALS you cannot test transactions, nor can you test Java clients that use the Advantage JDBC Driver.

The next two solutions permit you to use ADS, but these require some configuration of your computer's operating system. The first is to disable Window's DHCP media sensing behavior, which in most cases permits the IP stack to be loaded whether or not a network is detected. The second is to install the Microsoft Loopback Adapter. We recommend trying the first technique, described in the next section. If that doesn't work, try installing the Microsoft Loopback Adapter, described in the later section "Installing the Microsoft Loopback Adapter."

While one or the other should work, we have encountered an instance that required us to perform both of these configurations. Also, we have found that these techniques do not work with Windows 98/ME machines. Those machines must be connected to a network, or you must use ALS.

Finally, regardless of which of these techniques you use, you might have to disable your firewall client. Client applications communicate with ADS over UDP port 6262 (by default) or TCP port 6262 (the default when using the Advantage JDBC Driver). If your firewall is blocking these ports, you will not be able to use ADS with the firewall active.

Disabling DHCP Media Sensing

In order to prevent Windows from testing for a network connection you need to make a small change to your Windows registry. Use the following steps to make this change:

1. Select Run from the Start menu. Enter **Regedit.exe** in the Open field of the Run dialog box, and click OK to launch the Windows Registry Editor, shown in Figure A-1.

2. Select the HKEY_LOCAL_MACHINE root key in the Registry Editor.

3. Make the following subkey the current key:

   `SYSTEM\CurrentControlSet\Services\Tcpip\Parameters`

4. Select Edit | New | DWORD Value from the Registry Editor's main menu.

5. Change the name of the new value to **DisableDHCPMediaSense**.

6. Right-click the DisableDHCPMediaSense value and select Modify.

7. Change the value to **1**. Your screen should look something like that shown in Figure A-2.

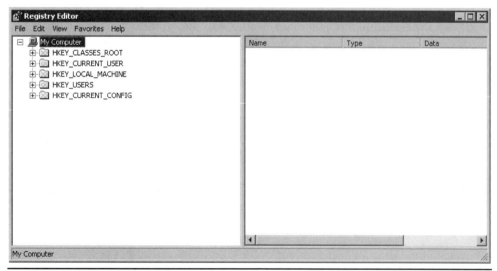

Figure A-1 *The Windows Registry Editor*

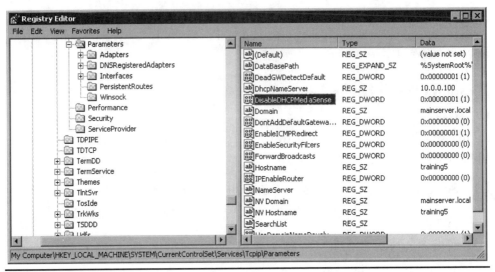

Figure A-2   *The new entry in the Windows registry*

8. Now reboot your computer. ADS should now run normally, whether or not you are connected to a network.

Installing the Microsoft Loopback Adapter

Disabling Window's DHCP media sensing is normally all you need to do to use ADS on a Windows machine that is not connected to a network. Another alternative, albeit one that is a little more involved, is to install the Microsoft Loopback Adapter. In our experience, we have come across only one laptop where the preceding steps failed (thereby requiring this step). If you cannot connect to ADS after making these registry changes, use the following steps to install the Microsoft Loopback Adapter.

NOTE

The steps given here are for Windows 2000. If you are using another operating system, the steps will be similar, though not identical. Use the displayed dialog boxes to get to the screen where you manually select hardware that you have already installed. From there, select to install a Network adapter, and when asked which one you want to install, select the Microsoft Loopback Adapter. You probably do not need your Windows installation disk handy, but it might be a good idea to have it available just in case.

1. Open the Control Panel and launch the Add/Remove Hardware applet.

2. From the Welcome screen, select Next.

3. On the Choose a Hardware Task dialog box, leave the Add/Troubleshoot a device radio button enabled, and click Next.

4. Windows will now search for hardware devices. Once this search is complete, you will see the Choose a Hardware Device dialog box.

5. Select Add A New Device and click Next.

6. From the Find New Hardware dialog box, select the No, I Want To Select A Hardware Item From A List Radio Button, and click Next.

7. From the Hardware Type dialog box, select Network Adapters, and click Next.

8. From the Select Network Adapter dialog box, set Manufacturers to Microsoft, and Network Adapter to Microsoft Loopback Adapter, as shown in Figure A-3. Select Next.

9. From the Start Hardware Installation dialog box, select Next.

10. From the Completed the Add/Remove Hardware Wizard dialog box, select Finish.

11. Reboot your computer.

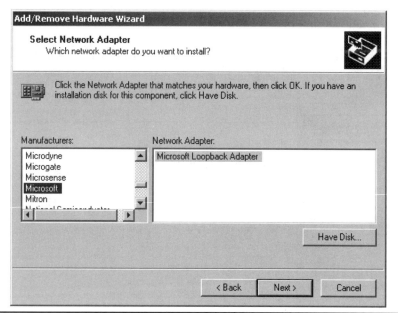

Figure A-3   *Selecting the Microsoft Loopback Adapter*

Getting Information About Advantage Error Codes

While building your client applications, you are likely to encounter an error generated by ADS now and then. These error codes indicate that a problem occurred while ADS or ALS was trying to perform a task that you instructed it to perform.

These errors almost always result in the display of a four-digit error code as well as a brief error message. For more information about a particular error, use the Advantage help files, which you can access either directly or from the Advantage Data Architect.

The following steps describe how to access additional information about an error returned by ADS or ALS:

1. From the Advantage Data Architect, select Help | Contents. Alternatively, to open the Help file directly, select Start | Programs | Advantage Database Server | Documentation | Advantage.

2. Select the Index tab of the Help dialog box.

3. Type the four-digit error code into the index field.

4. Once the error code is visible in the help index, double-click its entry to display a more detailed description of the error, like the one shown in Figure A-4.

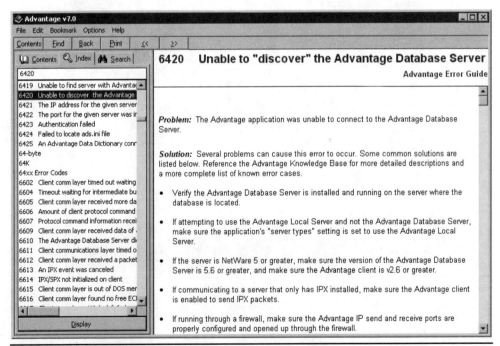

Figure A-4   *Detailed information about an error is displayed in the Advantage help index.*

TIP

Some developers find it handy to place a shortcut to the Advantage help file on their desktop. In Windows, this help file is located in c:\Program Files\Extended Systems\Advantage\Help by default.

The Error Table

ADS also keeps track of errors it encounters in a special DBF table named ads_err.dbf. The configuration of ADS specifies where this table is stored. To discover the location of this file, use the following steps:

1. Open the Advantage Data Architect.

2. Select Tools | Advantage Database Server Management.

3. Set Server Drive to the drive or share where the server is running. Use a UNC (universal naming convention) path if the server is running on another machine on your network. Click the Connect to Server button, which appears to the immediate right of the Server Drive field.

4. Once connected, click the Configuration Parameters tab, then click the Not Affecting Memory tag. The Error Log and Assert Log Path field displays the location where the ads_err.dbf file is stored.

Use the Advantage Data Architect to view this free DBF table, as described in the following steps:

1. From the Advantage Data Architect's main menu, select File | Open Table.

2. Set Path to the location where the ads_err.dbf file is stored.

3. Set Files to **ads_err.dbf** or use the Browse button to select the file.

4. Set Table Type to DBF/CDX.

5. Select the server type. Remember, all Advantage applications that are opening a single table (in this case, ads_err.dbf) should be using the same server type. Otherwise, 7008 errors are likely to occur. In other words, all applications that want to open the same table concurrently should either all be using ALS or all be using ADS to open that table.

6. Click OK.

Once you select the ads_err.dbf file, all errors that have been saved can be viewed. The most recent errors appear at the end of this table.

Exclusive Locks and Cursor Caching

ADS is a high-performance server; it uses a number of advanced techniques for optimizing the operations that it performs. One of these optimizations is to keep the cursor of a SELECT query in cache following the execution of the query. This technique improves performance since there is a high likelihood that a just executed query will be executed again very soon.

While this optimization increases performance, it has one major drawback. If you are working in an environment that permits you to place an exclusive lock on a table, that lock will fail if the table you are locking has an open cursor in the cursor cache. In other words, an exclusive lock may fail even though the table being locked is not being used by another user.

For those development environments that permit exclusive table locks, such as Delphi, or any development language that can make direct calls to the ACE (Advantage Client Engine) API (such as Delphi, Visual Basic, Visual C++, and C++Builder), there is a way to disable cursor caching. In short, you either call the AdsCloseCachedTables function to close all cursors in the cache or set the size of the cursor cache to 0.

> ### NOTE
> *Even if you are not interested in the following technique, we recommend that you check out the Technical Tip of the Month Web page. It contains many good articles that can help you use ADS better.*

A more detailed discussion of disabling cursor caching can be found online at the Advantage Database Server site, in one of the Advantage Monthly Tech Tips. To locate this tech tip, go to http://www.AdvantageDatabase.com. Look for Monthly Tech Tips in the Support section. This link takes you to the Technical Tip of the Month page. (Alternatively, use this Web site's search function to locate the Monthly Tech Tips page.) Scroll to the end of this page to find past technical tips, including the one titled "Closing Tables used in an SQL Statement."

Installing the Code Samples

IN THIS CHAPTER:

Installing the Sample Database and Code

Downloading the Code Samples

T he examples described throughout this book use a sample ADS database that you will find on the CD-ROM. This database includes table, index, and memo files.

This database does not include a data dictionary, nor does it include a number of other objects, such as additional tables, index orders, constraints, users, groups, referential integrity definitions, stored procedures, and triggers that are used in the examples described in this book. You will create these objects as you work through the various step-by-step instructions provided throughout.

In all cases, we have tried to make the creation of these additional objects easy for you. The additional tables, index orders, constraints, users, groups, and referential integrity definitions are relatively simple, and detailed instructions for creating these objects are provided in Part I.

Furthermore, not only do we provide you with the step-by-step instructions for creating stored procedures and triggers, but we also provide code in text files for the code listings that appear in Chapters 7 and 8, so that you do not have to type in all of the code while working with the examples in these chapters. The files are referred to in these chapters and follow the naming conventions of listing7-1.txt, listing7-2.txt, and so on. There are also two script files, ch8triggers.sql and ch10queries.sql, which contain SQL query examples for Chapters 8 and 10, respectively. Again, these are provided so that you do not have to enter all of the SQL code while working through the examples.

In addition, the sample applications described in Chapters 12–16 are found in the same compressed file that contains the sample database. See the appropriate chapter for the names of these files.

> **NOTE**
>
> *If you try to install the code samples and find that there is a problem, please download the sample database and code samples from this book's Web site, as described at the end of this appendix.*

Installing the Sample Database and Code

There are two compressed files that contain the database and all associated sample code files. For Windows developers, this compressed file is a self-extracting executable named adsbook.exe. For Linux developers, there is a compressed tar file named adsbook.tar.gz.

If you are a Windows developer, there are three ways for you to install the database and other code samples. The first uses the installation program on the CD-ROM. The following steps describe how to install the files using this approach:

1. If your computer is set up to auto-run inserted CD-ROMs, simply insert the CD-ROM into your CD-ROM drive once you have logged on to your computer. The installation program will automatically start.

   If you do not have auto-run enabled, insert the CD-ROM into your CD-ROM drive, open the Windows Explorer, and then run the install.exe on the CD-ROM's root directory.

2. Once the installation program is running, click the introduction button. Next click the install code samples now button. This will launch the adsbook.exe program, which will then prompt you for the directory into which you want to install its contents.

3. By default, adsbook.exe extracts its contents into a directory named ADSBook, located under the c:\Program Files\Extended Systems\Advantage directory. This is the same directory referred to in this book. If you wish to install the samples into some alternative directory, use the provided dialog box to select the alternative directory into which you want the files extracted.

The second way to install the files is to launch the adsbook.exe file manually. Use the following steps to install these files manually:

1. Insert the CD-ROM into your CD-ROM drive.

2. Open the Windows Explorer, and navigate to the \ads\book\ directory under your CD-ROM's root directory. There you will find the adsbook.exe file.

3. Right-click adsbook.exe and select Open.

4. Use the displayed dialog box to install the database and sample files.

The third way is to copy all of the files from the \ads\book\adsbook directory under the CD-ROM's root directory to your hard disk. This directory contains an uncompressed version of all of the files referred to in this book. You can copy the files to the directory referred to in the chapters of this book—C:\Program Files\ Extended Systems\Advantage\ADSBook\—or to a directory of your choice.

For Linux developers, you will find the adsbook.tar.gz file in the \ads\book\ directory under the root directory of the CD-ROM drive. Use the following instructions to install the sample files from this tar file:

1. From Linux, mount your CD-ROM drive.

2. Using your tool of choice, copy this file to the directory where you want to extract the files. For example, you may want to place this file in a directory named ADSBook under the directory where the installation disk will install your Linux version of ADS and the associated utilities and drivers. By default, this directory is /usr/local/advantage/.

3. Make the directory into which you copied adsbook.tar.gz the current directory.

4. Enter the following command to extract this file:

```
tar zxf bka_code.tar.gz
```

Alternatively, you can copy the uncompressed files from the ads\book\adsbook directory on the CD-ROM to the directory of your choosing on your hard drive.

Downloading the Code Samples

The sample code and database referred to throughout this book is also available online. To download this code, go to the Web site www.JensenDataSystems.com/adsbook.html. There you will find a link to download adsbook.exe (for Windows developers) and adsbook.tar.gz (for Linux developers). After you download the appropriate sample code file, extract it to the directory of your choice using the steps just provided. Note, however, that the compressed file will be located wherever you downloaded it to, and not on your CD-ROM drive (unless you copy the file to a CD-R or CD-RW disk).

Book Web Support Site

W̲e have provided a Web site, which supports this book and contains general information about it, related upcoming events (such as Advantage training and seminars), a link to this book's errata, a link for downloading the sample code (the same sample code that is included on the CD-ROM), and links to essential ADS-related sites. This site is located at http://www.JensenDataSystems .com/adsbook.html, or you can go to http://www.JensenDataSystems.com and follow the link for *Advantage Database Server: The Official Guide.*

One of the more interesting pages on this site is the errata page. Although we have taken great care to ensure the accuracy of the information, there is always the possibility that we will discover one or more errors after the book has gone to press. If errors are discovered, we will report these errors on the errata page, providing you with corrected information. You will also find a link on the errata page that you can use to report any errors that you discover in the book.

We hope that you will find this Web site useful. Please note, however, that we regret that we cannot provide free support for ADS development. For training, consulting, or development services using the Advantage Database Server, use the links located at http://www.JensenDataSystems.com. For example, lead author Cary Jensen offers onsite ADS training services, which you can use to train your development team on using ADS in the comfort of your own office.

Index

% (wildcard character), 283
* (multiplication), 245
* (select all), 276, 284, 294
+ (addition), 245–246
+ (concatenation), 245
+ (sign change), 244
– (sign change), 244
– (subtraction), 244–246
.NET. *See* Advantage .NET Data
   Provider
/ (division), 245
; (SQL statement separator),
   250–252
< (less than), 245–246
<= (less than or equal to), 245–246
<> (less than or greater than),
   244–246
=, 244–246
> (greater than), 245–246
>= (greater than or equal to),
   245–246
_ (wildcard character), 283
__error table, 174, 200
__input table, 173–174
__new table, 200
__old table, 200
__output table, 173–174

A

ABS() scalar function, 248
access rights. *See* granting access
   rights to tables; permissions
accessing ADS data. *See* connecting
   to ADS data; reading ADS data
ACE API. *See* Advantage Client
   Engine (ACE) API
ACOS() scalar function, 248
ActiveX data objects. *See* ADO
ADD file, 96
ADD reserved keyword, 239, 275
ADM file, 32

administrative user (ADSSYS),
   98–99, 300, 302–303, 315
ADO
   See also ADO.NET
   changing user passwords,
     394–395
   client-side cursors, 373
   connecting to ADS data with,
     376–380
   connecting using data link
     (UDL) files, 377–378
   connection parameters for,
     376–377
   creating tables, 392–393
   defined, 372–373
   drivers for ADS, 24
   executing parameterized
     queries, 381–383
   executing queries, 380–381
   executing stored procedures,
     385–386
   granting access rights to tables,
     392–393
   opening tables directly, 386–387
   overview, 6, 372–373
   reading and writing data,
     383–385
   scanning result sets, 390–391
   seeking records, 388–389
   server-side cursors, 373
   setting filters, 389–390
   setting indexes, 387–388
   using with ADS, 372–373
ADO.NET
   See also ADO; Advantage .NET
     Data Provider; C#Builder;
     Visual Basic .NET; Visual C#
   changing user passwords,
     414–417
   connecting to ADS data with,
     401–403

connection parameters for,
   401–424
creating tables, 412–414
drivers for ADS, 24
executing parameterized
   queries, 405–406
executing queries, 403–405
executing stored procedures,
   409–410
granting access rights to tables,
   412–414
overview, 26, 398–399
reading and writing data,
   406–409
scanning result sets, 410–411
ADS help, 11, 448–449
AdsAddCustomKey, 70
AdsDeleteCustomKey, 70
ADSSYS administrative user, 98–99,
   300, 302–303, 315
ads_err.dbf, 448
ADT file, 32, 38
ADT table format, 31–33
   See also tables
Advantage ANSI Collation Utility,
   18–20
Advantage Client Engine (ACE) API
   supported development
     environments, 24
   using with Delphi, 330
Advantage Clipper RDDs, 24
Advantage Configuration Utility,
   11–17
Advantage Data Architect
   message display option in,
     98–99
   overview, 17–18
Advantage data dictionaries. *See* data
   dictionaries
Advantage Database Manager,
   98–100

INTERNATIONAL CONTACT INFORMATION

AUSTRALIA
McGraw-Hill Book Company
Australia Pty. Ltd.
TEL +61-2-9900-1800
FAX +61-2-9878-8881
http://www.mcgraw-hill.com.au
books-it_sydney@mcgraw-hill.com

CANADA
McGraw-Hill Ryerson Ltd.
TEL +905-430-5000
FAX +905-430-5020
http://www.mcgraw-hill.ca

**GREECE, MIDDLE EAST, & AFRICA
(Excluding South Africa)**
McGraw-Hill Hellas
TEL +30-210-6560-990
TEL +30-210-6560-993
TEL +30-210-6560-994
FAX +30-210-6545-525

MEXICO (Also serving Latin America)
McGraw-Hill Interamericana Editores
S.A. de C.V.
TEL +525-1500-5108
FAX +525-117-1589
http://www.mcgraw-hill.com.mx
carlos_ruiz@mcgraw-hill.com

SINGAPORE (Serving Asia)
McGraw-Hill Book Company
TEL +65-6863-1580
FAX +65-6862-3354
http://www.mcgraw-hill.com.sg
mghasia@mcgraw-hill.com

SOUTH AFRICA
McGraw-Hill South Africa
TEL +27-11-622-7512
FAX +27-11-622-9045
robyn_swanepoel@mcgraw-hill.com

SPAIN
McGraw-Hill/
Interamericana de España, S.A.U.
TEL +34-91-180-3000
FAX +34-91-372-8513
http://www.mcgraw-hill.es
professional@mcgraw-hill.es

**UNITED KINGDOM, NORTHERN,
EASTERN, & CENTRAL EUROPE**
McGraw-Hill Education Europe
TEL +44-1-628-502500
FAX +44-1-628-770224
http://www.mcgraw-hill.co.uk
emea_queries@mcgraw-hill.com

ALL OTHER INQUIRIES Contact:
McGraw-Hill/Osborne
TEL +1-510-420-7700
FAX +1-510-420-7703
http://www.osborne.com
omg_international@mcgraw-hill.com

Sound Off!

Visit us at **www.osborne.com/bookregistration** and let us know what you thought of this book. While you're online you'll have the opportunity to register for newsletters and special offers from McGraw-Hill/Osborne.

We want to hear from you!

Sneak Peek

Visit us today at **www.betabooks.com** and see what's coming from McGraw-Hill/Osborne tomorrow!

Based on the successful software paradigm, Bet@Books™ allows computing professionals to view partial and sometimes complete text versions of selected titles online. Bet@Books™ viewing is free, invites comments and feedback, and allows you to "test drive" books in progress on the subjects that interest you the most.

"Advantage is fast, extremely reliable and costs less than other embedded database servers and the support is second to none."

Don Kitchen, CEO, Scancode Systems Inc.

Deploy Advantage Database Server today

Visit the official web site for this book: www.AdvantageDatabase.com/go/adsbook

- get details about regional Advantage technical training seminars, taught by qualified technical staff, including author Cary Jensen

- sign up for notifications of updated drivers, monthly technical tips and the latest information about Advantage Database Server

- take advantage of other special offers associated with this book (reference promotion code: ADSGuide6900)

Contact an Advantage sales representative in the United States, 208-322-7575 ext. 5030